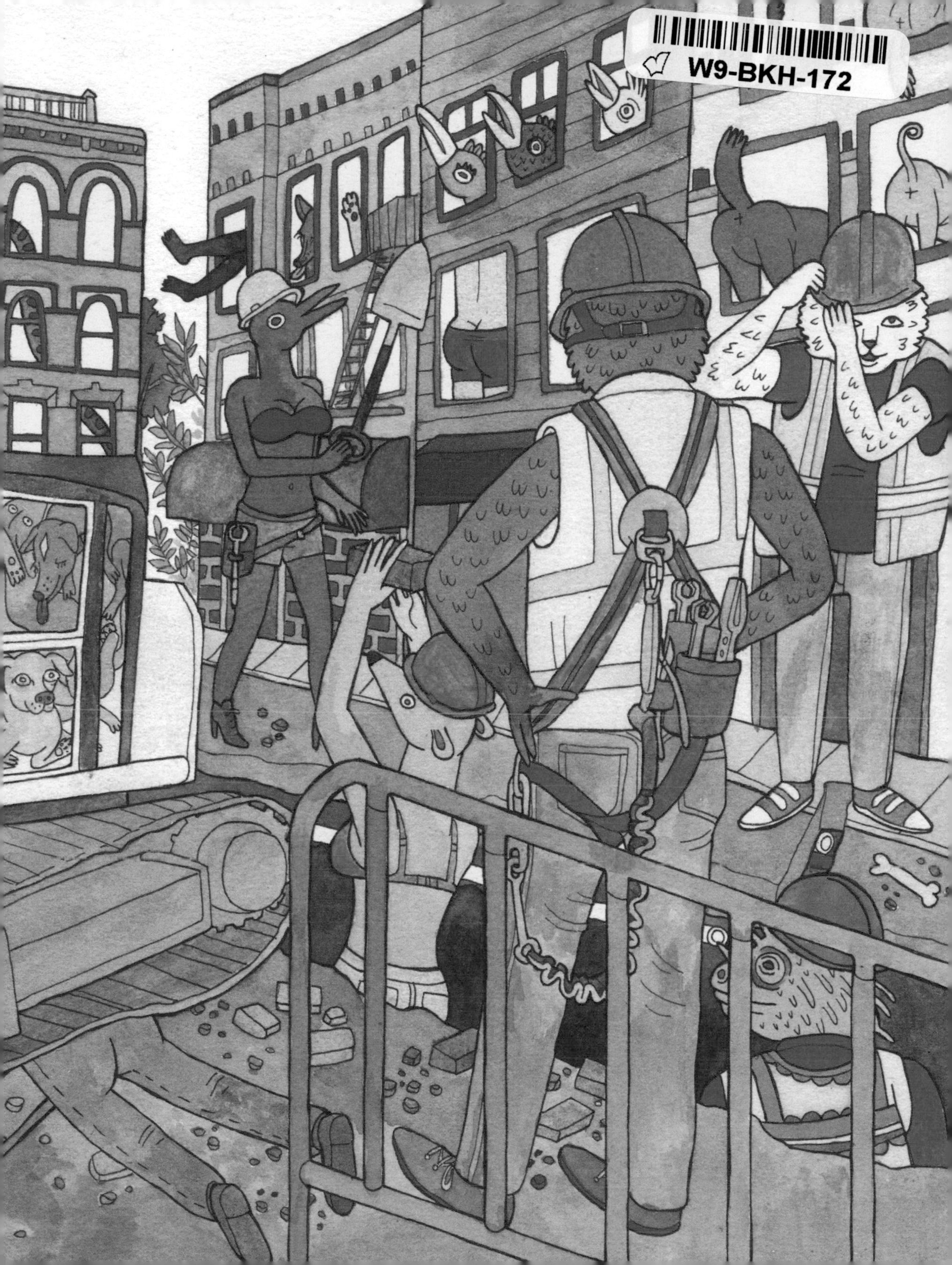

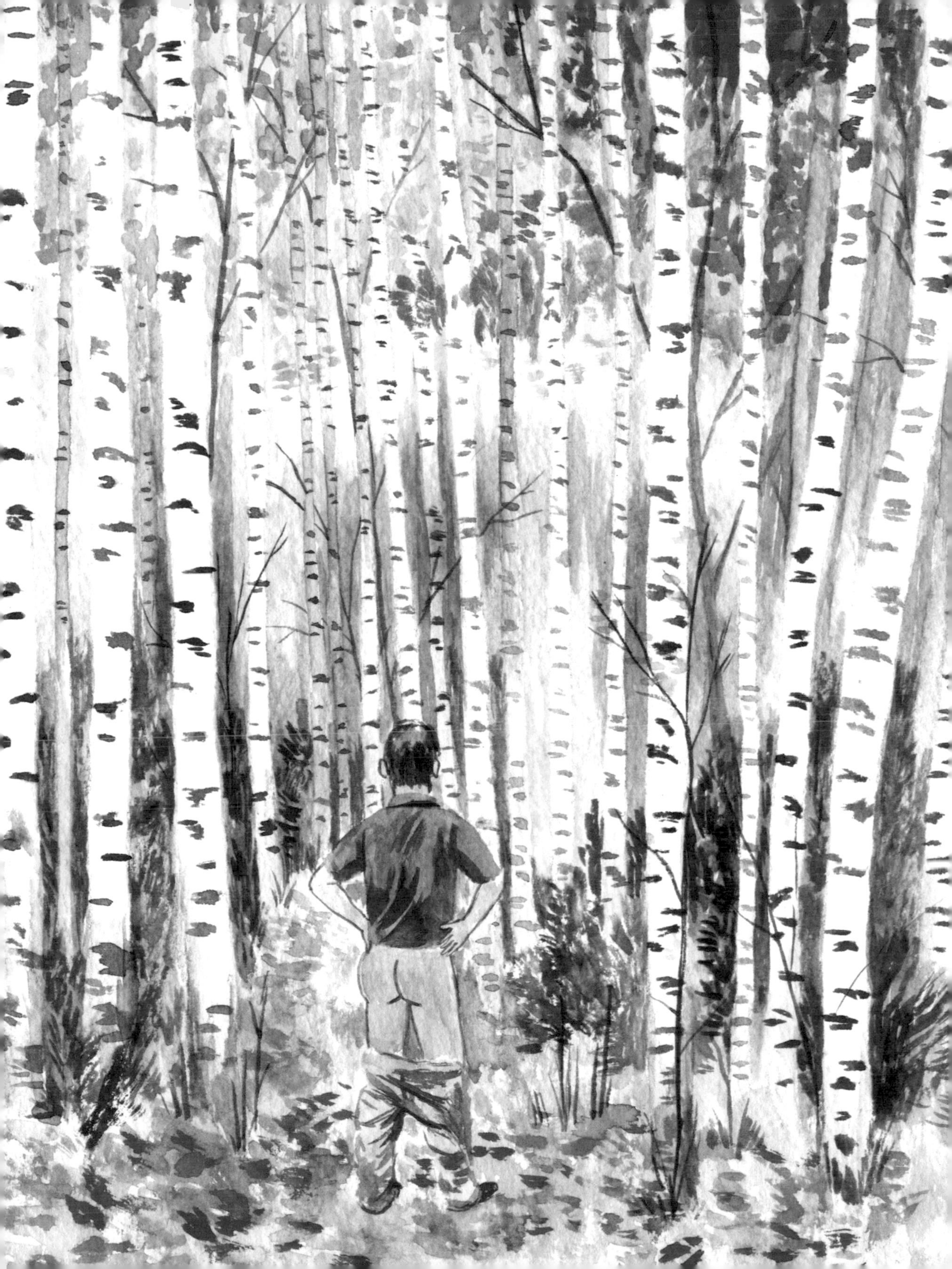

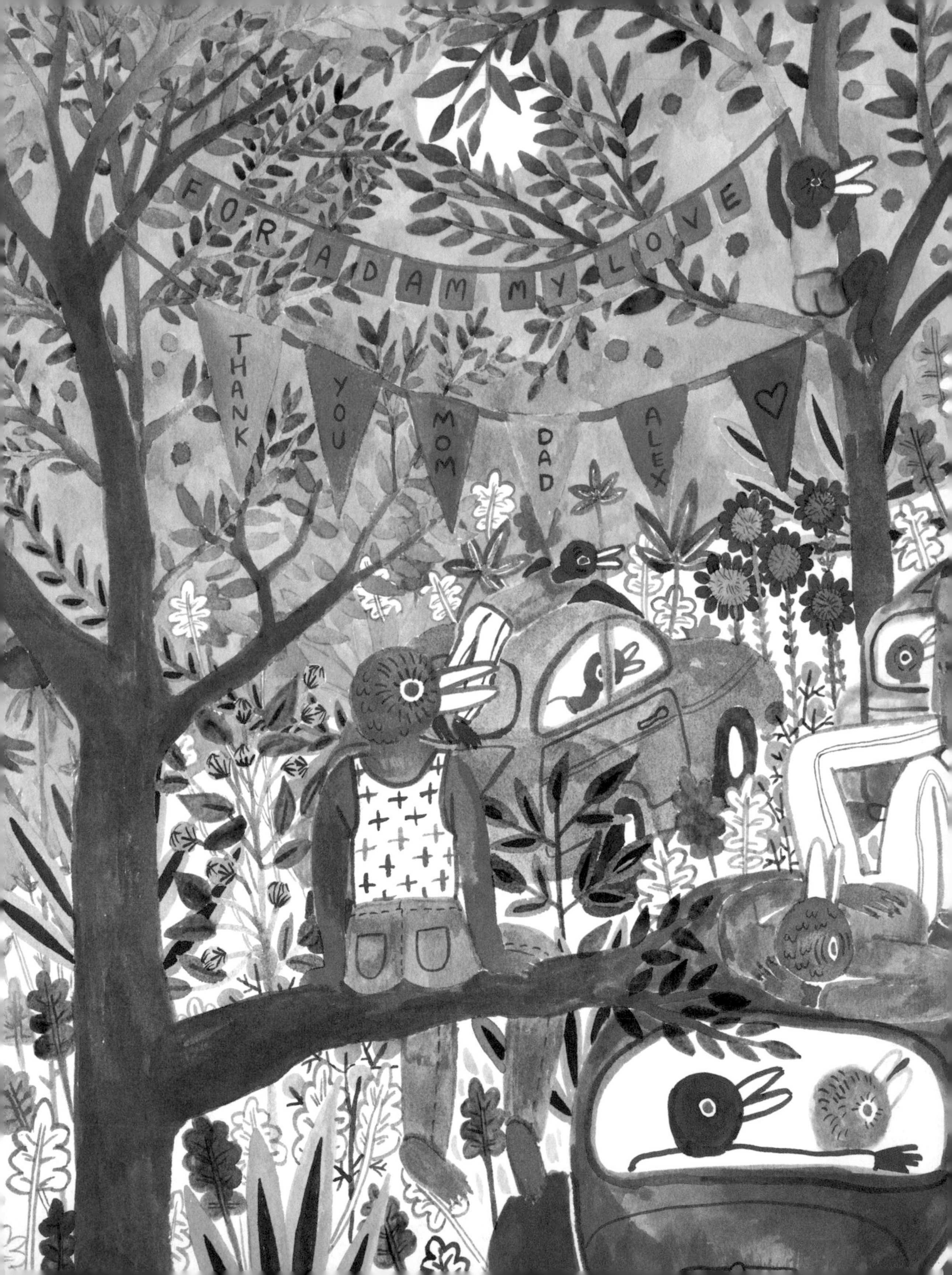
FOR ADAM MY LOVE
THANK YOU MOM DAD ALEX ♡

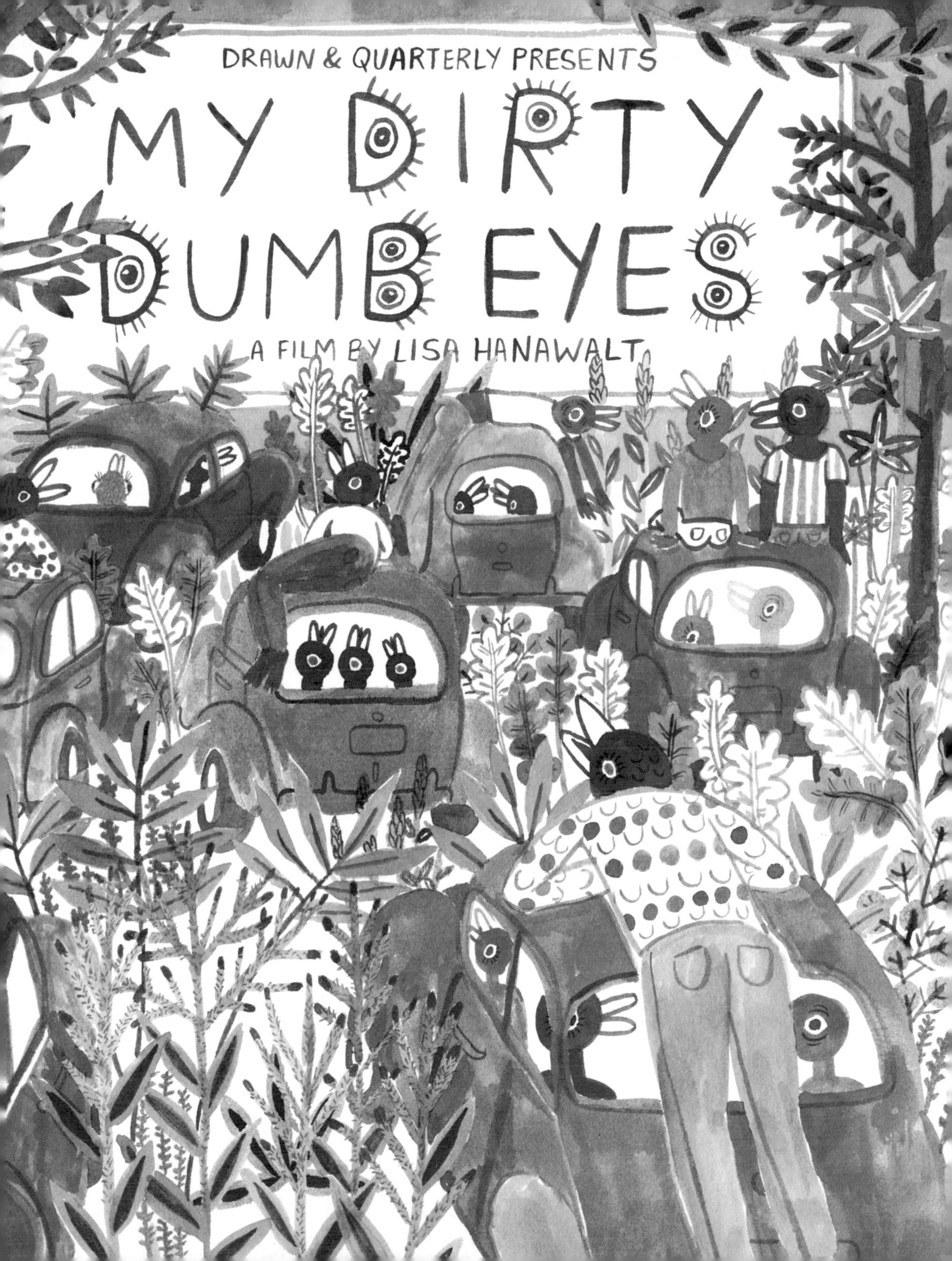

DRAWN & QUARTERLY PRESENTS
MY DIRTY DUMB EYES
A FILM BY LISA HANAWALT

WHAT DO DOGS WANT ??

① A HOUSE MADE OUT OF OLD FISH.

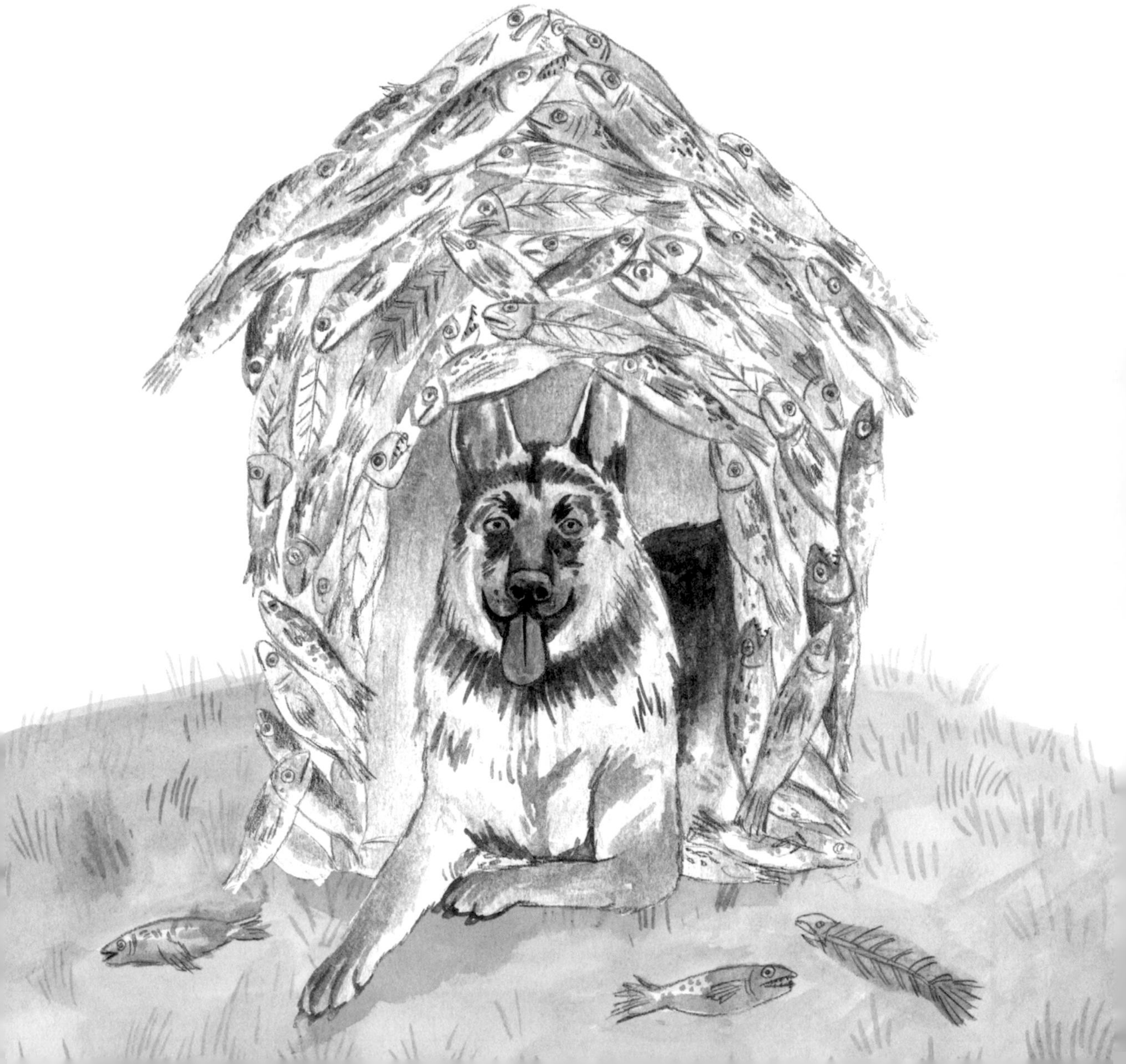

② A TENNIS-BALL BRIDE.

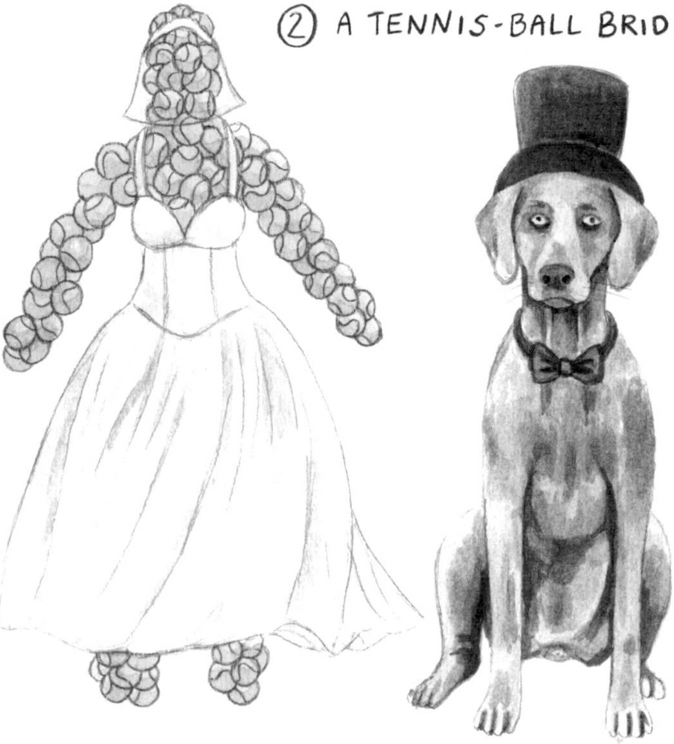

③ A SALT LICK IN THE SHAPE OF HUMAN LEGS.

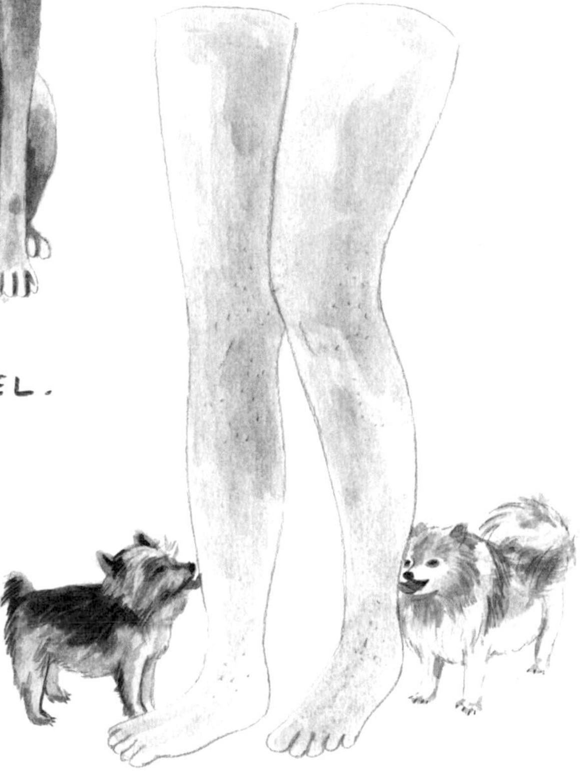

④ THE CHANCE TO SIT DOWN AND CHAT WITH A SQUIRREL.

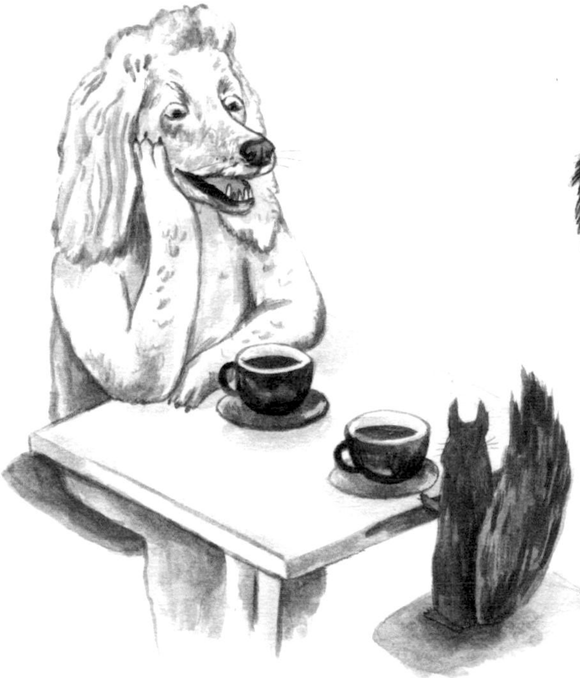

⑤ AN ENDLESS LAWN OF GRASS, LEAVES, AND SNOW, TO POOP ON.

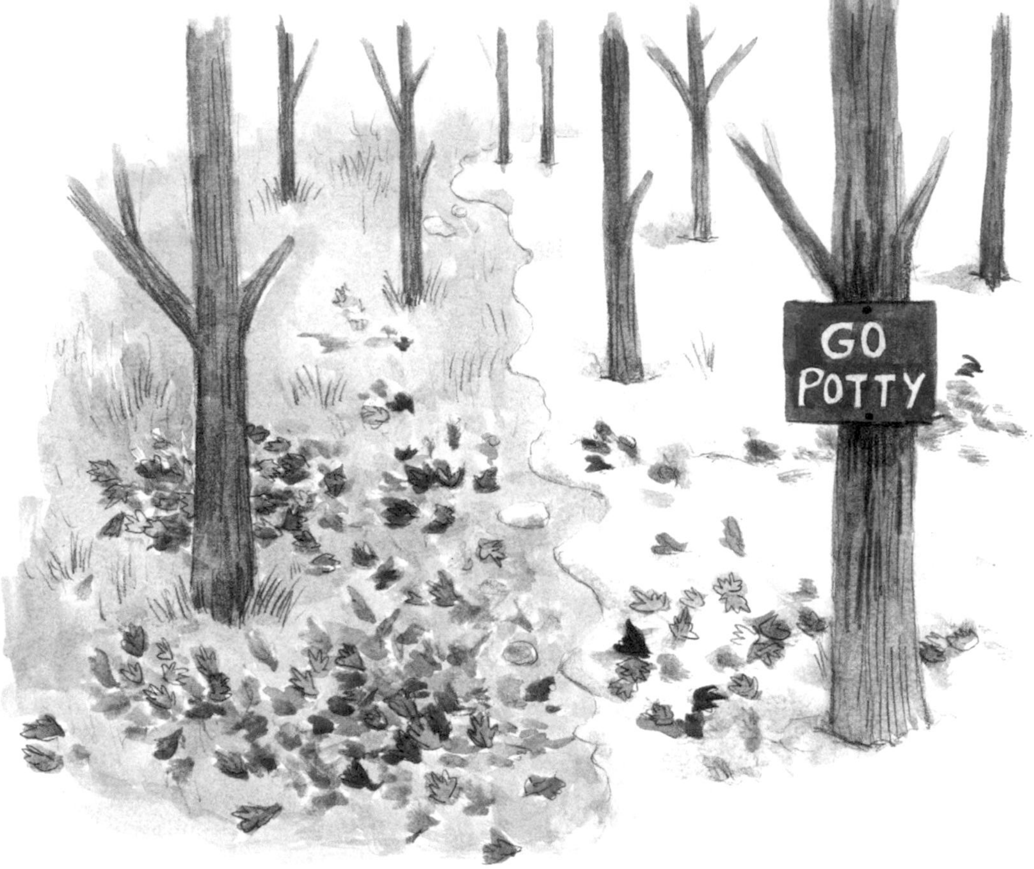
GO
POTTY

⑥ A FANCY MEAL.

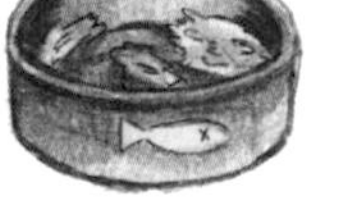

TUNA CAN TO LICK.

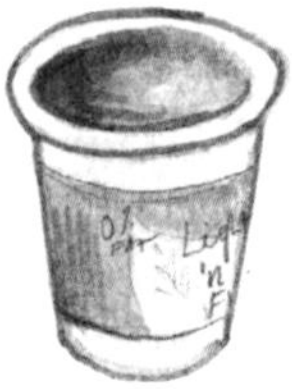

YOGURT CUP TO LICK.

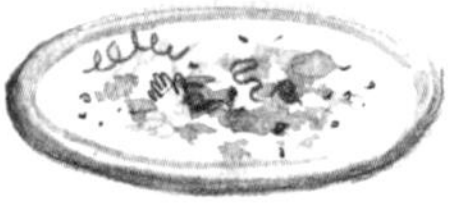

LINT AND FLOOR CRUMBS.

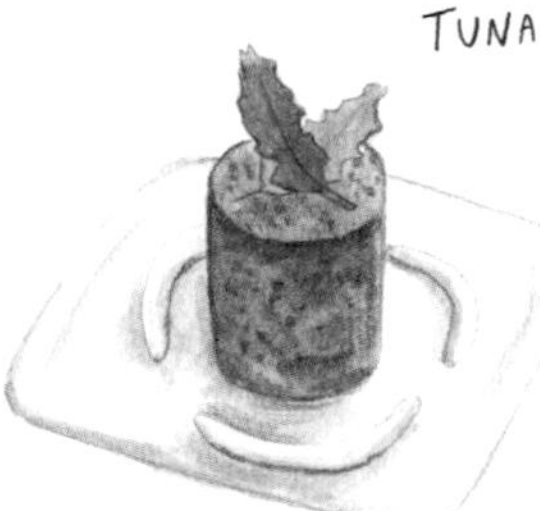

ALPO® WITH MILK-BONE® INFUSED MAYONNAISE AND DRIED LEAF GARNISH.

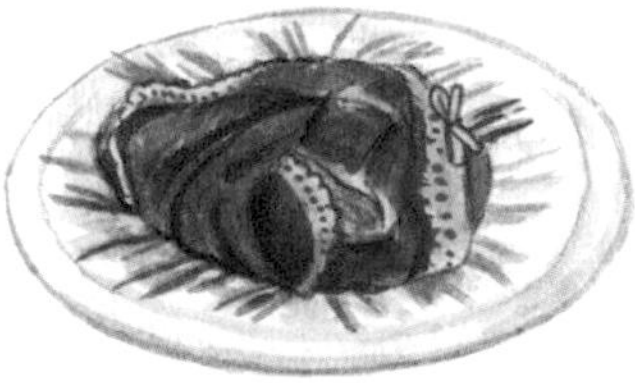

DIRTY UNDERWEAR ON A BED OF REGURGITATED GRASS, WITH CAT POOP REDUCTION.

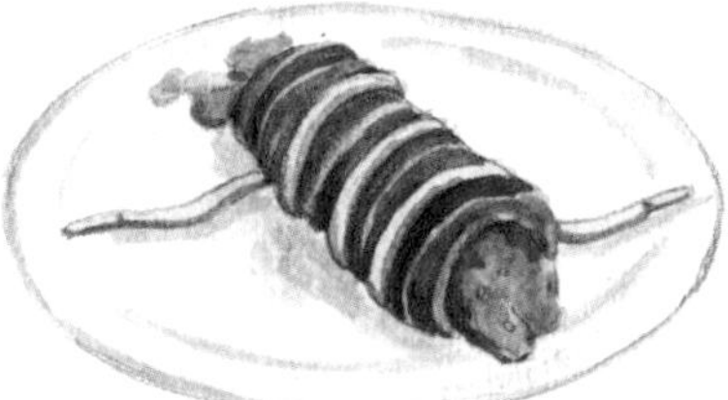

BACON- AND SHOELACE-WRAPPED PEANUT BUTTER.

⑦ TO BE MADE OUT OF RUBBER BANDS.

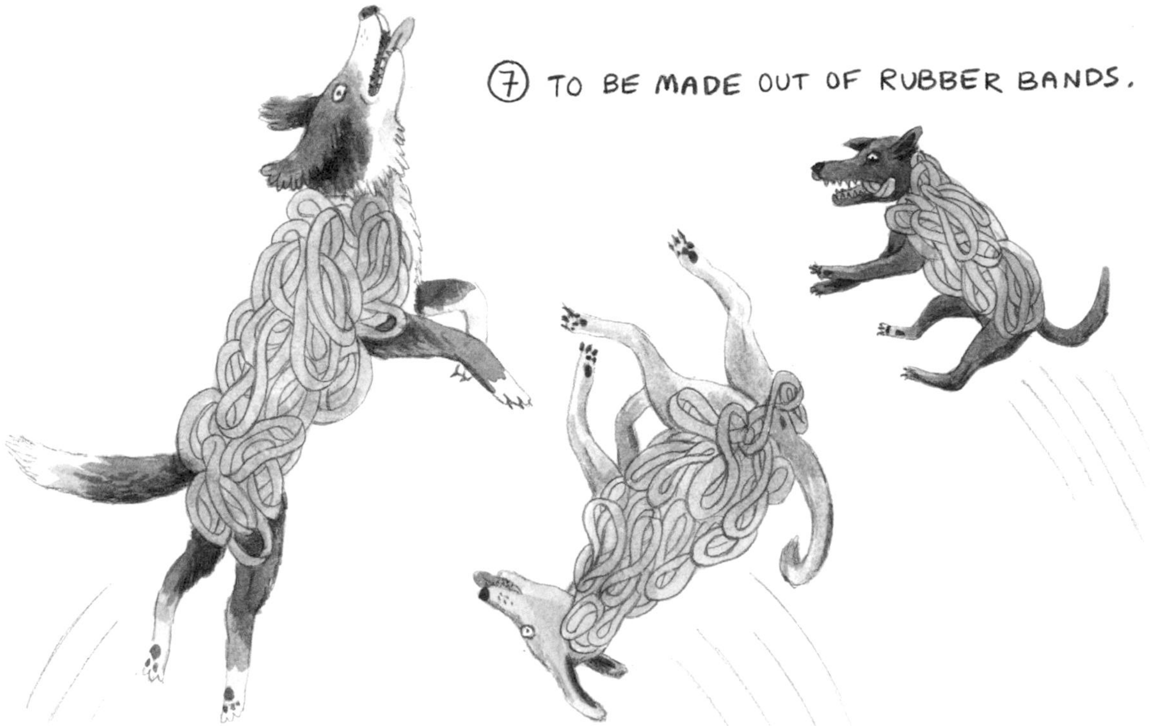

⑧ TO CHASE PIGEONS WITH HOT DOGS IN THEIR BEAKS.

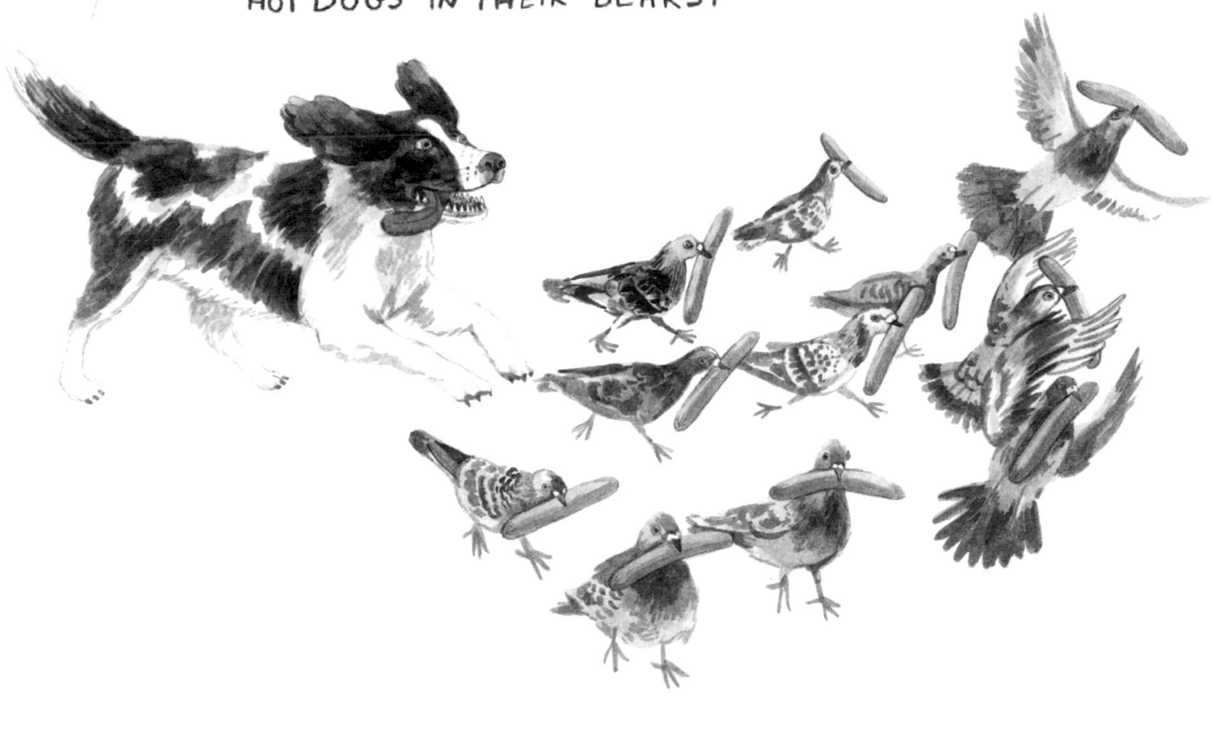

⑨ A JOB.

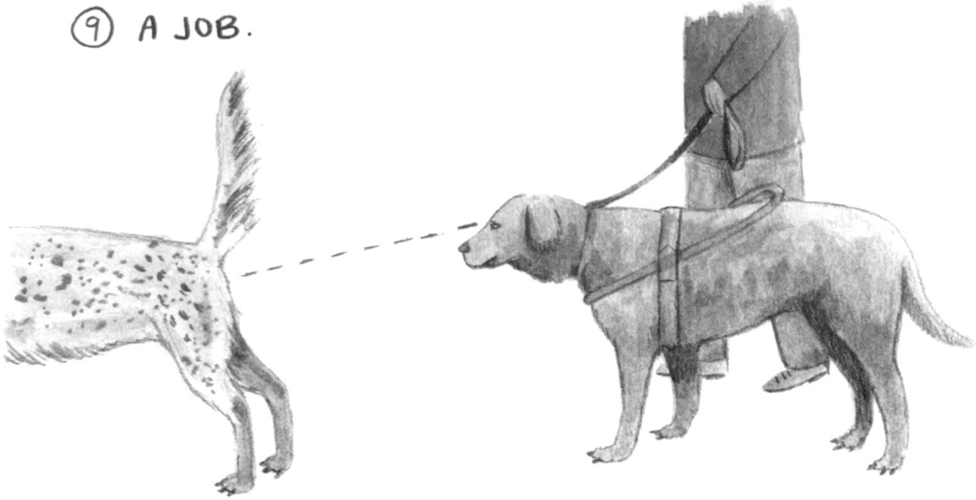

SEEING-EYE DOG.

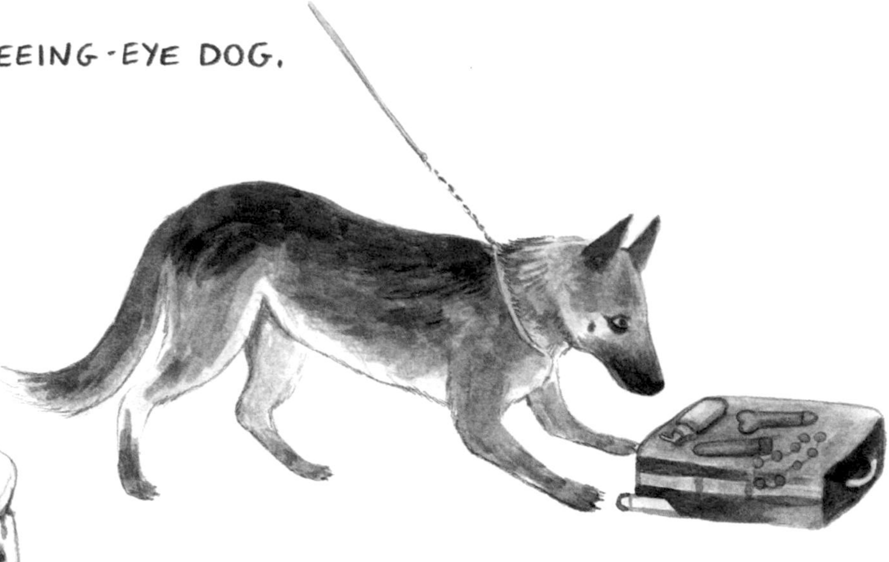

DRUG-SNIFFING DOG.

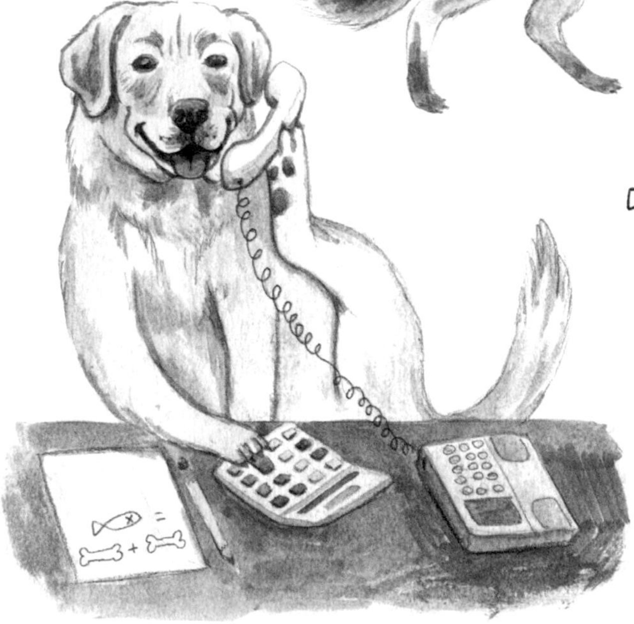

CERTIFIED PUBLIC ACCOUNTANT DOG.

(10) FOR US TO STOP EATING THEIR BISCUITS.

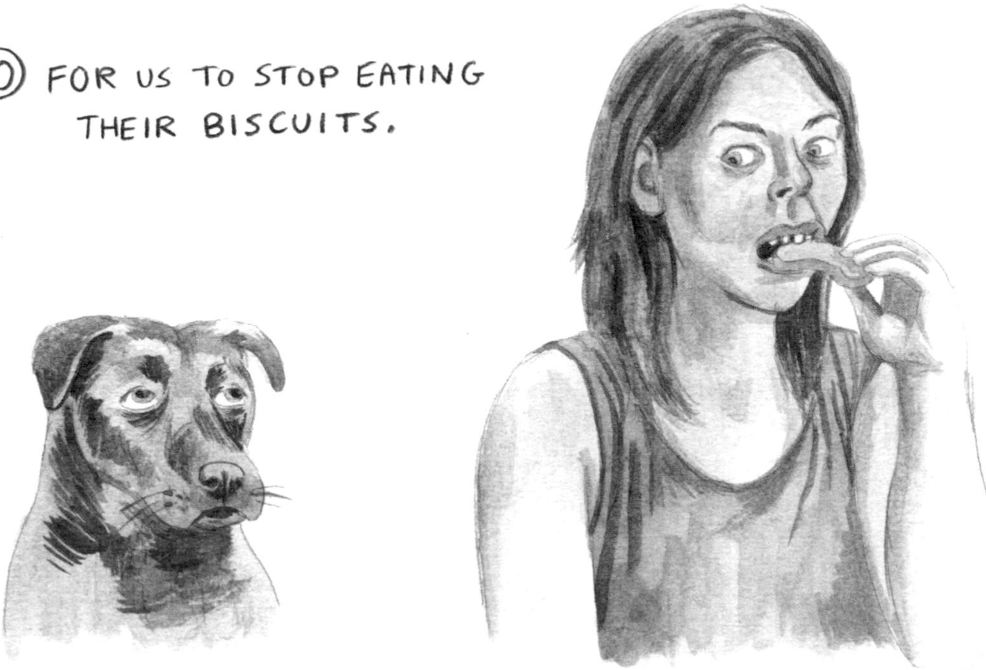

(11) THE DRIED, POWDERED URINE OF OTHER DOGS.

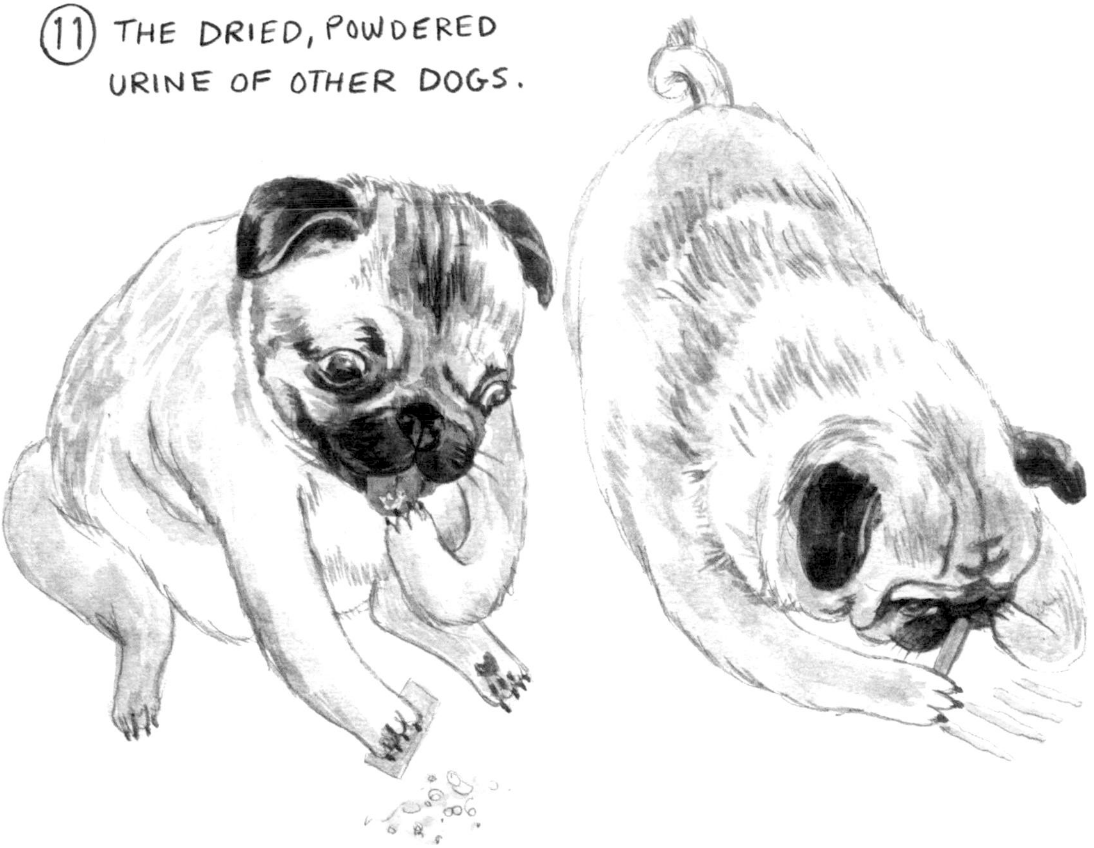

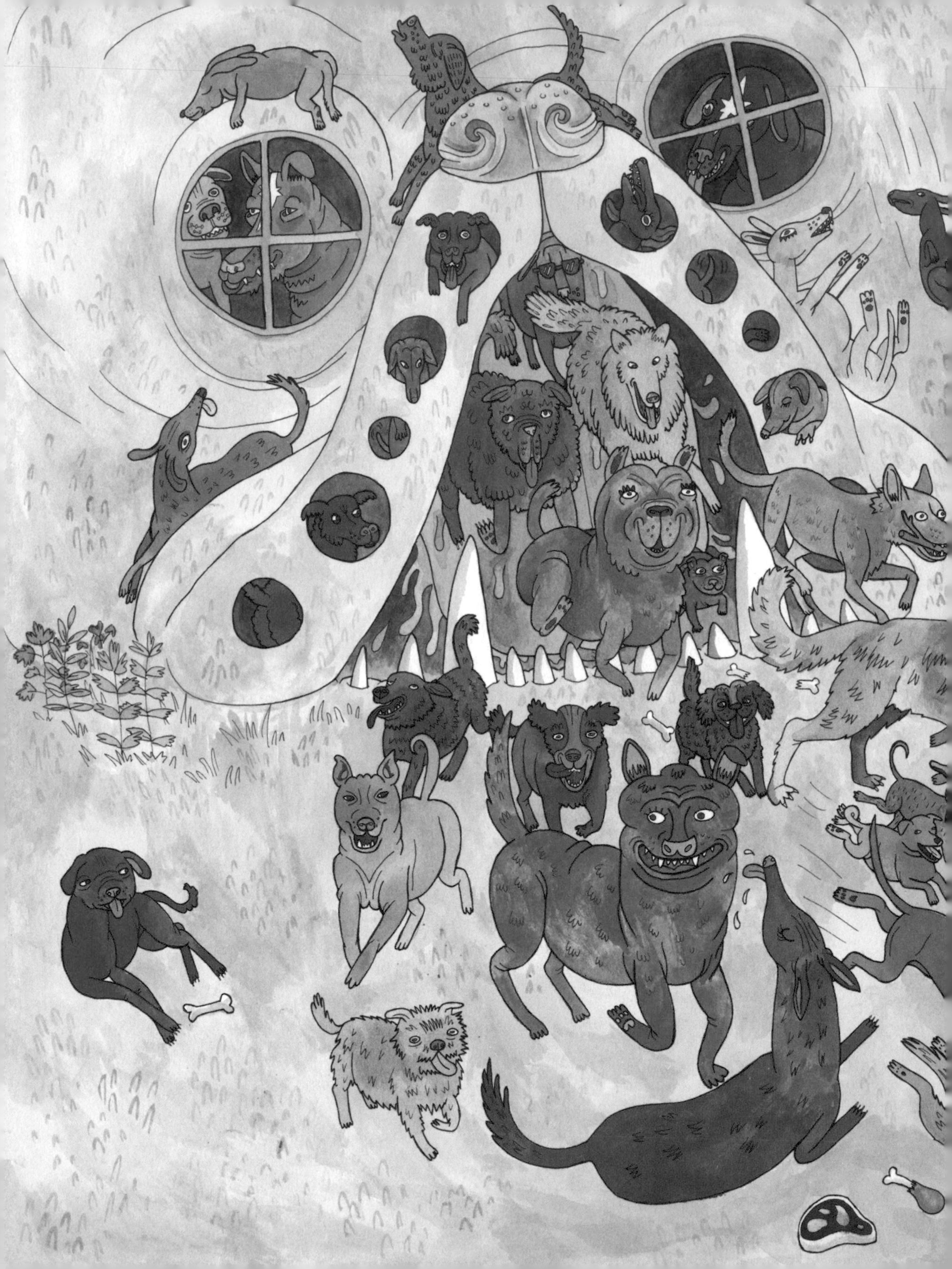

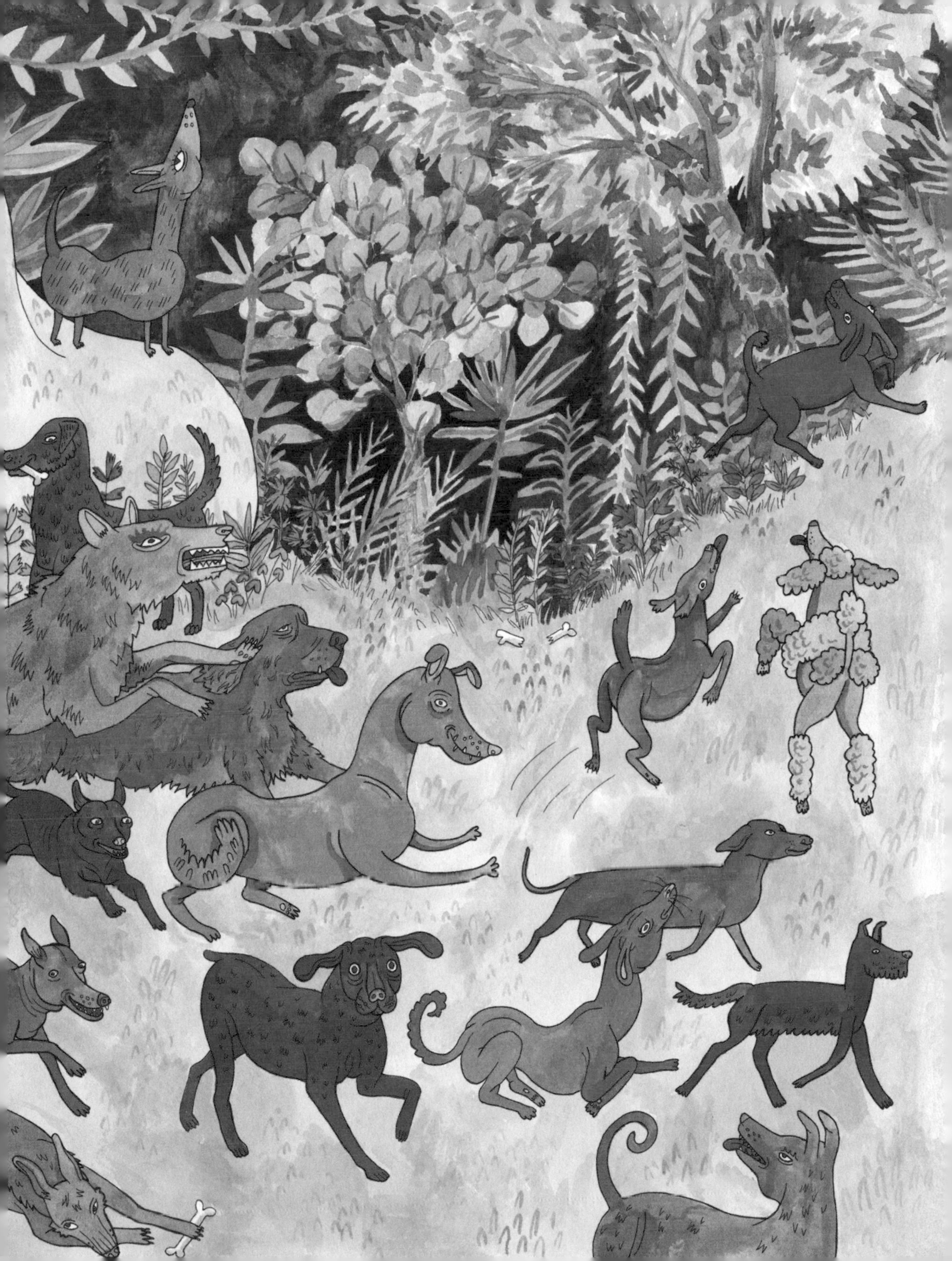

FASHION WEEK ANIMALS IN HATS

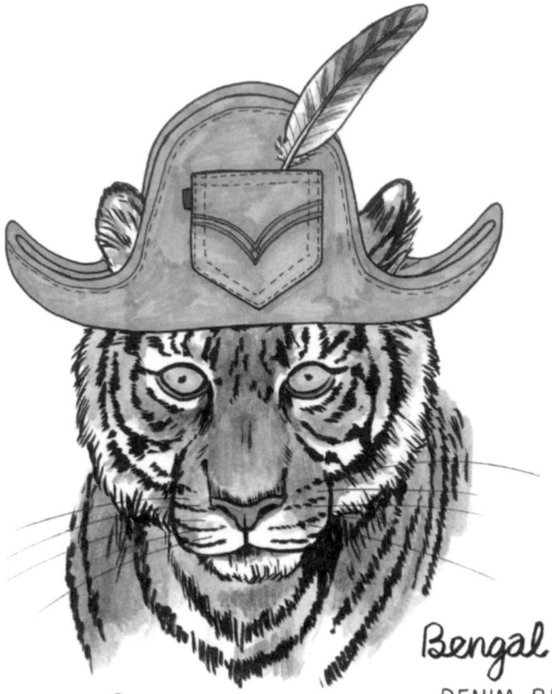

Bengal Tiger
DENIM BICORNE

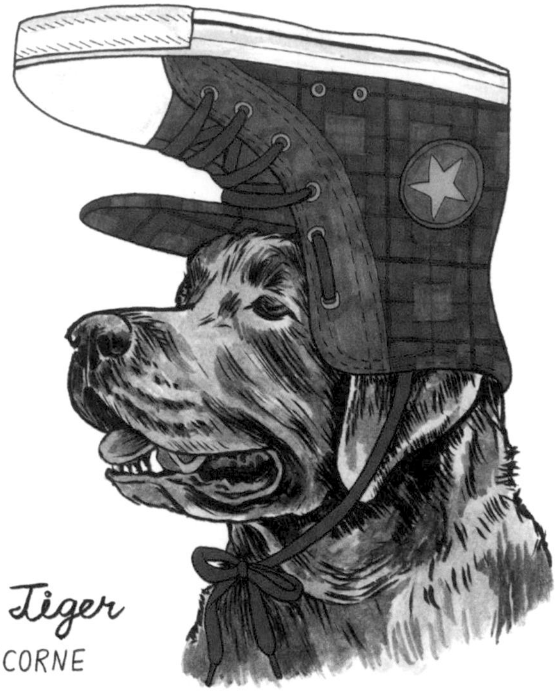

Labrador
ICONIC SNEAKER HUNTING CAP

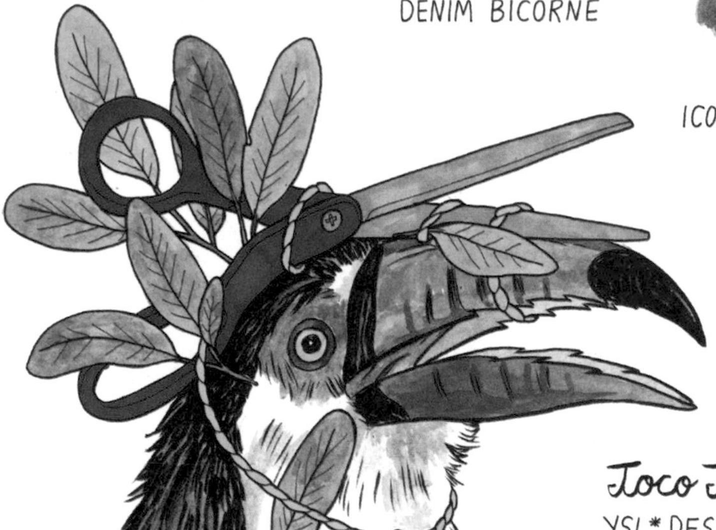

Toco Toucan
YSL* DESIGNER HAT

*YARN, SCISSORS, AND LEAVES

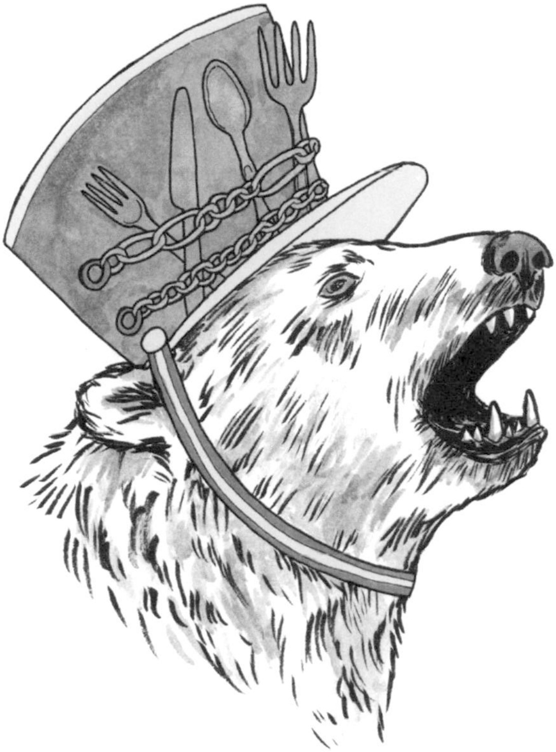

Polar Bear

MILITARY-INSPIRED UTENSIL HAT

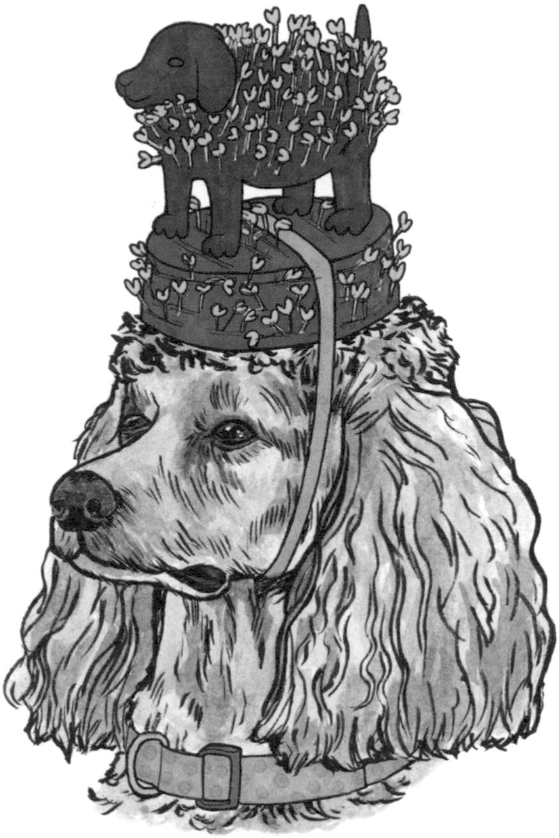

Standard Poodle

CHIA PET PILLBOX

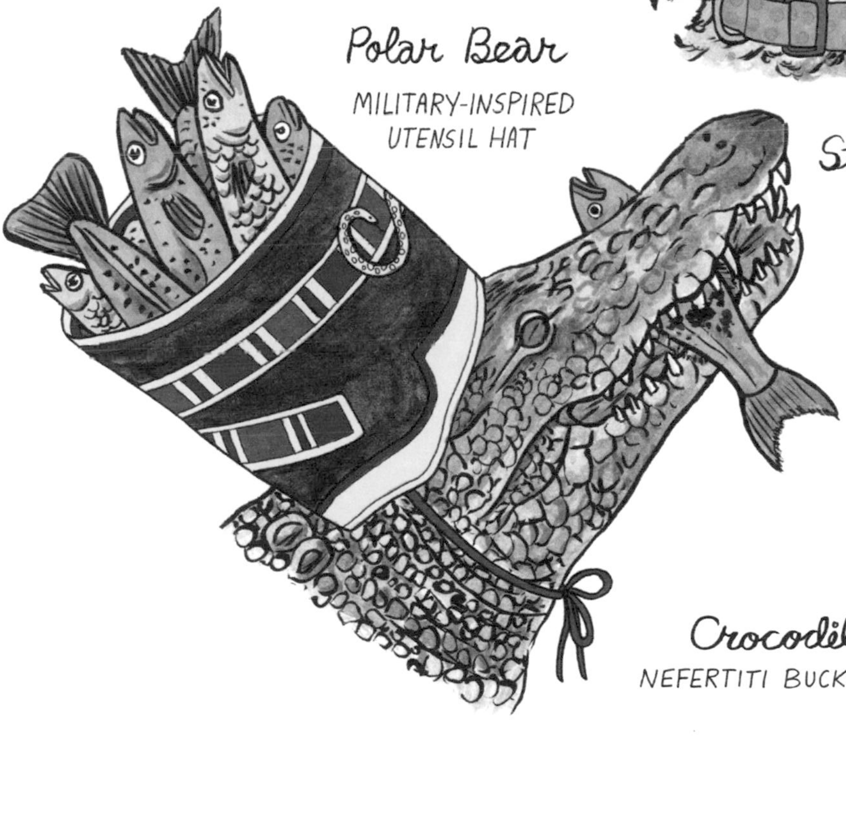

Crocodile

NEFERTITI BUCKET HAT

Hippopotamus

SWIMMING CAP (WITH FINGERS)

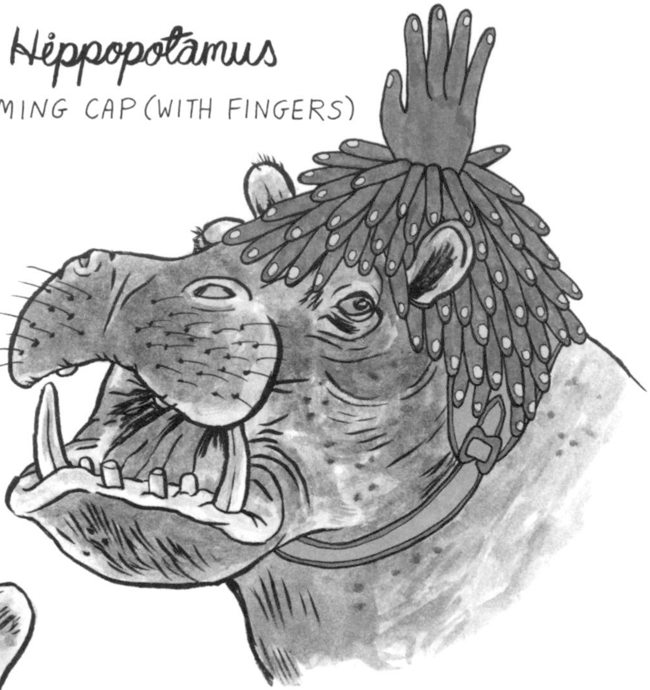

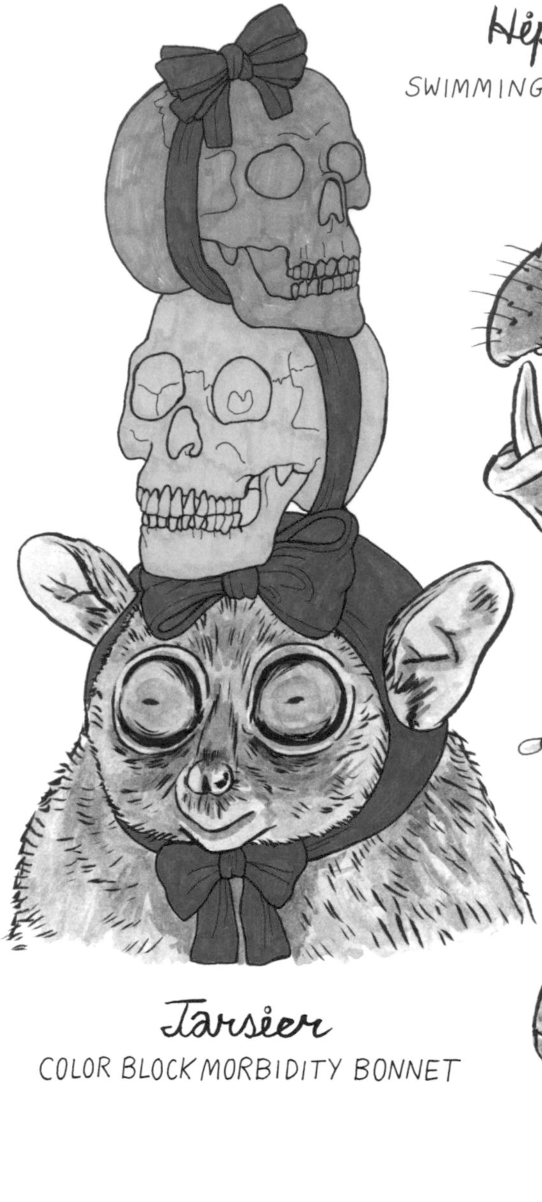

Tarsier

COLOR BLOCK MORBIDITY BONNET

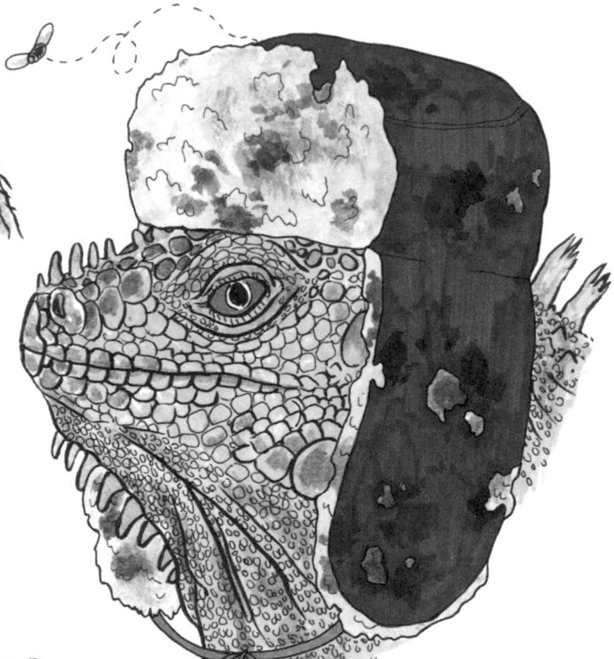

Iguana

SLOWLY ROTTING USHANKA

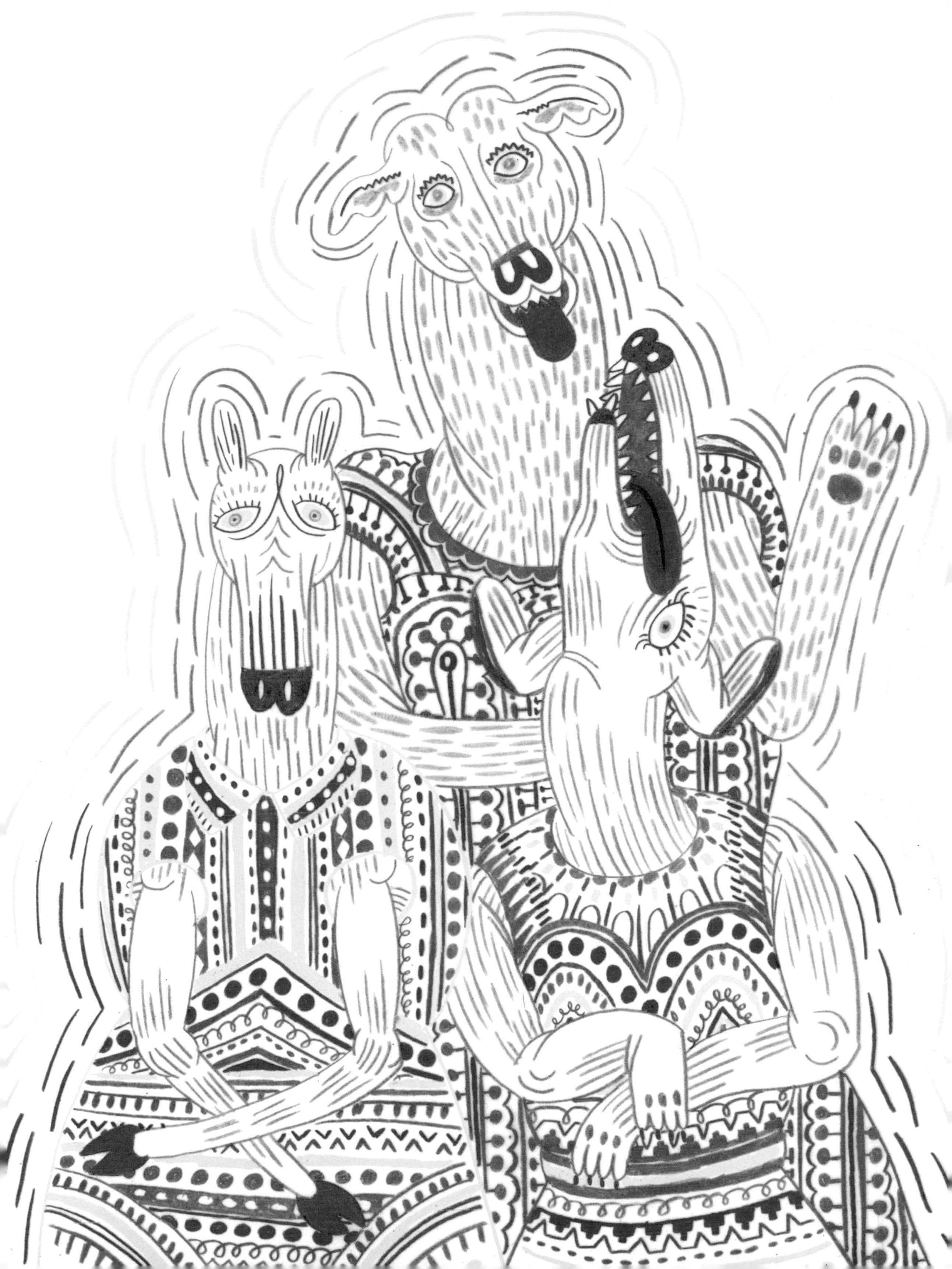

STOOL CHART

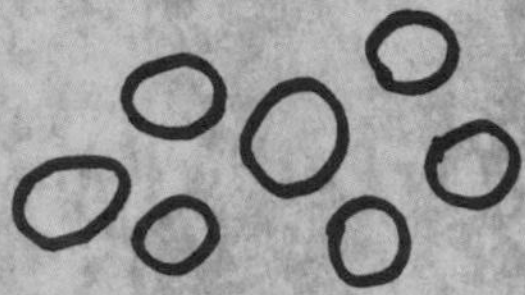

TYPE 1 YOU ARE A RABBIT

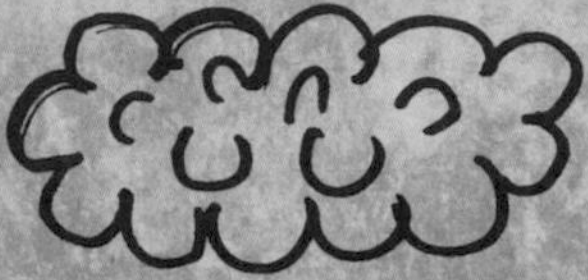

TYPE 2 YOU ARE A BEAR

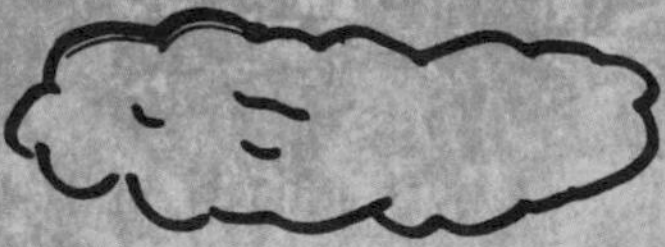

TYPE 3 YOU ARE A SMALL BEAR OR A HUMAN

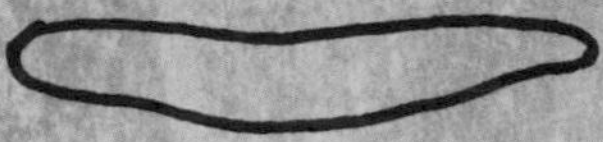

TYPE 4 YOU ARE A HUMAN

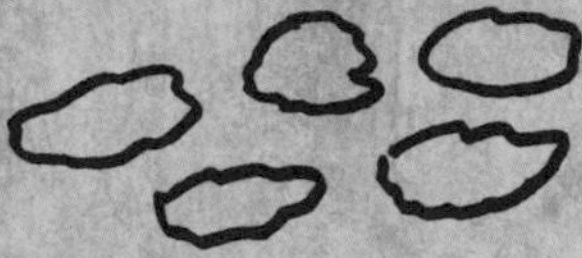

TYPE 5 YOU ARE A FRUIT

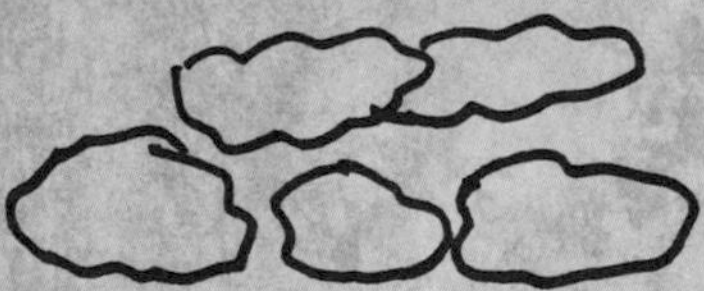

TYPE 6 YOU ARE A SICK HUMAN

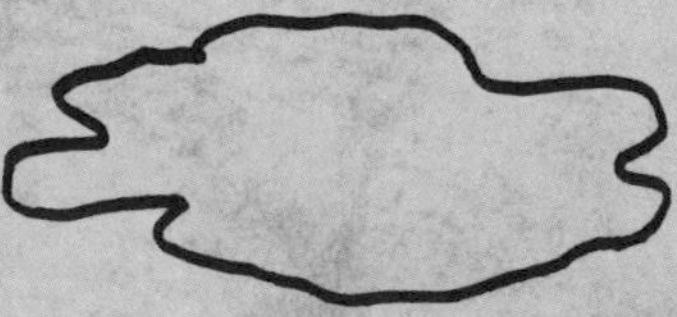

TYPE 7 YOU ARE A CAR

AN ILLUSTRATED MOVIE REVIEW

RISE OF THE PLANET OF THE APES

I DON'T GET IT. WHY DO PEOPLE LOVE MONKEYS SO MUCH? CHIMPANZEES AREN'T CUTE; THEY LOOK LIKE OLD MEN WITH HORMONAL IMBALANCES. THEY'RE UNCANNY AND CREEPY. PLUS THEIR HAIR LOOKS WIRY AND UNPLEASANT TO PET. I KNOW APES AND MONKEYS AREN'T THE SAME THING, BUT I LUMP THEM TOGETHER AS THE POOP-HURLERS OF THE ANIMAL KINGDOM.

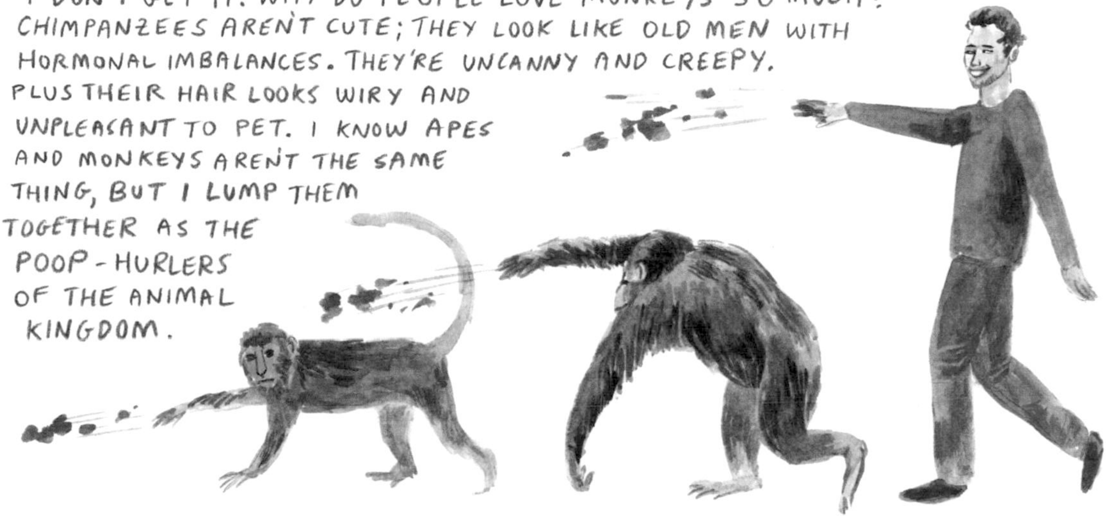
MONKEY
APE
JAMES FRANCO

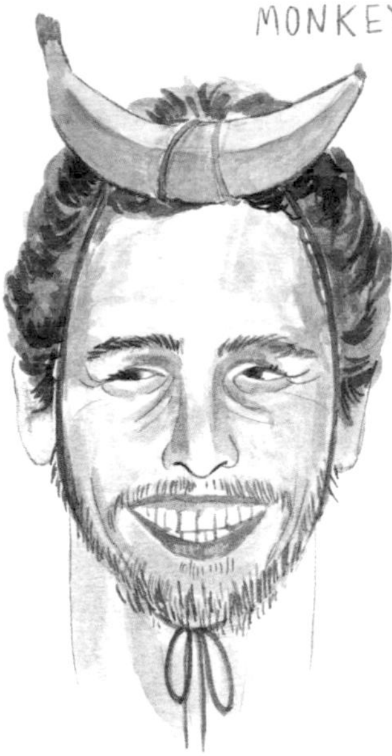

BANANA FRANCO

MY MONKEY-LOVING BOYFRIEND DRAGGED ME TO SEE "RISE OF THE PLANET OF THE APES" ON AN OPENING FRIDAY NIGHT WITH A ROWDY AUDIENCE. HERE ARE MY NOTES AND DRAWINGS:

- THIS AUDIENCE IS SO PRO-APE FROM THE START; THEY CLEARLY ALL CAME ON OPENING NIGHT BECAUSE THEY LOVE CHIMPS. WILL I STICK OUT AS AN APE HATER?
- I JUST WROTE "MONKEYS ARE HORRIBLE" IN MY NOTEBOOK, BUT I'M HUNCHING OVER IT SO NOBODY CAN SEE.
- THE MOVIE IS OFF TO A FAST- AND STUPID-PACED START AND I LIKE IT!
- JAMES FRANCO IS CAST AS THE LEAST PROFESSIONAL RESEARCH SCIENTIST TO EVER EXIST.

- THE BOSS CHARACTER, JACOBS, JUST SHOUTED, "I RUN A BUSINESS, NOT A PETTING ZOO!" HEY, PETTING ZOOS ARE TOTALLY A BUSINESS.

- ALSO, PETTING ZOOS ARE FUN TO OWN AND THEY'RE VIRTUALLY RECESSION-PROOF! HERE ARE SOME TIPS FOR RUNNING A SUCCESSFUL PETTING ZOO:

CHARGE A HUGE MARKUP ON CONES FILLED WITH PELLETS.

TRAIN ANIMALS TO PICK POCKETS.

PAD YOUR ZOO WITH BARGAIN-PRICED ANIMALS, LIKE POST-EASTER BUNNIES & CHICKS.

- SORRY, I ZONED OUT DURING THE BORING JOHN LITHGOW PARTS AND WENT OFF ON THAT PETTING ZOO TANGENT.

- JACOBS HAS ALL THE BEST LINES. "YOU KNOW EVERYTHING ABOUT THE HUMAN BRAIN, EXCEPT HOW IT WORKS." THAT'S SUCH A BURN TO A SCIENTIST. HOW BRAINS WORK IS 99% OF WHAT THERE IS TO KNOW ABOUT BRAINS!

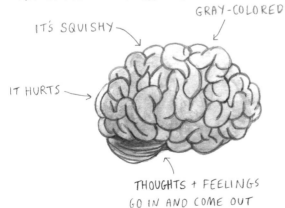

IT'S SQUISHY

GRAY-COLORED

IT HURTS

THOUGHTS + FEELINGS GO IN AND COME OUT

- JAMES FRANCO AND FREIDA PINTO HAVE THE MOST BEAUTIFUL SMILES. "FRANCO & FREIDA" SHOULD BE THE NAME OF A FANCY FURNITURE STORE.

- CAESAR HAS JUST LEARNED SIGN LANGUAGE, AND IT'S MAKING THE AUDIENCE GO, "AWW!" BUT MOST OF HIS GESTURES JUST LOOK OBSCENE.

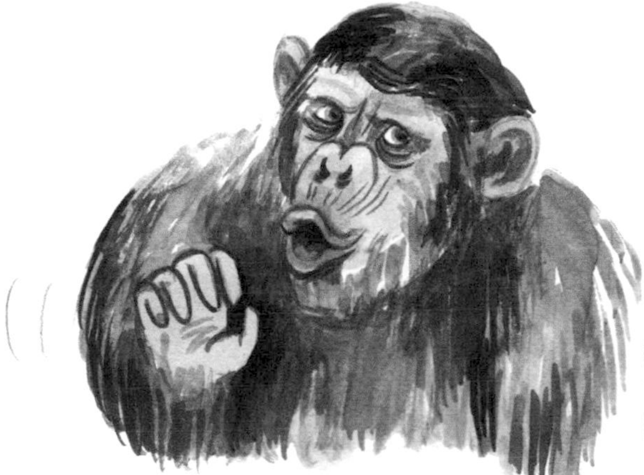

I WANT ICE CREAM.

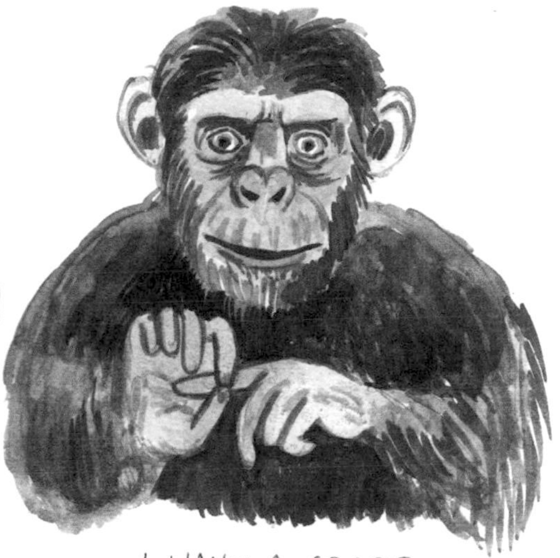

I WANT A GRAPE.

- THE PLOT JUST JUMPED AHEAD NEARLY TEN YEARS. CAESAR LOOKS LIKE HE'S BEEN IN TWO WARS AND SEEN EIGHT GHOSTS, WHILE FRANCO & FREIDA HAVEN'T AGED A DAY OR EVEN CHANGED THEIR HAIRCUTS.
- ALSO, THESE CHARACTERS HAVE BEEN DATING FOR FIVE YEARS AND ONLY NOW DOES SHE NOTICE AN ENTIRE ROOM OF HIS HOUSE IS DEVOTED TO CHARTING THE EFFECTS OF DRUGS ON HIS PET CHIMPANZEE. THE WALLS ARE COMPLETELY PLASTERED WITH RESEARCH AND SCIENCEY GRAPHS AND STUFF. BOY DOES SHE LOOK SURPRISED!

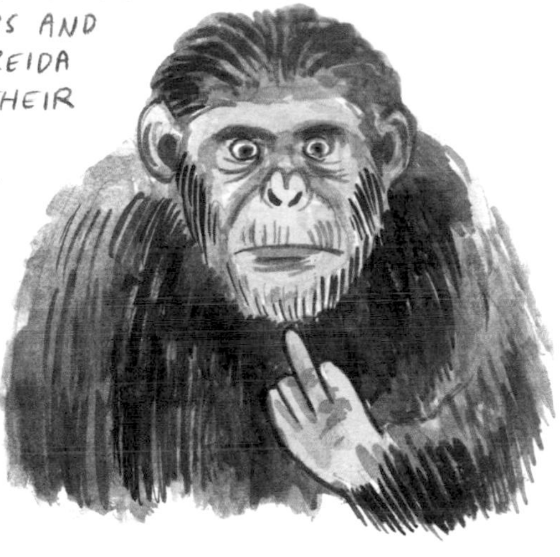

GIVE ME A BANANA.

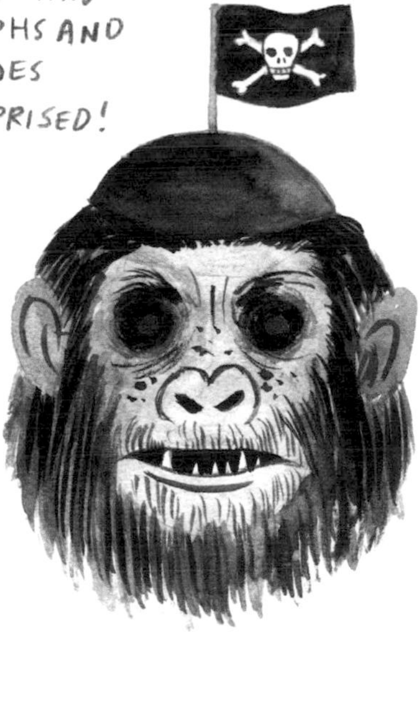

- WE ARE GETTING EVERY POSSIBLE VISUAL CUE THAT THIS PARTICULAR CHIMP IS THE EVIL CHIMP.

- I HATE IT WHEN, IN ORDER TO INDICATE DEADLY ILLNESS, SCREENWRITERS HAVE THE CHARACTERS COUGH BLOOD INTO HANKIES, OR SNEEZE BLOOD ALL OVER EACH OTHER'S FACES, OR MOONWALK ACROSS A FLOOR COVERED IN THEIR OWN LIQUEFIED INTERNAL ORGANS. IT'S SO CLICHÉ!

- OKAY, I GUESS I DO LIKE SOME PRIMATES, BECAUSE "CIRCUS ORANGUTAN" IS MY NEW FAVORITE ANIMAL. HE LOOKS TOO COOL TO THROW HIS OWN POOP.

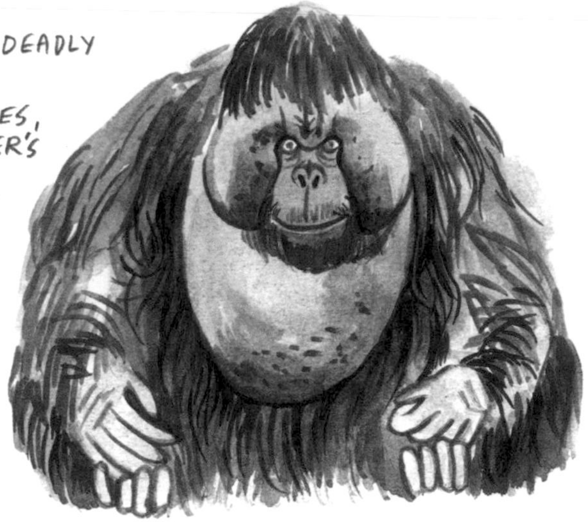

CIRCUS ORANGUTAN

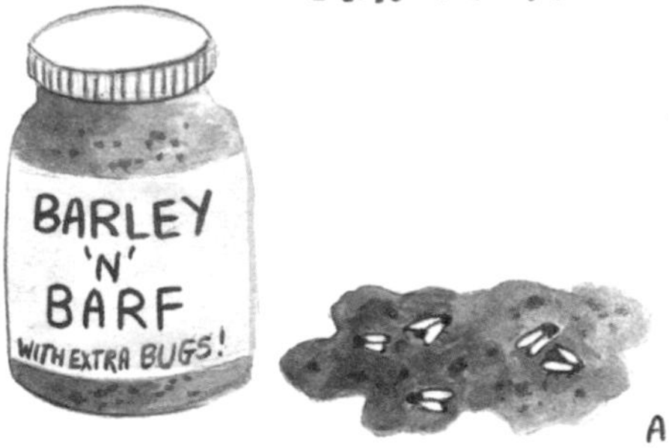
BARLEY 'N' BARF
WITH EXTRA BUGS!

- THE PROP MASTER DESERVES PROPS (SORRY) FOR MAKING THE CHIMP SANCTUARY FOOD LOOK SO DISGUSTING.

- CAESAR JUST REACHED INTO A FRIDGE TO GRAB A CAN OF DEADLY VIRUS AND A DUDE BEHIND US SHOUTED "FOUR LOKO!!"

- THIS AUDIENCE IS GETTING TOTALLY JAZZED ABOUT THE APES BECOMING POWERFUL AND REBELLIOUS BUT THIS IS MY WORST NIGHTMARE.

- MEANWHILE, MY BOYFRIEND'S IN HEAVEN. HE JUST LEANED OVER TO SAY, "I WISH I WAS A MONKEY." IS THERE A CHIMPANZEE VERSION OF SWIMMING WITH DOLPHINS? BECAUSE THAT WOULD BE THE BEST PRESENT I COULD EVER GET HIM.

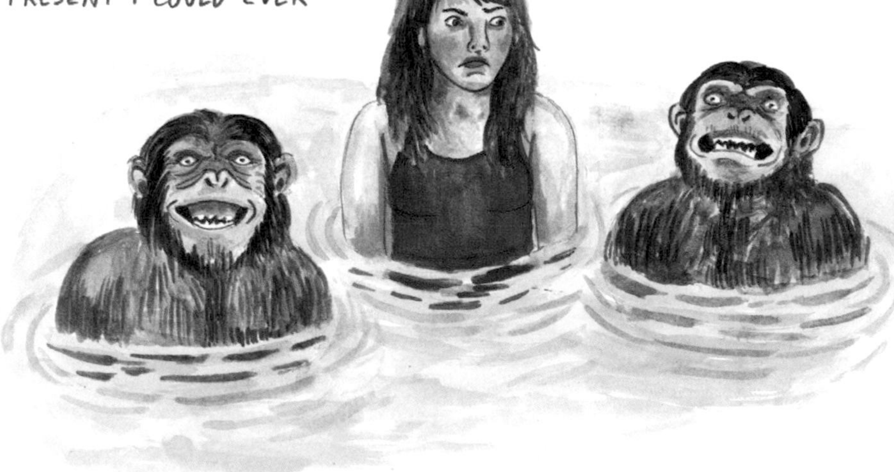

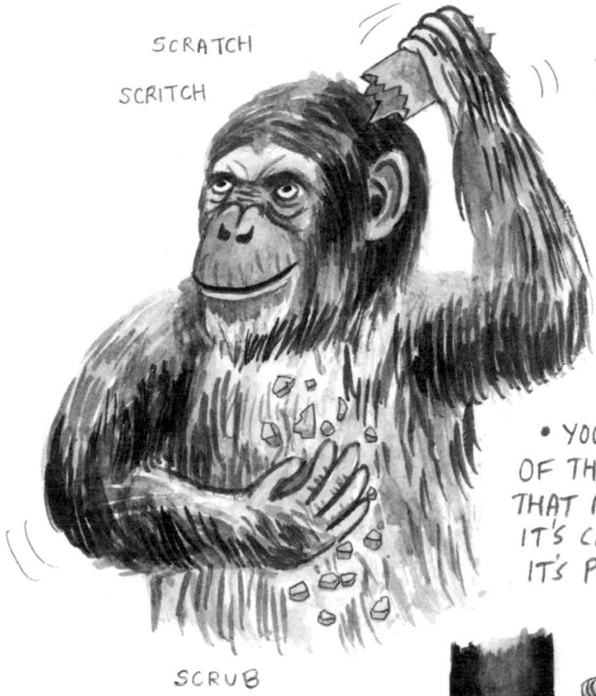
SCRATCH
SCRITCH
SCRUB

- ONE OF THE CHARACTERS JUST GOT ELECTROCUTED, AND A LADY SITTING NEAR ME WHISPERED, "WATER CONDUCTS ELECTRICITY!!"

- IF THERE'S ONE THING I'VE LEARNED FROM THIS MOVIE, IT'S THAT APES ARE CONSTANTLY JUMPING THROUGH GLASS WINDOWS. THE SHATTERING GLASS MUST FEEL GOOD ON THEIR FUR?

- YOU KNOW WHAT I'D LIKE TO SEE? "RISE OF THE PLANET OF THE DOGS"! EXCEPT THAT MOVIE HAS ALREADY BEEN MADE. IT'S CALLED "HOTEL FOR DOGS" (AND IT'S PRETTY GOOD).

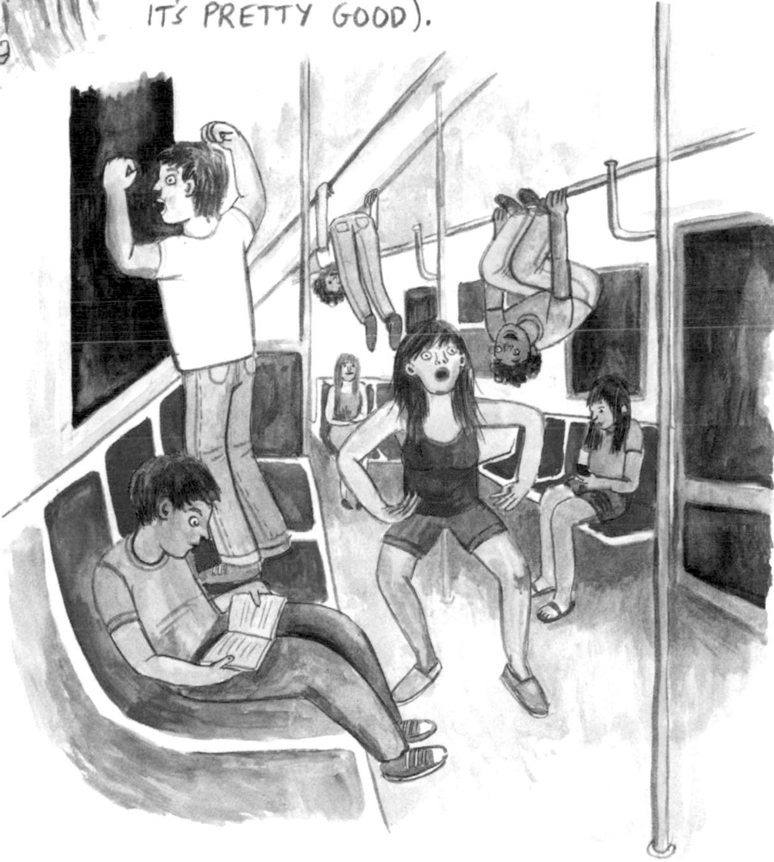

- ON THE SUBWAY RIDE HOME, IT'S EASY TO POINT OUT OTHER PEOPLE WHO HAVE JUST SEEN "RISE OF THE PLANET OF THE APES."

- IN CONCLUSION: YOU WILL LOVE THIS MOVIE IF YOU LOVE APES. IF YOU DON'T LIKE APES, THIS MOVIE WILL MAKE YOU FEEL MORE STRONGLY ABOUT NOT LIKING THEM. I GIVE IT FIVE-OUT-OF-FIVE APES!

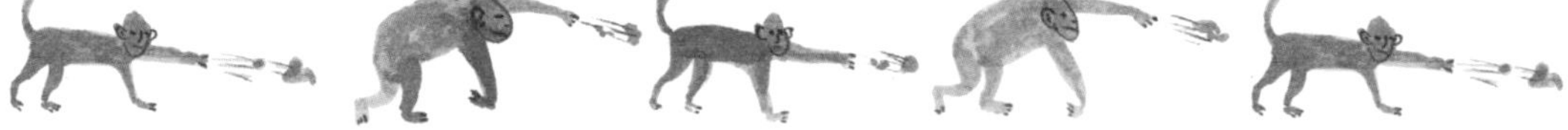

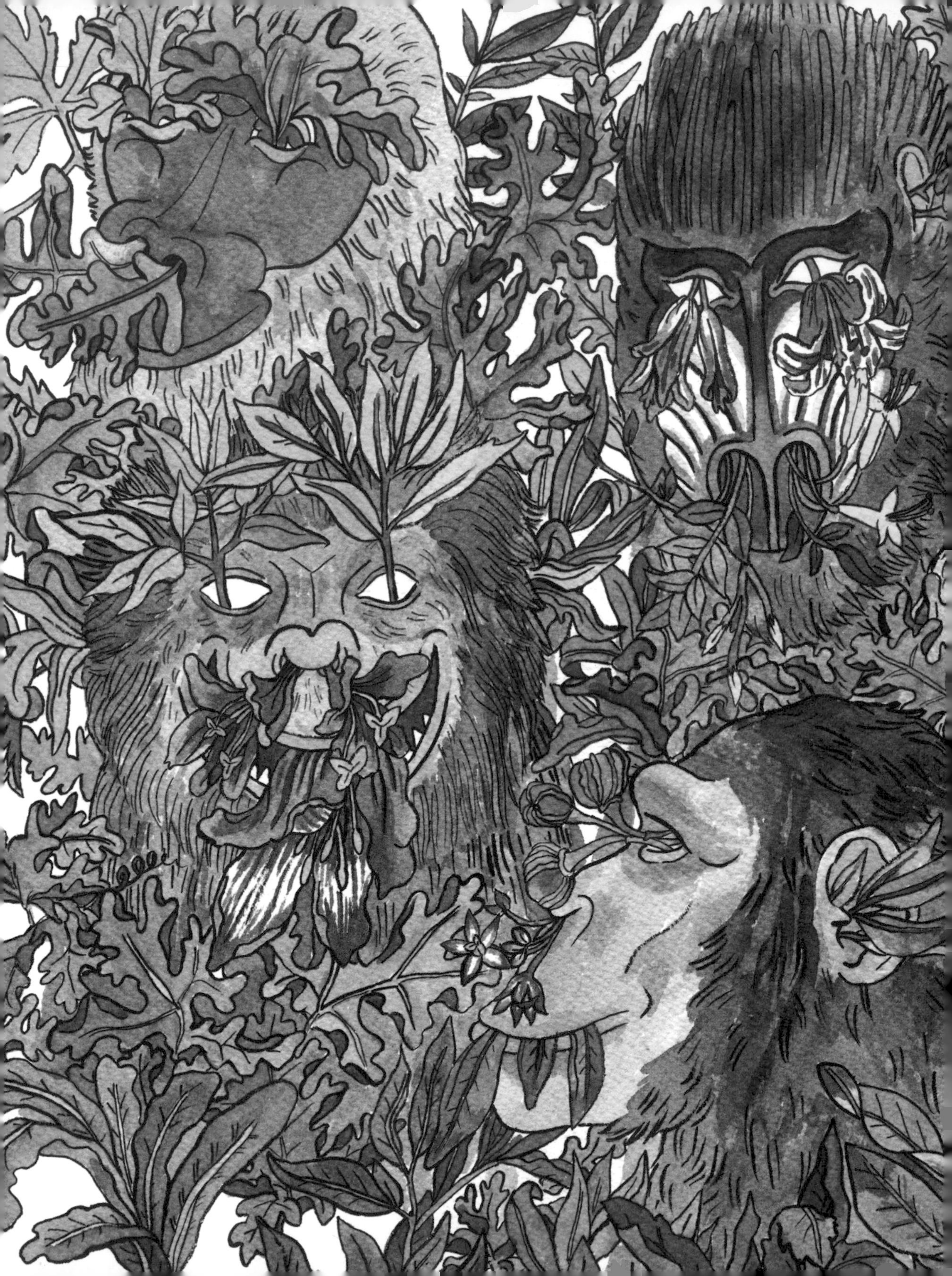

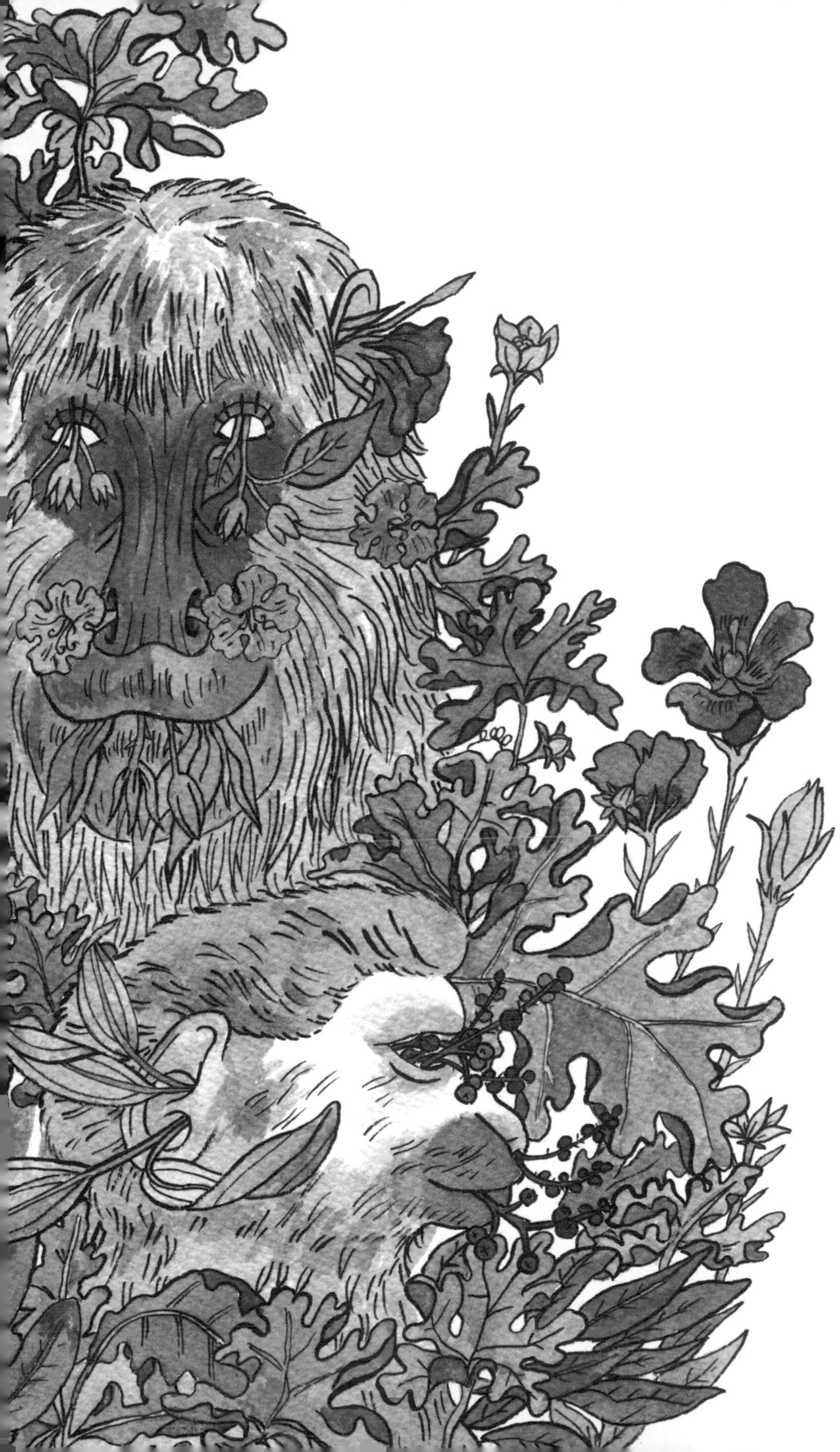

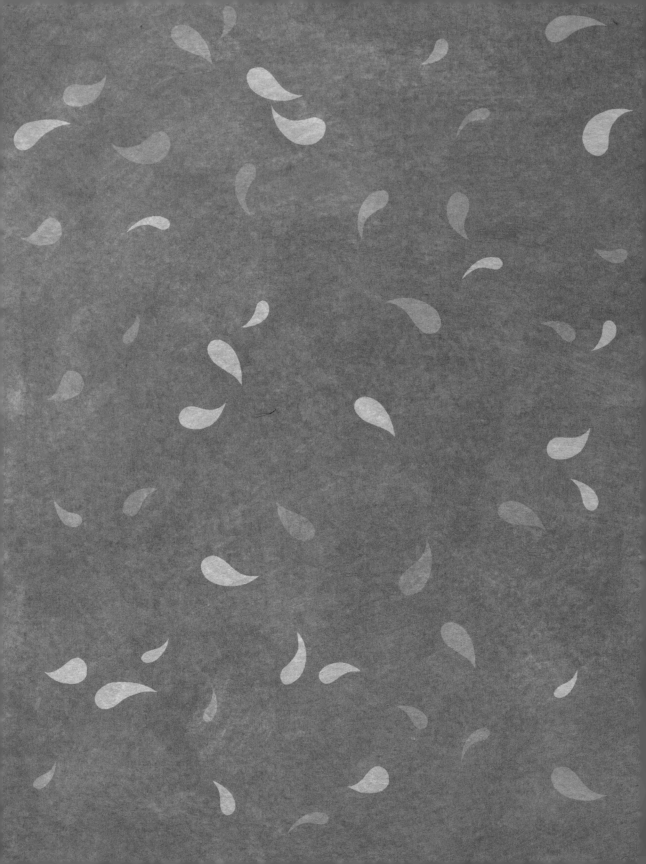

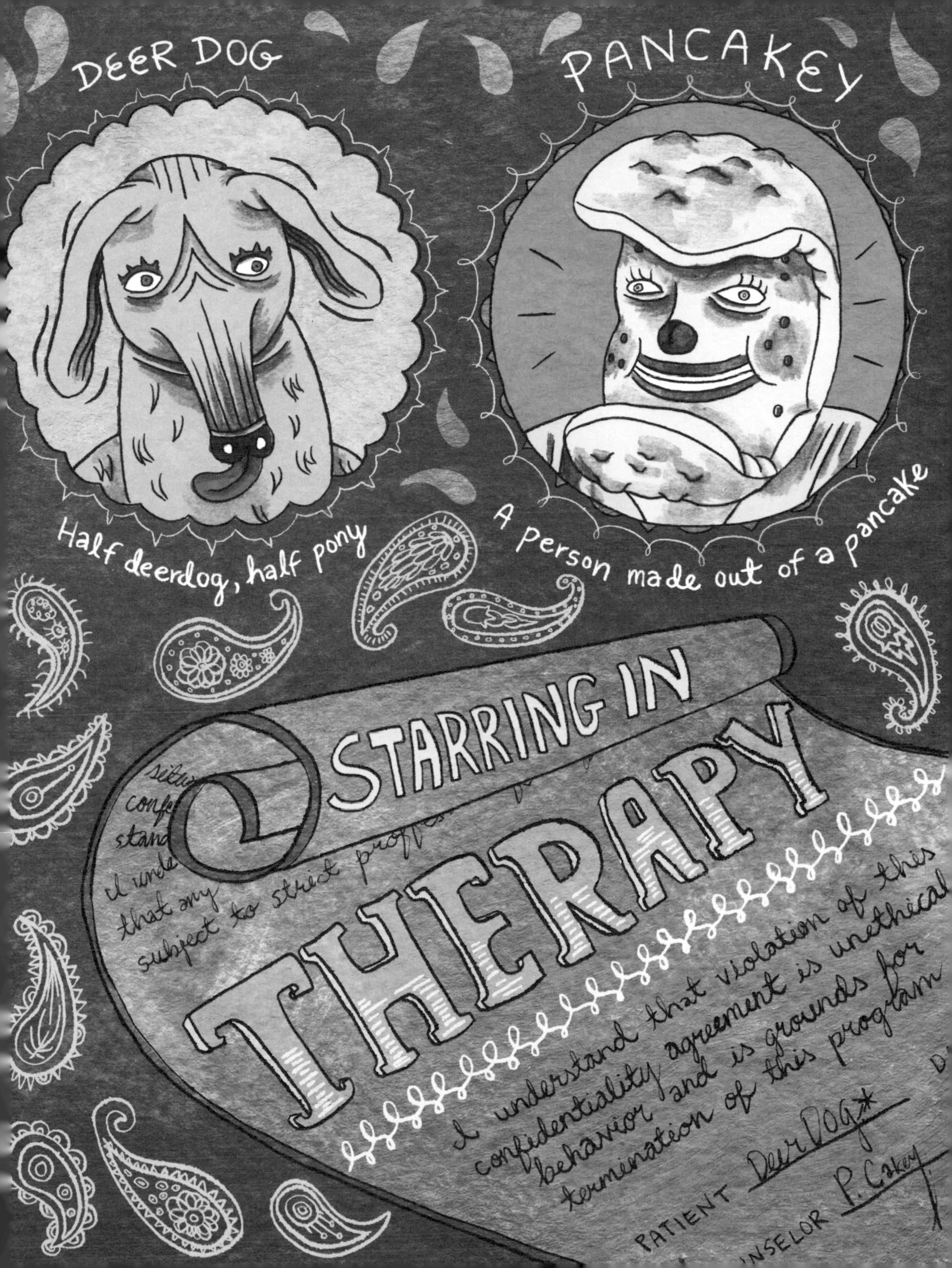
DEER DOG
PANCAKEY
Half deerdog, half pony
A person made out of a pancake
STARRING IN
THERAPY
I understand that violation of this confidentiality agreement is unethical behavior and is grounds for termination of this program
subject to strict proffes
PATIENT Deer DOG*
NSELOR P. Cakey

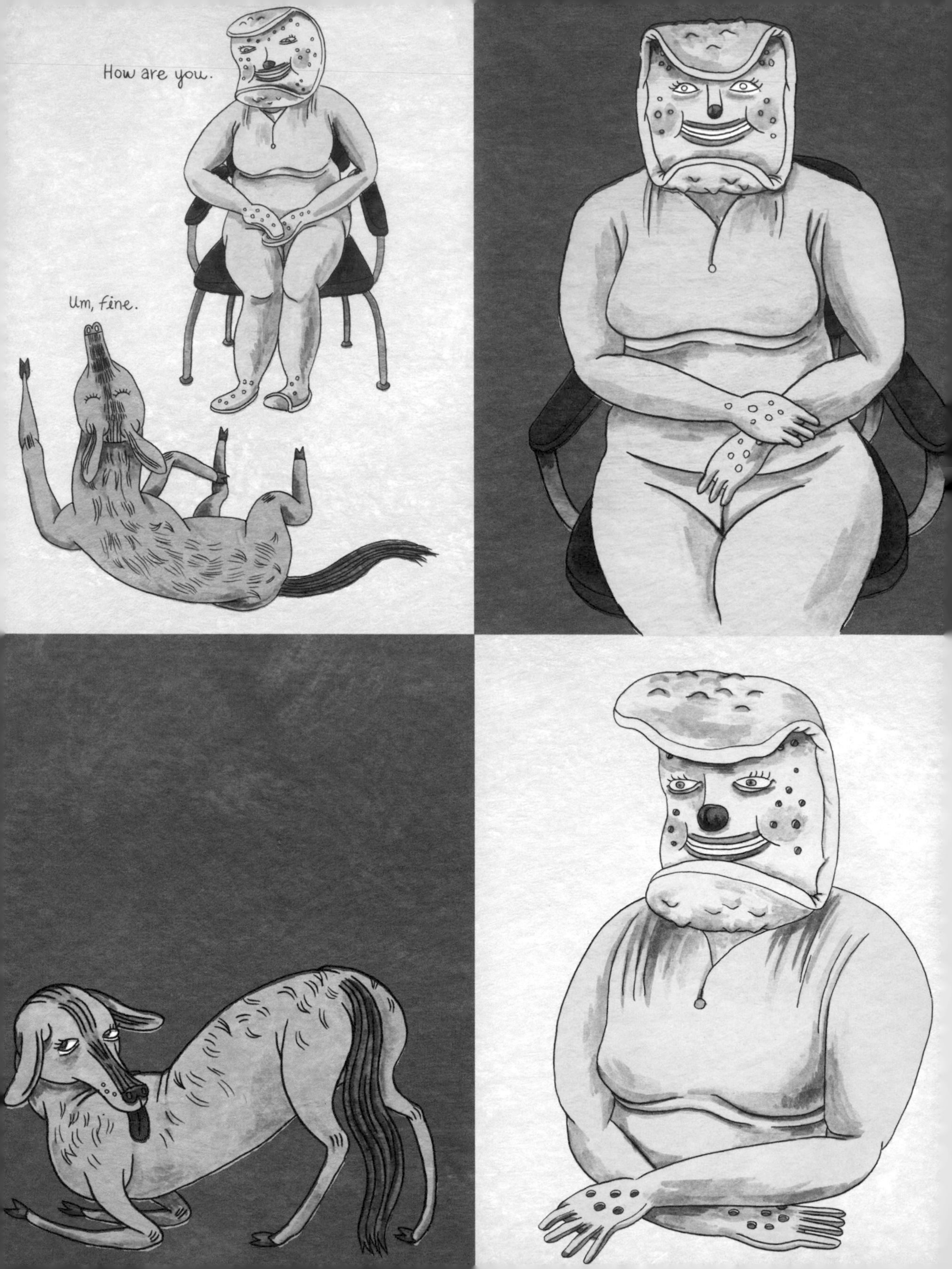
How are you.
Um, fine.

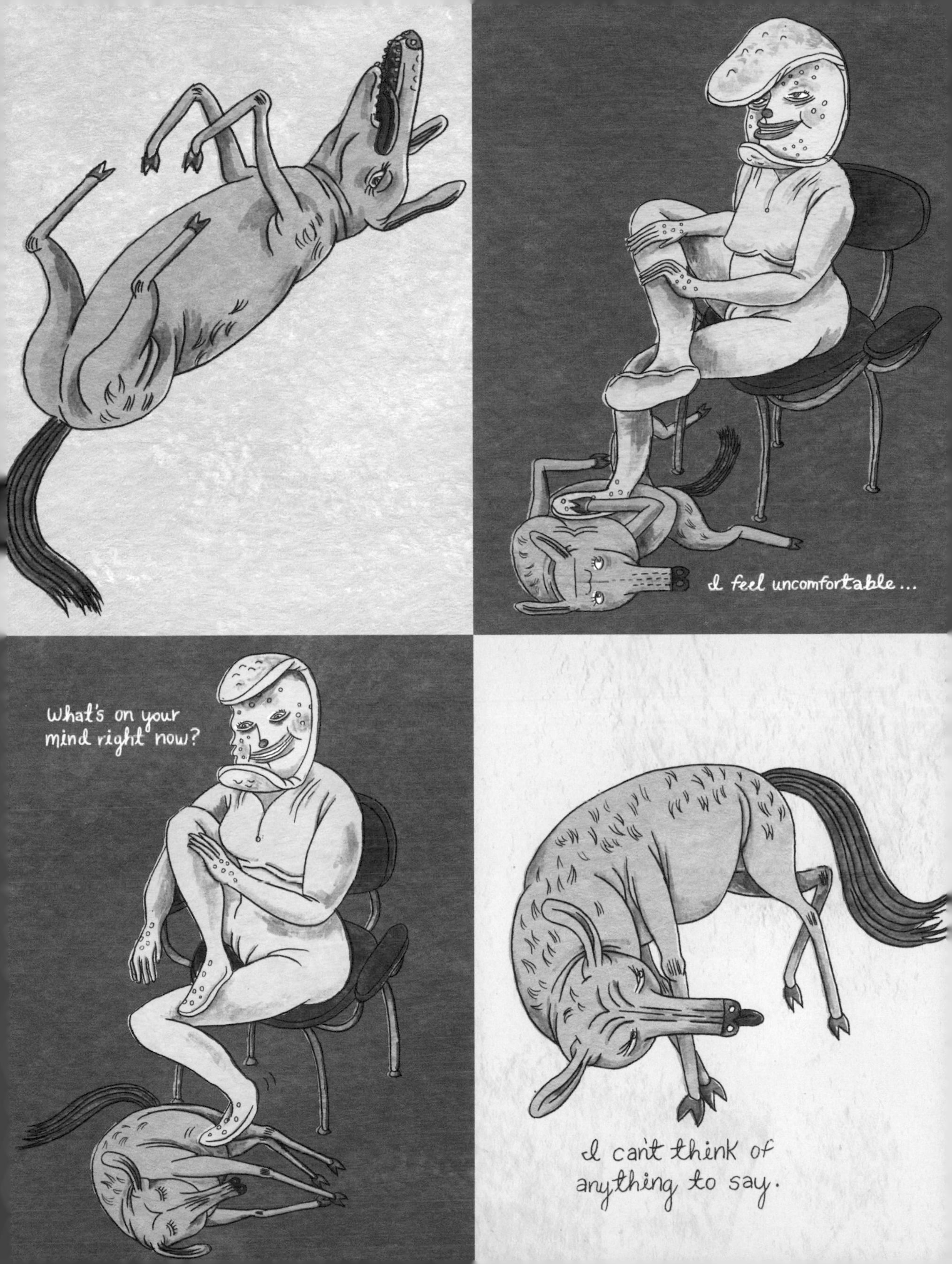
I feel uncomfortable...
What's on your mind right now?
I can't think of anything to say.

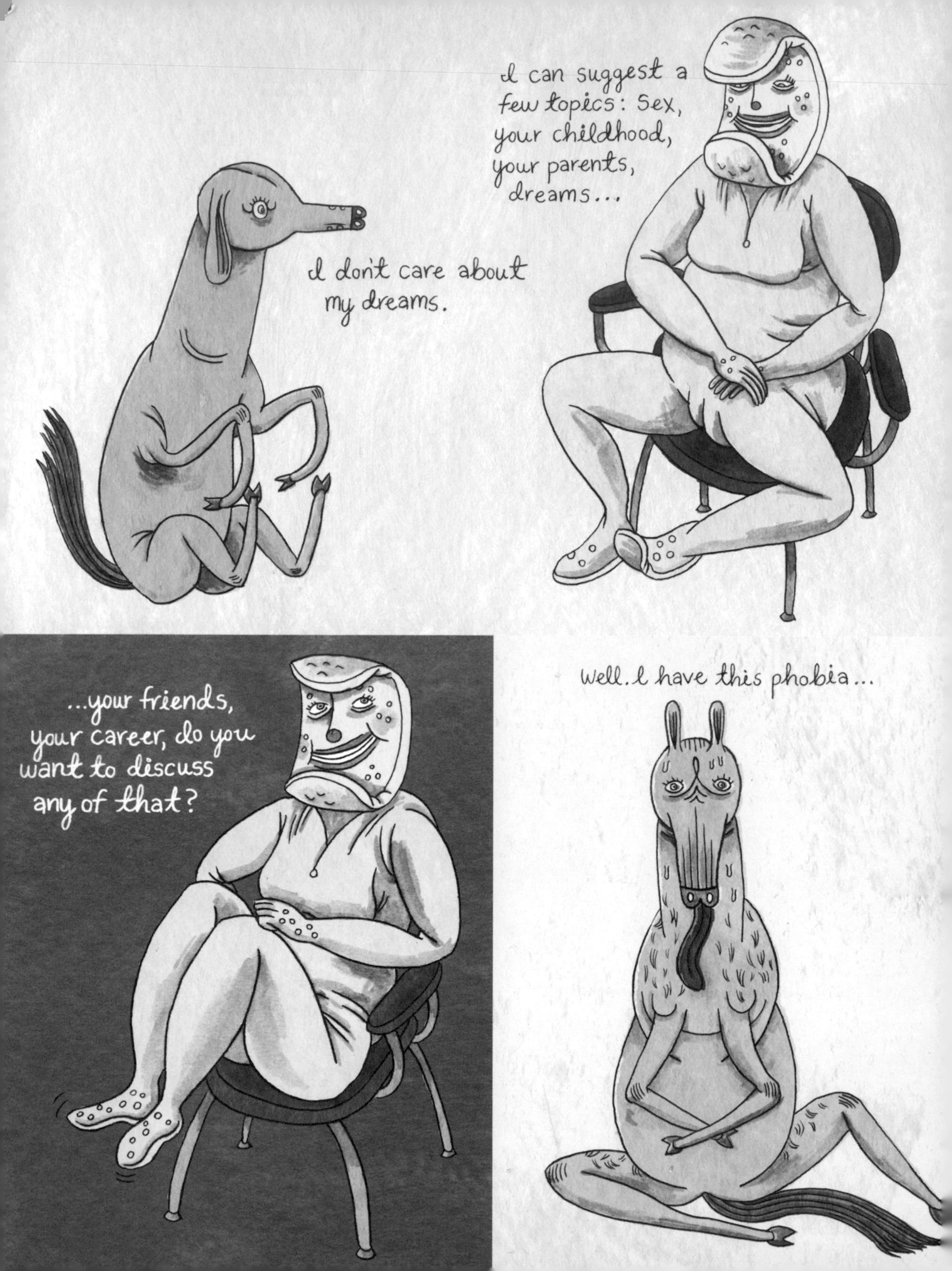
I can suggest a few topics: Sex, your childhood, your parents, dreams...
I don't care about my dreams.
...your friends, your career, do you want to discuss any of that?
Well. I have this phobia...

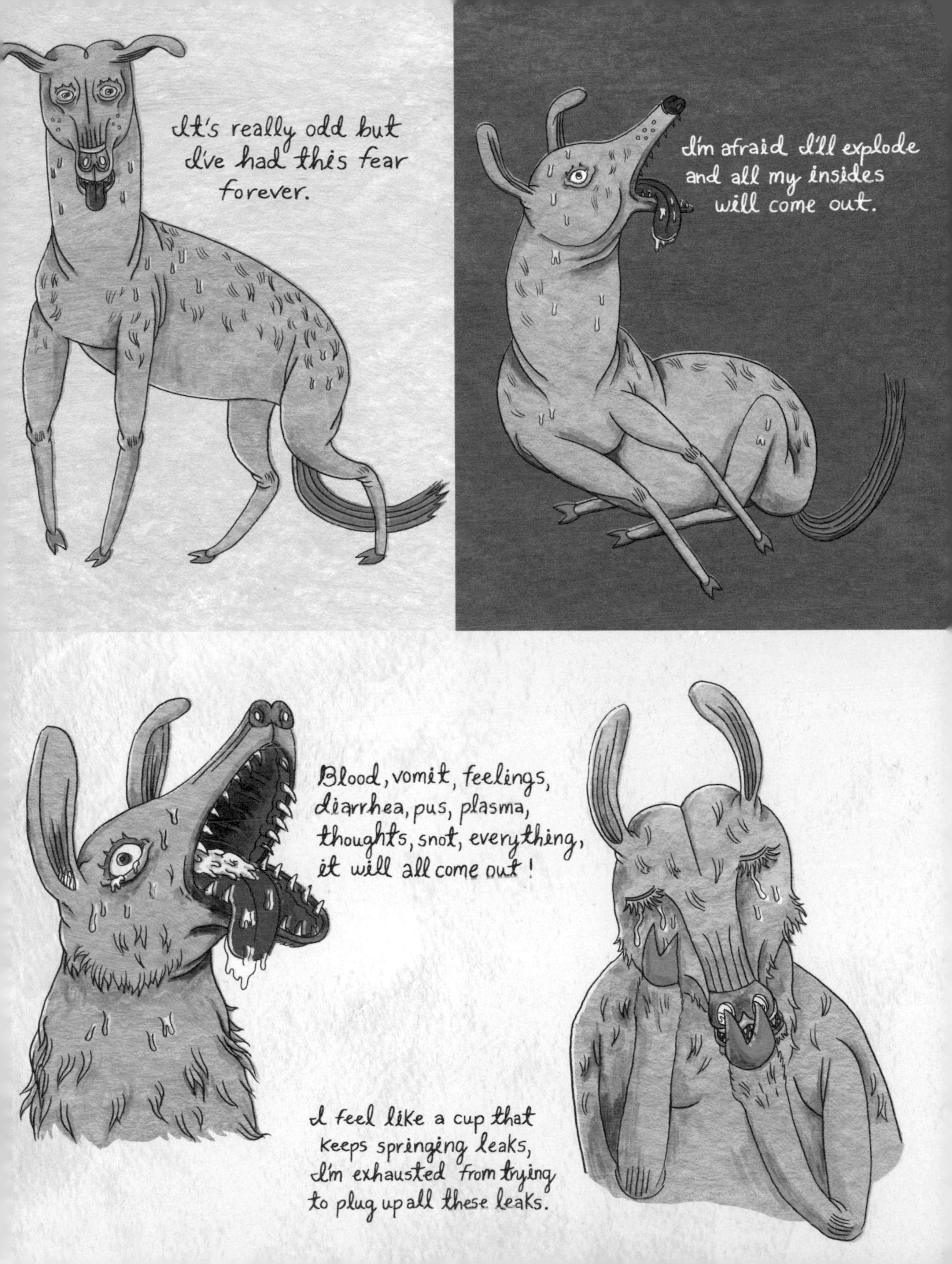
It's really odd but I've had this fear forever.
I'm afraid I'll explode and all my insides will come out.
Blood, vomit, feelings, diarrhea, pus, plasma, thoughts, snot, everything, it will all come out!
I feel like a cup that keeps springing leaks, I'm exhausted from trying to plug up all these leaks.

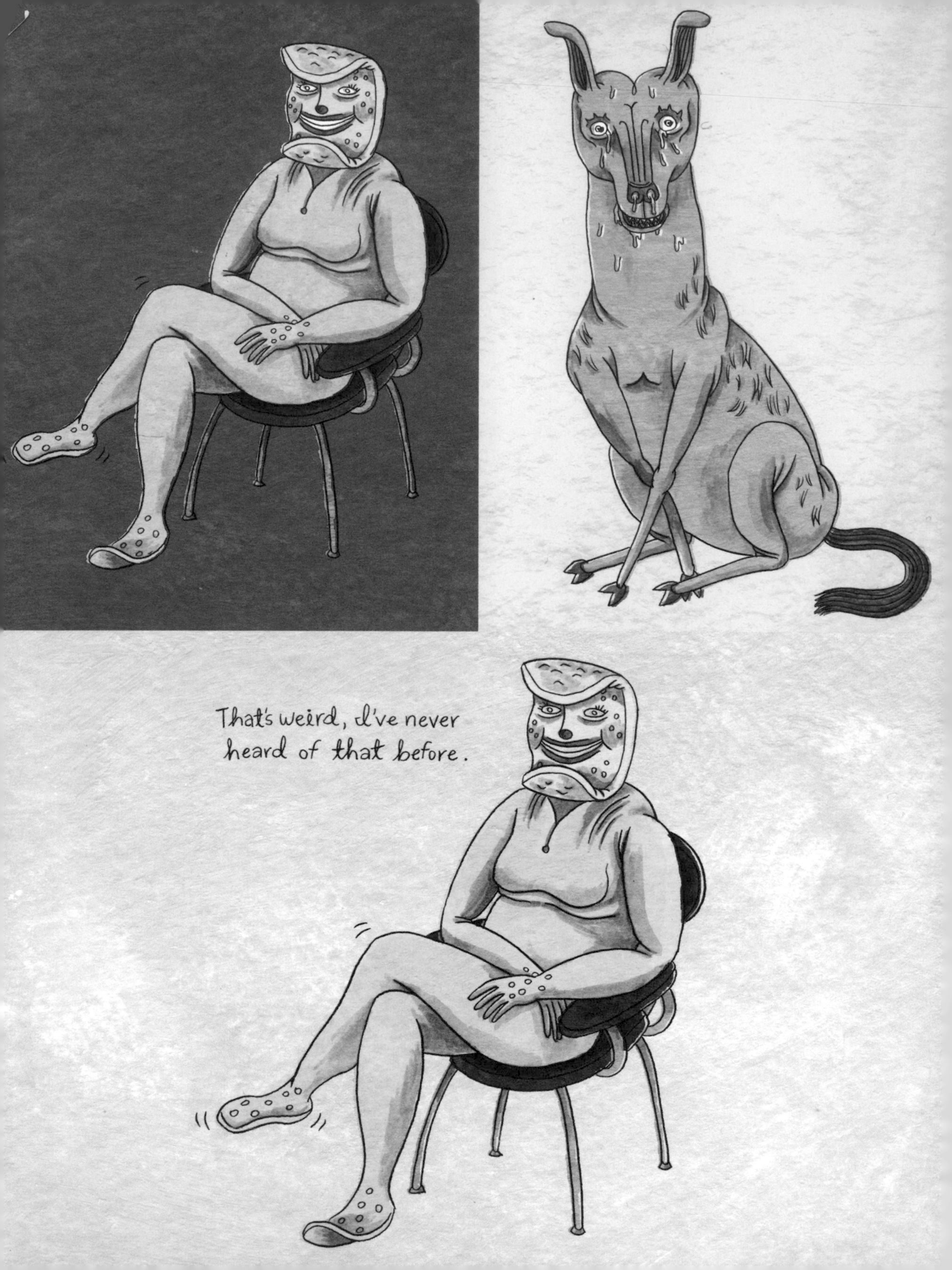
That's weird, I've never heard of that before.

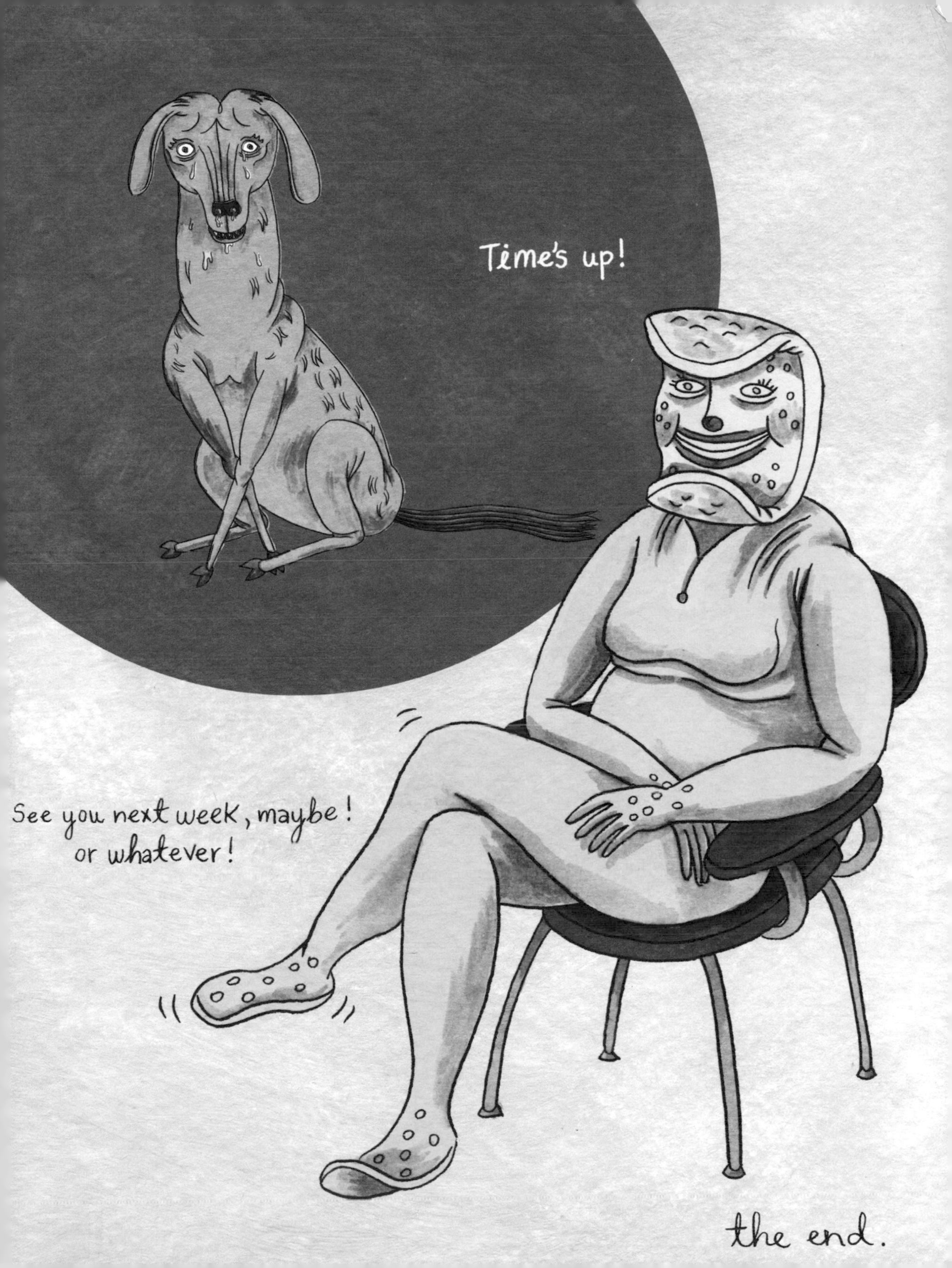
Time's up!
See you next week, maybe! or whatever!
the end.

RUMORS I'VE HEARD ABOUT ANNA WINTOUR

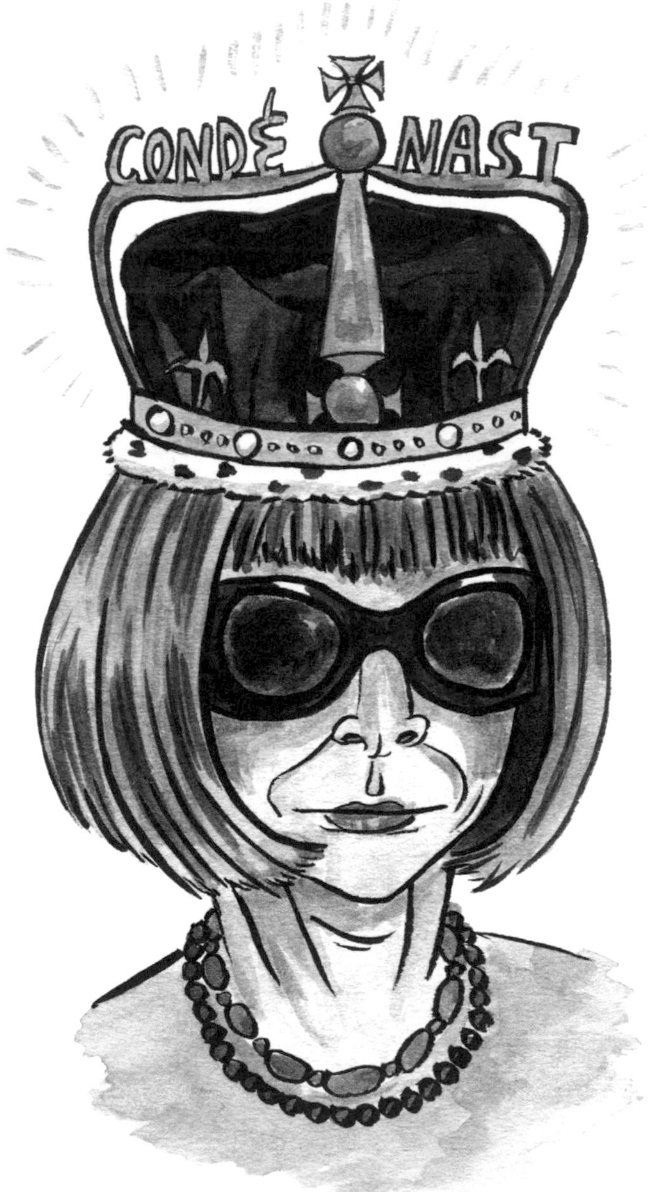
CONDÉ NAST

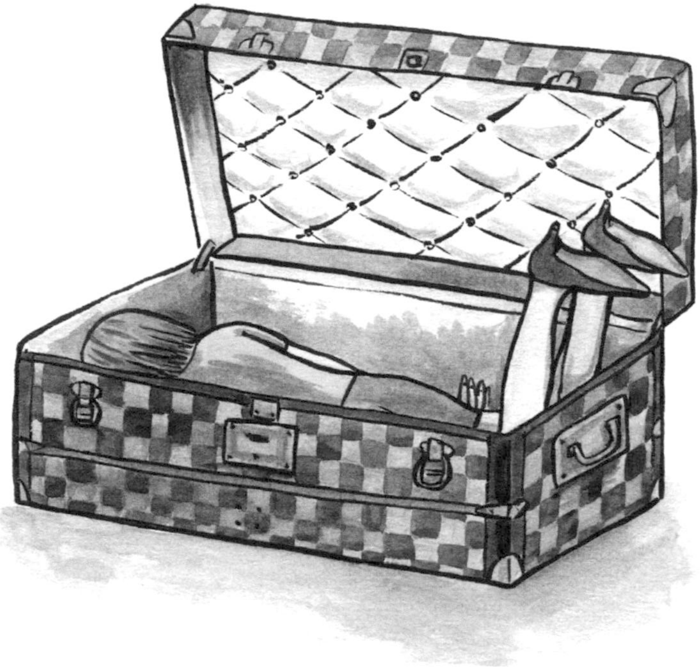

SHE KEEPS A LOUIS VUITTON TRUNK IN HER OFFICE FOR POWER NAPS.

ANNA WINTOUR WON'T HIRE FAT PEOPLE BECAUSE SHE'S A CLOSETED CHUBBY CHASER.

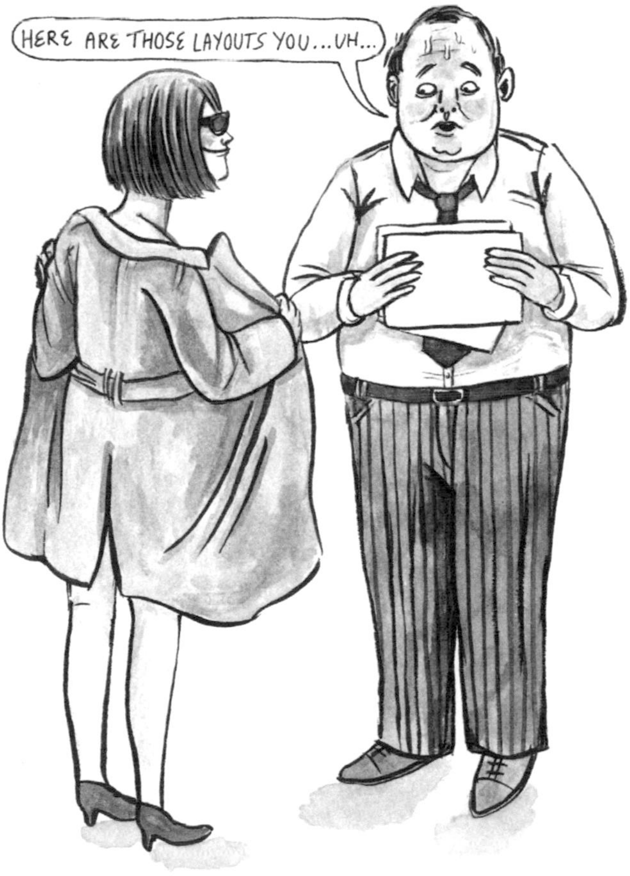
HERE ARE THOSE LAYOUTS YOU...UH...

IF ANNA LETS YOU REST YOUR HEAD IN HER LAP, YOUR BRAND WILL BE FEATURED IN *VOGUE'S* SEPTEMBER ISSUE.

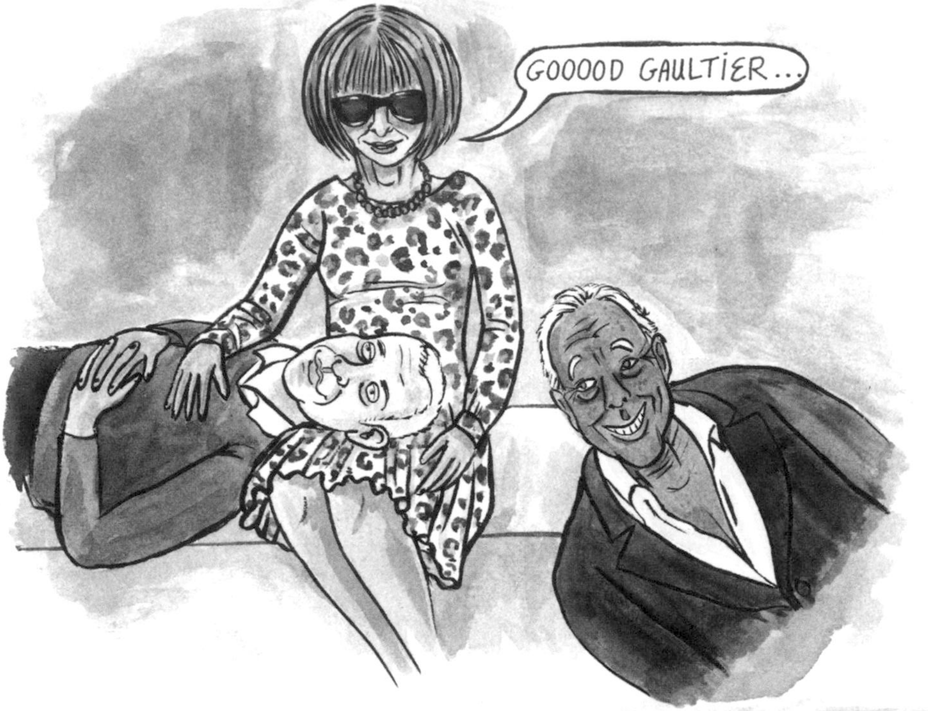
GOOOOD GAULTIER...

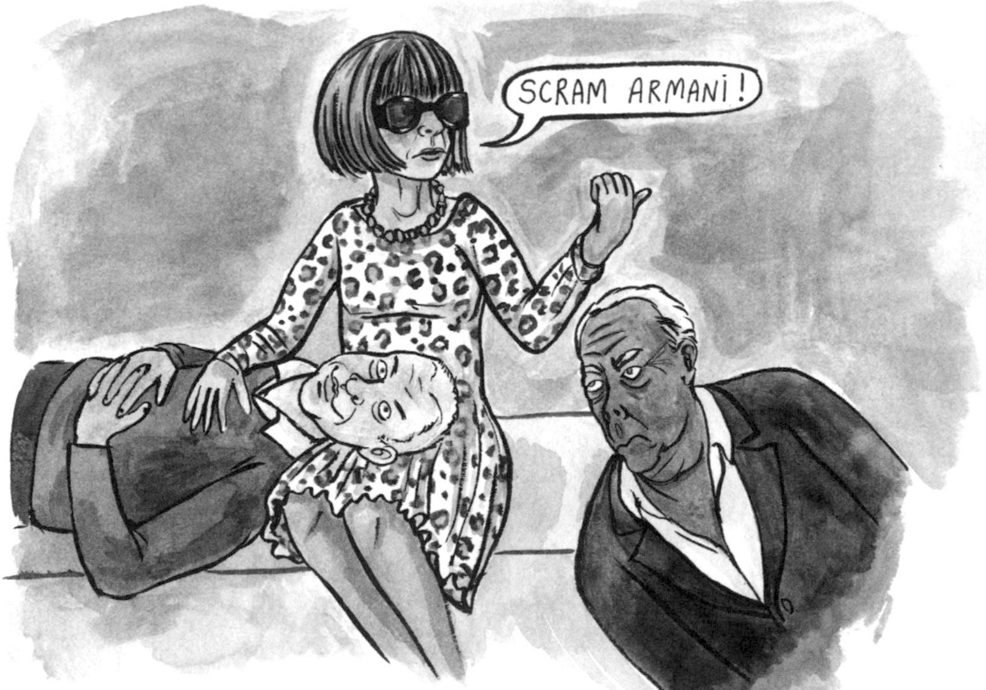
SCRAM ARMANI!

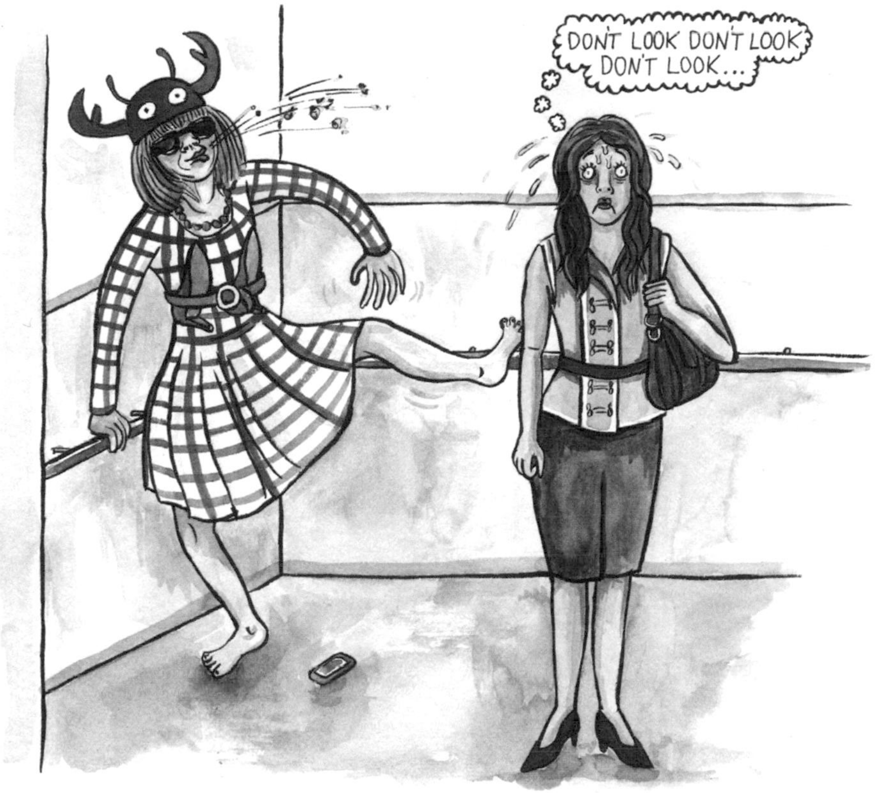
DON'T LOOK DON'T LOOK DON'T LOOK...

JUNIOR STAFFERS ARE NOT ALLOWED TO LOOK AT ANNA WINTOUR.

HER DISPLAYS OF AFFECTION ARE UNUSUAL.

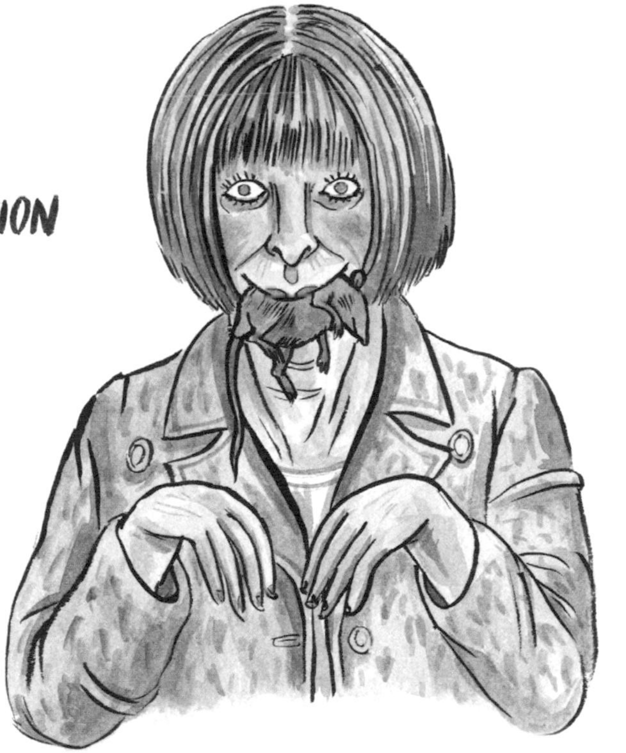

SHE WILL SACRIFICE VOGUE'S REPUTATION FOR A GOOD PRACTICAL JOKE.

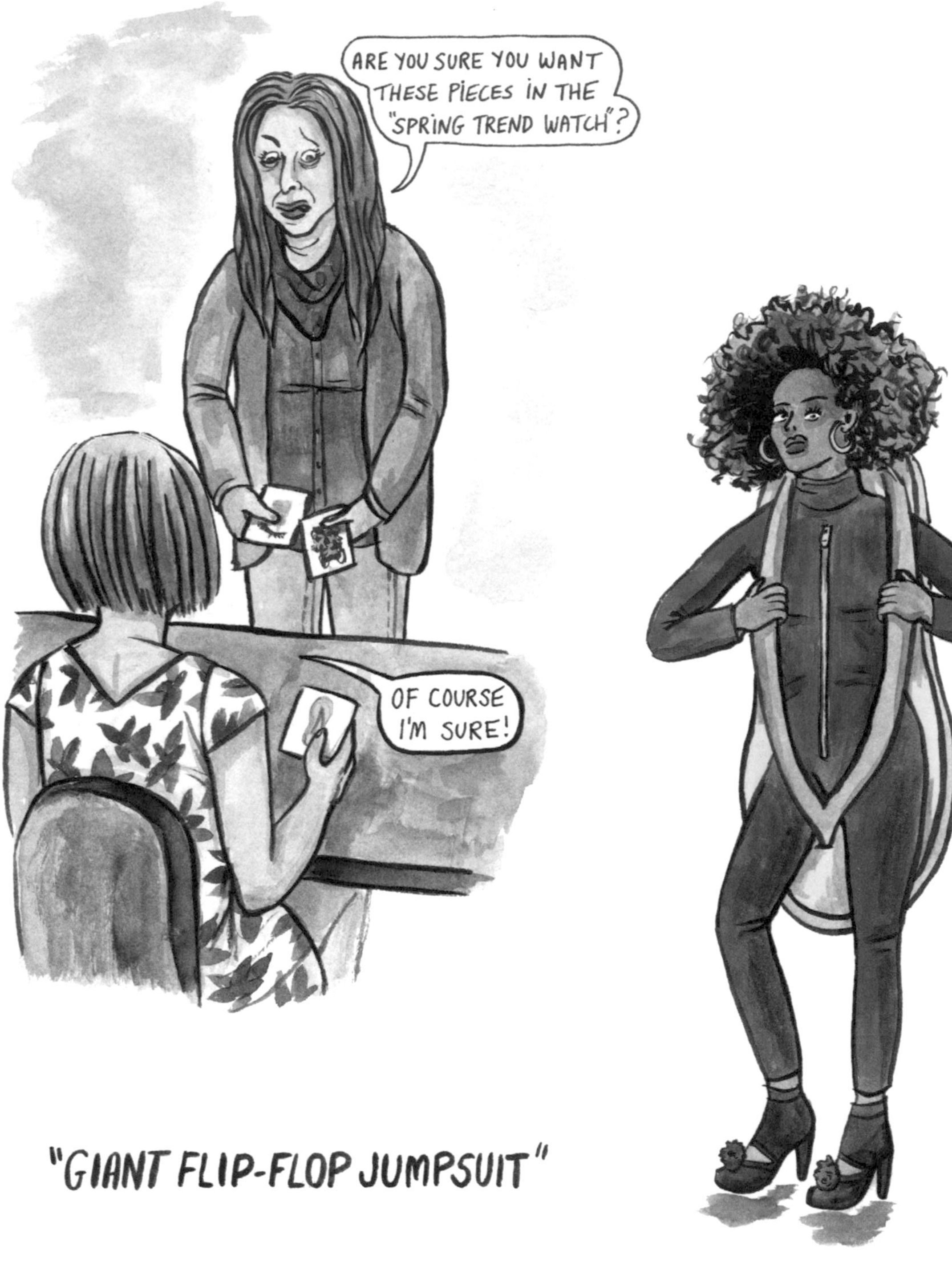
ARE YOU SURE YOU WANT THESE PIECES IN THE "SPRING TREND WATCH"?
OF COURSE I'M SURE!

"GIANT FLIP-FLOP JUMPSUIT"

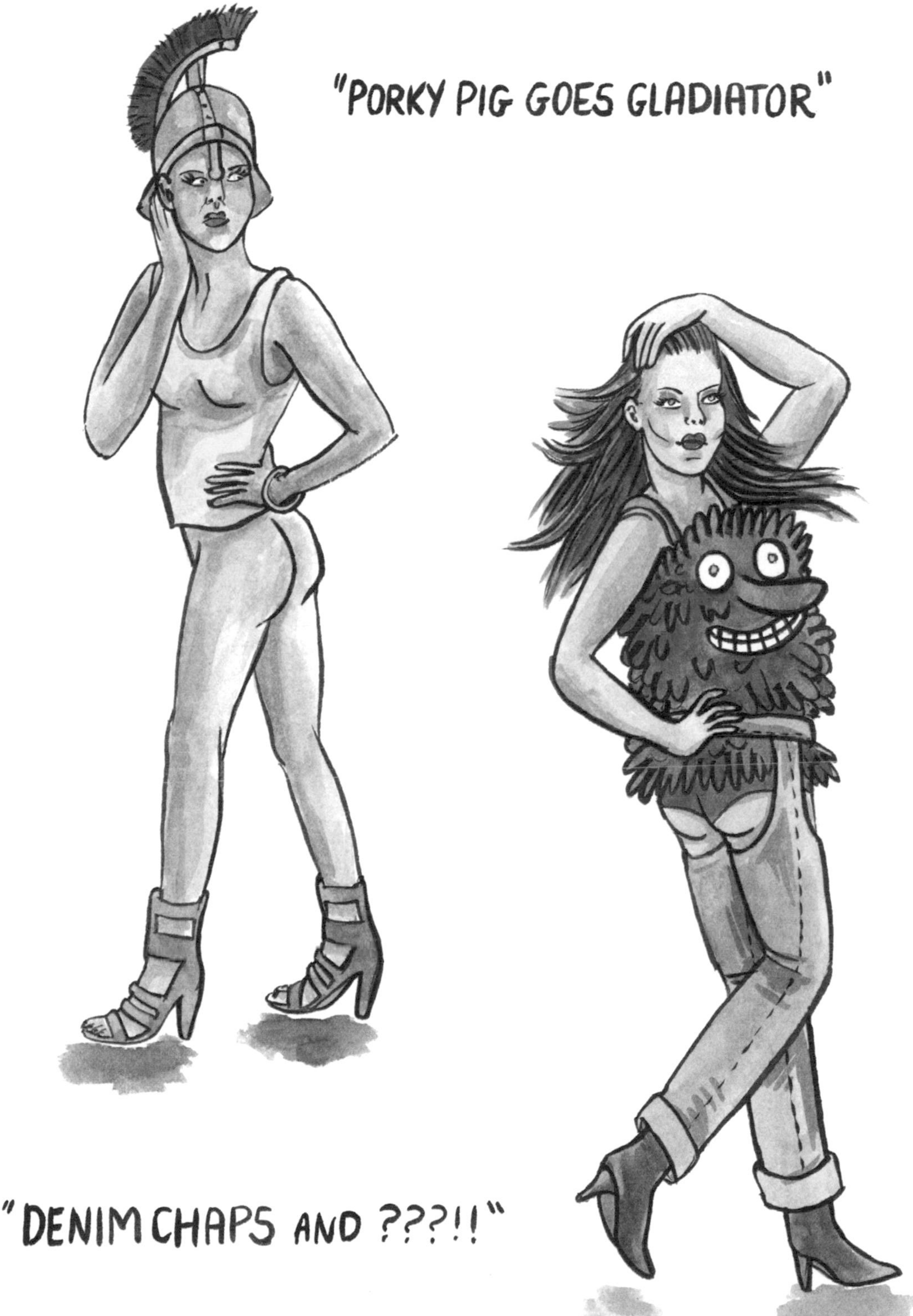
"PORKY PIG GOES GLADIATOR"
"DENIM CHAPS AND ???!!"

HER POWER ANIMAL IS THE OSTRICH.

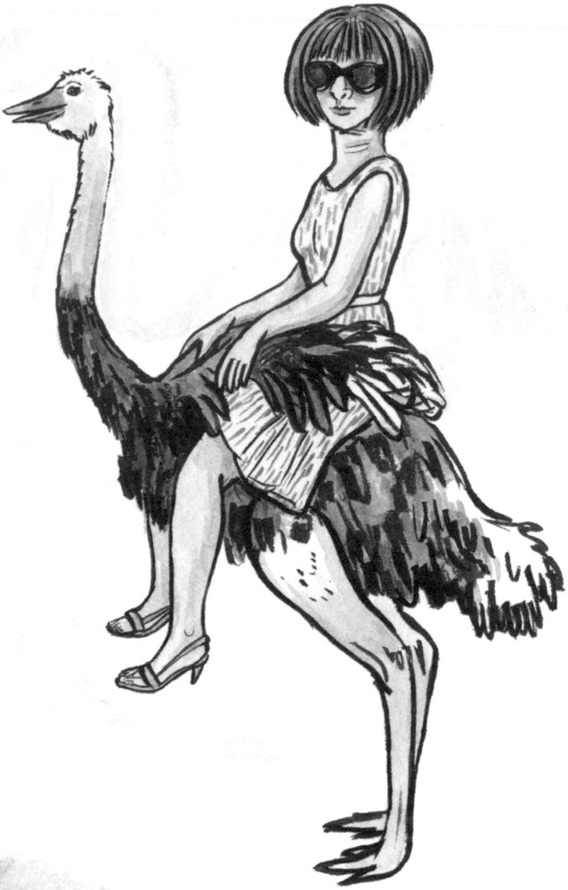

STAFFERS KNOW NOT TO DISTURB HER DURING OSTRICH TIME.

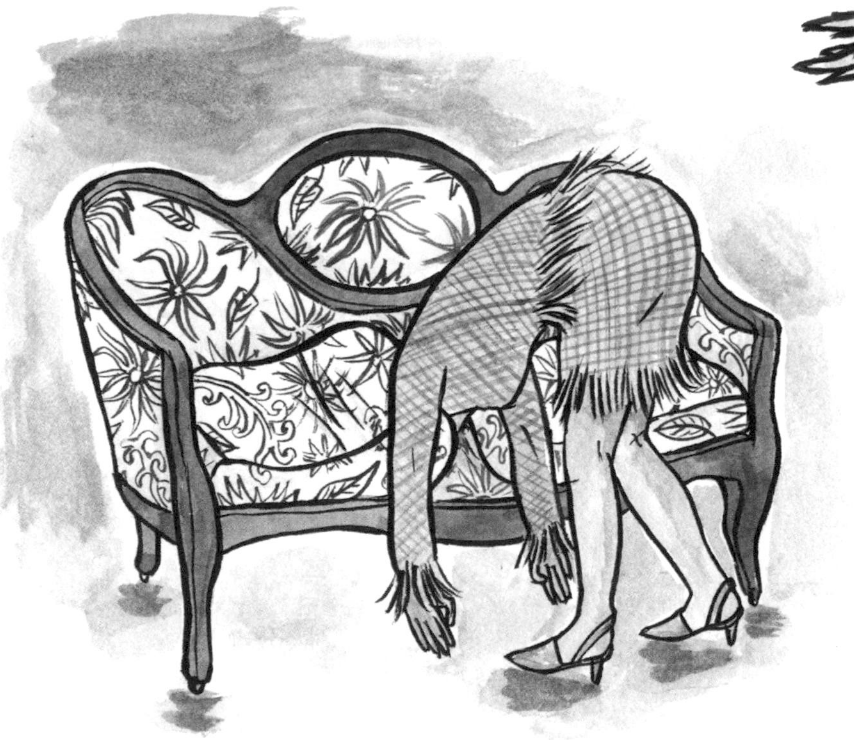

ANNA WINTOUR DOES NOT HAVE BOWEL MOVEMENTS.

BUT SHE DOES LAY STUNNING EGGS.

INCUBATION DUTIES ARE ASSIGNED TO ASSISTANTS AND SENIOR EDITORS.

HER OFFSPRING ARE HIGHLY SOUGHT AFTER AS PETS.

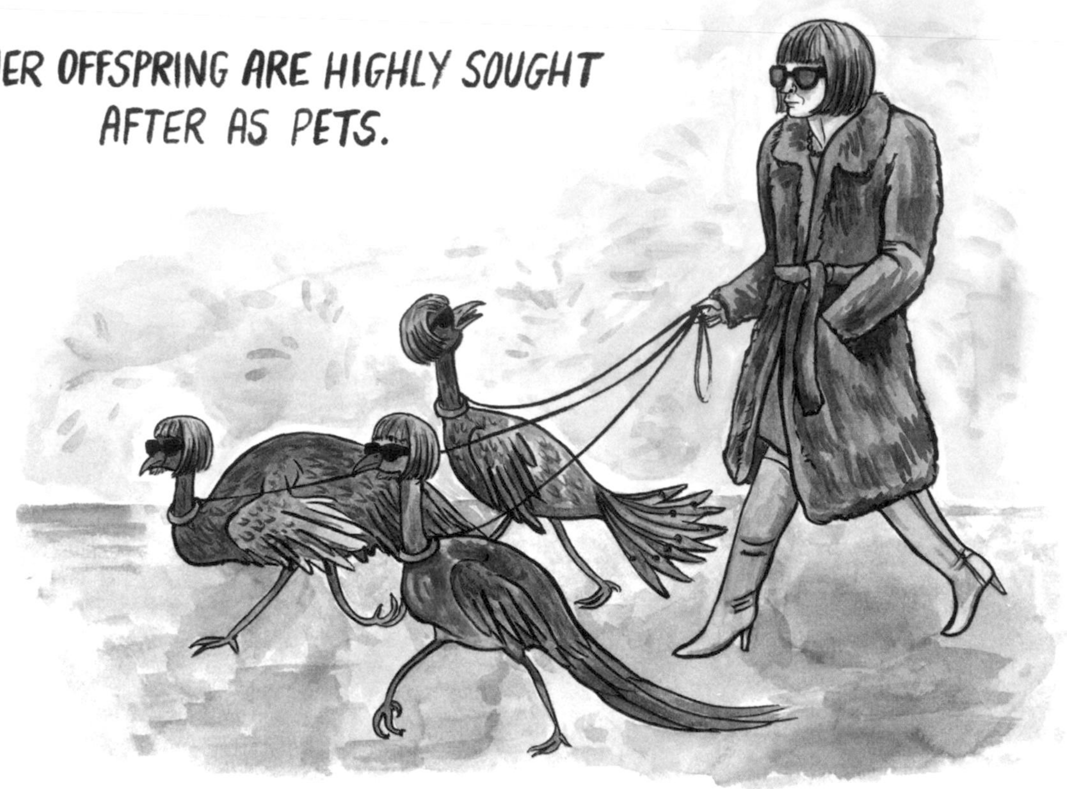

SHE SHOPS AT FOREVER 21 AND HATES HERSELF FOR IT.

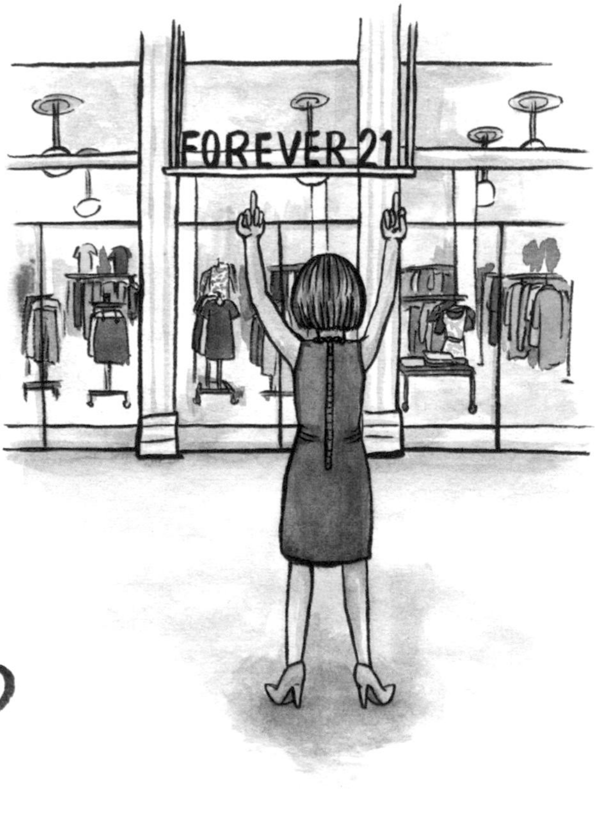
FOREVER 21

THE END

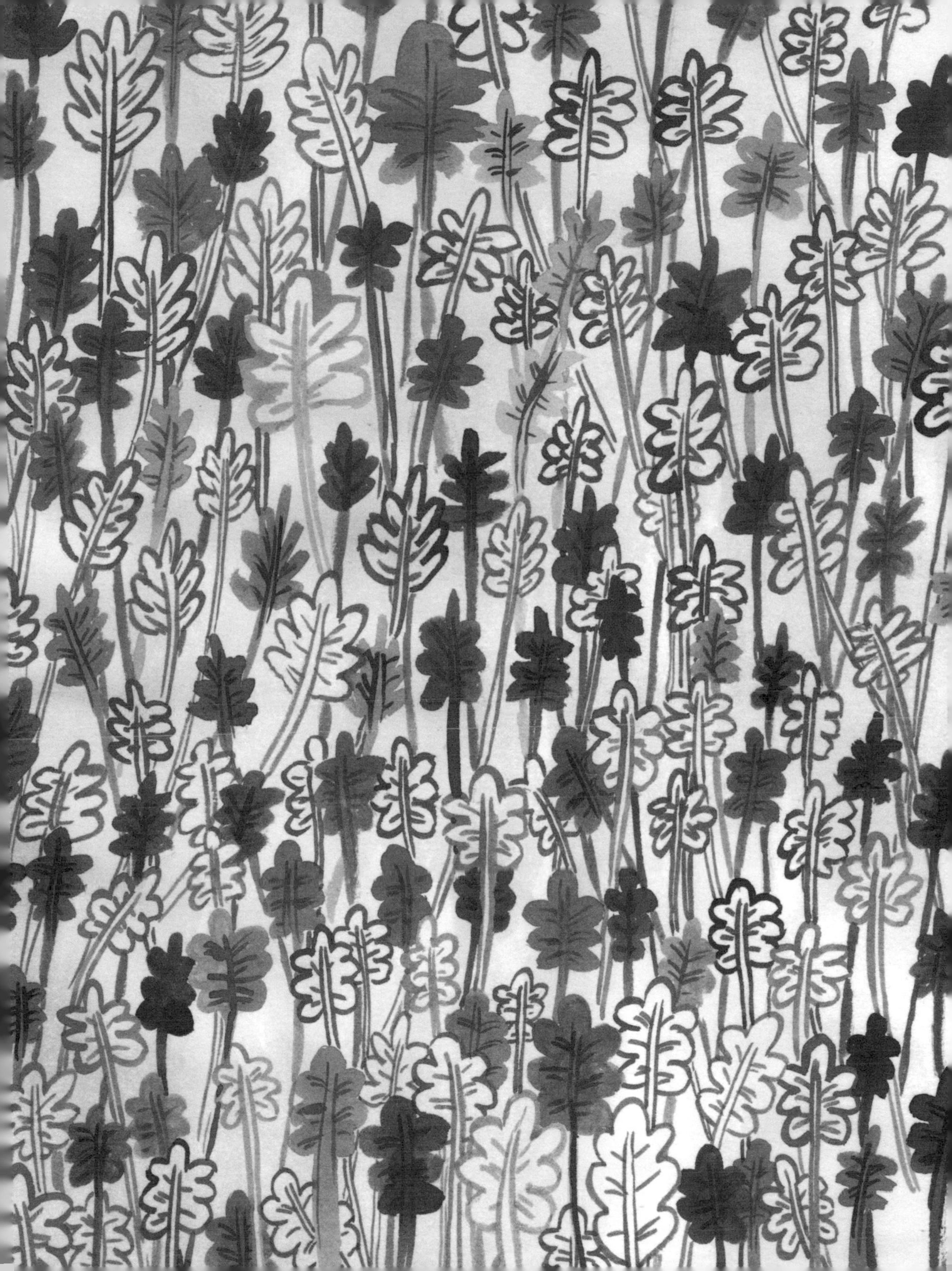

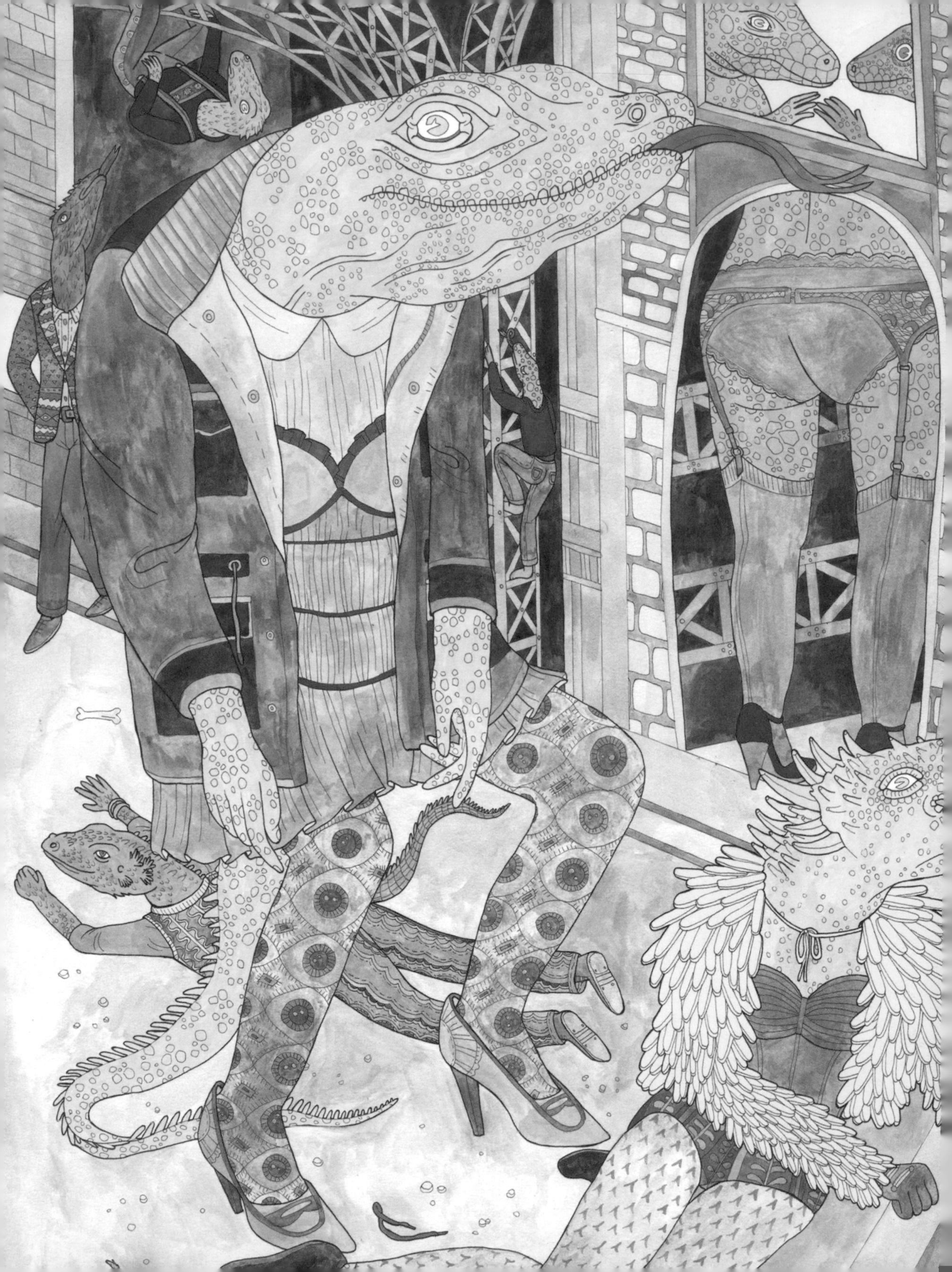

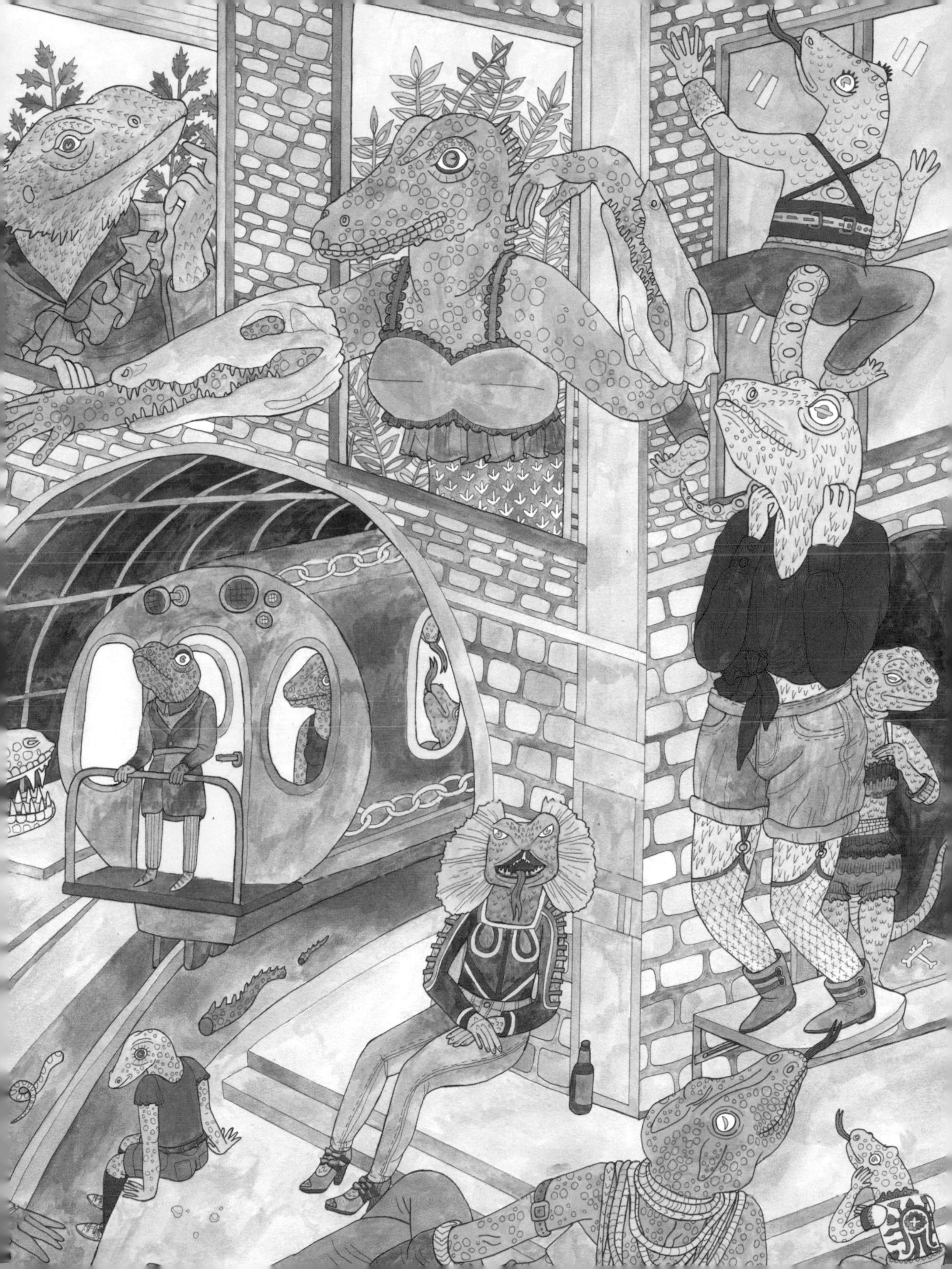

Moosefingers

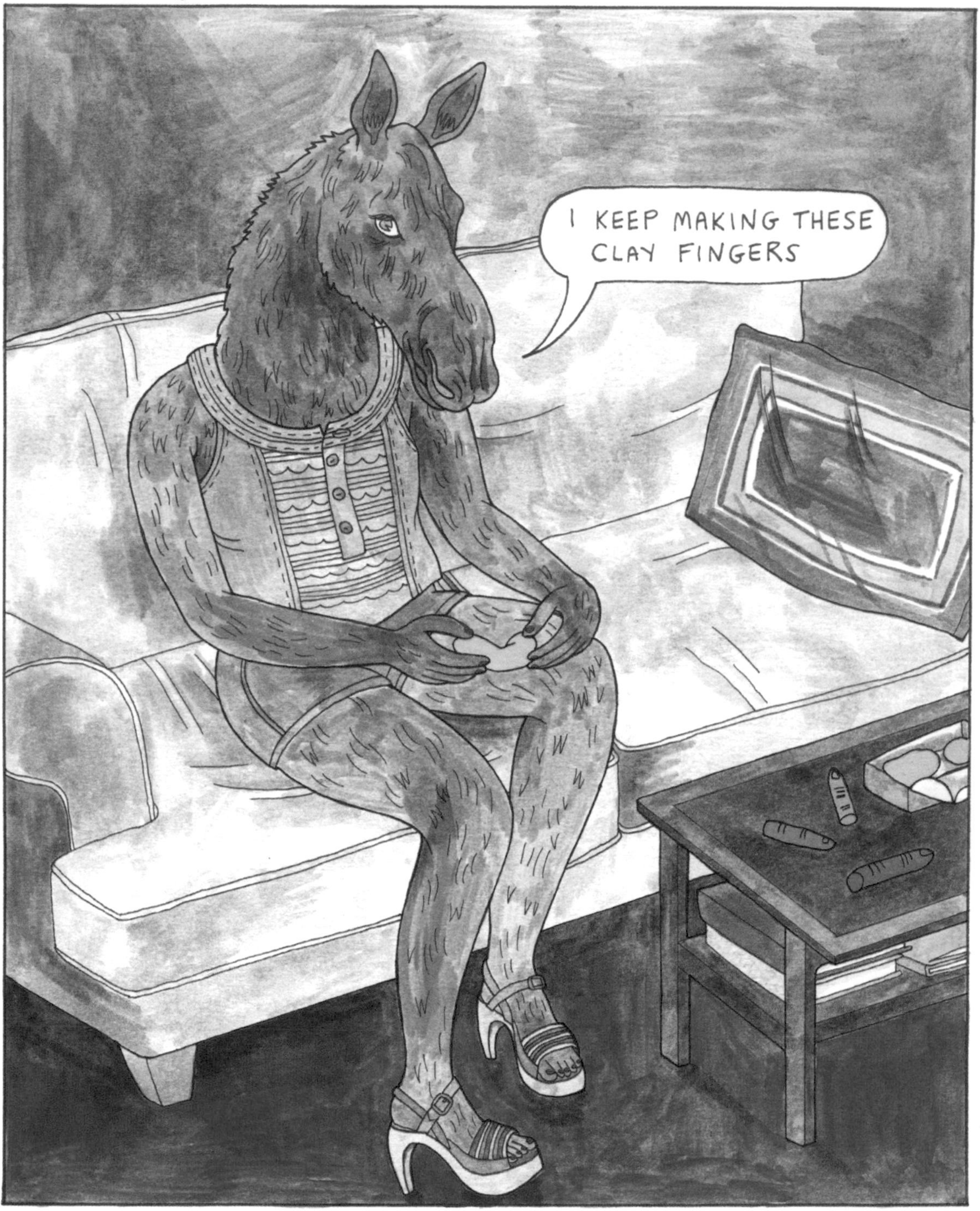
I KEEP MAKING THESE CLAY FINGERS

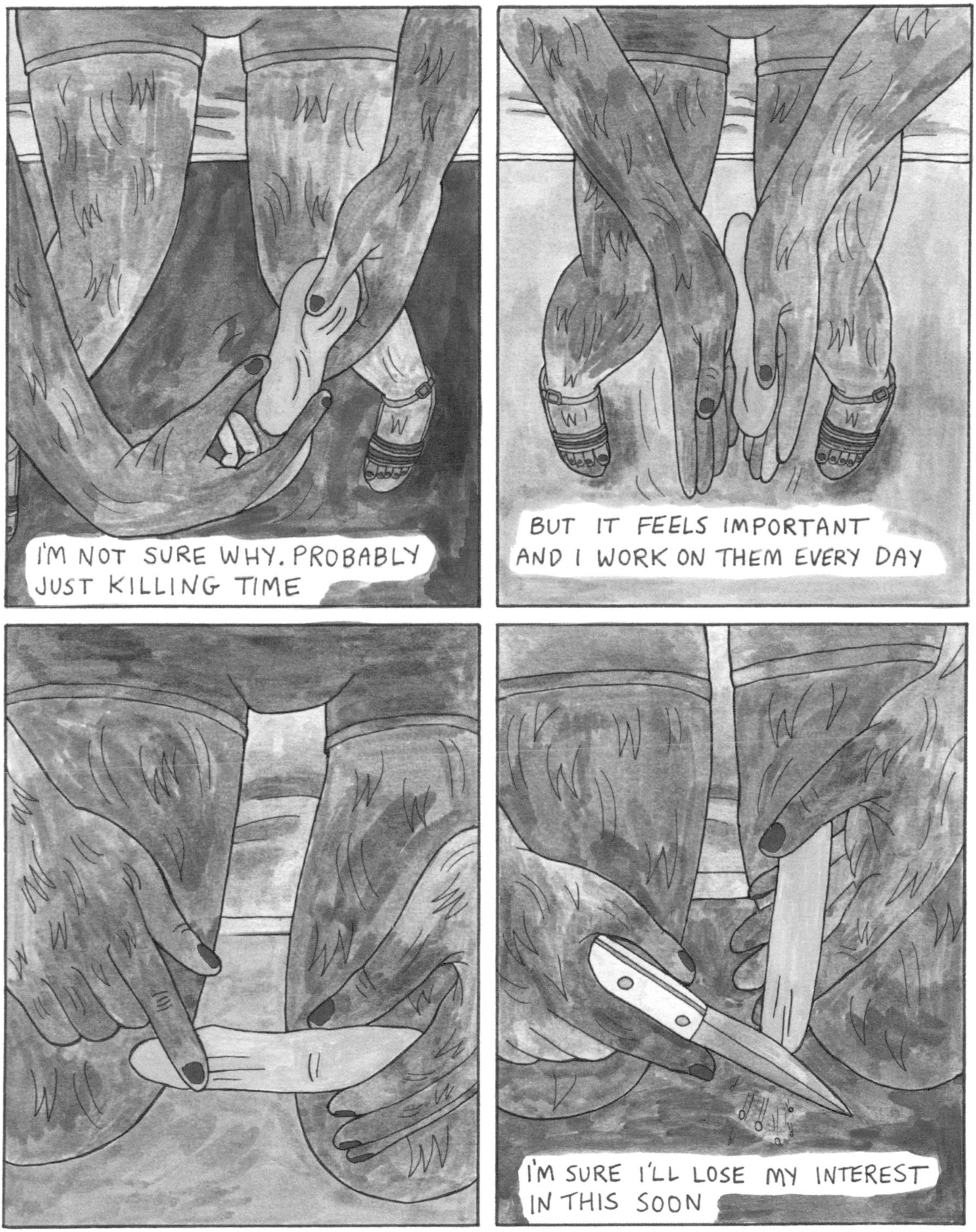
I'M NOT SURE WHY. PROBABLY JUST KILLING TIME
BUT IT FEELS IMPORTANT AND I WORK ON THEM EVERY DAY
I'M SURE I'LL LOSE MY INTEREST IN THIS SOON

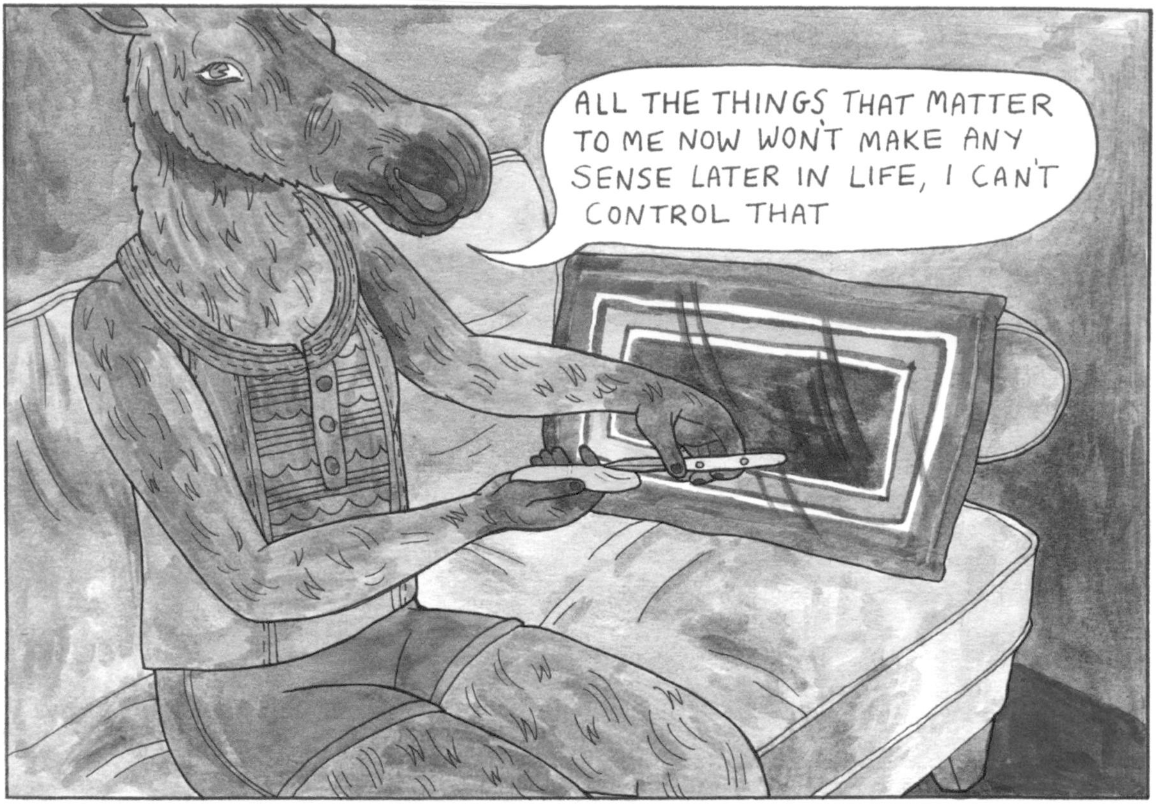
ALL THE THINGS THAT MATTER TO ME NOW WON'T MAKE ANY SENSE LATER IN LIFE, I CAN'T CONTROL THAT

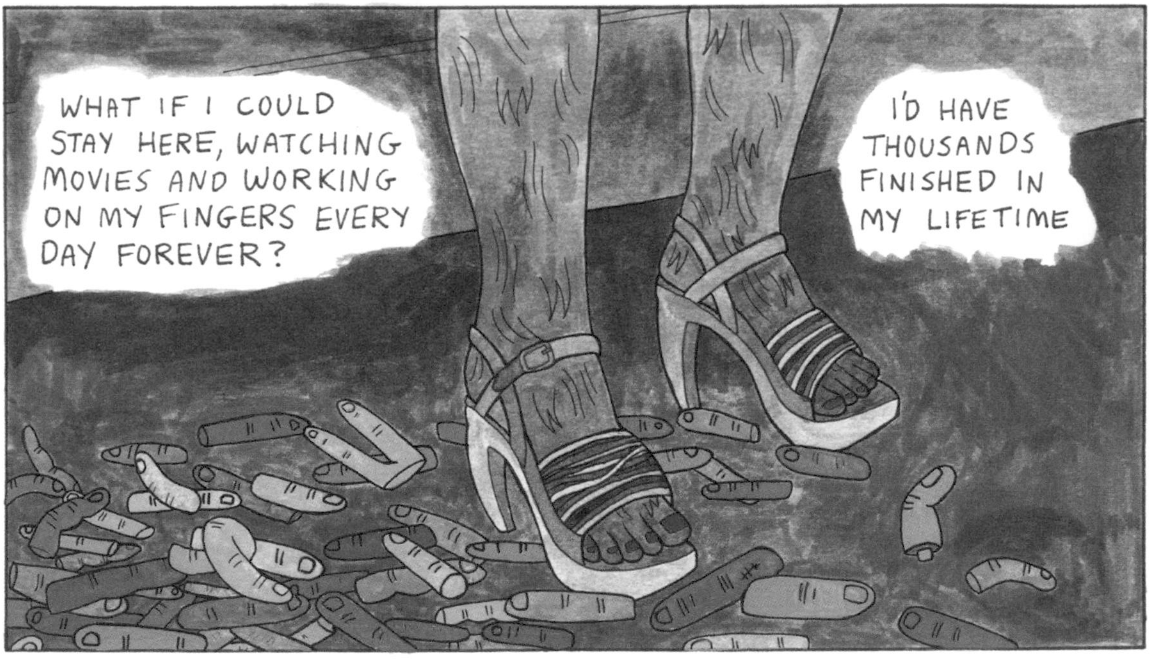
WHAT IF I COULD STAY HERE, WATCHING MOVIES AND WORKING ON MY FINGERS EVERY DAY FOREVER?
I'D HAVE THOUSANDS FINISHED IN MY LIFETIME

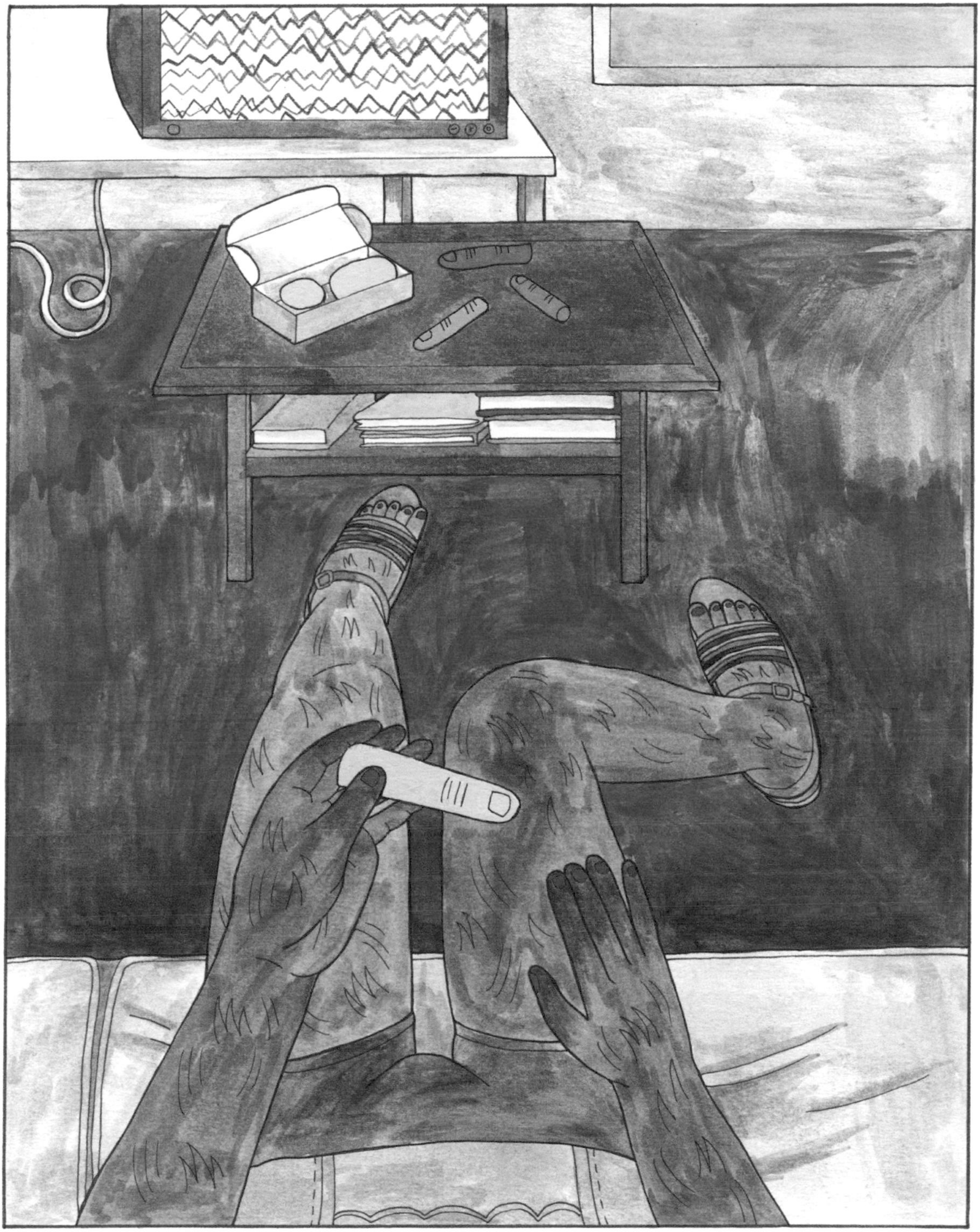

Movie Night

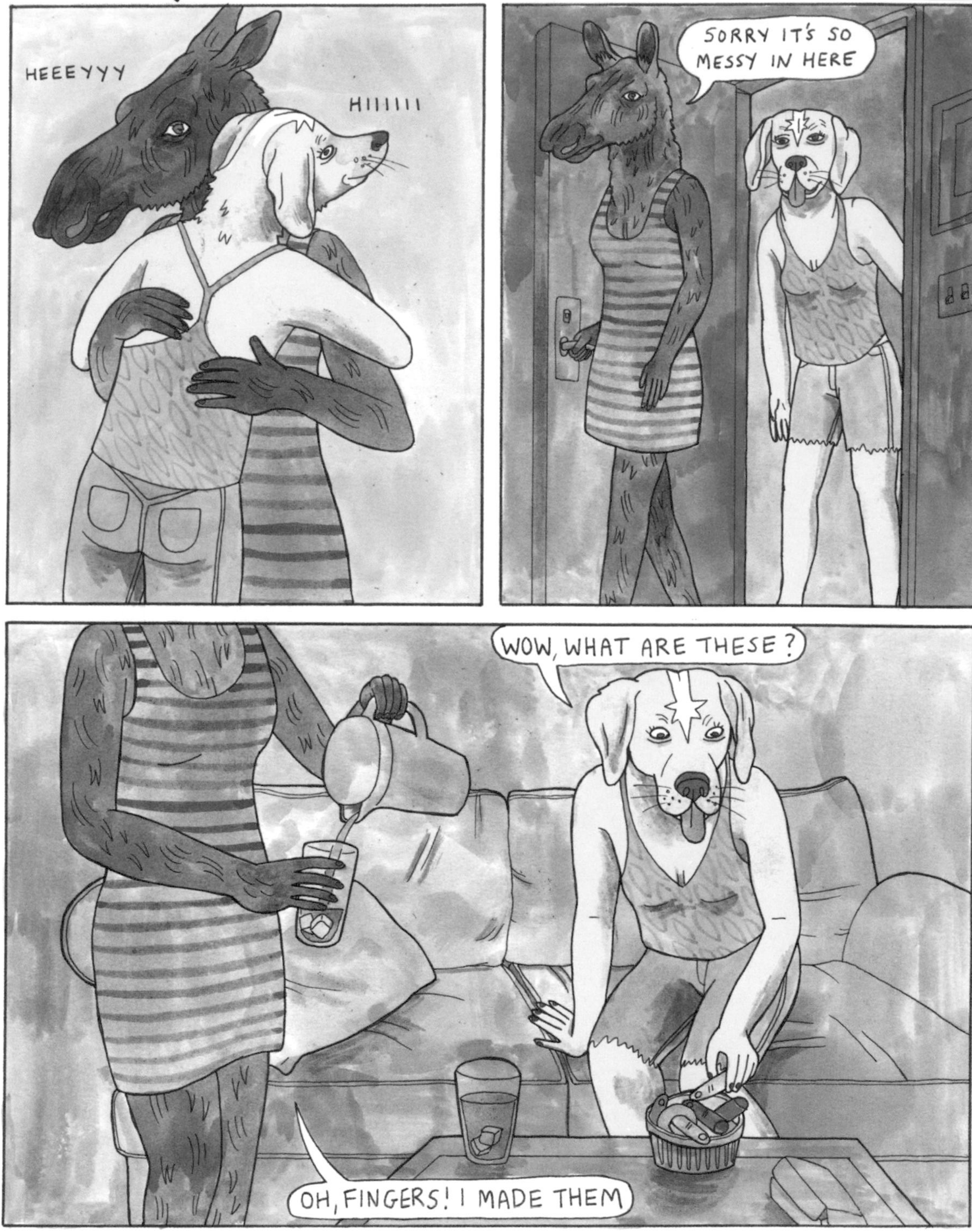
HEEEYYY
HIIIIII
SORRY IT'S SO MESSY IN HERE
WOW, WHAT ARE THESE?
OH, FINGERS! I MADE THEM

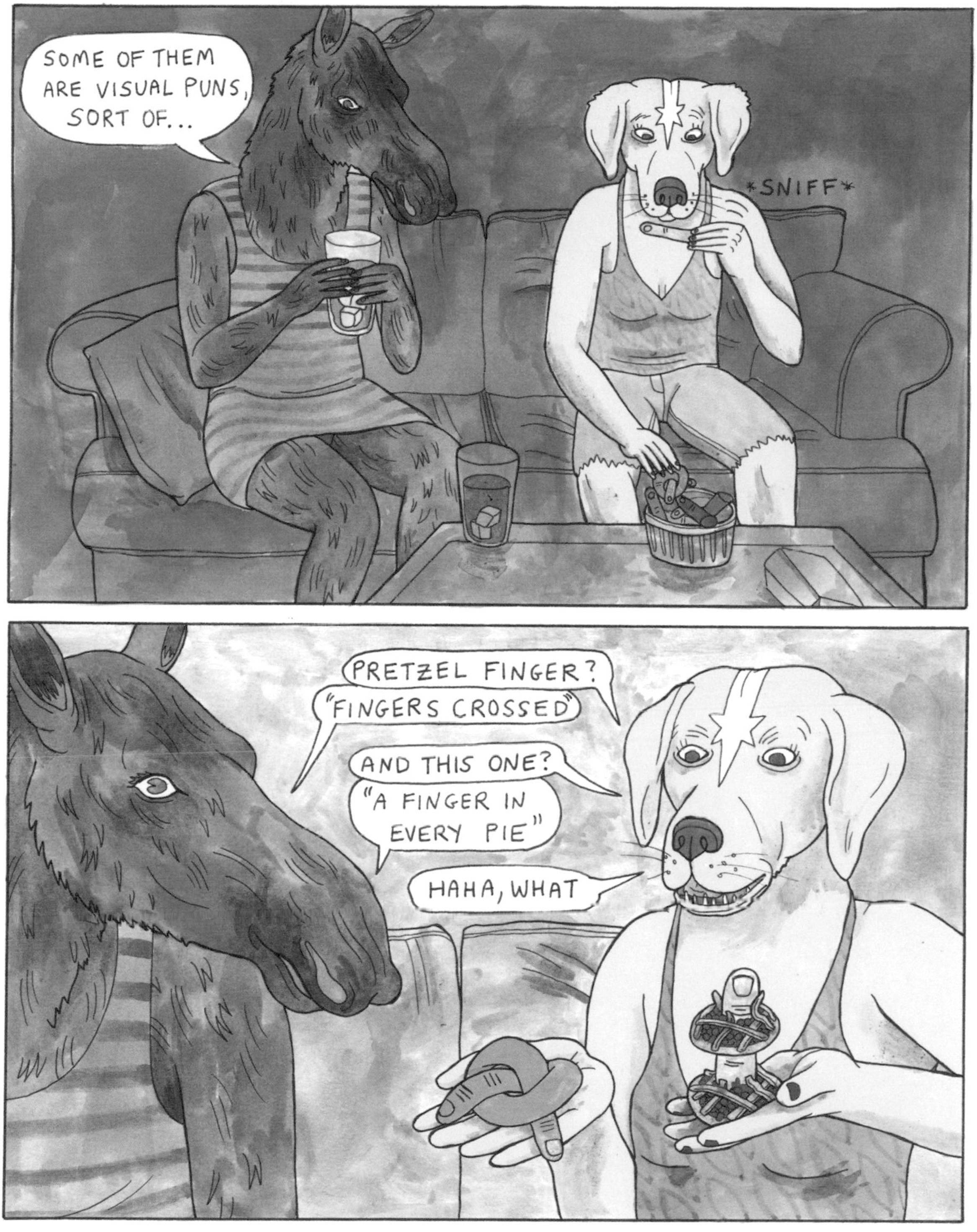
SOME OF THEM ARE VISUAL PUNS, SORT OF...
SNIFF
PRETZEL FINGER? "FINGERS CROSSED"
AND THIS ONE? "A FINGER IN EVERY PIE"
HAHA, WHAT

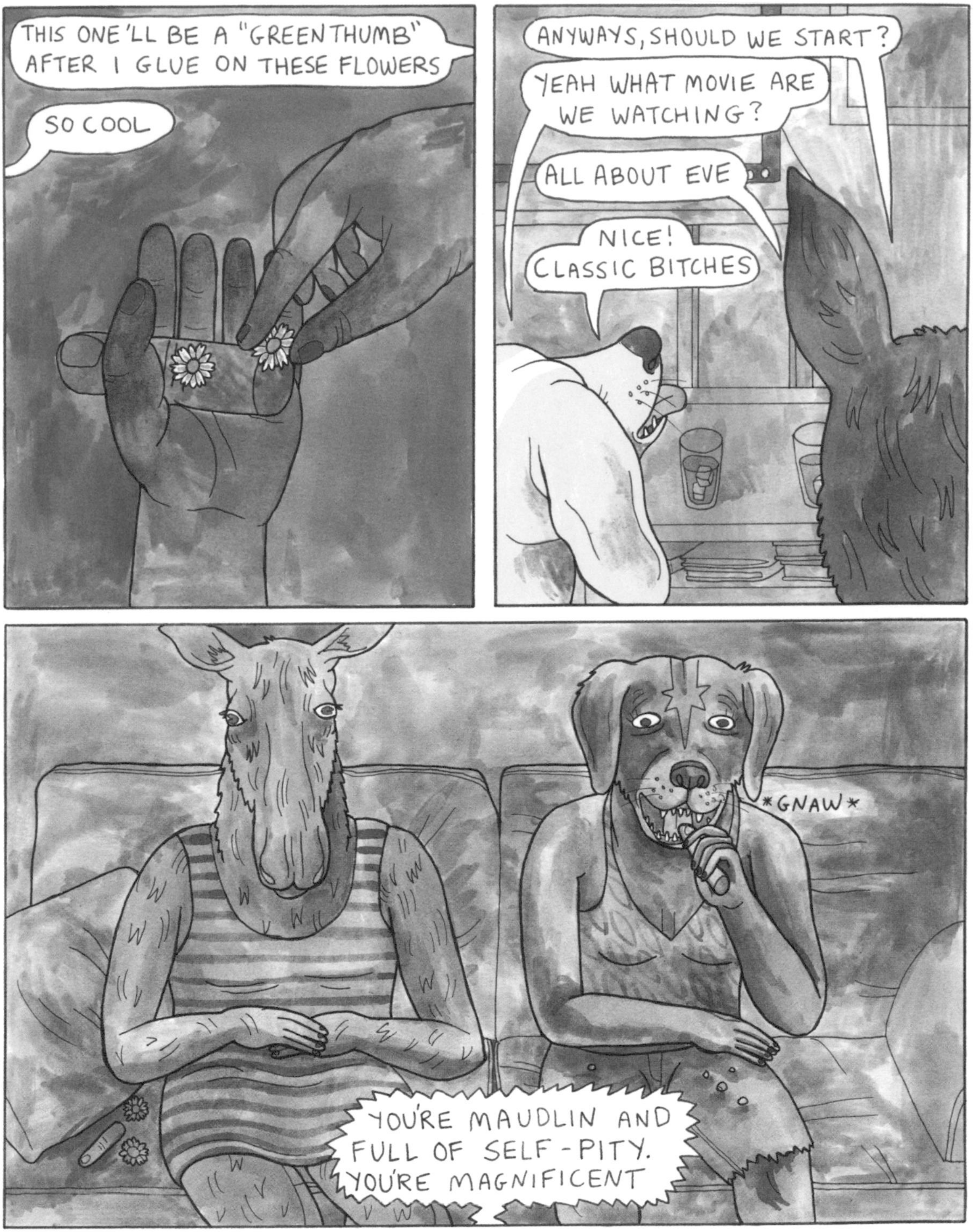
THIS ONE'LL BE A "GREENTHUMB" AFTER I GLUE ON THESE FLOWERS
SO COOL
ANYWAYS, SHOULD WE START?
YEAH WHAT MOVIE ARE WE WATCHING?
ALL ABOUT EVE
NICE! CLASSIC BITCHES
GNAW
YOU'RE MAUDLIN AND FULL OF SELF-PITY. YOU'RE MAGNIFICENT

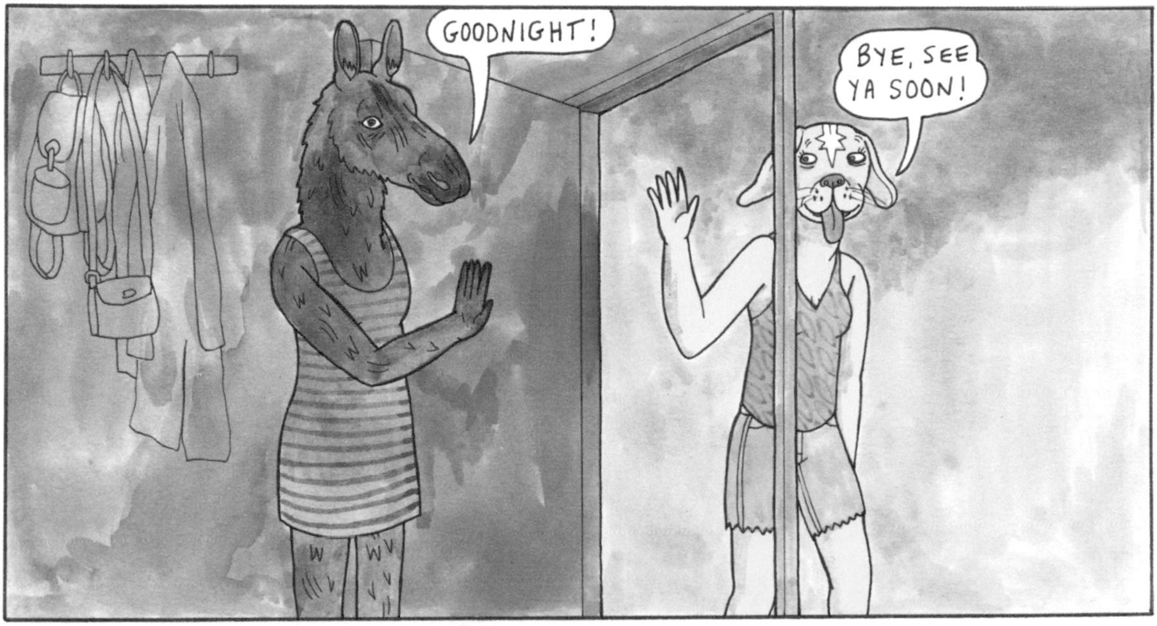
GOODNIGHT!
BYE, SEE YA SOON!

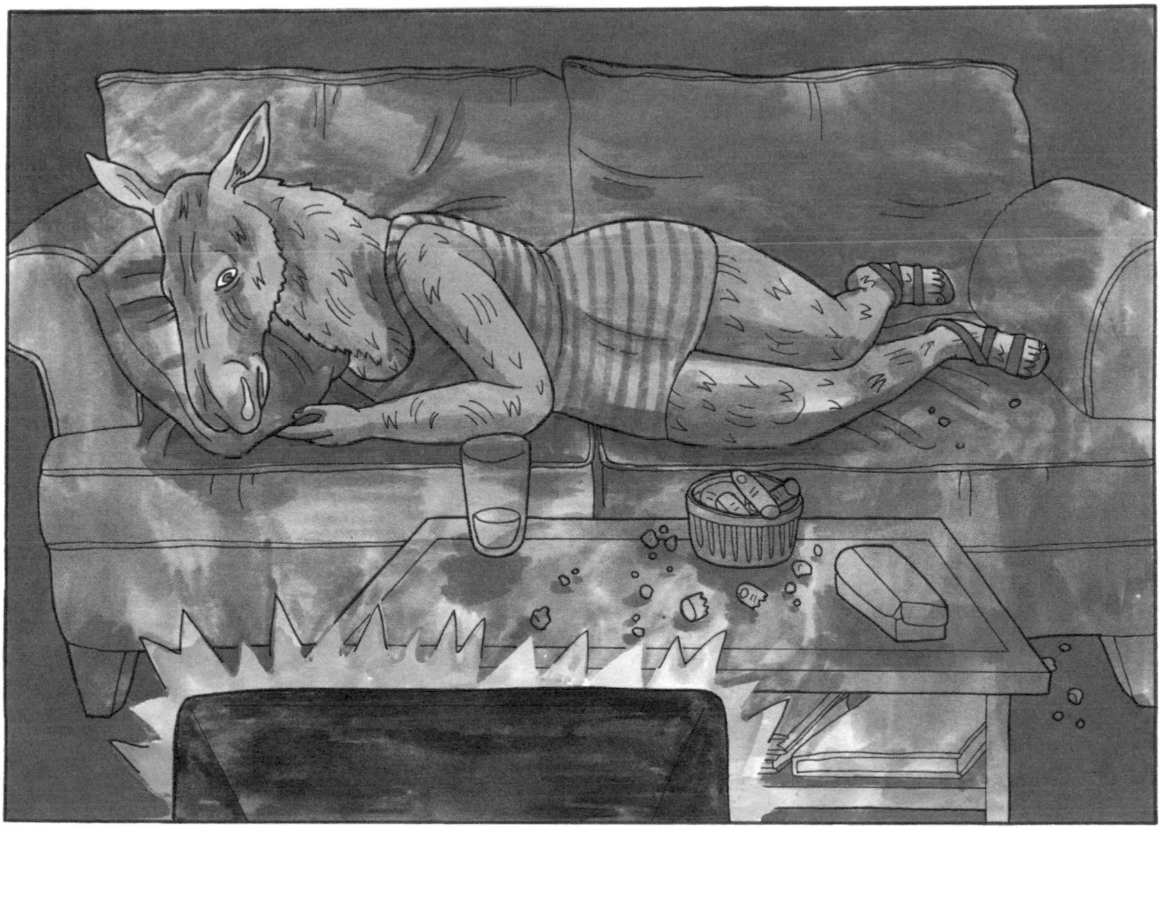

Bedtime

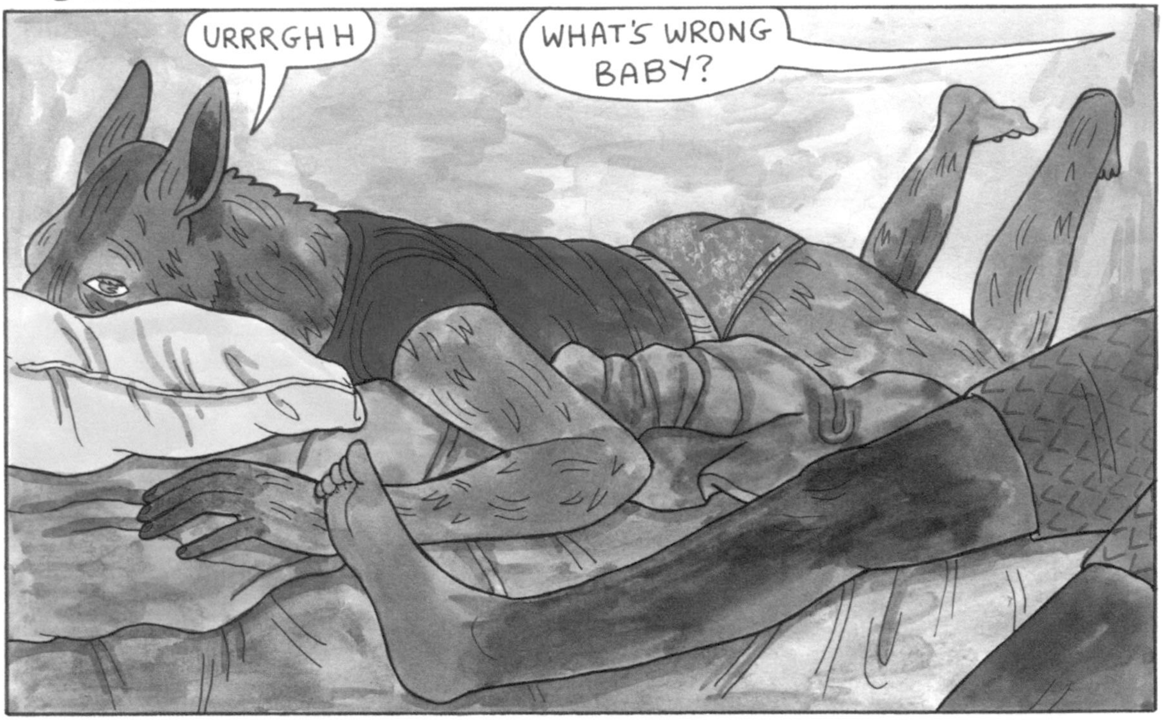
URRRGHH
WHAT'S WRONG BABY?

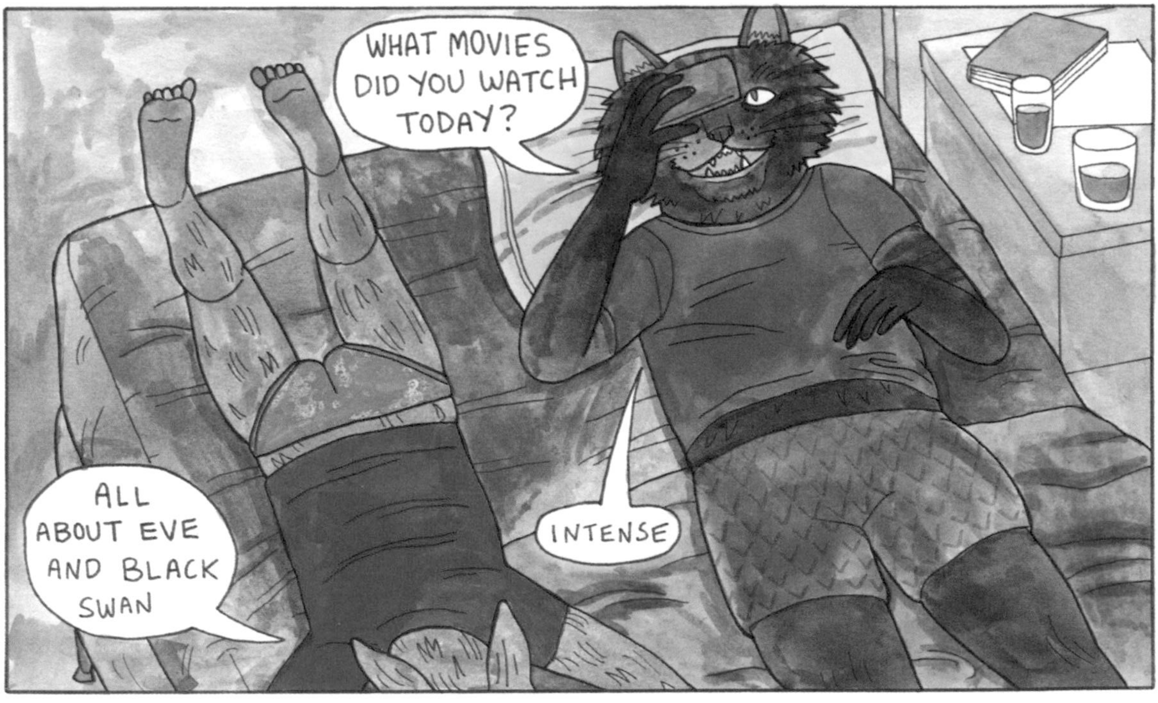
WHAT MOVIES DID YOU WATCH TODAY?
ALL ABOUT EVE AND BLACK SWAN
INTENSE

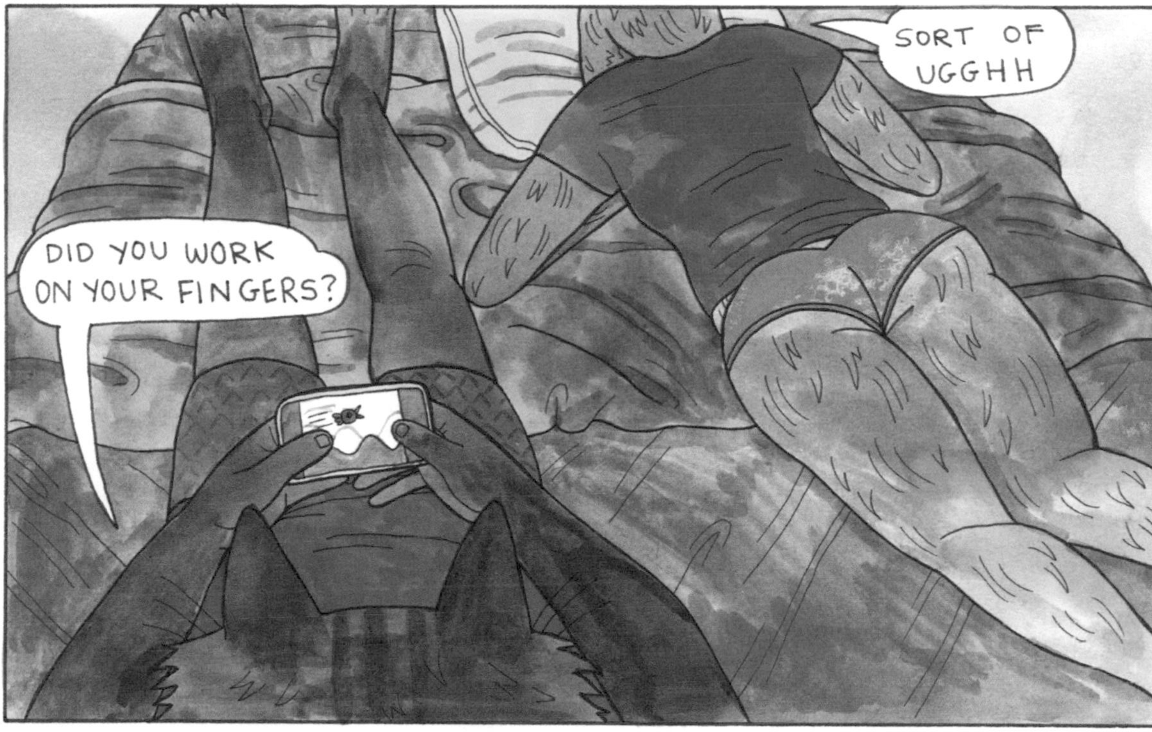
DID YOU WORK ON YOUR FINGERS?
SORT OF UGGHH

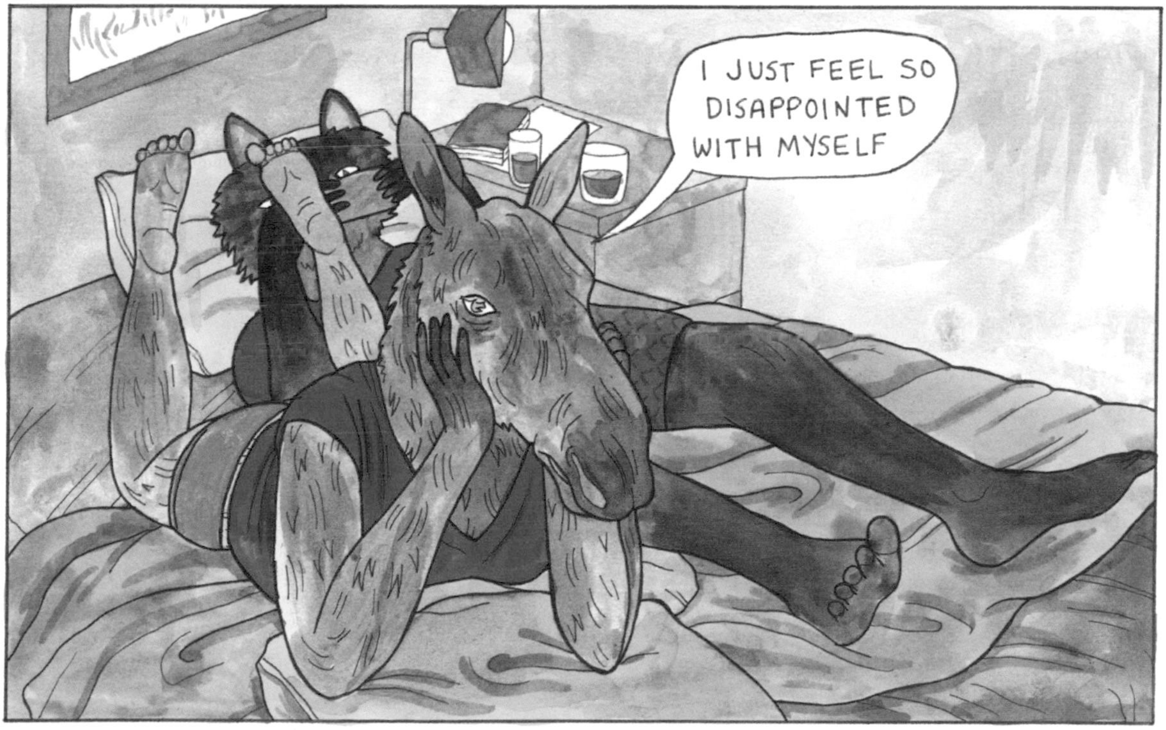
I JUST FEEL SO DISAPPOINTED WITH MYSELF

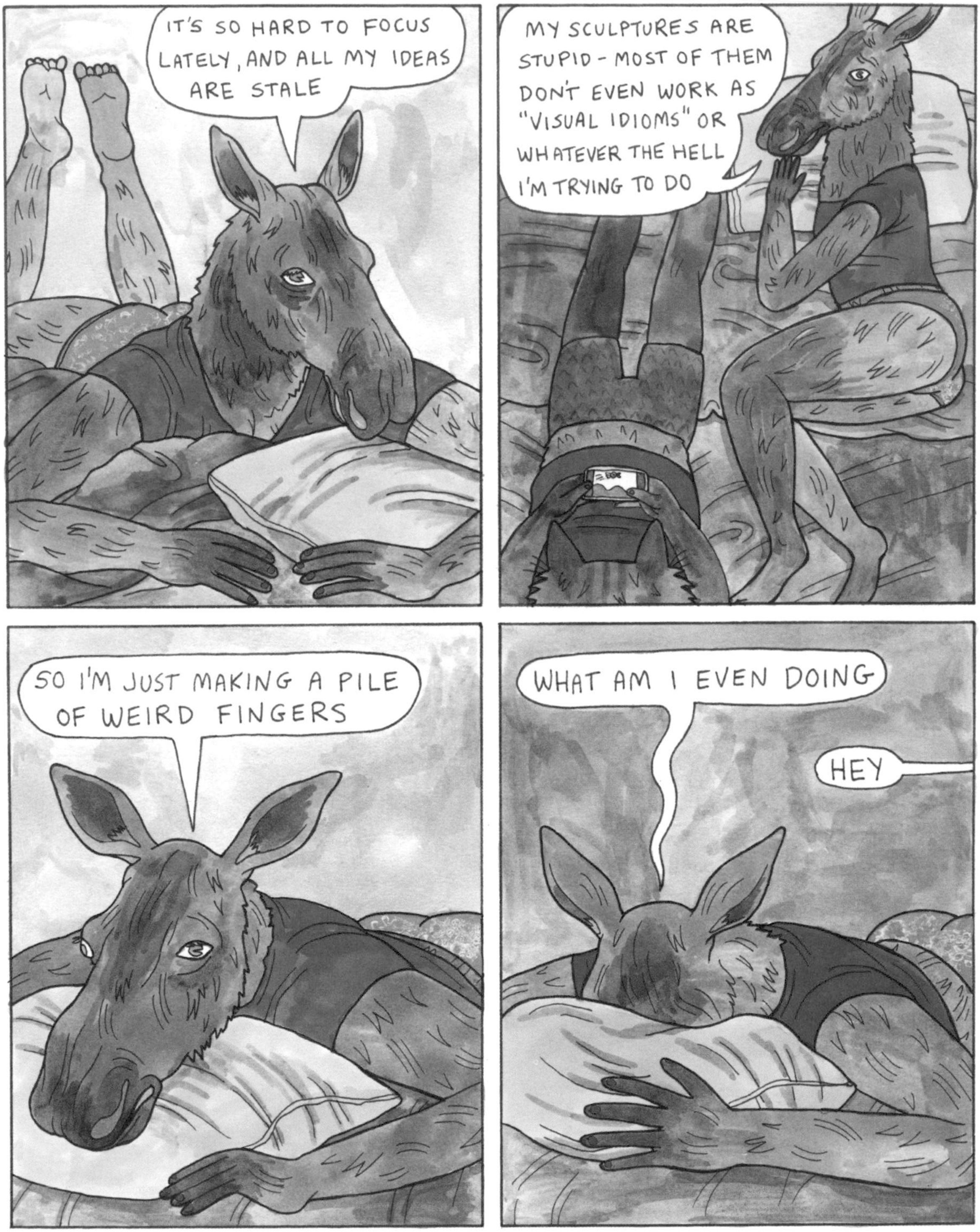
IT'S SO HARD TO FOCUS LATELY, AND ALL MY IDEAS ARE STALE
MY SCULPTURES ARE STUPID - MOST OF THEM DON'T EVEN WORK AS "VISUAL IDIOMS" OR WHATEVER THE HELL I'M TRYING TO DO
SO I'M JUST MAKING A PILE OF WEIRD FINGERS
WHAT AM I EVEN DOING
HEY

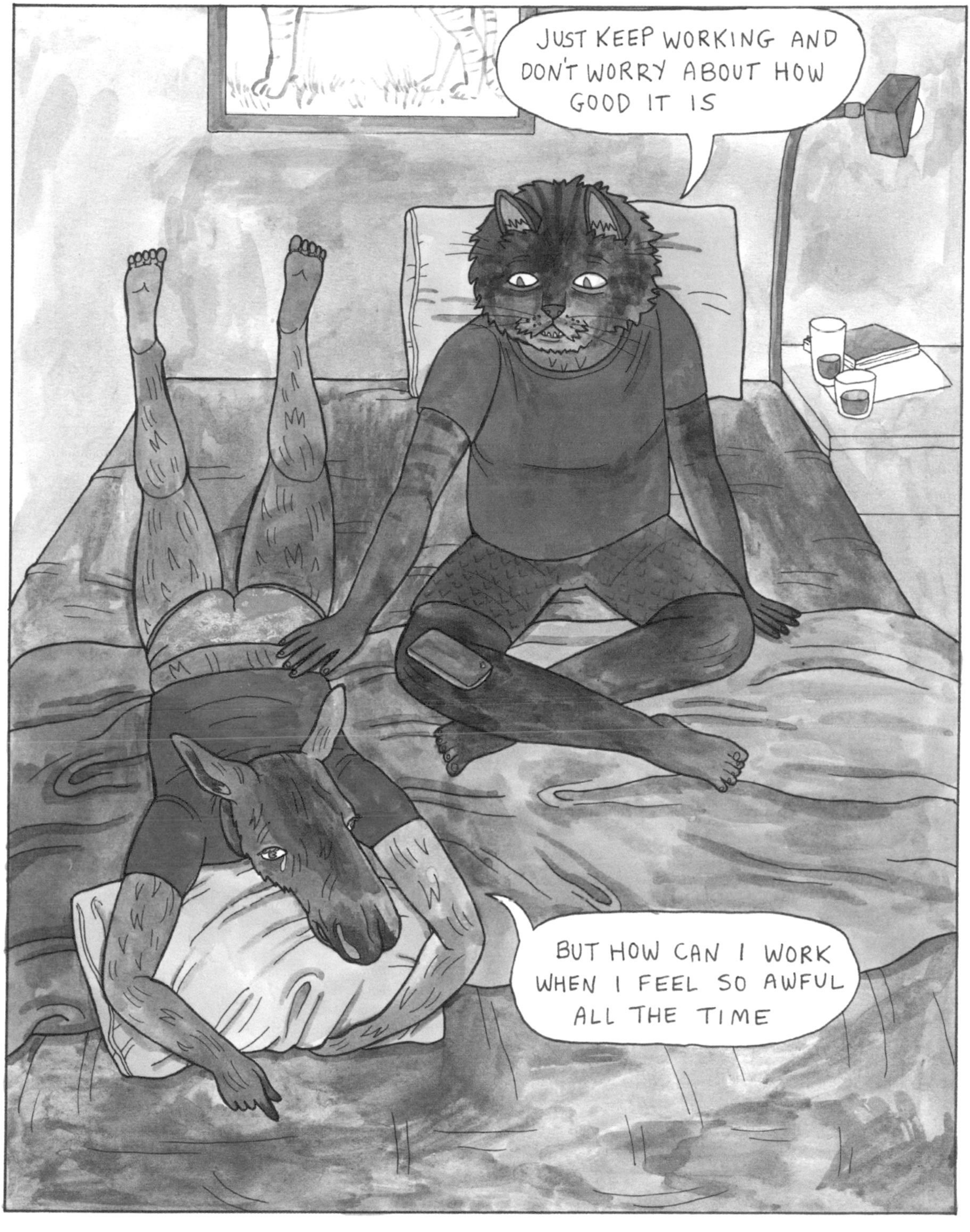
JUST KEEP WORKING AND DON'T WORRY ABOUT HOW GOOD IT IS
BUT HOW CAN I WORK WHEN I FEEL SO AWFUL ALL THE TIME

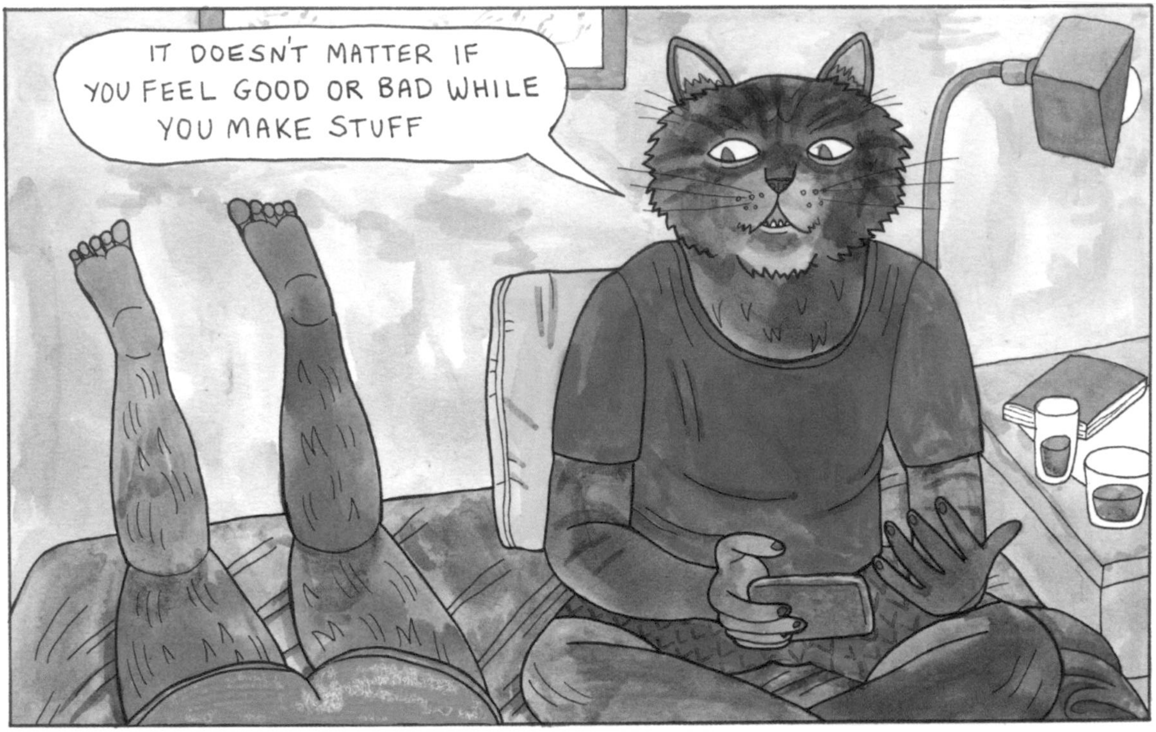
IT DOESN'T MATTER IF YOU FEEL GOOD OR BAD WHILE YOU MAKE STUFF

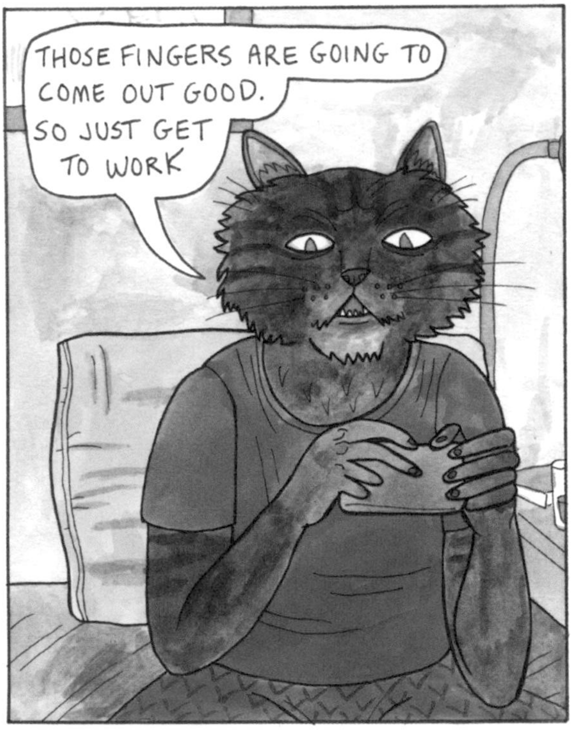
THOSE FINGERS ARE GOING TO COME OUT GOOD. SO JUST GET TO WORK

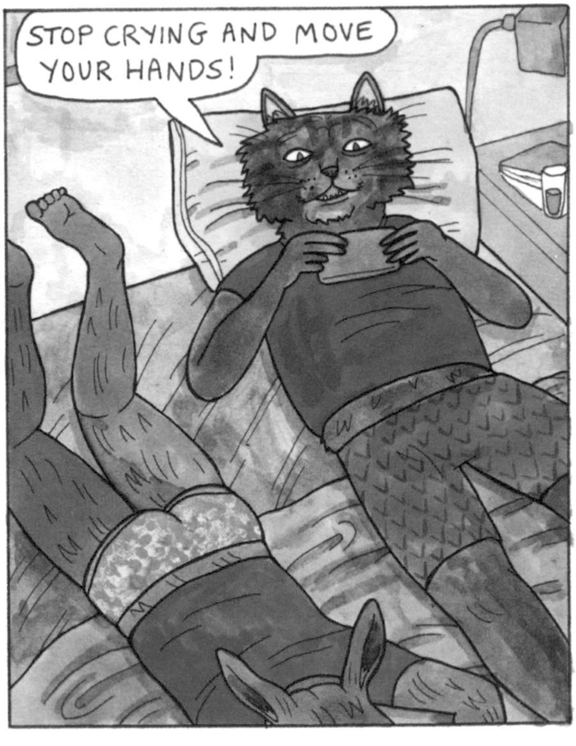
STOP CRYING AND MOVE YOUR HANDS!

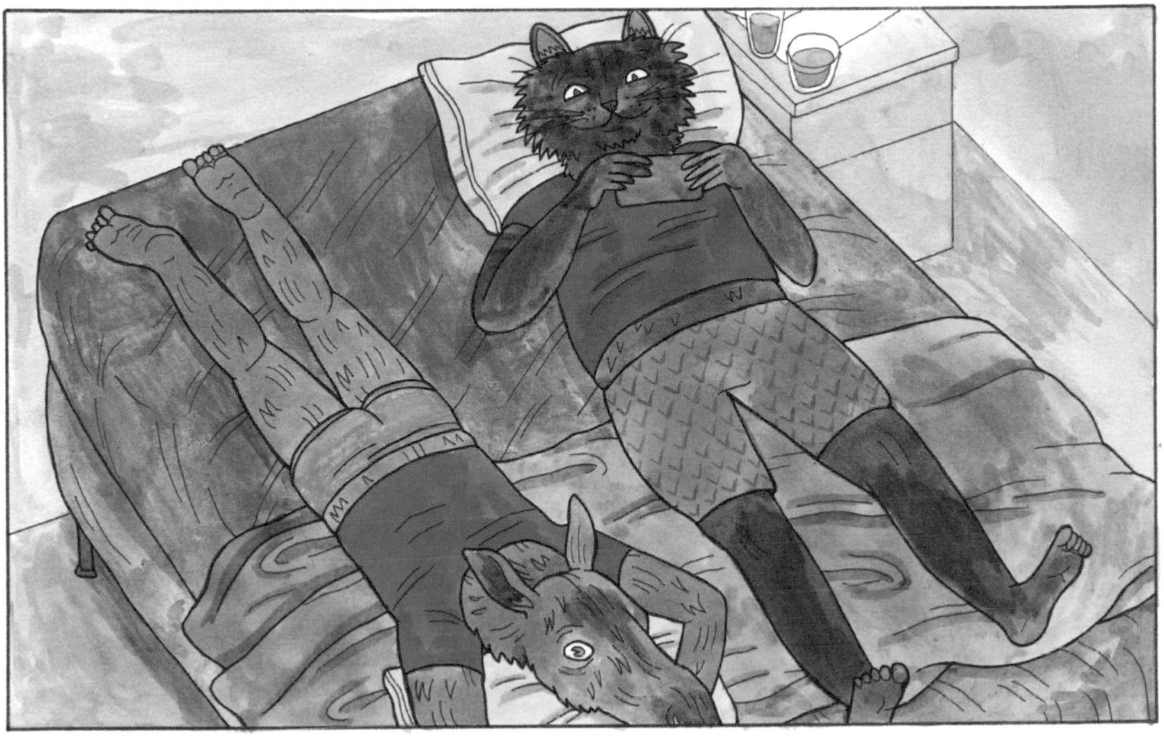
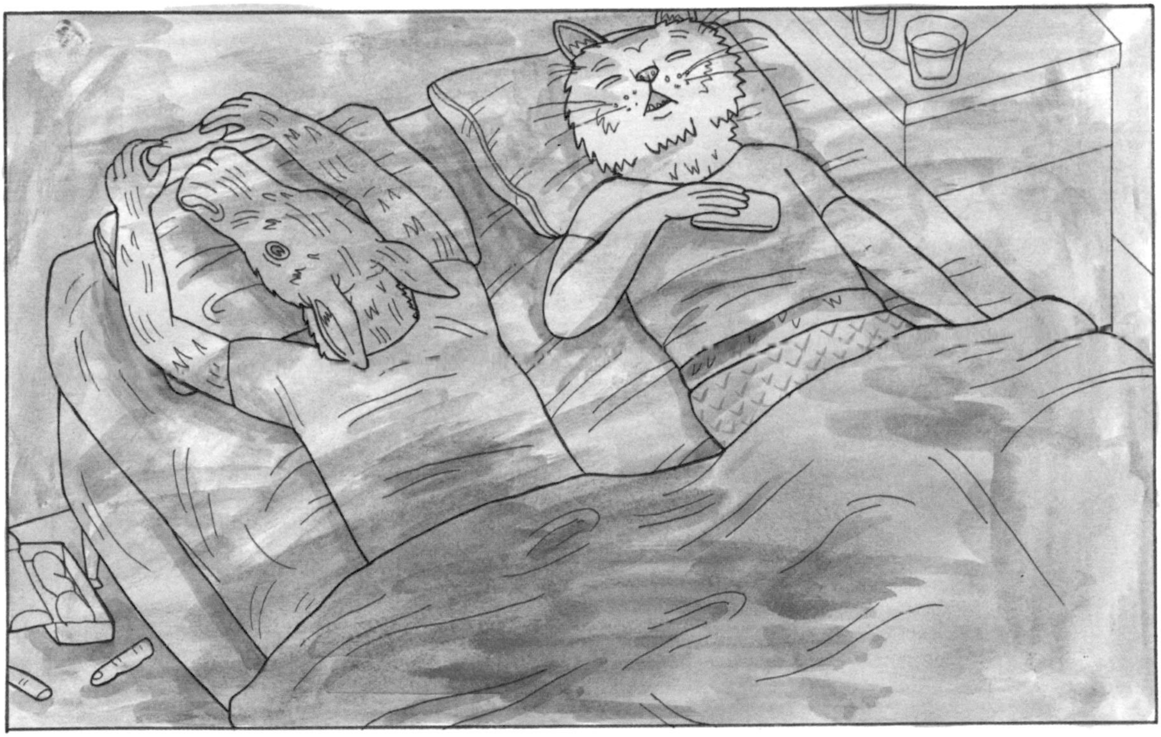

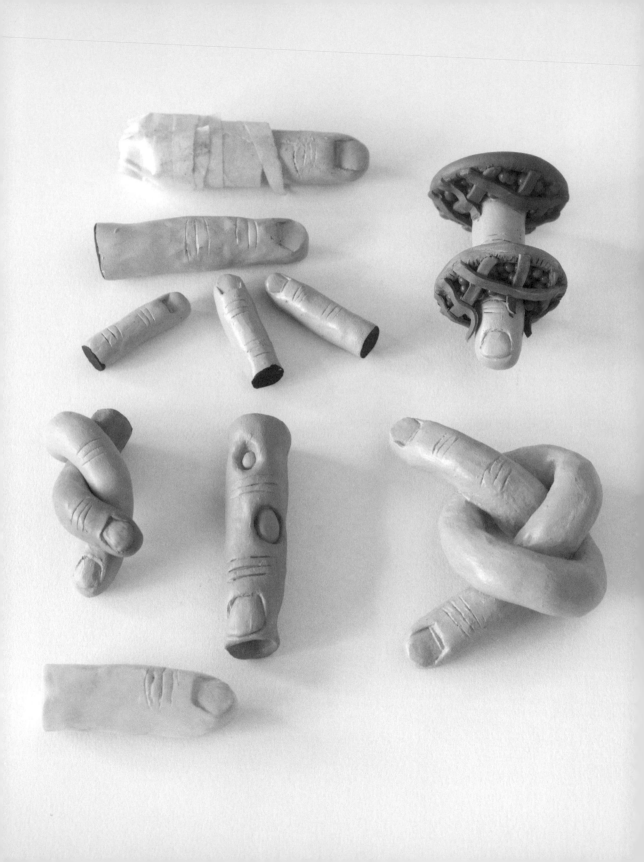

THE REMEMBERING GAME

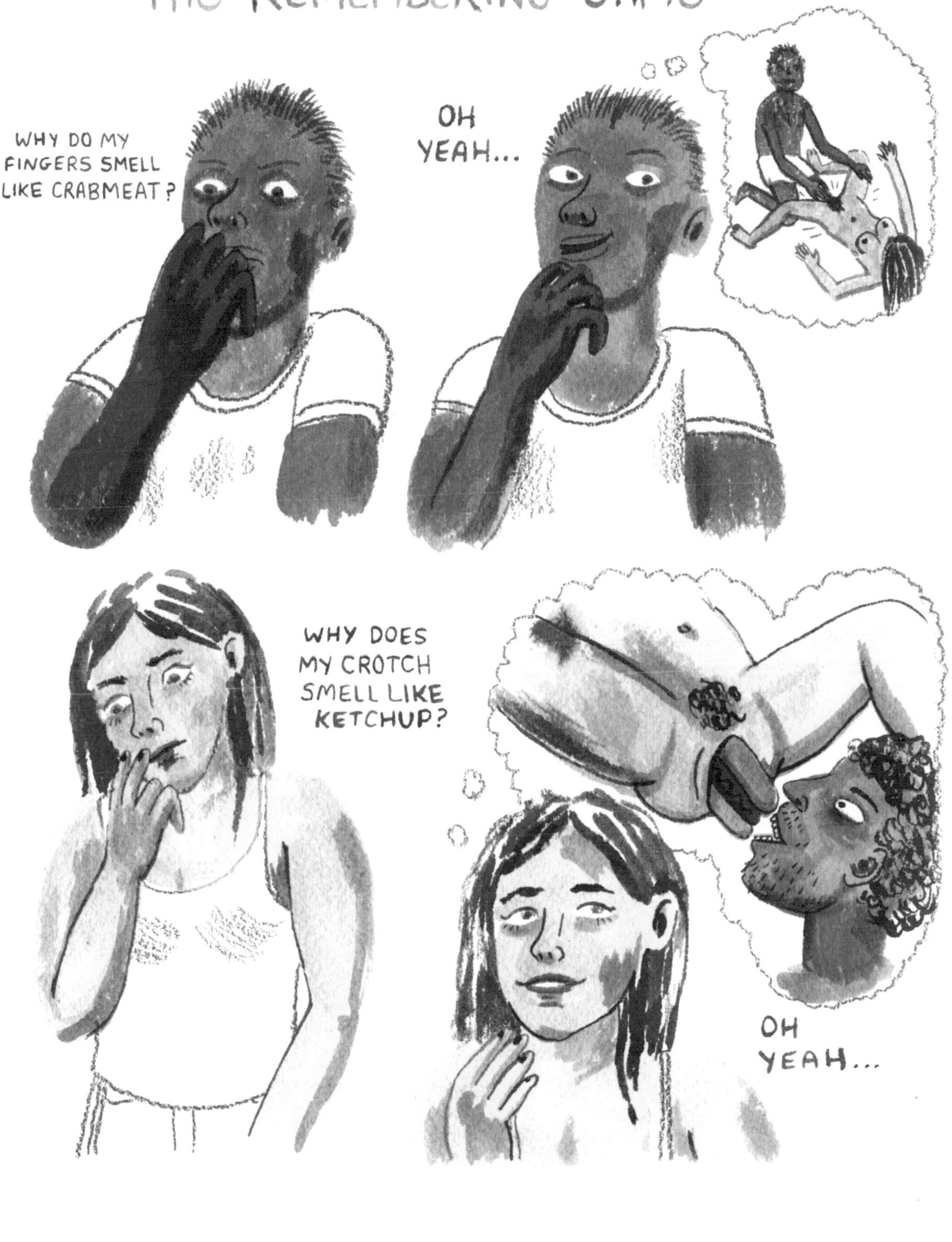
WHY DO MY FINGERS SMELL LIKE CRABMEAT?
OH YEAH...
WHY DOES MY CROTCH SMELL LIKE KETCHUP?
OH YEAH...

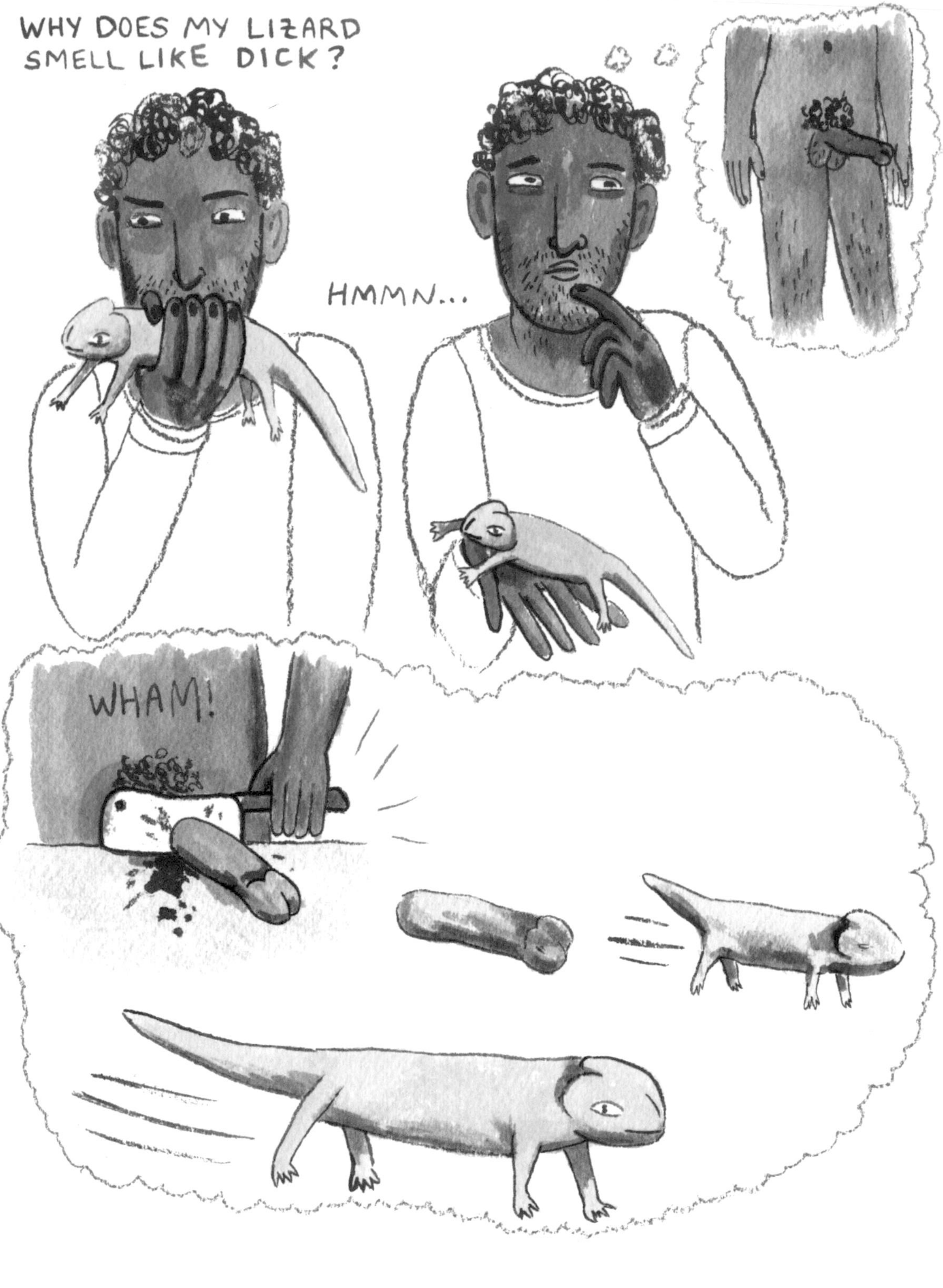
WHY DOES MY LIZARD SMELL LIKE DICK?
HMMN...
WHAM!

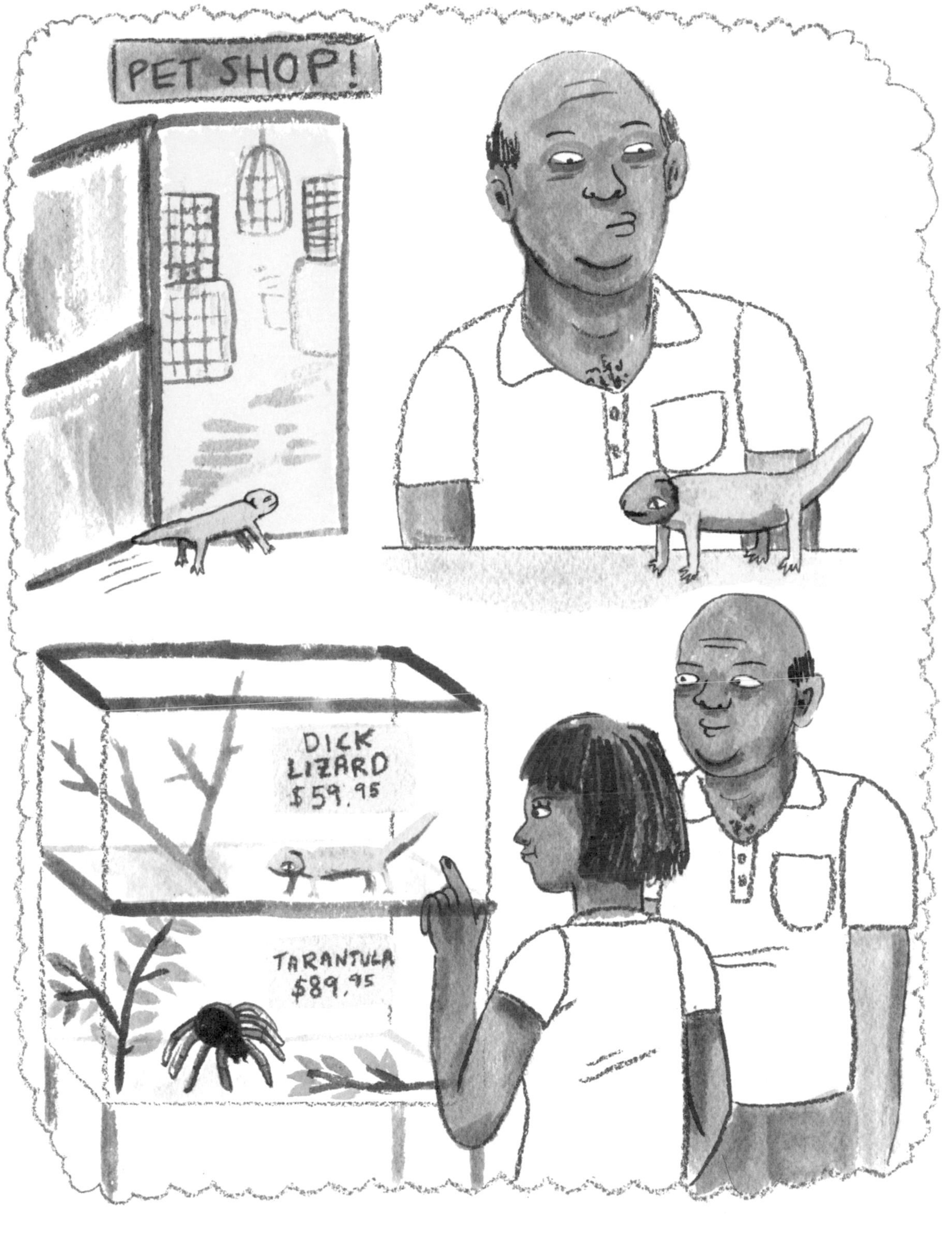
PET SHOP!
DICK LIZARD $59.95
TARANTULA $89.95

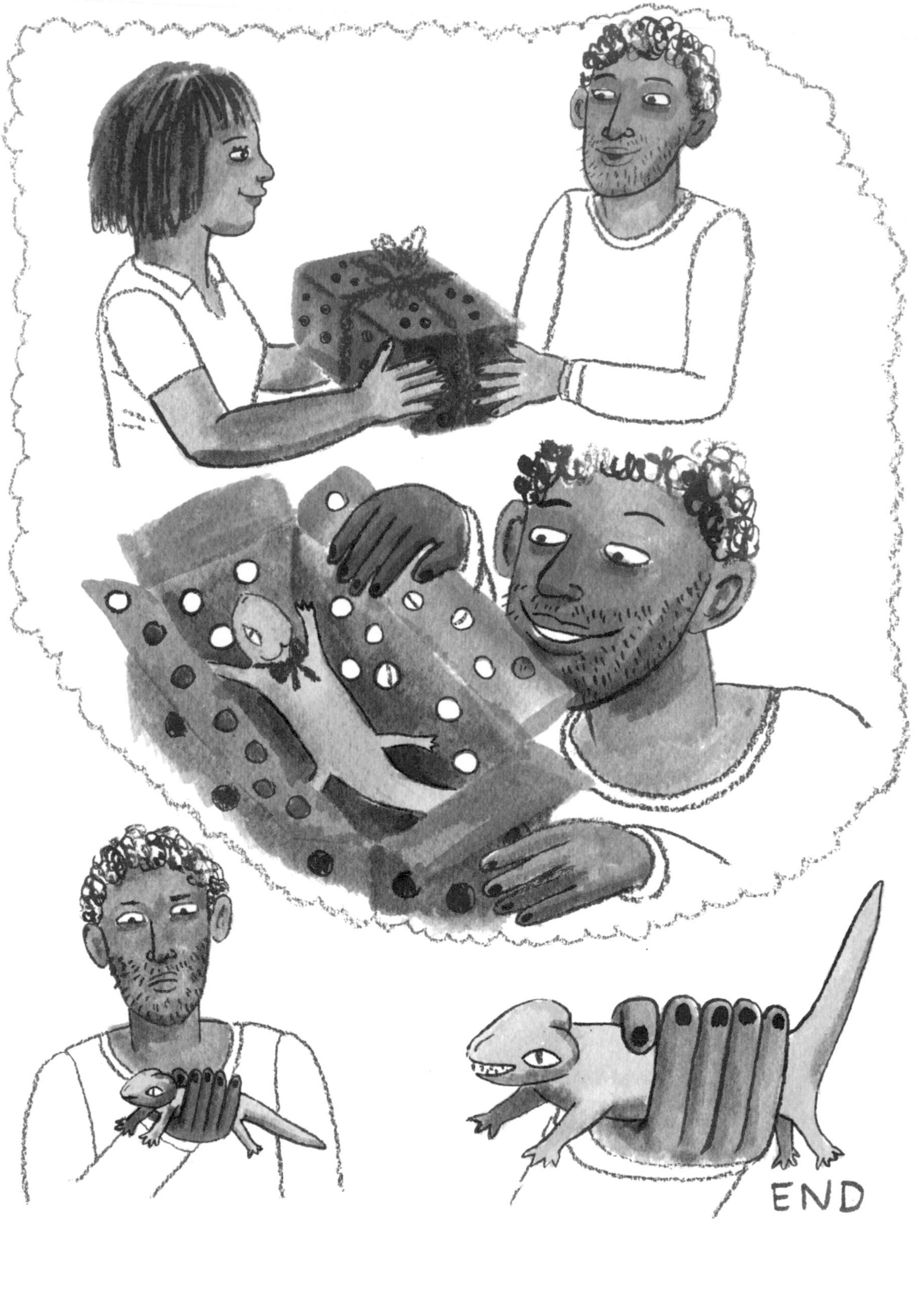
END

SEX FANTASIES INSPIRED BY MOVIES

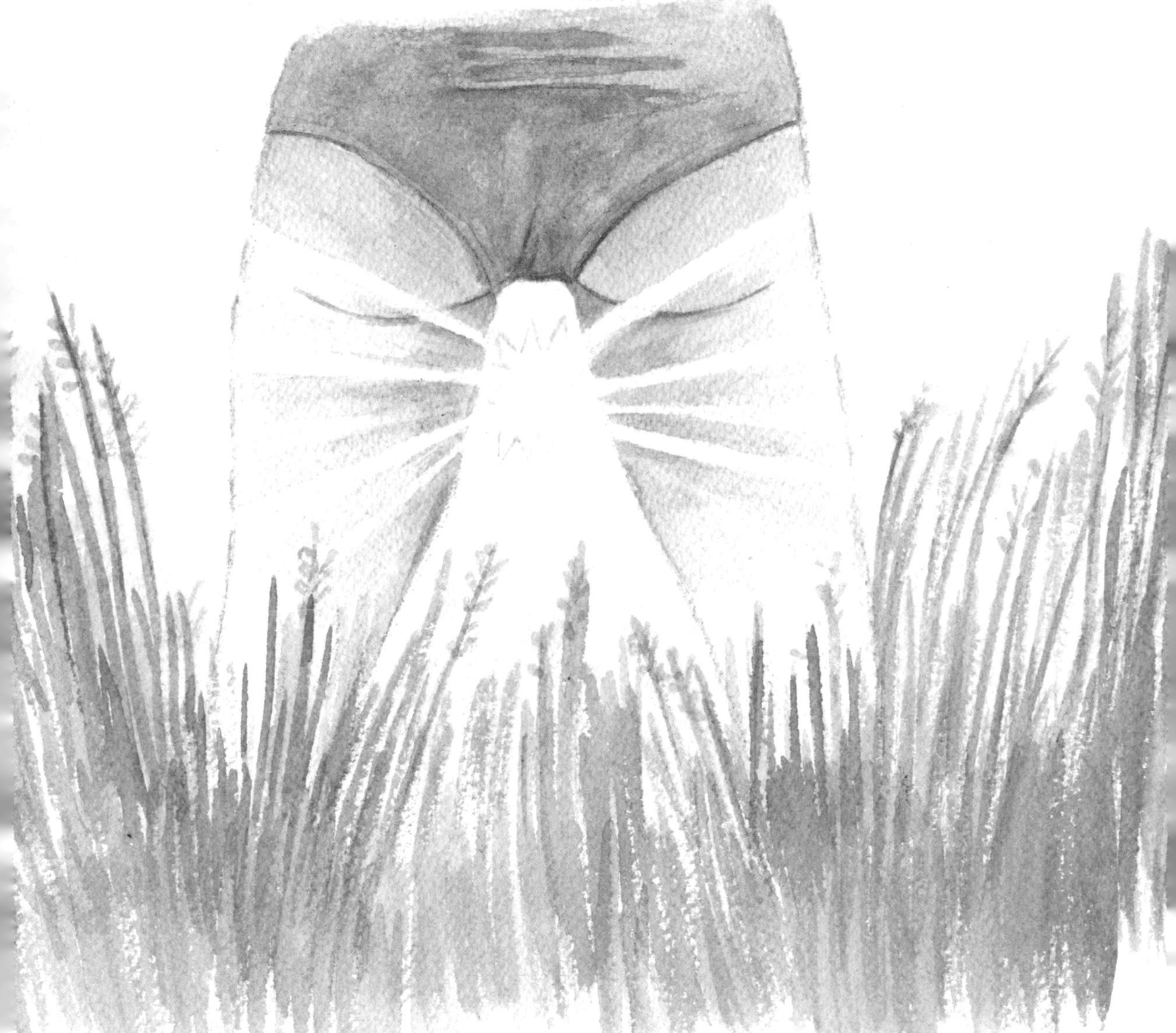

ANY MOVIE BY TERRENCE MALICK

I'M STANDING IN A FIELD, BEING PLEASURED BY LENS FLARE AS A HUSKY VOICE-OVER NARRATOR WHISPERS TO ME.

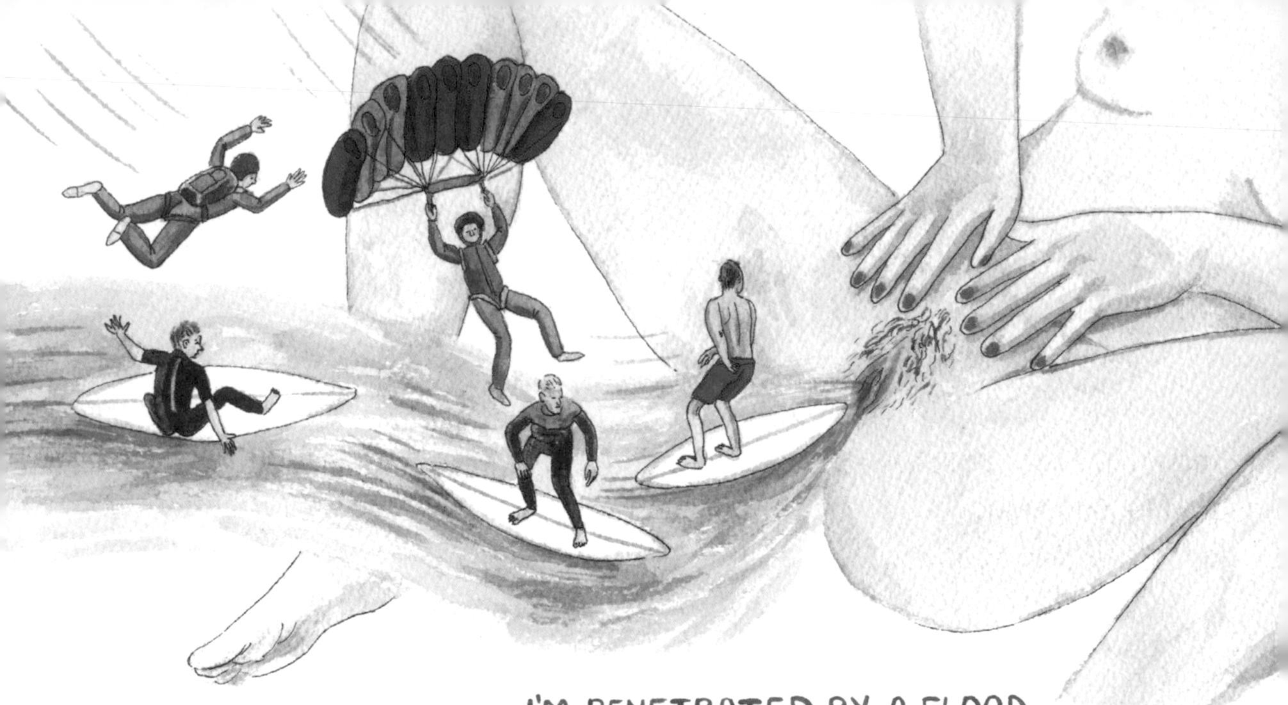

POINT BREAK

I'M PENETRATED BY A FLOOD OF TINY ADRENALINE JUNKIES.

TRANSFORMERS

I'M A TRANSFORMABABE.

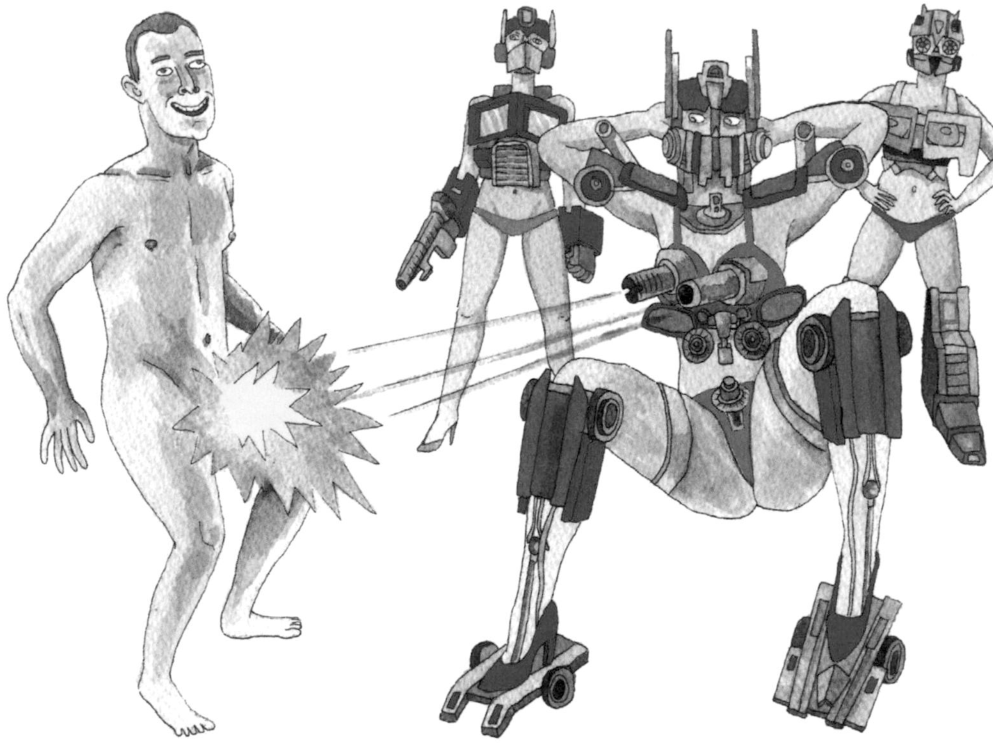

THE AVENGERS

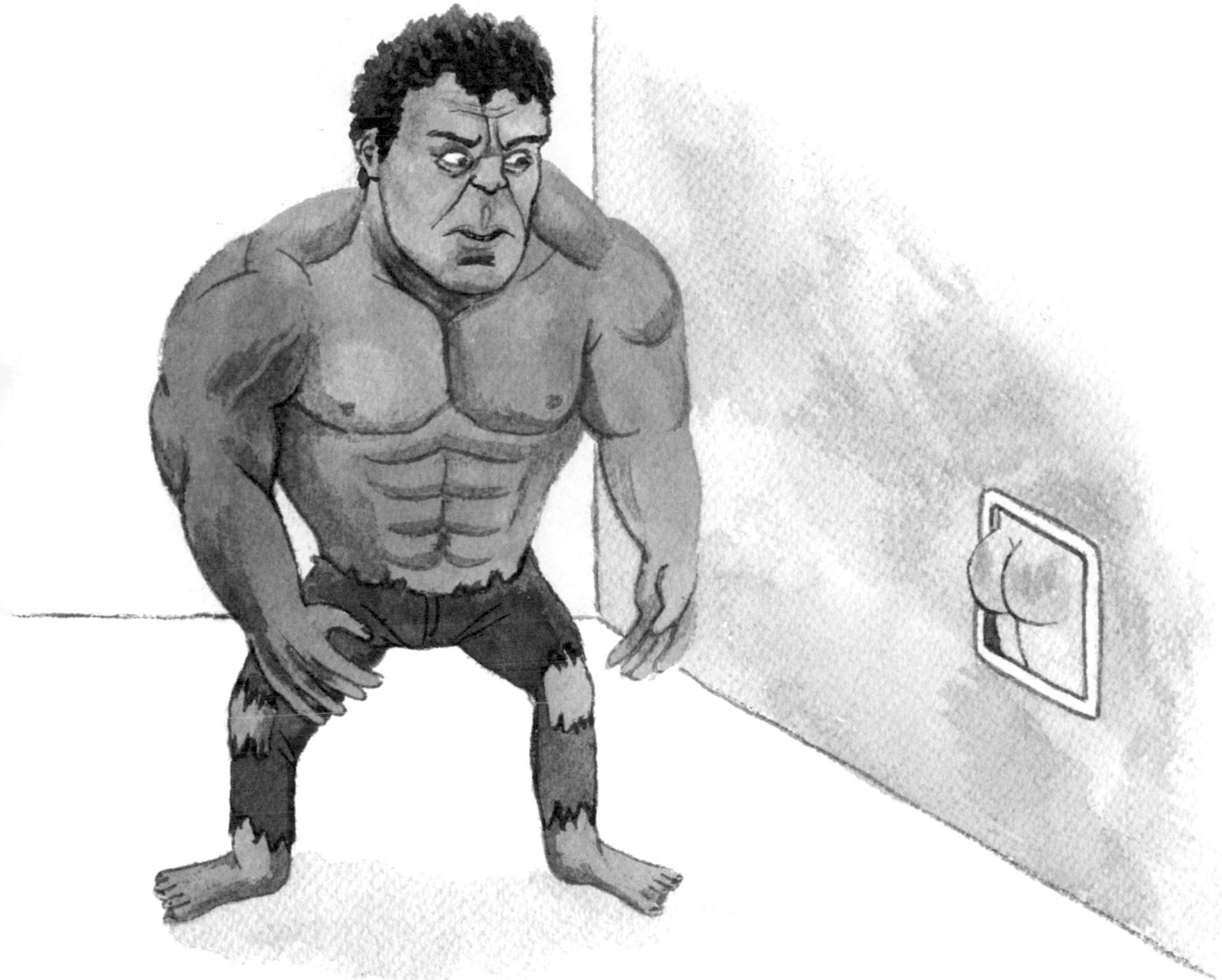

THE HULK IS TRAPPED IN A ROOM CONTAINING *NOTHING* EXCEPT MY BUTT.

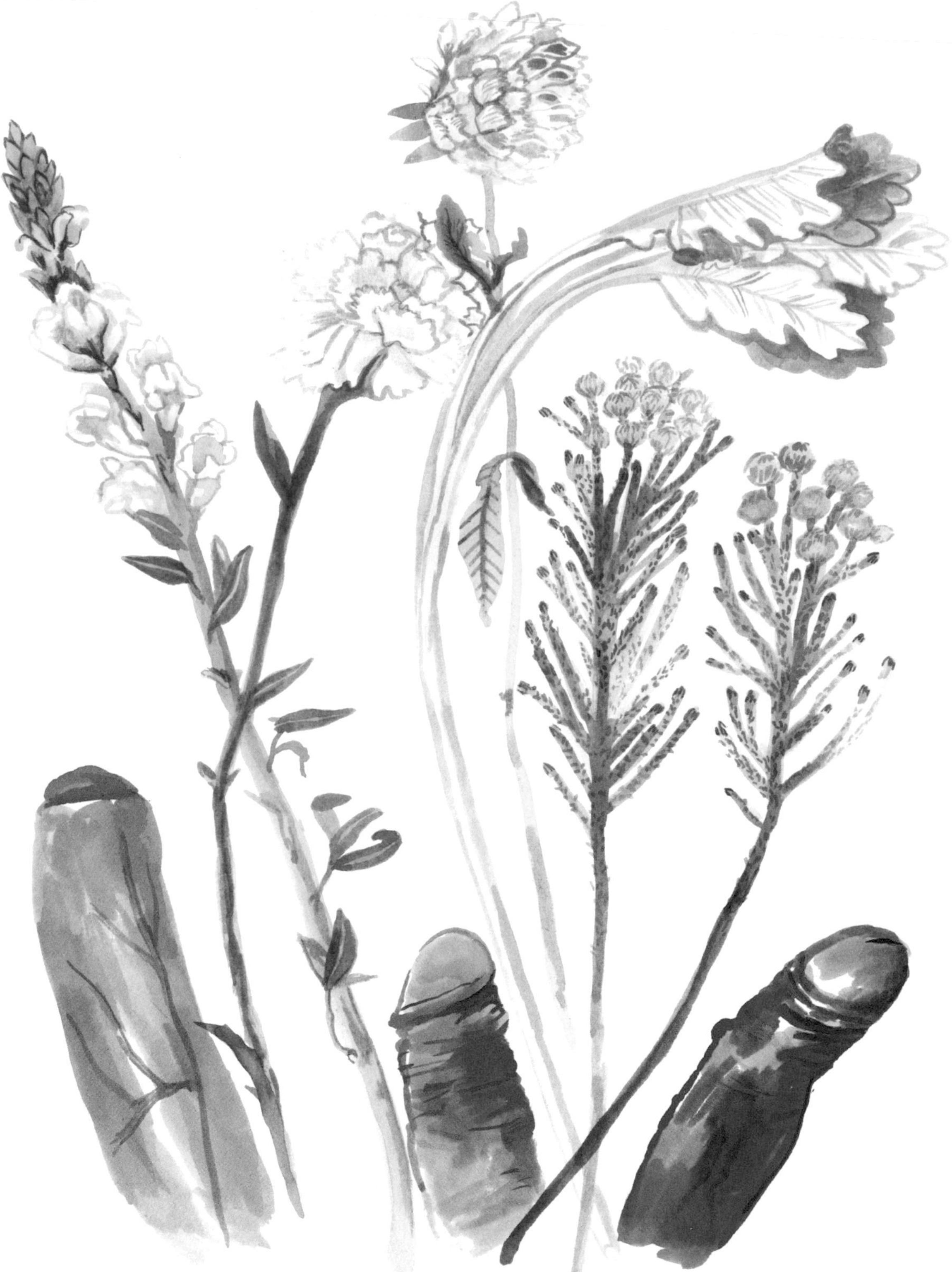

TIPS FOR LIVING WITH A SIGNIFICANT OTHER

① PREPARE FOR THE STATISTICAL LIKELIHOOD OF BREAKING UP BY LABELING YOUR POSSESSIONS AHEAD OF TIME.

HIS
HIS
MINE
MINE
HIS
HIS

② ADMIT YOU HAVE SOME ANNOYING HABITS YOU COULD WORK ON QUITTING.

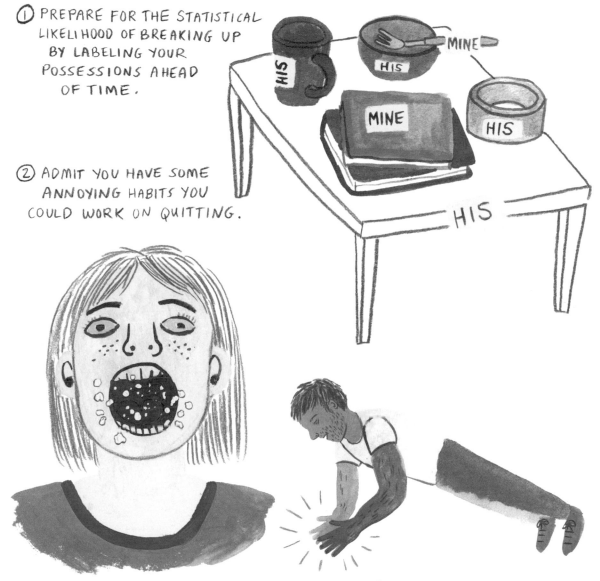

EX 1: YOU HAVE A HORRIBLE EATING FACE.

EX 2: YOU THINK CLAPPING PUSH-UPS ARE A COOL WAY TO DANCE.

③ SHOW THAT YOU'RE WILLING TO ADDRESS YOUR SHORTCOMINGS AND IMPROVE YOURSELF.

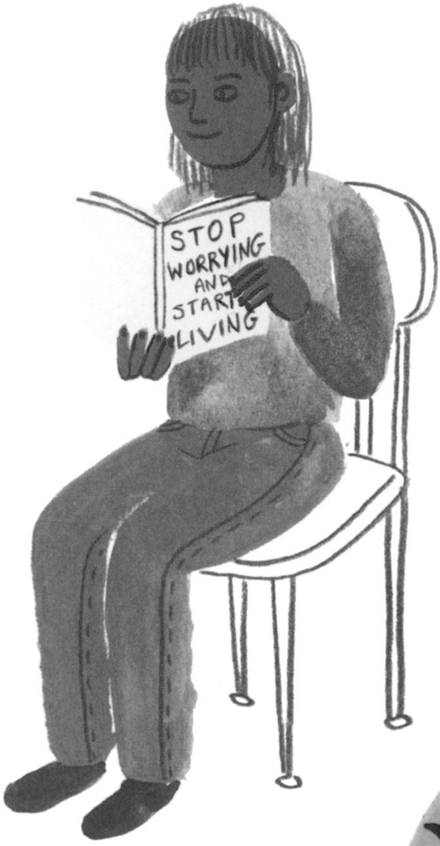
STOP WORRYING AND START LIVING

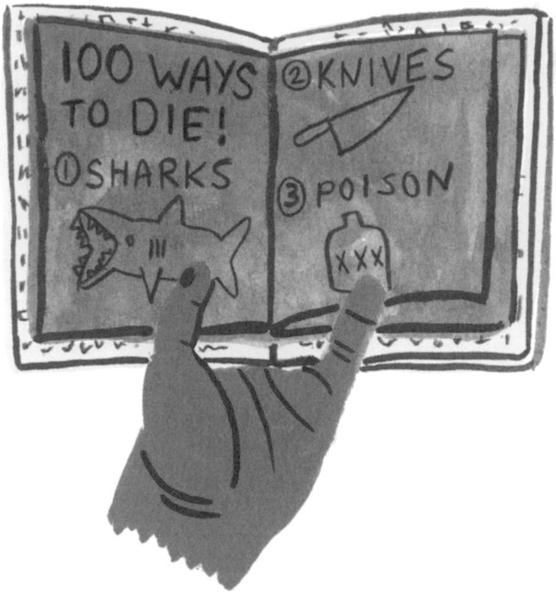
100 WAYS TO DIE!
①SHARKS
②KNIVES
③POISON
XXX

(OR AT LEAST MAKE IT LOOK LIKE YOU ARE.)

④ IT'S NORMAL FOR YOUR SEXUAL HABITS AND NEEDS TO CHANGE — WORK OUT A SYSTEM WITH YOUR PARTNER.

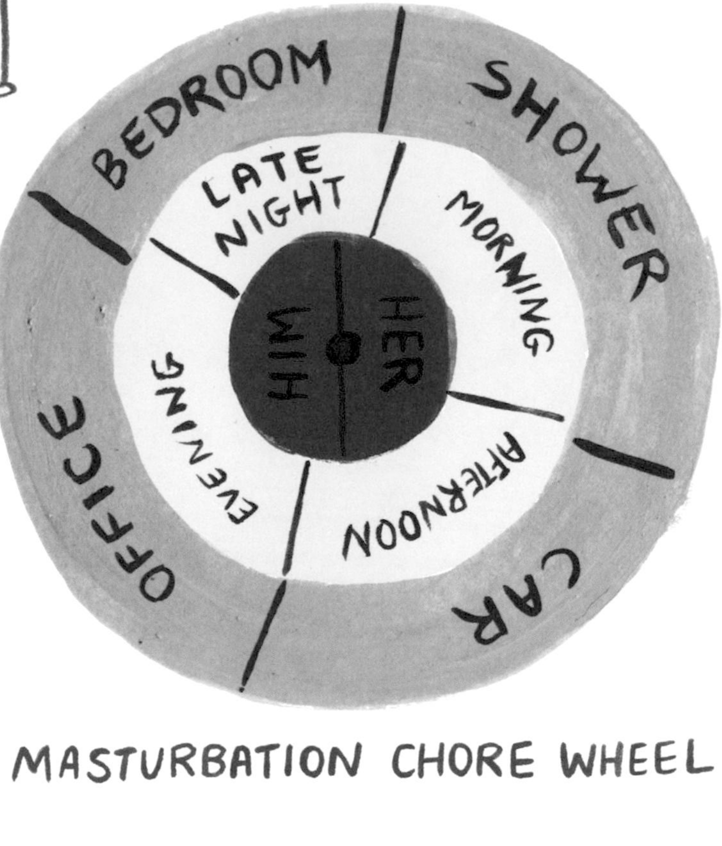
BEDROOM
SHOWER
CAR
OFFICE
LATE NIGHT
MORNING
AFTERNOON
EVENING
HIM
HER

MASTURBATION CHORE WHEEL

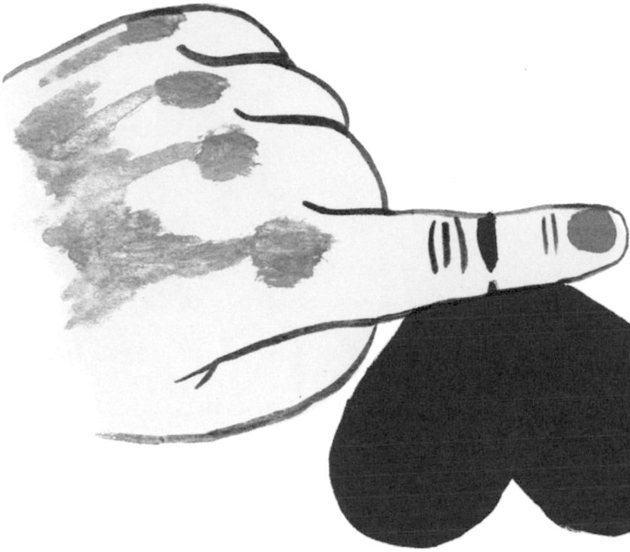

⑤ A GOOD WAY OF TESTING YOUR PARTNER IS TO SLICE YOUR FINGER OPEN.

DO THEY HELP YOU? DO THEY PASS OUT? OR DO THEY STARE AND LAUGH?

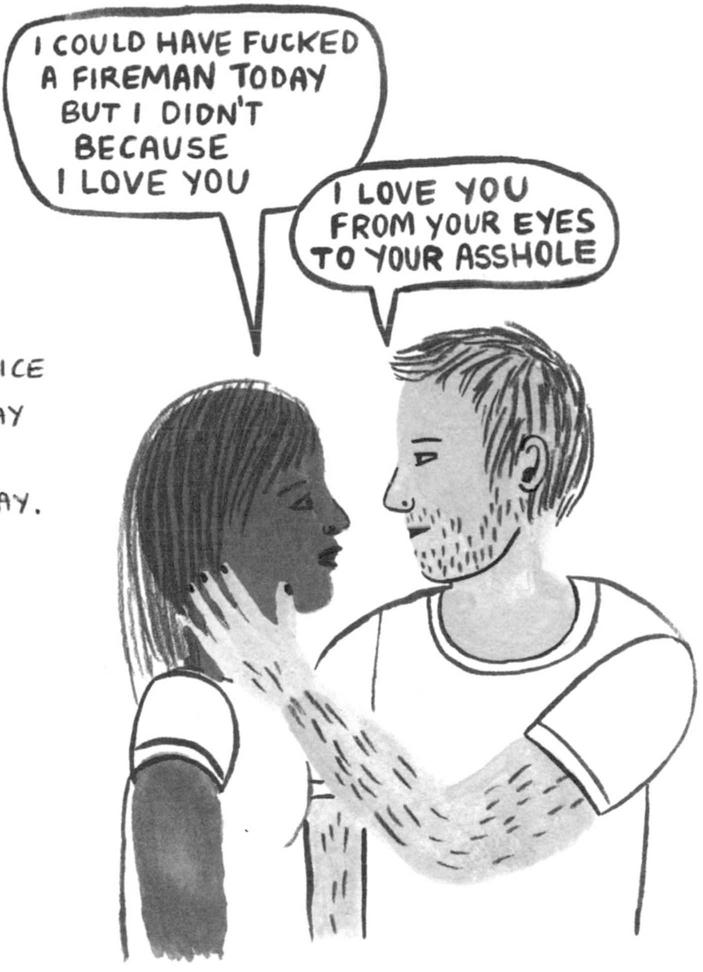
I COULD HAVE FUCKED A FIREMAN TODAY BUT I DIDN'T BECAUSE I LOVE YOU
I LOVE YOU FROM YOUR EYES TO YOUR ASSHOLE

⑥ THINK OF A FEW NICE THINGS YOU CAN SAY TO BRIGHTEN YOUR PARTNER'S DAY.

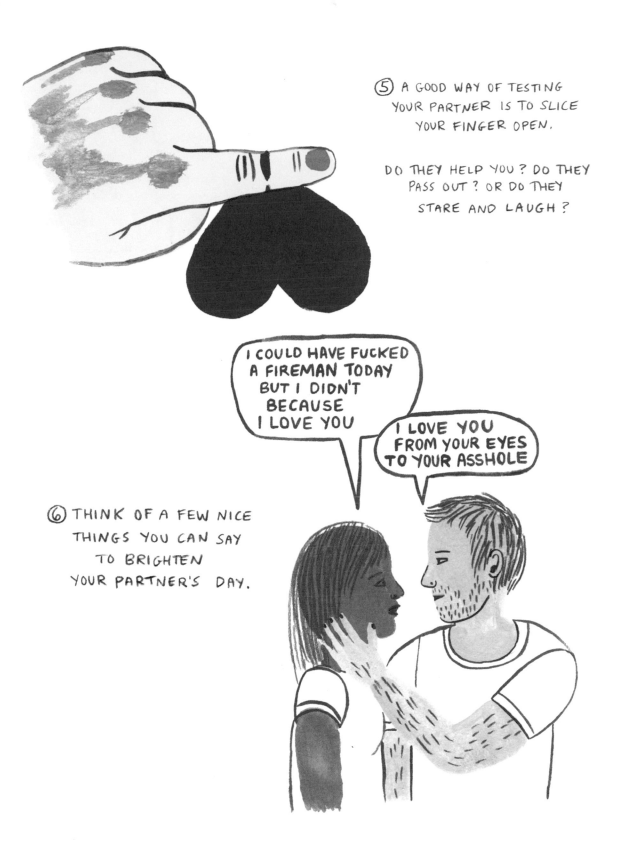

⑦ IT'S GOOD TO EXPERIMENT, BUT AVOID THE FOLLOWING SEX POSITIONS. THEY'RE ALL VERY BAD.

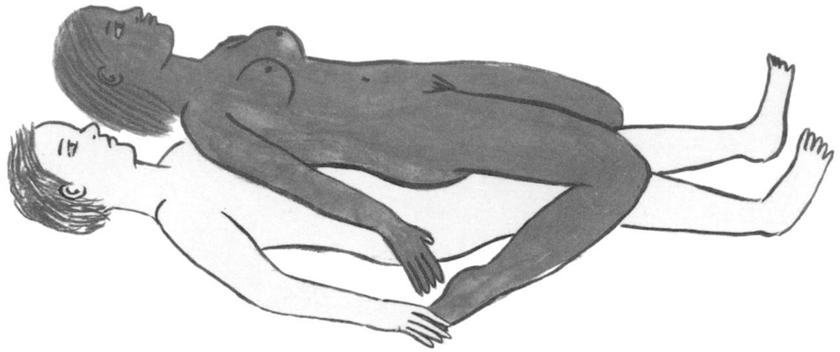

THE LUKEWARM LIE-DOWN

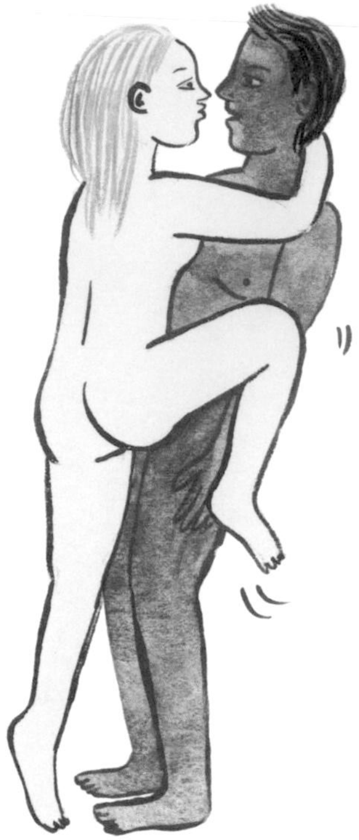

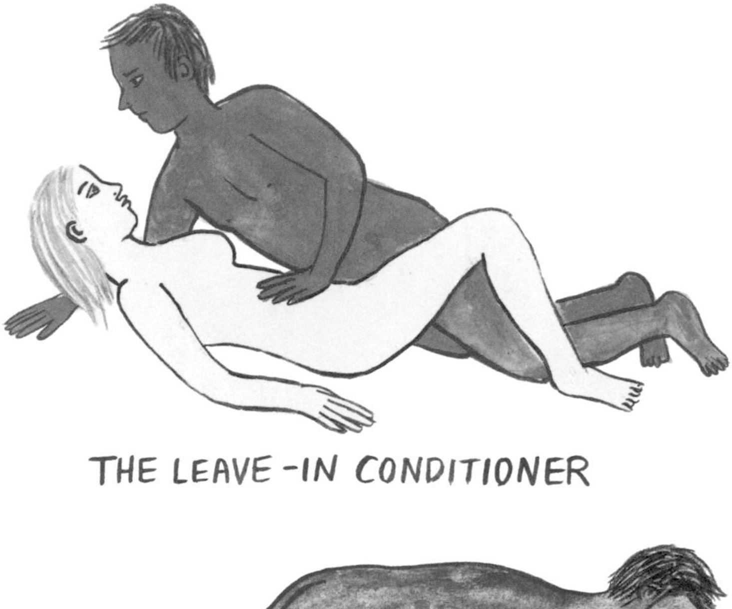

THE LEAVE-IN CONDITIONER

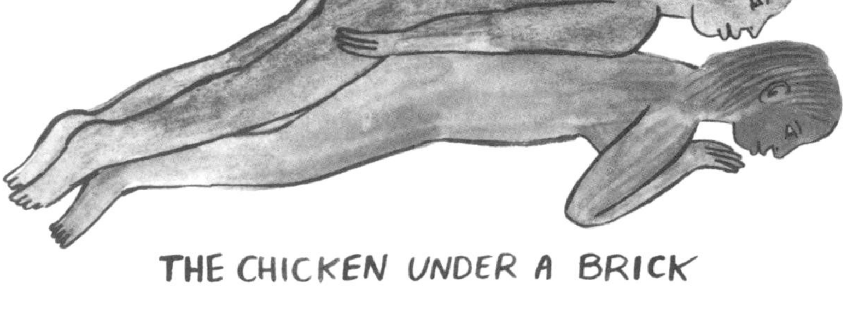

THE CHICKEN UNDER A BRICK

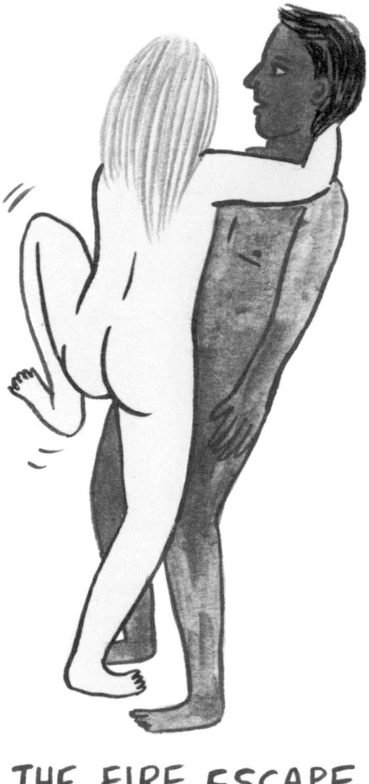

THE FIRE ESCAPE

8 LEARN TO COMMUNICATE OPENLY AND DON'T LET BAD FEELINGS FESTER.

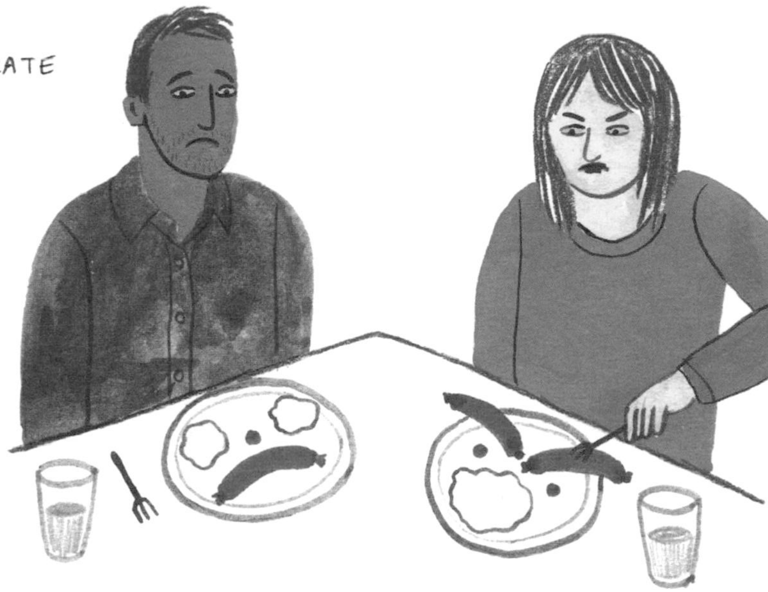

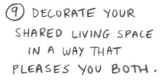

9 DECORATE YOUR SHARED LIVING SPACE IN A WAY THAT PLEASES YOU BOTH.

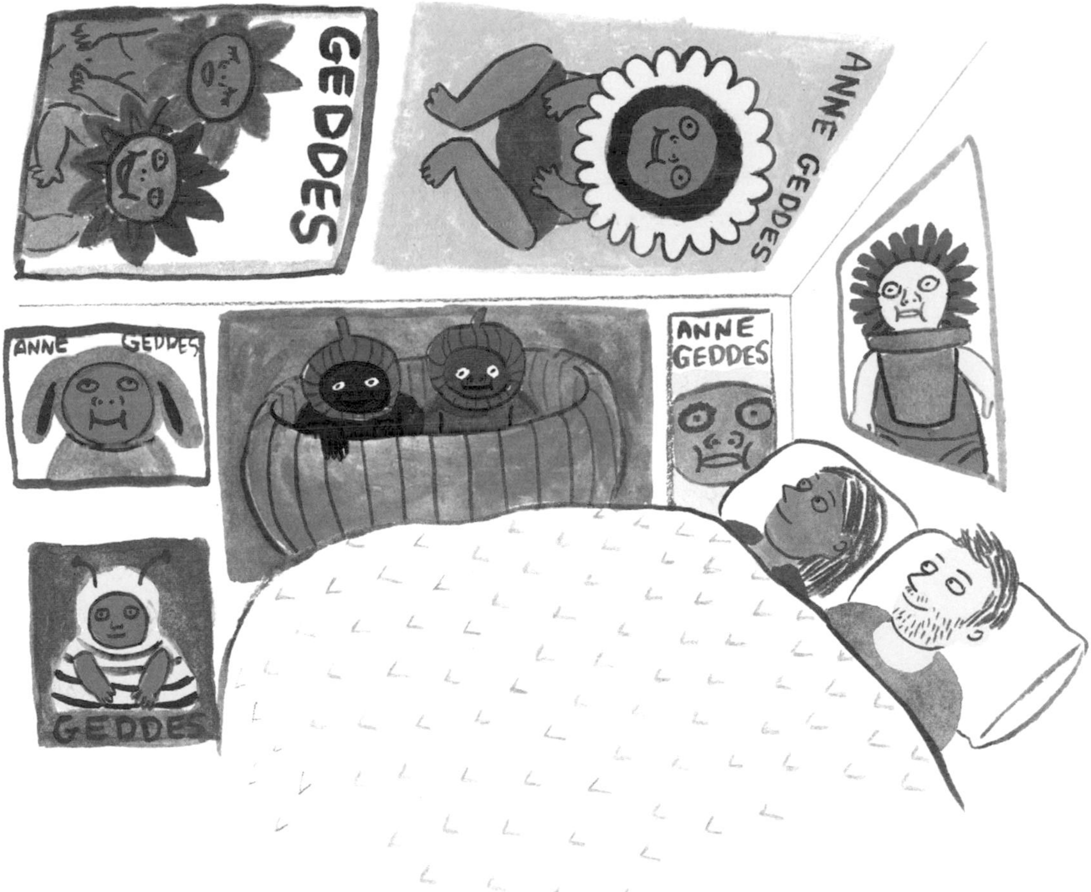
GEDDES
ANNE GEDDES
ANNE GEDDES
ANNE GEDDES
GEDDES

WEDDING REGISTRY

WE PUT THESE THINGS ON A LIST
AND THEN YOU BOUGHT THEM FOR US.

APPLIANCE

GLASSWARE

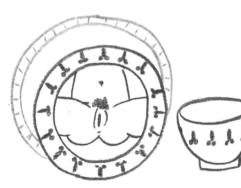

DISH

TOOLS

WHAT ARE THESE?

MORE APPLIANCE

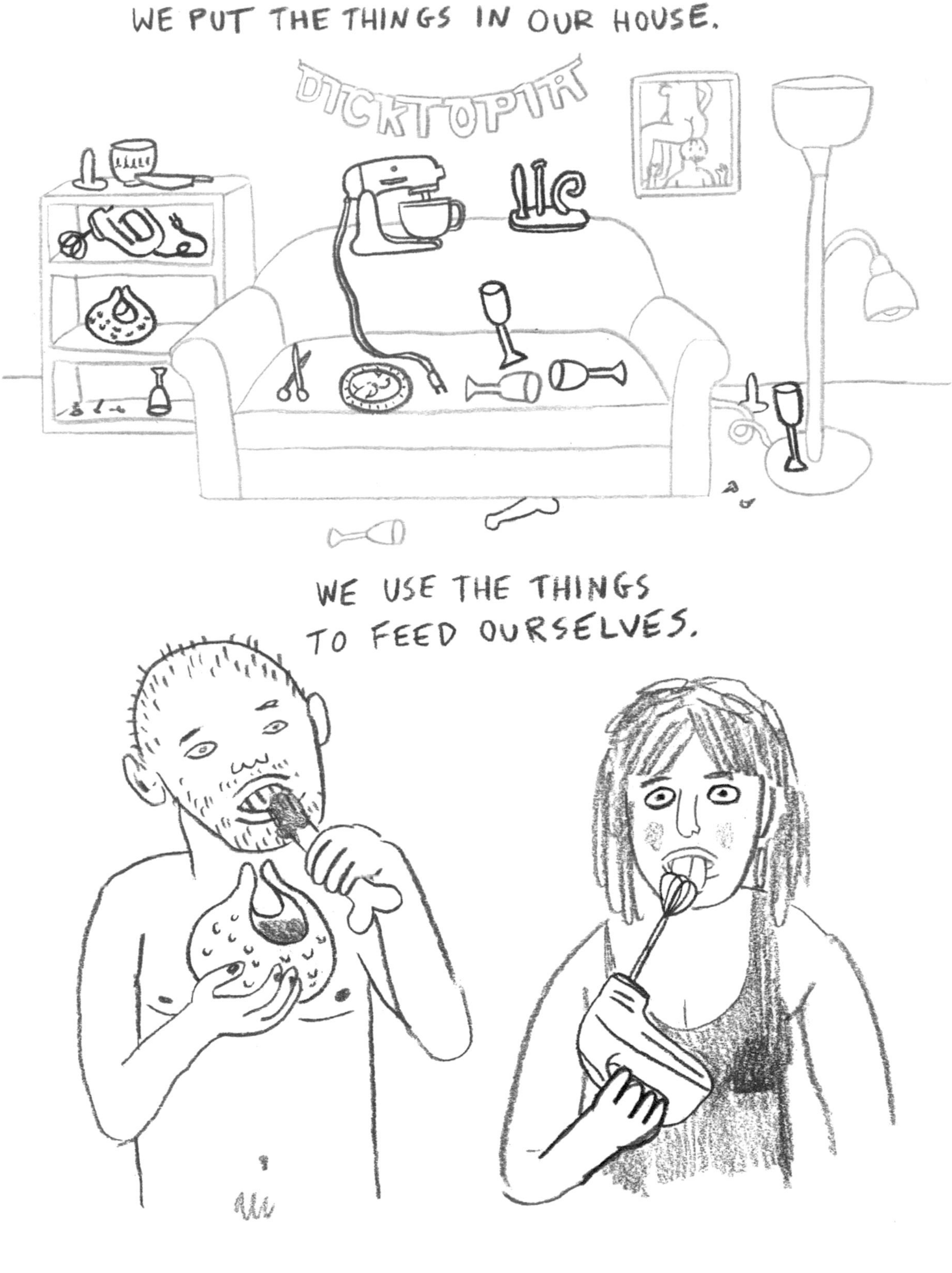
WE PUT THE THINGS IN OUR HOUSE.
DICKTOPIA
WE USE THE THINGS
TO FEED OURSELVES.

WE USE THE THINGS ON OUR BODIES.

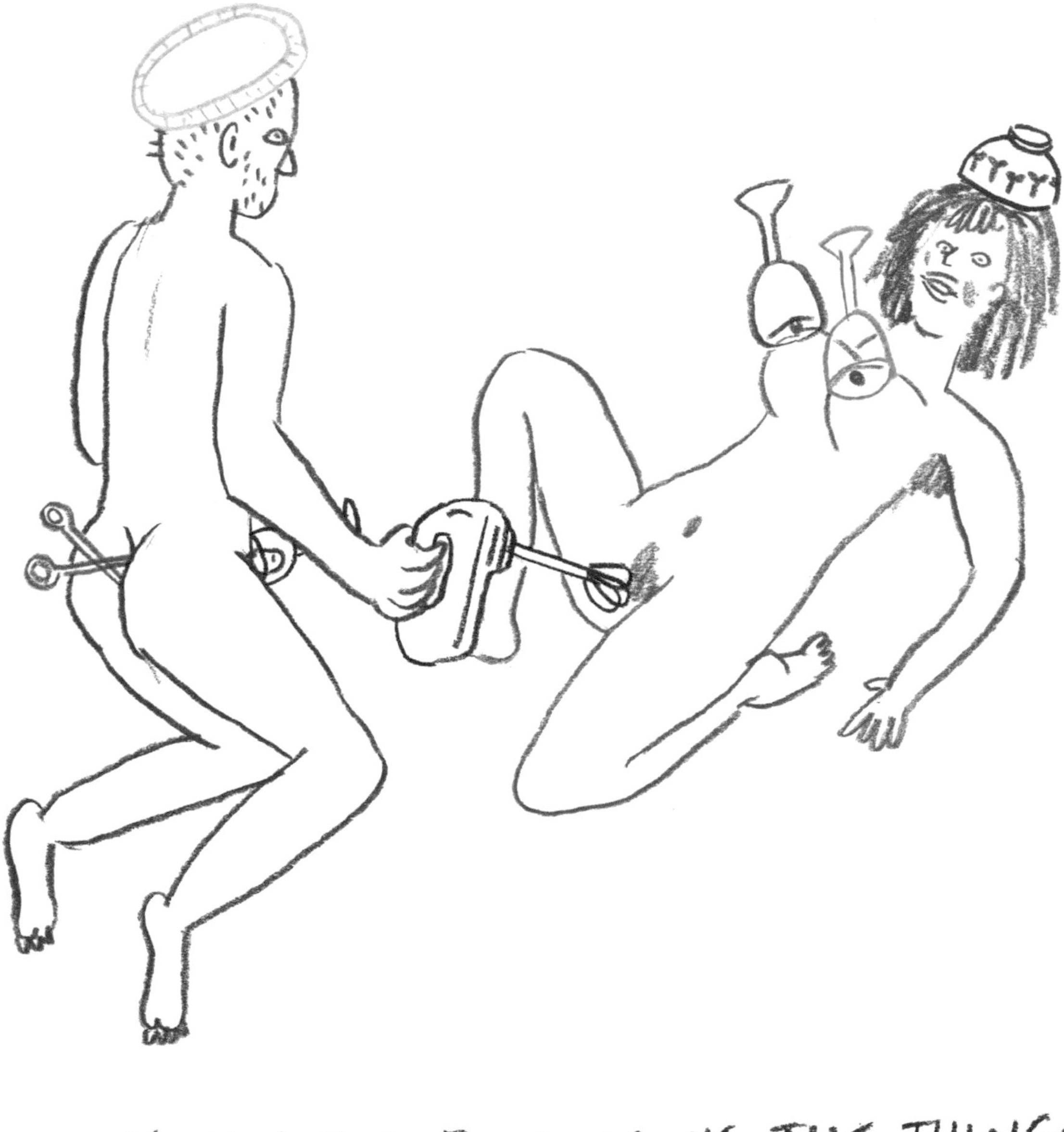

THANK YOU FOR BUYING US THE THINGS.

THE VOW

AN ILLUSTRATED MOVIE REVIEW

- I WENT TO A MIDNIGHT SCREENING OF "THE VOW," WHICH I GUESSED WOULD BE EMPTY BUT WAS IN FACT PACKED WITH SQUEALING WOMEN. I CANNOT OVEREMPHASIZE HOW EXCITED THE AUDIENCE WAS!

- "THE VOW" IS ABOUT A COUPLE OF LOVEBIRDS WHO GET IN A CAR ACCIDENT, LEAVING THE WIFE (RACHEL MCADAMS) WITH AMNESIA. THE FILMMAKERS LEFT OUT THE PARTS WHERE SHE FORGETS HOW TO WALK, CAN'T GO TO THE BATHROOM BY HERSELF, AND LAUGHS/CRIES AT INAPPROPRIATE MOMENTS BECAUSE OF HER PERMANENT BRAIN DAMAGE.

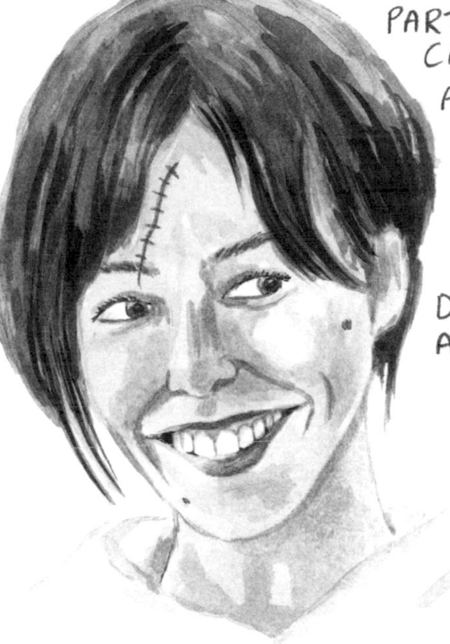

STARRING RACHEL MCADAMS AS PHINEAS GAGE

- CHANNING TATUM IS A TOTAL CHARMER BUT THE WAY HE MUMBLES MAKES ME THINK THE TATUM WRANGLERS HAD TO SPREAD PEANUT BUTTER ON HIS LIPS TO GET HIM TO "TALK."

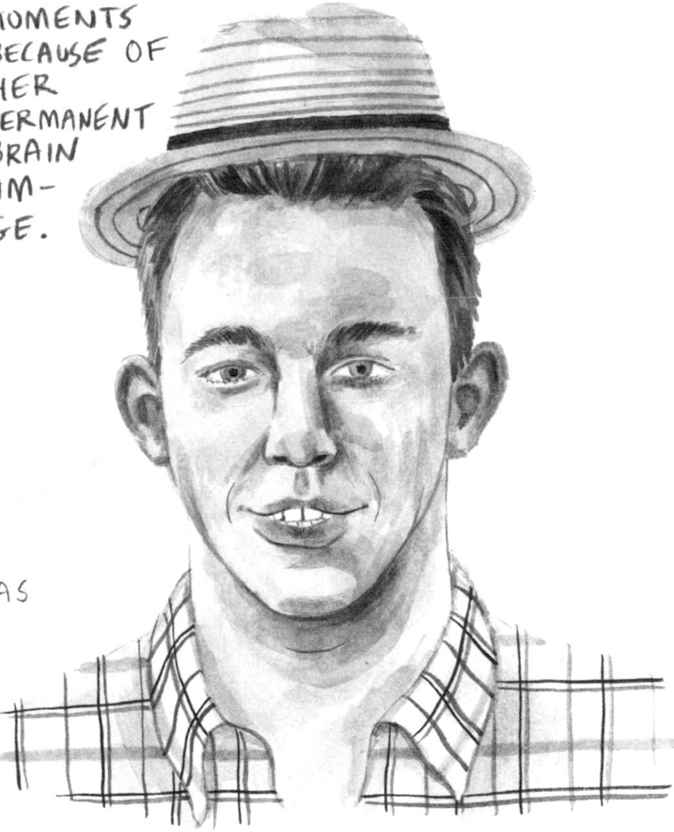

AND CHANNING TATUM AS "MR. ED"

• WHEN CHANNING TATUM WEARS A STRAW HAT IN AN EARLY SCENE, HE LOOKS SO MUCH LIKE A LABRADOR THAT I CRACK UP. HE LOOKS LIKE YOU COULDN'T LEAVE HIM UNATTENDED IN A ROOM WITH FOOD LEFT OUT.

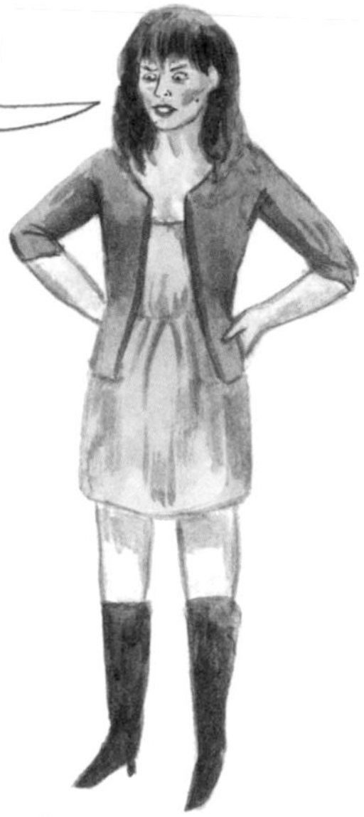
AW, WHAT THE? YOU ATE ALL THE CHOCOLATE AND MY PHONE BILL?!

• HEY, SAM NEILL AND JESSICA LANGE ARE HERE! I THINK THEY WERE CAST AS A CLEVER WINK TO THE FACT THAT THIS MOVIE IS NOWHERE NEAR AS GOOD AS "JURASSIC PARK" OR "TOOTSIE."

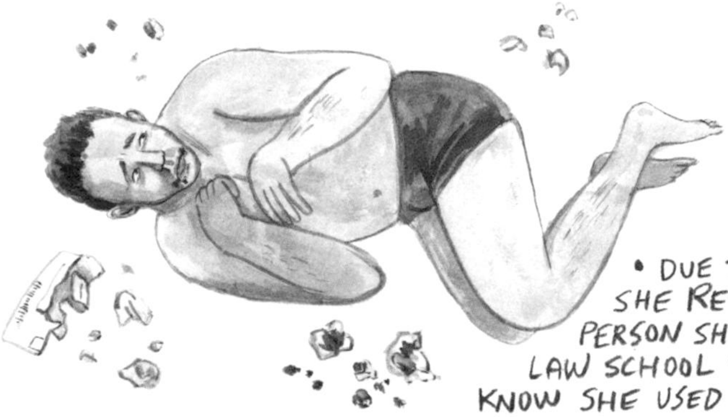

• DUE TO THE WIFE'S MEMORY LOSS, SHE REVERTS TO BEING THE PERSON SHE WAS BEFORE SHE QUIT LAW SCHOOL TO BE AN ARTIST. WE KNOW SHE USED TO BE A HUGE ASSHOLE BECAUSE SHE STARTS ORDERING BLUEBERRY MOJITOS. BLUEBERRY. MOJITOS.

• ACCORDING TO THE SCREENWRITERS, AN ARTIST IS SOMEBODY WHO CUTS OFF ALL TIES WITH FAMILY AND OLD FRIENDS, SLEEPS ON A MATTRESS ON THE FLOOR, AND HASTILY SWITCHES FROM J.CREW TO ANTHROPOLOGIE. SOUNDS ABOUT RIGHT!

• WE'RE MEANT TO BELIEVE THAT THE WIFE WAS SUCH A GREAT SCULPTOR THAT SHE WAS COMMISSIONED TO SCULPT THINGS FOR THE LOBBY OF THE CHICAGO TRIBUNE, BUT HER SCULPTURES ARE SO BORING I CAN DRAW THEM ALL FROM MEMORY:

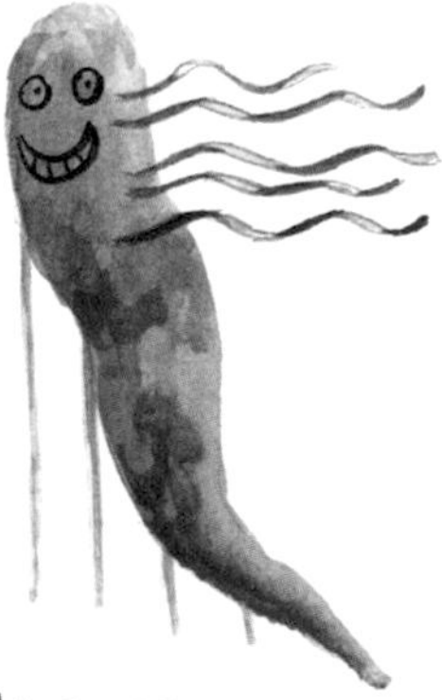
"ANTHROPOMORPHIC ROOT VEGETABLE"

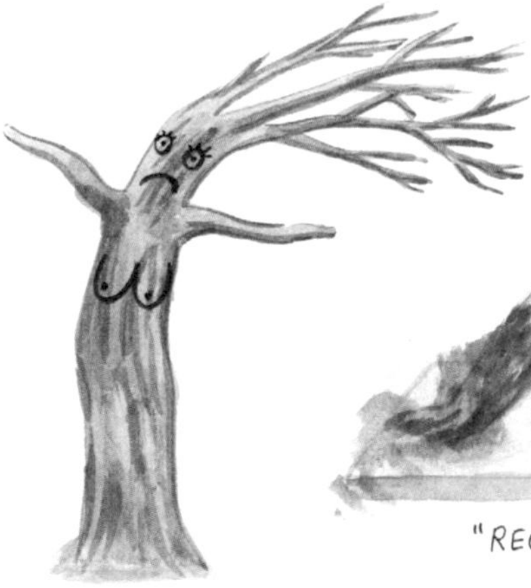
"ANTHROPOMORPHIC TREE"

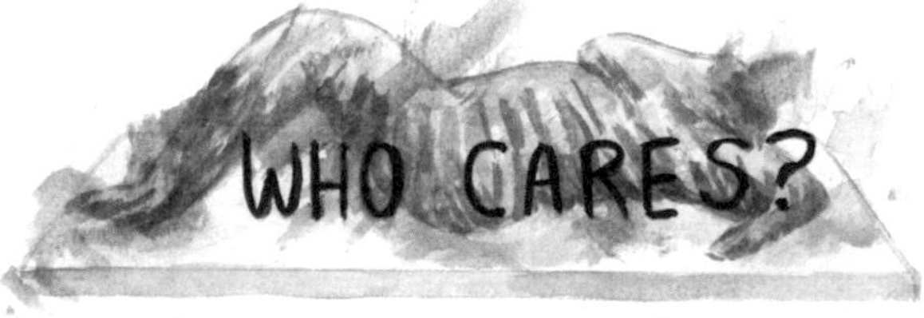
WHO CARES?
"RECLINING LADY PLANT"

• THE HUSBAND HAS LIKE FIVE HIP, FUNNY BUDDIES AND THERE'S NOT ENOUGH TIME TO BECOME FAMILIAR WITH ANY OF THEM. IT'S LIKE THE CASTING DIRECTOR WENT AROUND SCOOPING UP ALL THE QUIRKY FRIENDS FROM FAILED SITCOMS. HERE THEY ARE, TO THE BEST OF MY RECOLLECTION:

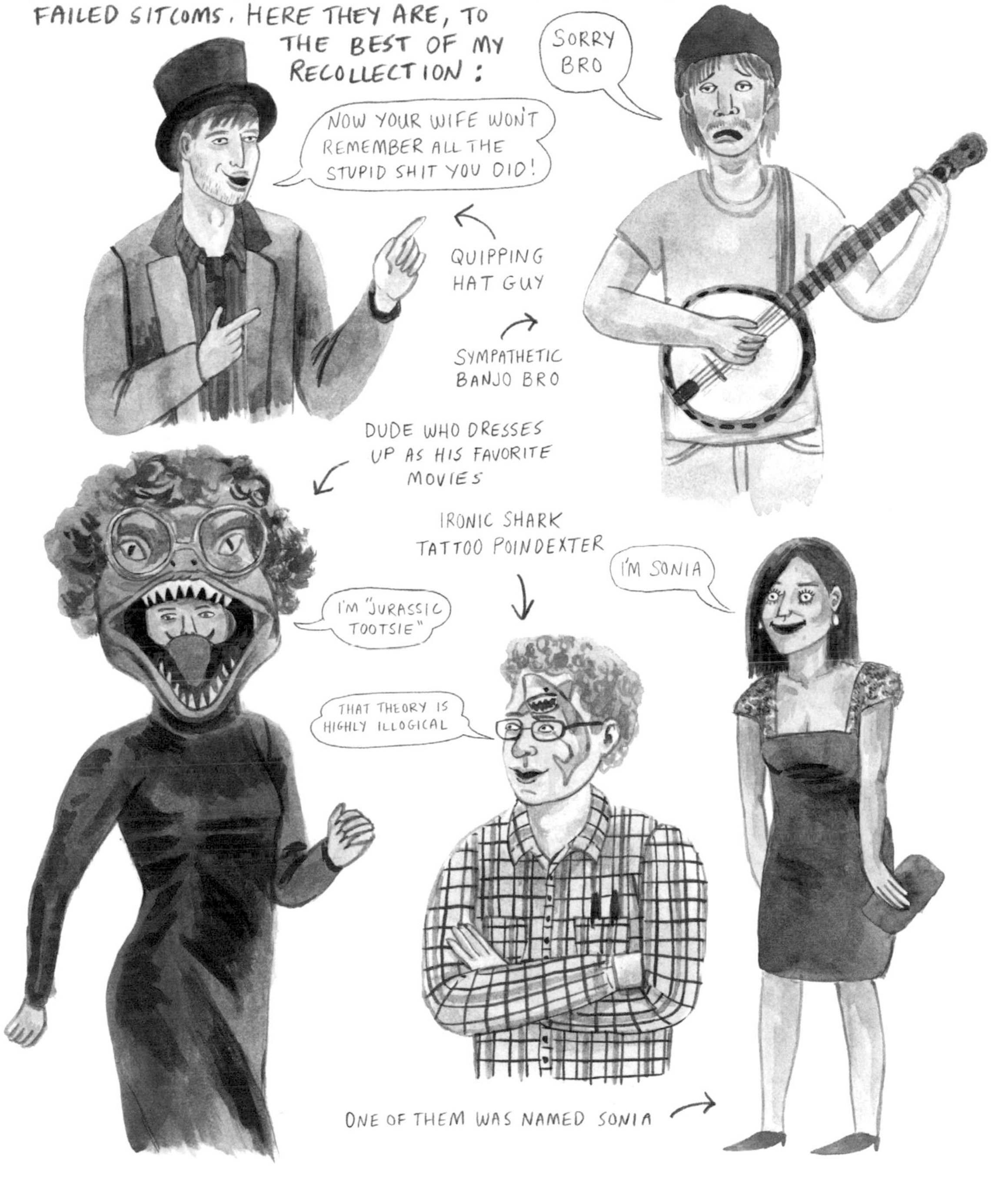
SORRY BRO
NOW YOUR WIFE WON'T REMEMBER ALL THE STUPID SHIT YOU DID!
QUIPPING HAT GUY
SYMPATHETIC BANJO BRO
DUDE WHO DRESSES UP AS HIS FAVORITE MOVIES
IRONIC SHARK TATTOO POINDEXTER
I'M SONIA
I'M "JURASSIC TOOTSIE"
THAT THEORY IS HIGHLY ILLOGICAL
ONE OF THEM WAS NAMED SONIA

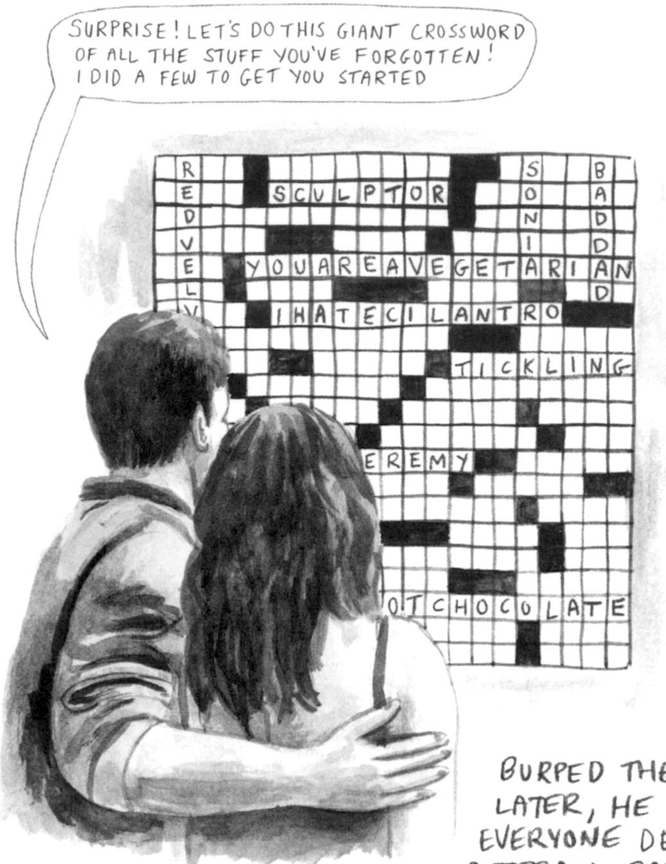
SURPRISE! LET'S DO THIS GIANT CROSSWORD OF ALL THE STUFF YOU'VE FORGOTTEN! I DID A FEW TO GET YOU STARTED
SCULPTOR
YOUAREAVEGETARIAN
IHATECILANTRO
TICKLING
BADDAD

• HUBBY DECIDES TO THROW WIFEY A SURPRISE PARTY WHEN SHE GETS HOME FROM THE HOSPITAL, SO SHE'S SUDDENLY SURROUNDED BY FORTY FRIENDS SHE DOESN'T REMEMBER. WHAT'S A MORE BONEHEADED THING YOU COULD DO FOR AN AMNESIAC?

• DURING THE PART WHERE HER PARENTS ARE SUPPOSED TO HATE HIM, TATUM GIVES A TOTALLY REASONABLE SPEECH ABOUT WHY RECORDING STUDIOS ARE STILL VALUABLE DESPITE THE DYING MUSIC INDUSTRY AND THE ENTIRE FAMILY STARES AT HIM LIKE HE JUST BURPED THE ALPHABET. MINUTES LATER, HE QUOTES THOM YORKE AND EVERYONE DECIDES HE'S NOT SO BAD AFTERALL. RADIOHEAD, THE GREAT EQUALIZER!

HERE ARE THE TWO SCENES THAT MADE THE AUDIENCE SCREAM THE LOUDEST:

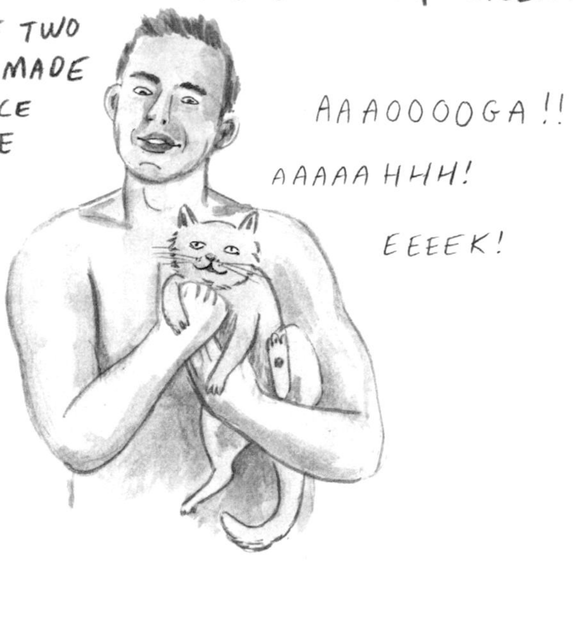
AAAOOOOGA!!
AAAAAHHH!
EEEEK!

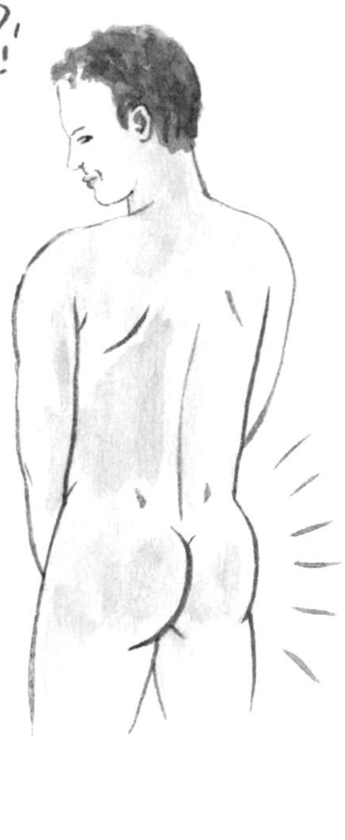

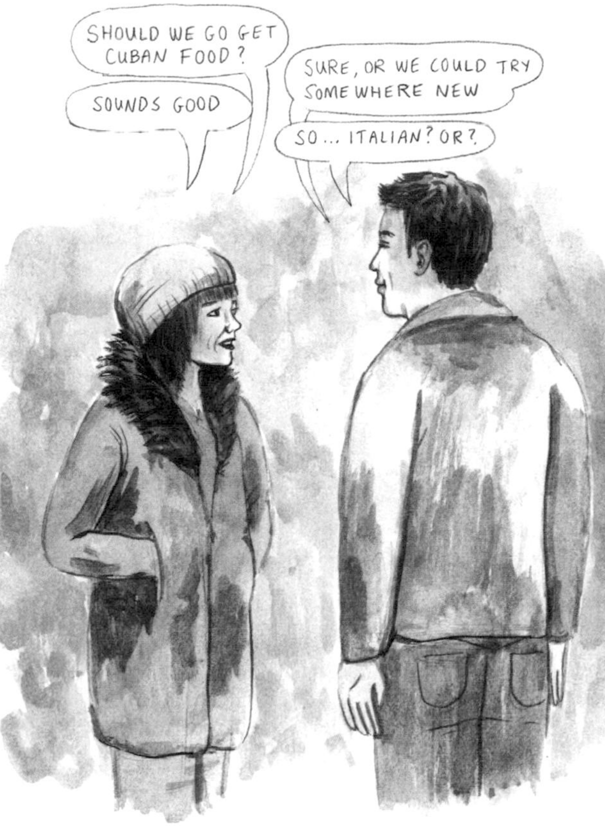
SHOULD WE GO GET CUBAN FOOD?
SURE, OR WE COULD TRY SOMEWHERE NEW
SOUNDS GOOD
SO... ITALIAN? OR?

• WHAT, THE MOVIE ENDS SO ABRUPTLY! I PAID TO SEE A SMOOCHY MOVIE! I WANT A PASSIONATE KISSING-IN-THE-RAIN SCENE, OR SHE SHOULD HAVE MADE A SCULPTURE INSPIRED BY HER FEELINGS FOR HIM! WE DON'T EVEN GET A MONTAGE - INSTEAD THEY JUST TALK ABOUT WHERE TO HAVE DINNER.

• I TOOK AN INFORMAL POLL AFTER THE CREDITS ROLLED (I.E., EAVESDROPPED) AND THE REST OF THE AUDIENCE SEEMED DISSATISFIED. ONE GIRL STARTED TO DEFEND THE ENDING, "WELL MAYBE IT WAS OPEN-ENDED AND YOU CAN MAKE OF IT WHAT YOU WANT..." BUT WAS SHOT DOWN BY HER FRIEND, "I WANT A BIG KISS."

♥ ♥ The End ♥ ♫

• I GIVE "THE VOW" TWO-OUT-OF-FIVE KISSES. ON THE WAY HOME FROM THE THEATRE I SAW A RAT WHO FOUND A CHURRO AND IT WAS MORE ROMANTIC THAN ANYTHING IN THE ENTIRE MOVIE.

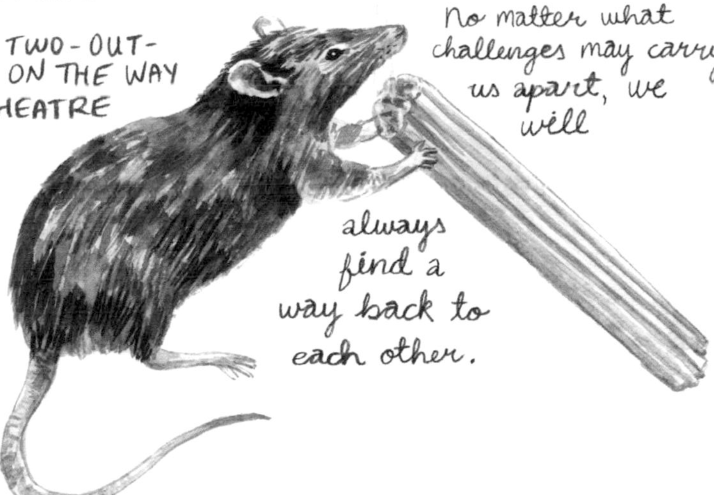

No matter what challenges may carry us apart, we will always find a way back to each other.

NO WOMEN ALLOWED ON THIS PAGE THIS IS A MAN PAGE FOR MAN THINGS

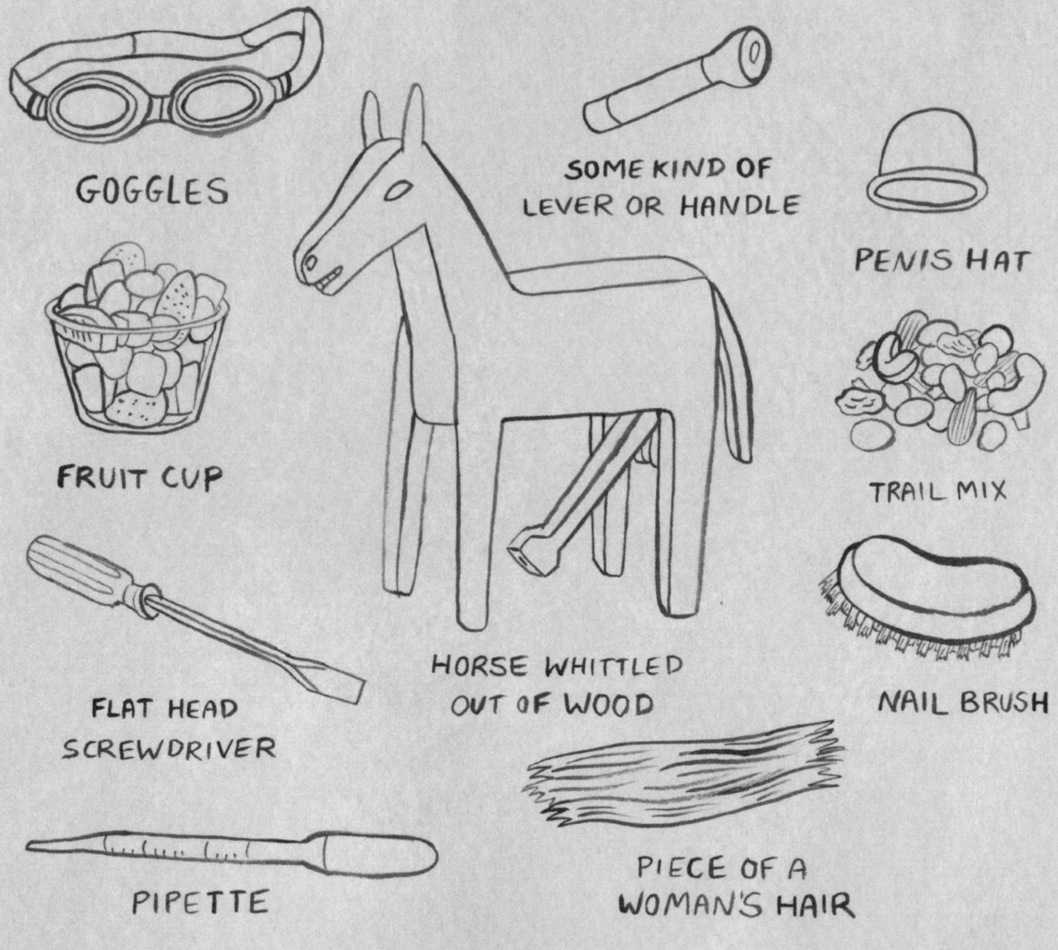

GOGGLES

SOME KIND OF
LEVER OR HANDLE

PENIS HAT

FRUIT CUP

TRAIL MIX

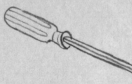

FLAT HEAD
SCREWDRIVER

HORSE WHITTLED
OUT OF WOOD

NAIL BRUSH

PIPETTE

PIECE OF A
WOMAN'S HAIR

ONLY WOMEN ARE ALLOWED TO SEE THIS PAGE
ALL MEN CLOSE YOUR EYES OR ONLY LOOK AT OTHER PAGES

HEY WOMEN: THESE ARE IMPORTANT WOMAN TOOLS

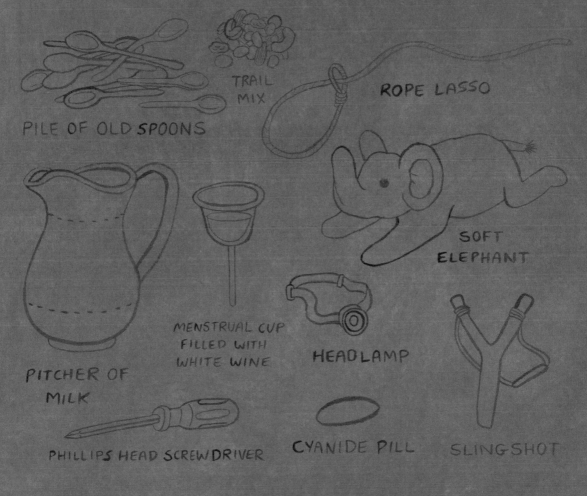

PILE OF OLD SPOONS

TRAIL MIX

ROPE LASSO

PITCHER OF MILK

MENSTRUAL CUP FILLED WITH WHITE WINE

HEADLAMP

SOFT ELEPHANT

PHILLIPS HEAD SCREWDRIVER

CYANIDE PILL

SLINGSHOT

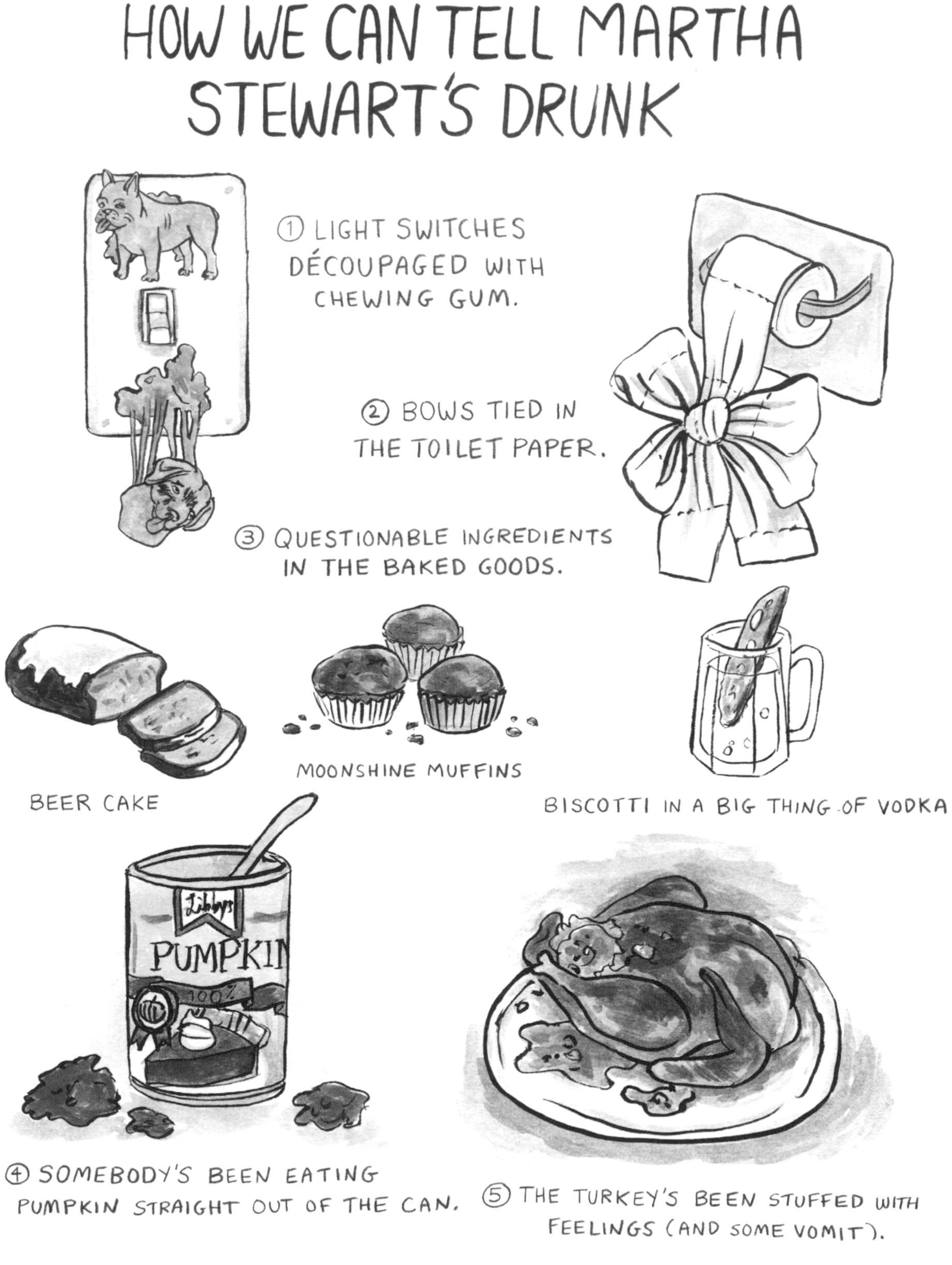
HOW WE CAN TELL MARTHA STEWART'S DRUNK
① LIGHT SWITCHES DÉCOUPAGED WITH CHEWING GUM.
② BOWS TIED IN THE TOILET PAPER.
③ QUESTIONABLE INGREDIENTS IN THE BAKED GOODS.
BEER CAKE
MOONSHINE MUFFINS
BISCOTTI IN A BIG THING OF VODKA
Libby's
PUMPKIN
100%
④ SOMEBODY'S BEEN EATING PUMPKIN STRAIGHT OUT OF THE CAN.
⑤ THE TURKEY'S BEEN STUFFED WITH FEELINGS (AND SOME VOMIT).

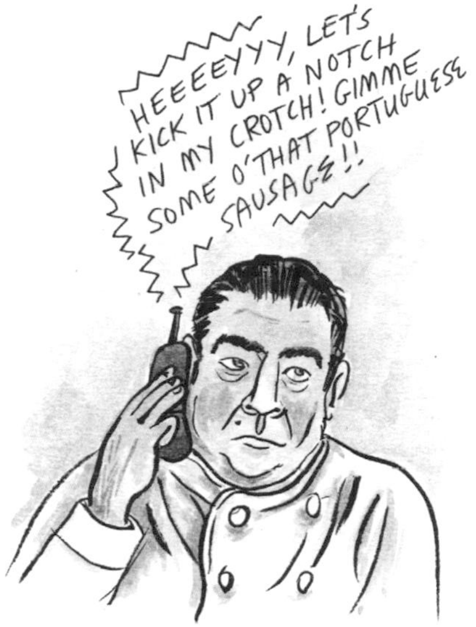
HEEEEYYY, LET'S KICK IT UP A NOTCH IN MY CROTCH! GIMME SOME O'THAT PORTUGUESE SAUSAGE!!

⑥ SHE KEEPS BOOTY CALLING EMERIL.

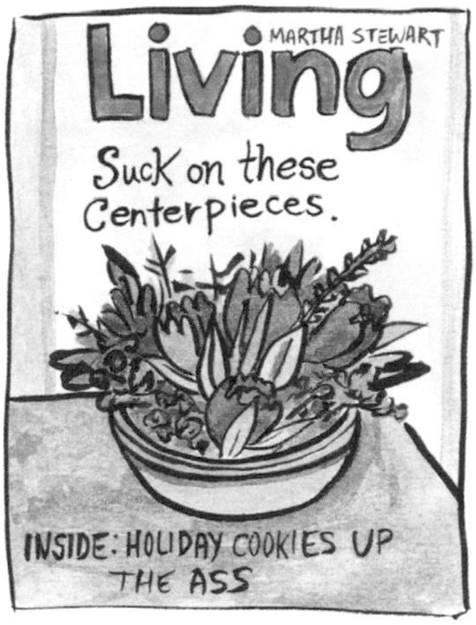
MARTHA STEWART
Living
Suck on these Centerpieces.
INSIDE: HOLIDAY COOKIES UP THE ASS

⑦ THAT LAST ISSUE OF MARTHA STEWART LIVING WAS CRAZY.

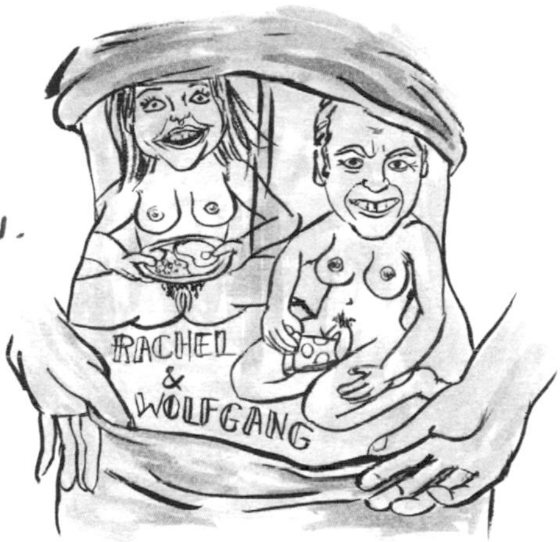
RACHEL & WOLFGANG

⑧ SHE KEEPS SHOWING OFF THE TATTOO SHE GOT IN PRISON.

⑨ DILDOS HOT-GLUED TO THE OVEN KNOBS.

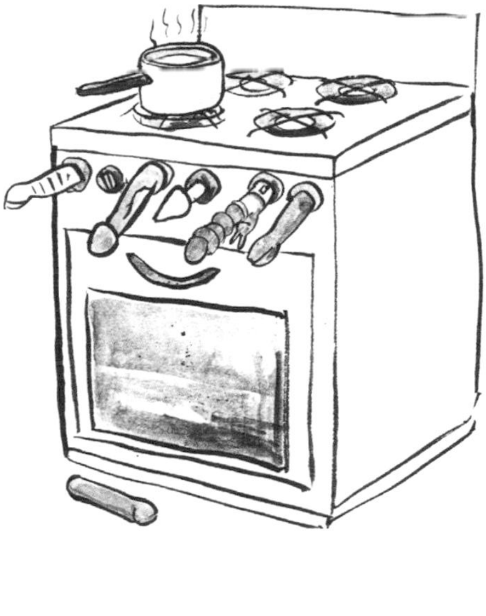

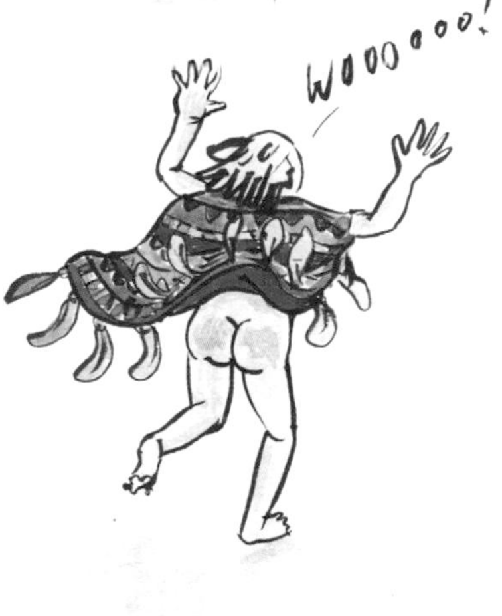
WOOOOOOO!

THE SECRET LIVES OF CHEFS

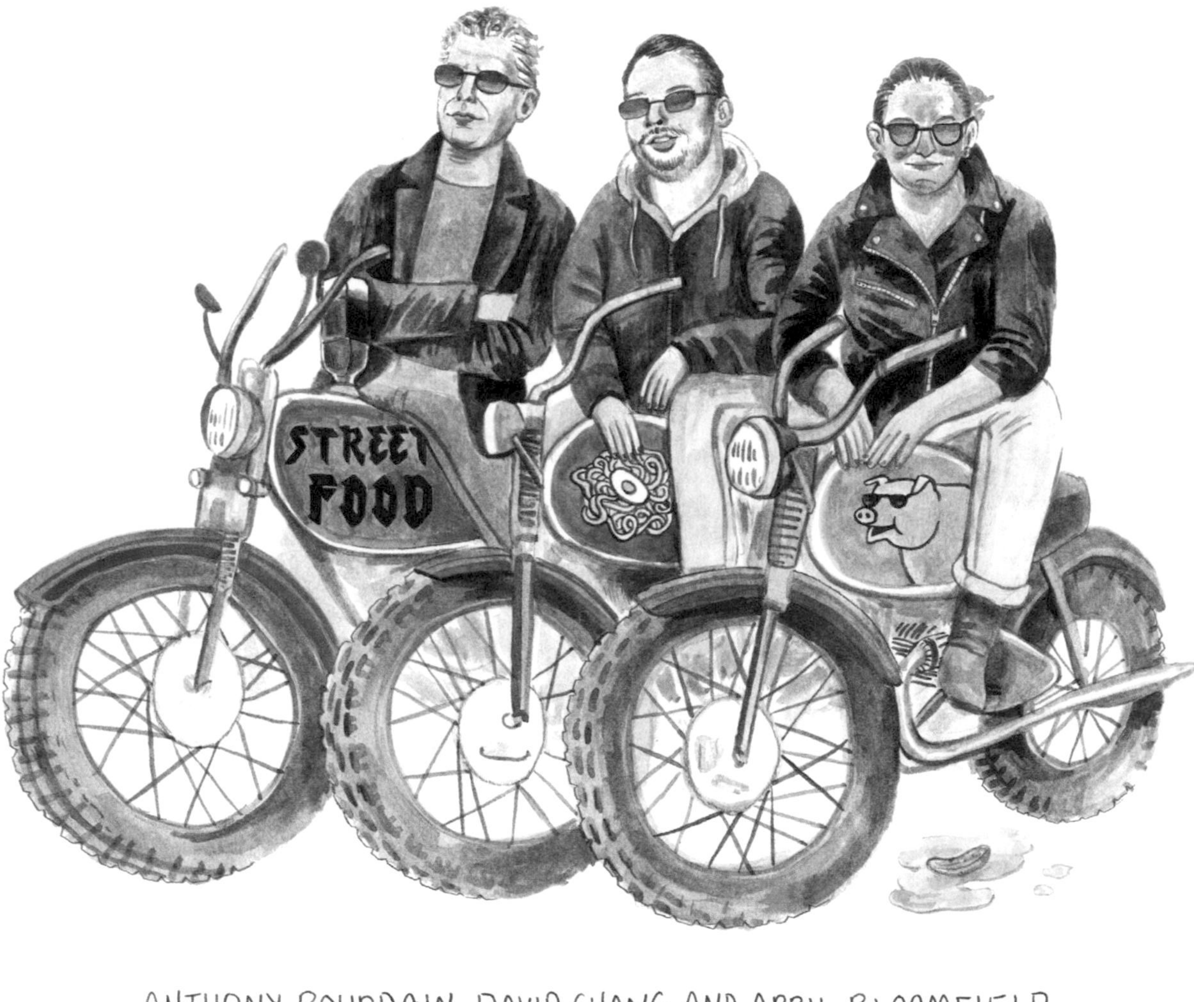
STREET FOOD

ANTHONY BOURDAIN, DAVID CHANG, AND APRIL BLOOMFIELD ARE IN A BIKER GANG AND THEIR MOTORCYCLES RUN ON PICKLE JUICE, PORK BROTH, AND WHISKEY.

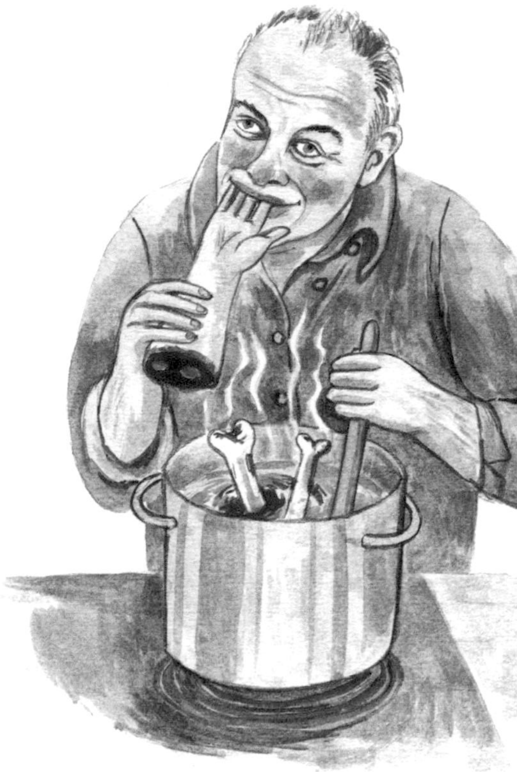

MARK BITTMAN IS A VEGAN
BEFORE 6PM AND A
CANNIBAL AFTER 11 PM.

MARIO BATALI CARRIES A
BRIEFCASE FULL OF PIZZA
FIXINGS EVERYWHERE HE GOES.

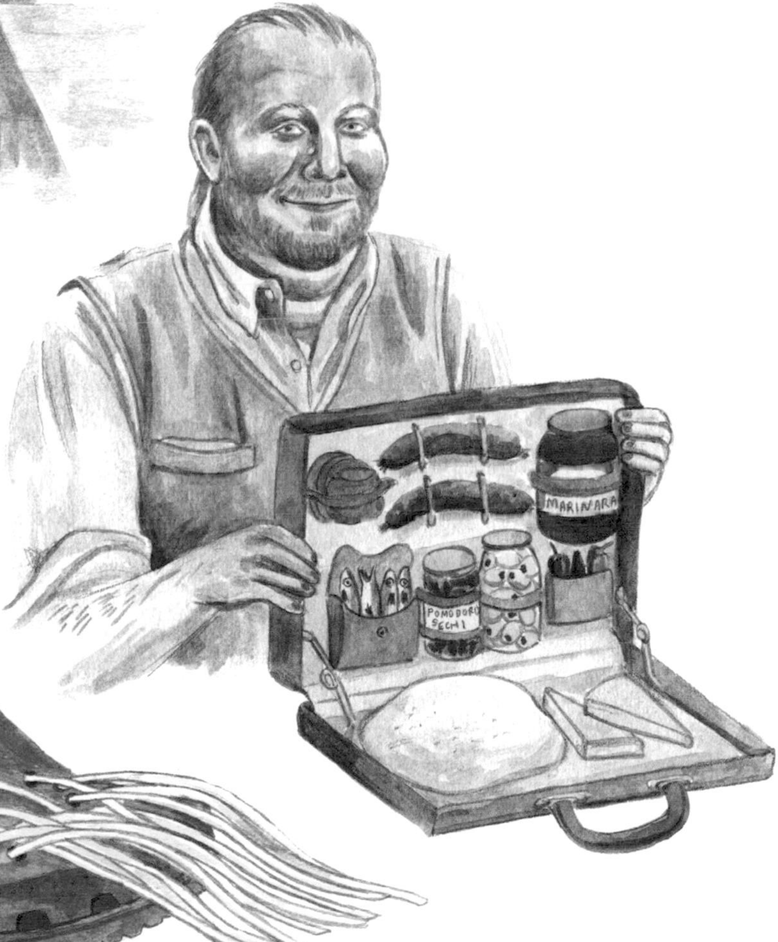
MARINARA
POMODORO SECHI

ALSO, BATALI'S
CROCS™ DOUBLE
AS PASTA MAKERS.

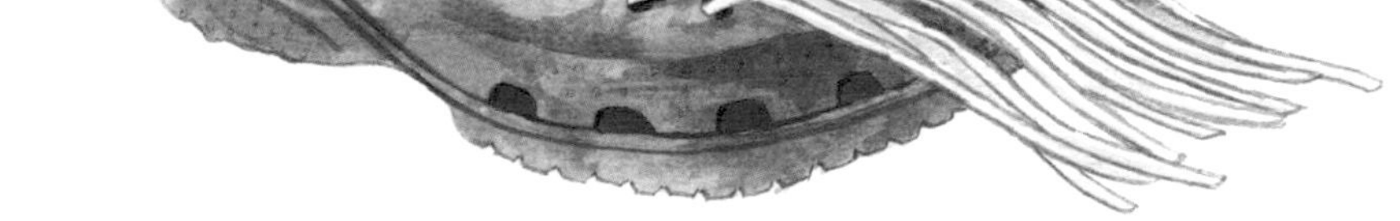

DAN BARBER AND THOMAS KELLER ARE PUT OUT TO PASTURE FOR A FEW WEEKS EVERY SPRING.

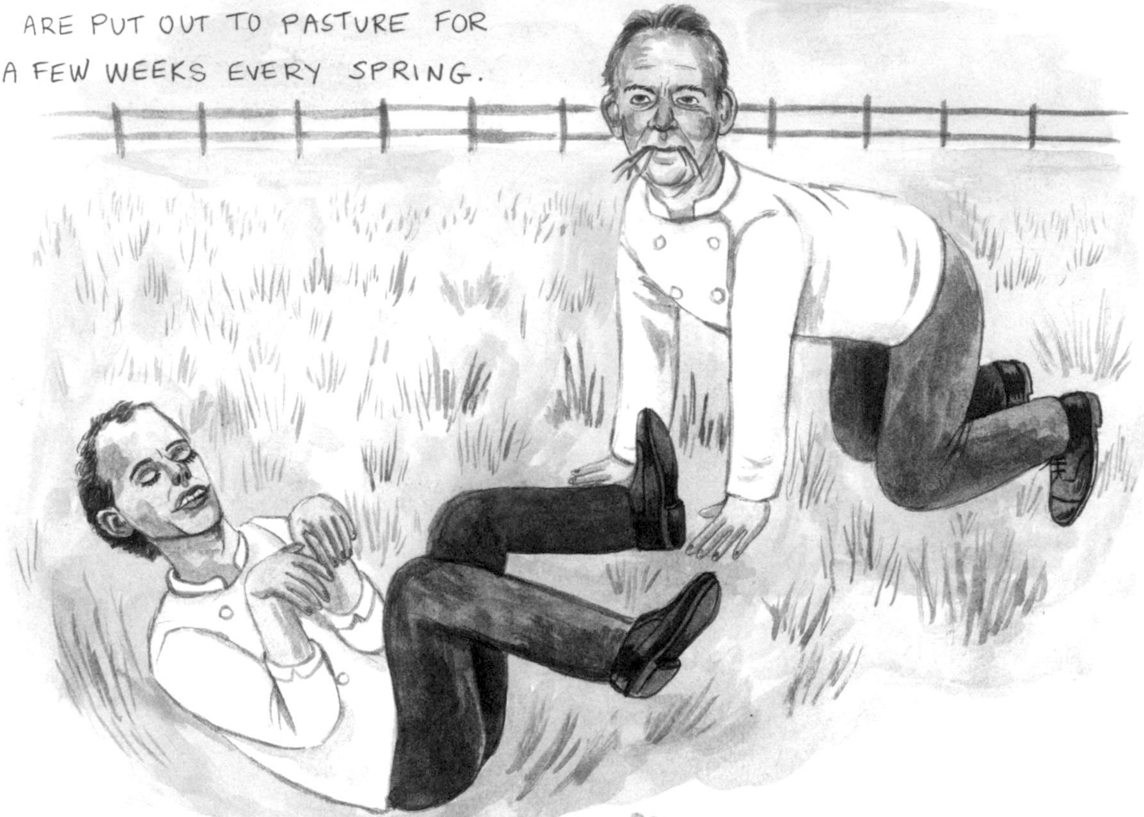

JULIA CHILD USED BÉCHAMEL SAUCE AS A MOISTURIZER AND WROTE HER CORRESPONDENCE WITH BROWN ROUX.

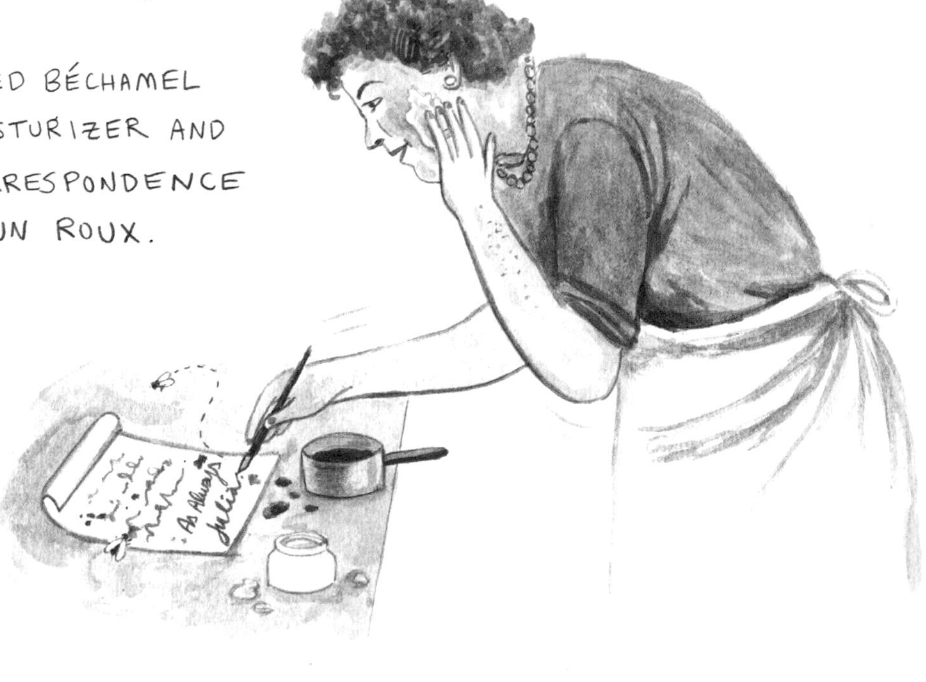
As Always,
Julia

WYLIE DUFRESNE AND GRANT ACHATZ ENJOY LIQUID NITROGEN FOOD FIGHTS.

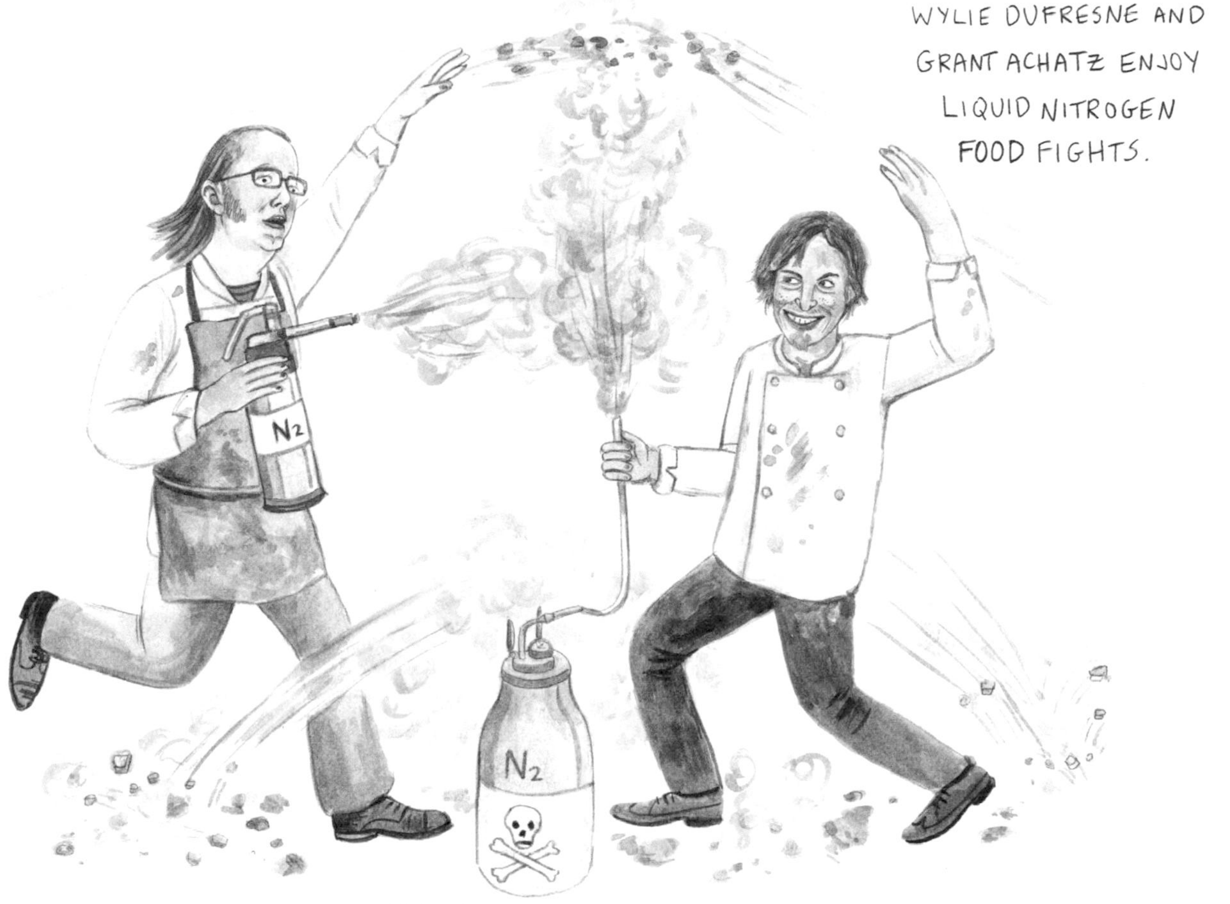
N_2
N_2

CHRISTINA TOSI EMPLOYS A CHILD THINK TANK TO COME UP WITH RECIPES FOR MILK BAR.

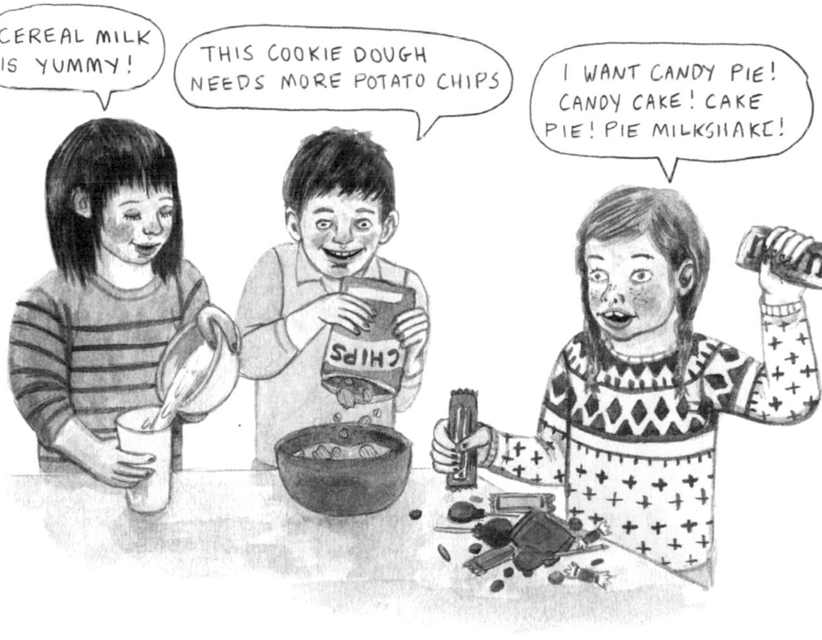
CEREAL MILK IS YUMMY!
THIS COOKIE DOUGH NEEDS MORE POTATO CHIPS
I WANT CANDY PIE! CANDY CAKE! CAKE PIE! PIE MILKSHAKE!
CHIPS

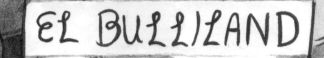

FERRAN ADRIÀ'S DREAM IS TO OPEN
A FOAM THEME PARK.

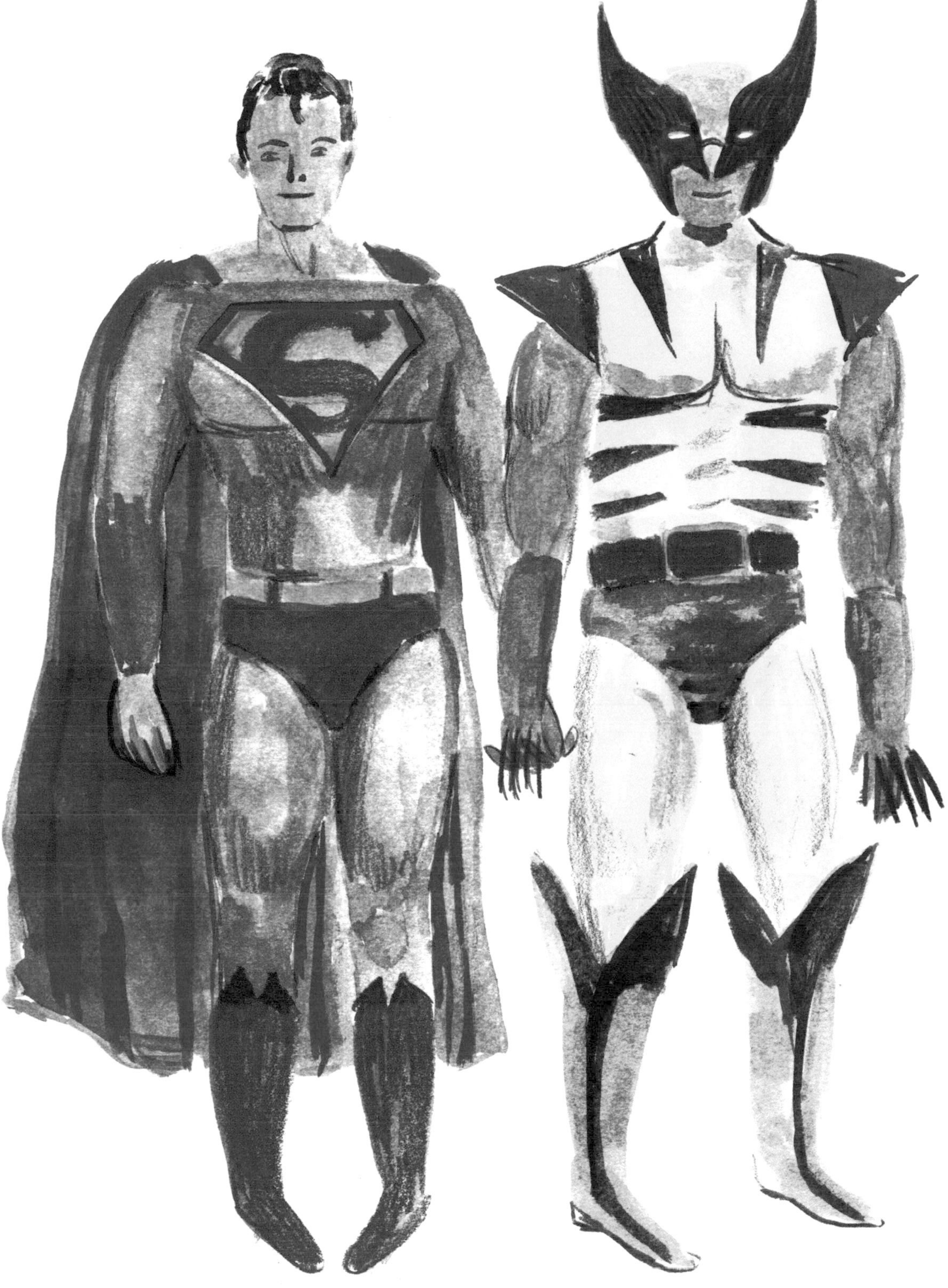

VISIONS OF

CORNUCOPIA
(HORN OF PLENTY)

HAND TURKEY

CORNUCATTA
(HORN OF CATS)

FOOT TURKEY

CORNUCORNUA
(HORN OF HORNS)

BOTTOM TURKEY

THANKSGIVING

CREAMY POTATOES
W/ BUTTER

BREAD CRUMBS

HILLY POTATOES
W/ BROCCOLI TREES

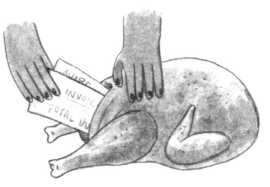

UNPAID BILLS

TURBULENT POTATOES
W/ SKINS

EXPIRED MEDICATION

NORTH AMERICAN WILDLIFE AND HATS

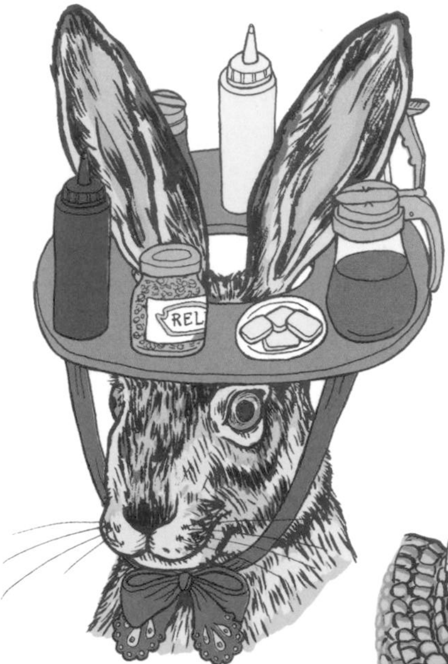
REL

Desert Hare

LAZY SUSAN HAT WITH HOT DOG AND PANCAKE CONDIMENTS

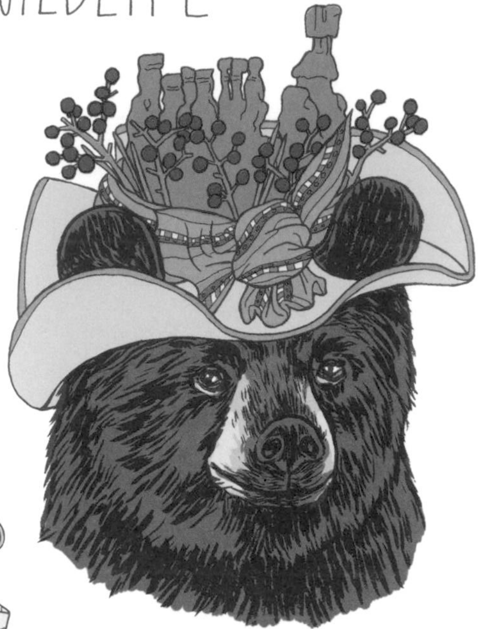

Black Bear

BRYCE CANYON BERRY HAT

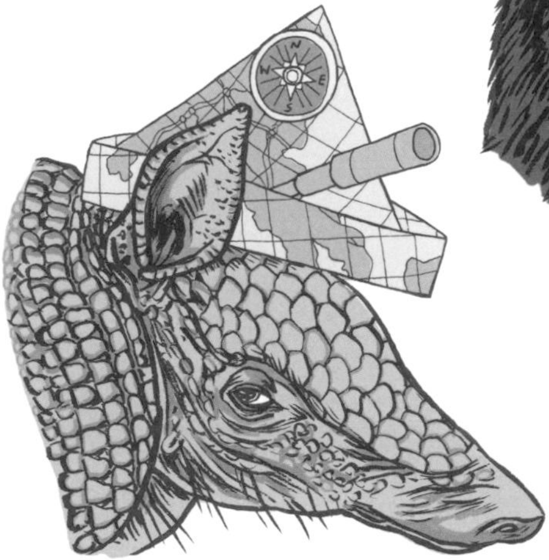
N
E
S

Armadillo

NAVIGATION HAT

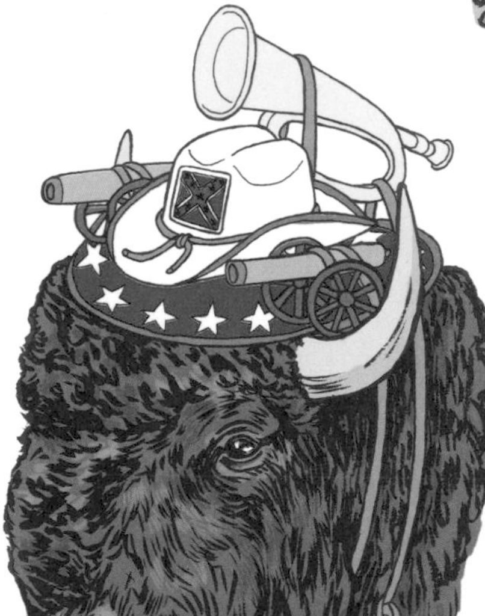

Bison

CIVIL WAR BUGLE HAT (PLAYS "REVEILLE," "TAPS," AND "SLEDGEHAMMER")

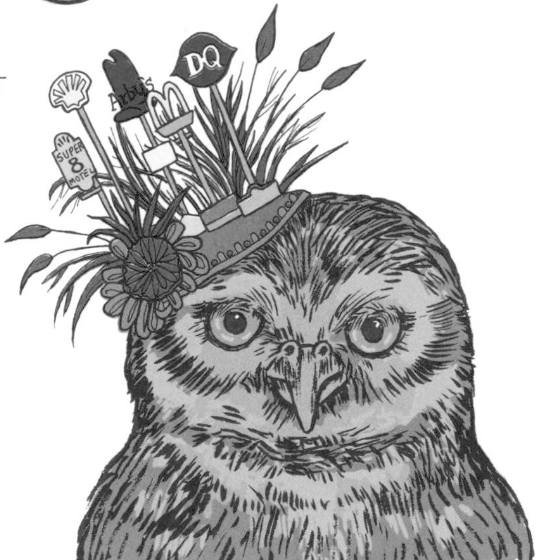
DQ
SUPER 8 MOTEL

Spotted Owl

REST STOP FASCINATOR

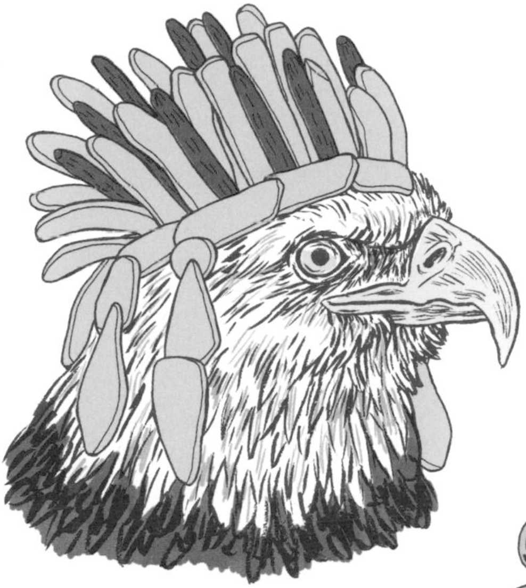

Bald Eagle

NATIVE AMERICAN HEADDRESS (MADE OUT OF AMERICAN CHEESE + SLIM JIMS®)

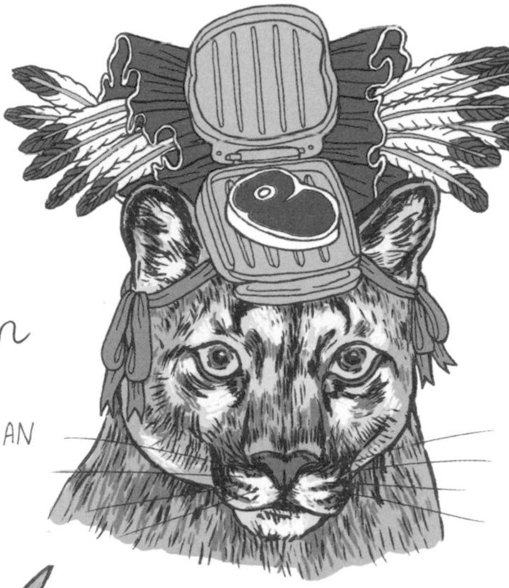

Mountain Lion

GEORGE FOREMAN GRILL® HAT

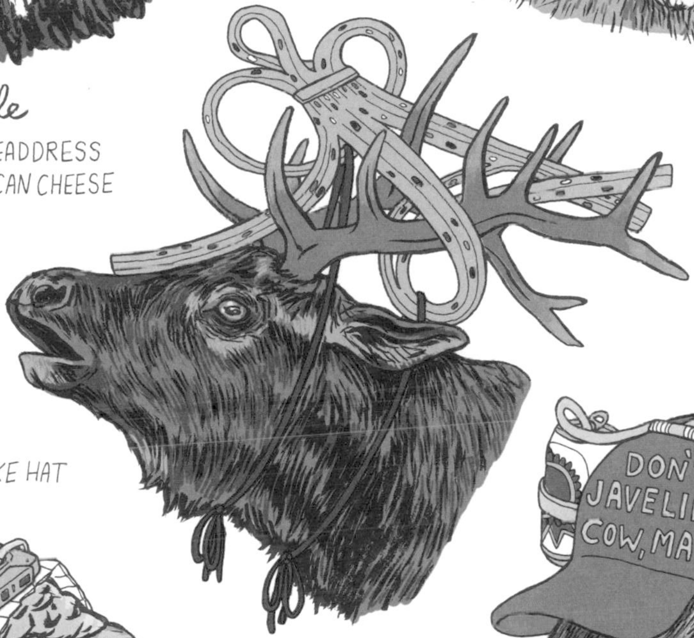

Elk

NEW JERSEY TURNPIKE HAT

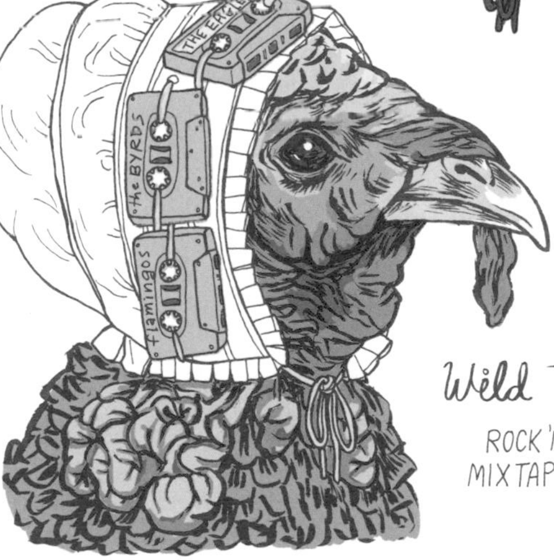
THE EAGLES
the BYRDS
flamingos

Wild Turkey

ROCK 'N' ROLL MIXTAPE BONNET

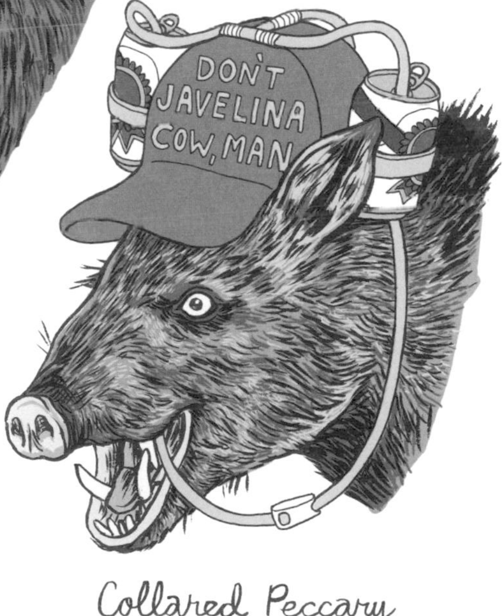
DON'T JAVELINA COW, MAN

Collared Peccary

TRUCKER DRINKING HAT

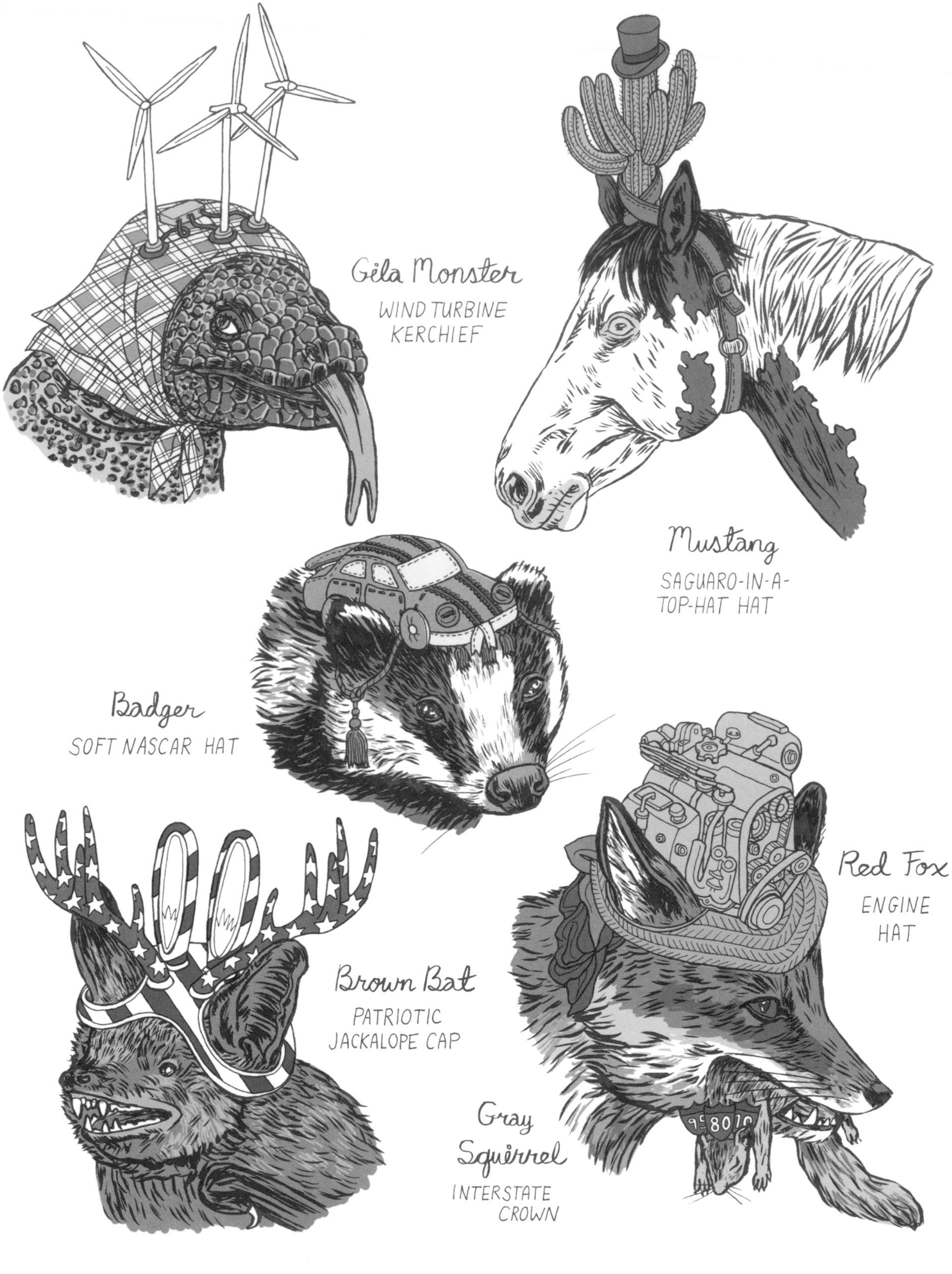
Gila Monster
WIND TURBINE KERCHIEF
Mustang
SAGUARO-IN-A-TOP-HAT HAT
Badger
SOFT NASCAR HAT
Red Fox
ENGINE HAT
Brown Bat
PATRIOTIC JACKALOPE CAP
Gray Squirrel
INTERSTATE CROWN

THE TOY FAIR

• THE TOY FAIR ISN'T FOR KIDS. THE SHOW'S HELD YEARLY AT THE JAVITS CENTER, MANHATTAN'S MAIN CONVENTION FACILITY (AKA MASSIVE GRAY BOX), AND IT'S FULL OF SERIOUS ADULTS IN BUSINESS SUITS WITH CORPORATE ACCOUNTS. IT'S NOT SUPPOSED TO BE FUN. WE'LL SEE ABOUT THAT!

• TOY FAIR BADGES ARE ONLY AVAILABLE FOR PROS, SO A RELATIVE GENEROUSLY REGISTERED ME AND MY FRIEND TIM AS EMPLOYEES OF HER CHIA SEED COMPANY. MY BADGE SAYS "CHIA POWER / ASSISTANT BUYER." WE'LL AVOID WALKING BY CHIA PRODUCTS FOR FEAR OF HAVING TO HOLD OUR OWN IN A CHIA CONVERSATION.

• I WANT TO PRETEND WE'RE HERE FOR LEGITIMATE REASONS, SO TIM AND I WORK OUT A COVER STORY: "WE DISTRIBUTE CHIA PRODUCTS BUT WE'RE LOOKING TO BRANCH OUT INTO TOYS AND ATHLETICS."

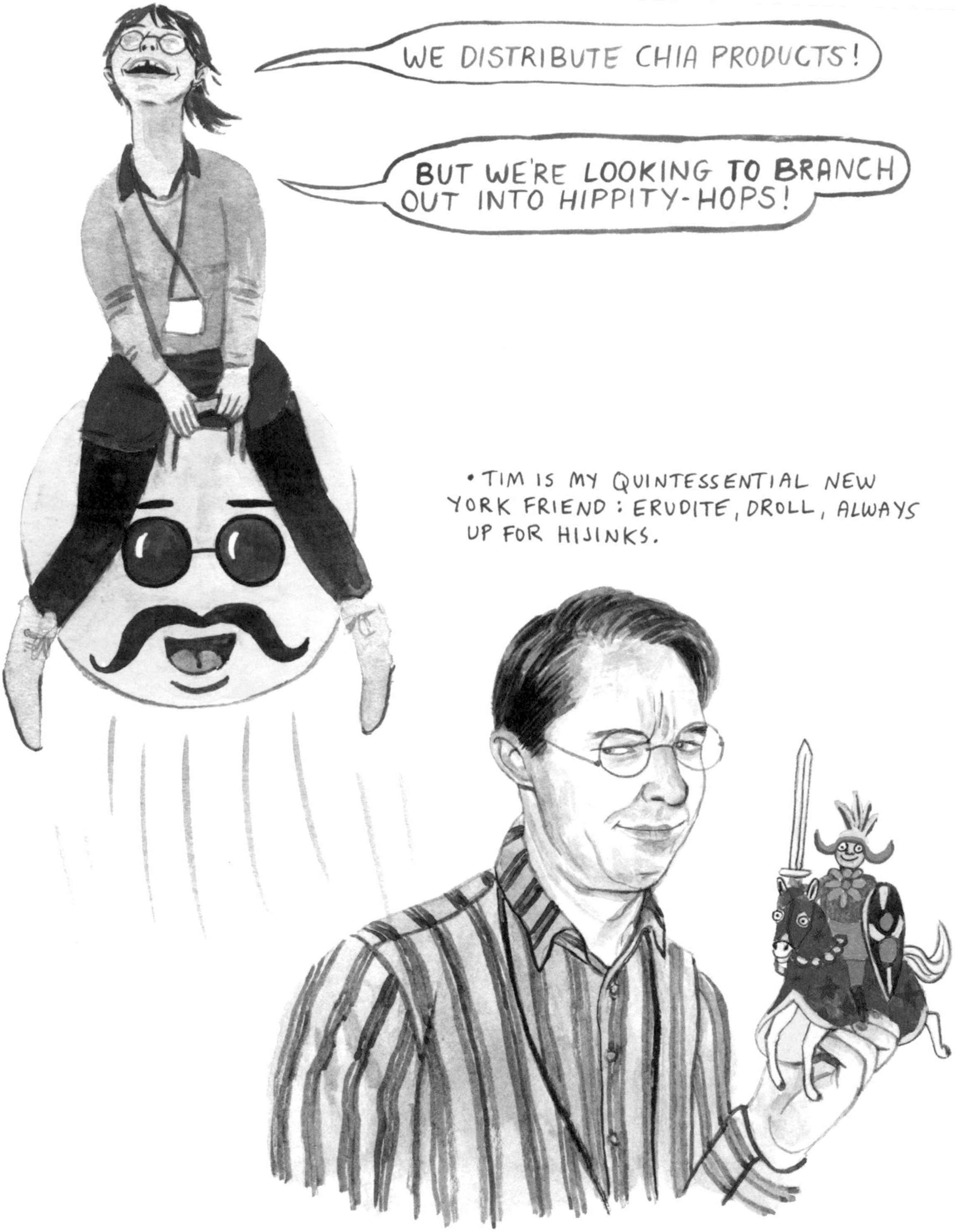
WE DISTRIBUTE CHIA PRODUCTS!
BUT WE'RE LOOKING TO BRANCH OUT INTO HIPPITY-HOPS!
• TIM IS MY QUINTESSENTIAL NEW YORK FRIEND: ERUDITE, DROLL, ALWAYS UP FOR HIJINKS.

TIM THOUGHT THIS TOY LOOKED STUPID

• AS SOON AS WE GET PAST SECURITY, TIM POINTS TO THE BEDAZZLING STATION AND SAYS, "I'M GOING TO LET ONE OF THOSE PRETTY GIRLS GIVE ME A GLITTER TATTOO." SURE, NO HARM IN MARKING OURSELVES AS EAGER TOY FAIR PARTICIPANTS.

TIM GETTING A GLITTER TATTOO

TIM'S DRAGONFLY

MY "HEART PAW"

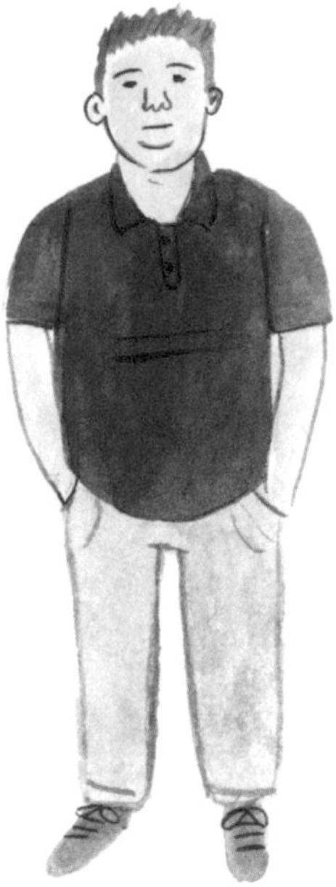

POLO SHIRT + KHAKIS

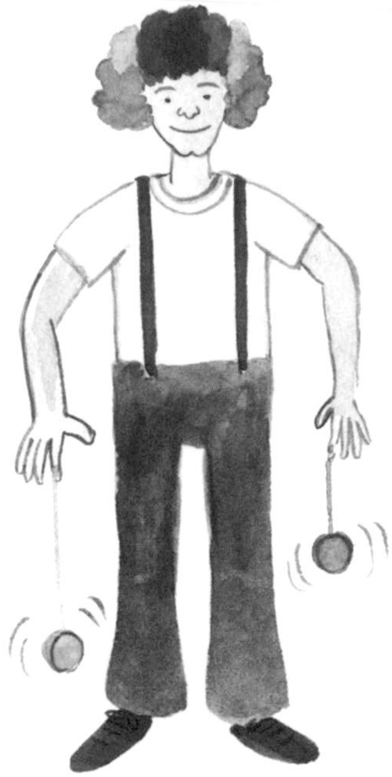

DESPERATION CASUAL

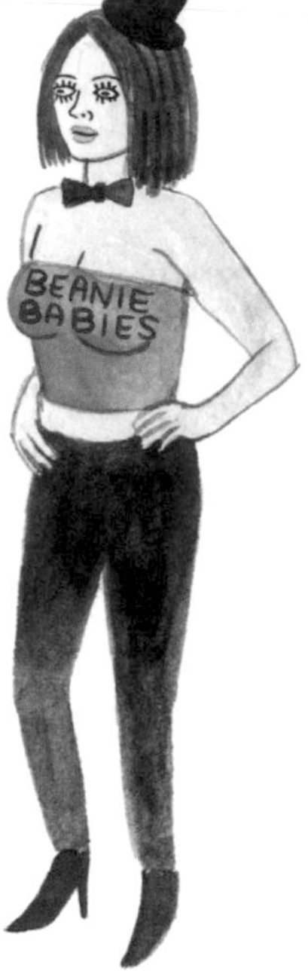
BEANIE BABIES

BOOTH BABE FORMAL

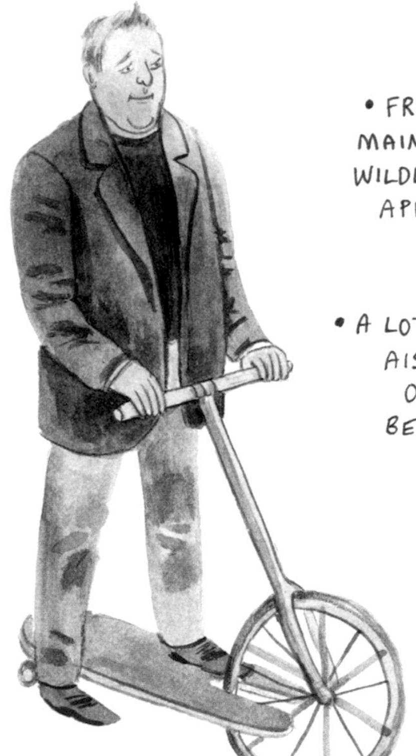

- FRESHLY GLITTERED, WE TAKE A LOOK AROUND THE MAIN EXHIBITION HALL. "THESE VENDORS HAVE WILDLY DIFFERING IDEAS ON WHAT MAKES FOR APPROPRIATE CONVENTION WEAR," TIM SAYS.

- A LOT OF BUSINESSMEN ARE WHIZZING AROUND THE AISLES ON LITTLE SCOOTERS AND THINGS. THE ONES SELLING MINIATURE VEHICLES SEEM TO BE HAVING MORE FUN THAN EVERYONE ELSE.

THIS GUY THOUGHT HE WAS THE COOLEST DUDE ON THE PLANET.

• THE MOST UPTIGHT VENDORS ARE THE GERMAN ARTISANAL STUFFED ANIMAL SALESMEN.

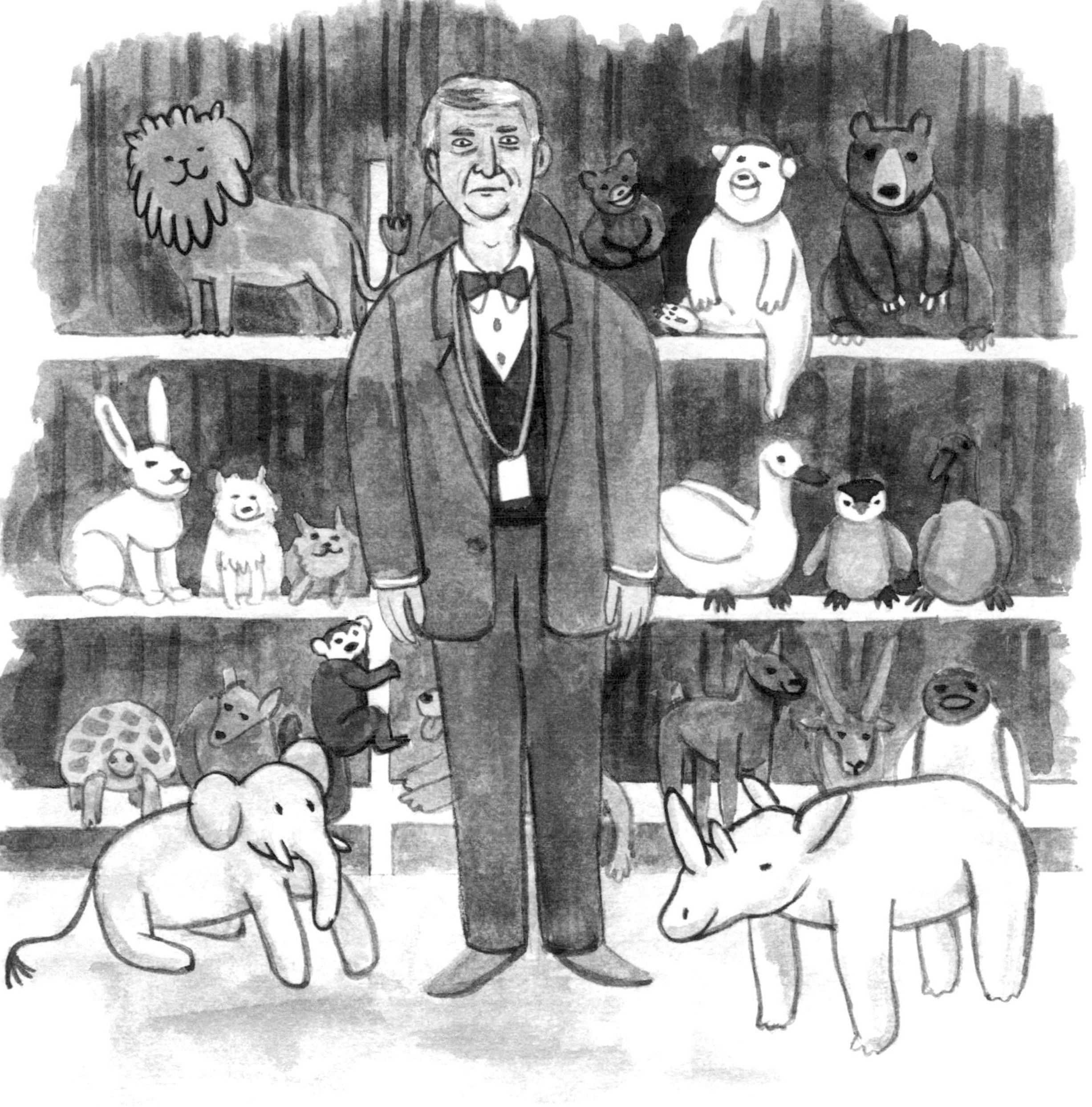

- I DO A DOUBLE-TAKE AT THE TEDDY TANKS BOOTH, WHERE LIVE FISH ARE SWIMMING INSIDE OF TEDDY BEARS. A BORED GUY GIVES US A SPIEL, "WE PUT THE ANIMATE IN THE INANIMATE. THAT'S OUR CONCEPT. WE BRING IT TO LIFE."

HE DEMONSTRATES HOW TO POUR FISH FOOD INTO THE STUFFED BEAR'S MOUTH, THEN REPEATS, "WE PUT THE ANIMATE IN THE INANIMATE." WHAT. NEVER MIND THAT IT'S A TERRIBLE SLOGAN, DOESN'T ANYONE REALIZE THAT TO A CHILD, A TEDDY BEAR IS ANIMATE? AND WON'T IT BE HORRIFYING WHEN ENCASING A LIVE FISH TANK IN TEDDY'S PLUSH FLESH CAUSES HIM TO ROT FROM THE INSIDE?

WEEK 1

WEEK 8

WEEK 14

- A LOT OF THESE TOYS COULD BENEFIT FROM BEING WORKSHOPPED WITH ACTUAL CHILDREN.

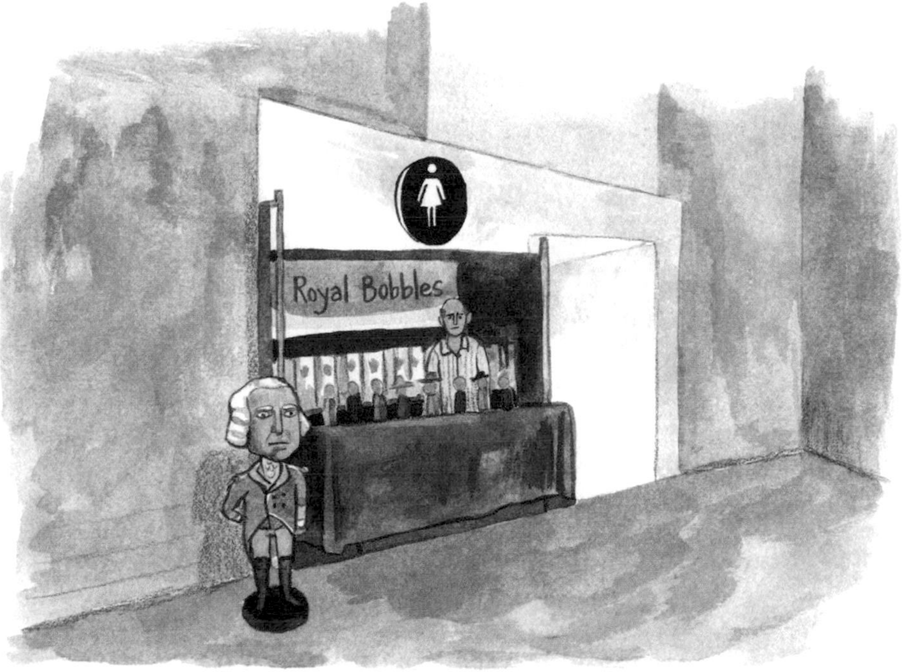
Royal Bobbles

HISTORICAL BOBBLEHEAD BOOTH BY THE WOMEN'S RESTROOM

• I HOPE THE OWNER OF ROYAL BOBBLES GOT HIS BOOTH AT A DISCOUNTED RATE.

• WE CIRCUMVENT EDUCATIONAL TOYS UNTIL I SPOT A FAUX ARCHAEOLOGICAL DIGASAURS SANDBOX WITH FAKE DINO BONES AND BRUSHES. HOW COOL! BONE BRUSHING HAS TO BE THE BEST PART OF BEING A PALEONTOLOGIST. I BET PALEONTOLOGISTS ARE CONSTANTLY FIGHTING OVER WHO GETS TO BRUSH BONES.

• OOH LOOK, IT'S AN INFLATABLE SHARK! TIM AND I BOTH COVET SHARKY, BUT WHO COULD FIT HIM IN THEIR APARTMENT AND AFFORD HIS DIET OF CONSTANT FRESH HELIUM?

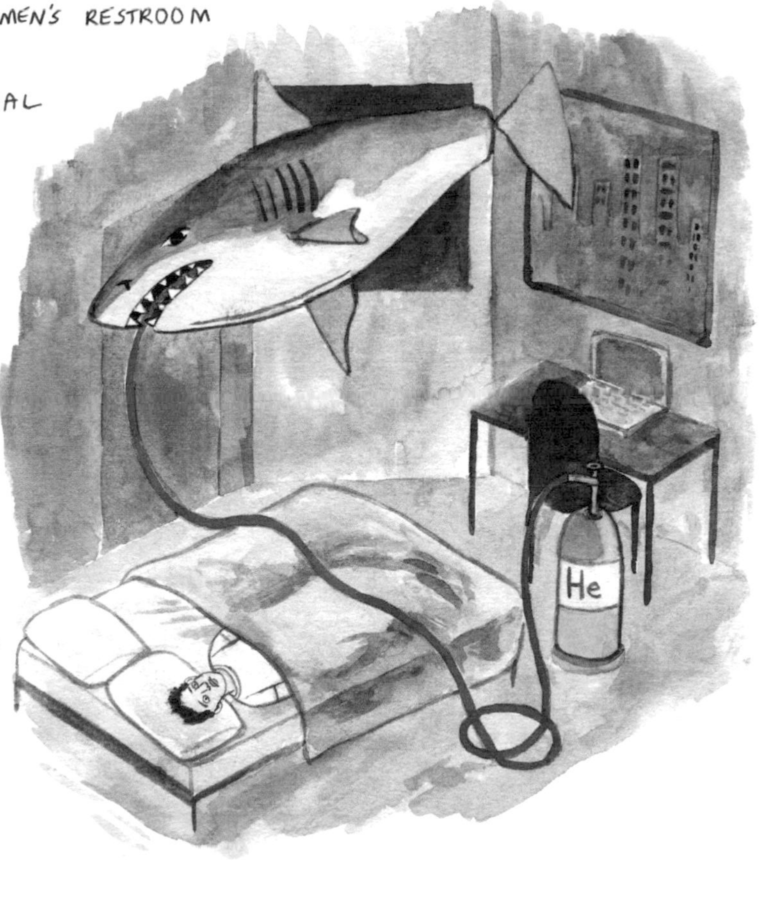
He

• HERE'S AN UNCOMFORTABLE OBSERVATION: I NOTICE MY ATTRACTION TO CERTAIN TOYS FEELS KIND OF... SEXUAL? A LOT OF THEM HAVE FLIRTATIOUS DESIGNS; FOR EXAMPLE, THE MY LITTLE PONIES HAVE VOLUPTUOUS RUMPS AND PERFUMED HAIR. IT MAKES ME UNEASY.

• I'M WANDERING AROUND THE COLLECTIBLE FIGURINES SECTION WHEN I SEE A "LIMITED EDITION RED STAY PUFT" AND FEEL THUNDERSTRUCK. HE LOOKS ANGRY, YET SUPPLE AND INVITING. HE LOOKS A BIT LIKE A DILDO.

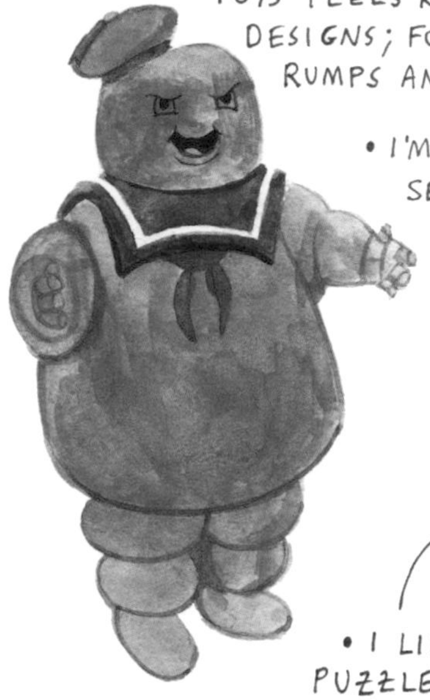

LIMITED EDITION RED STAY PUFT

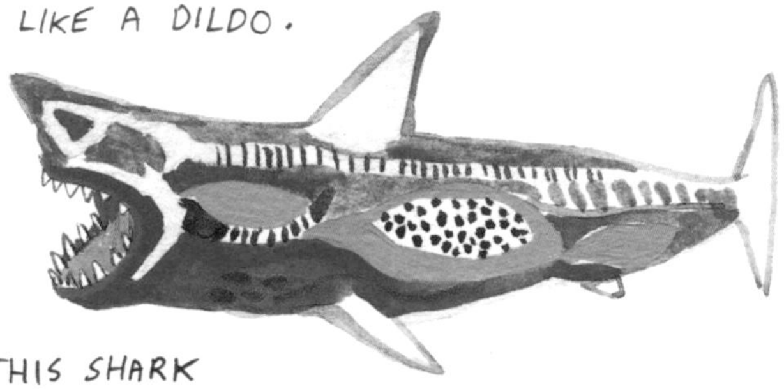

4D SHARK ANATOMY PUZZLE

• I LIKE THIS SHARK PUZZLE TOO; HE'D MAKE A FINE FRIEND FOR RED STAY PUFT.

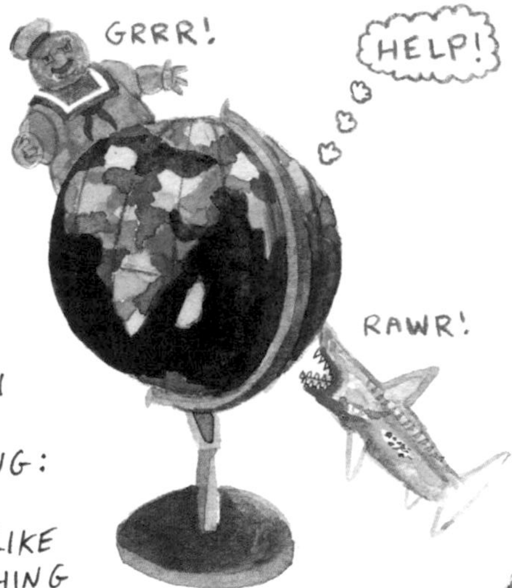
GRRR!
HELP!
RAWR!

• I WANT THIS STYLISH BLACK & NEON GLOBE TOO.

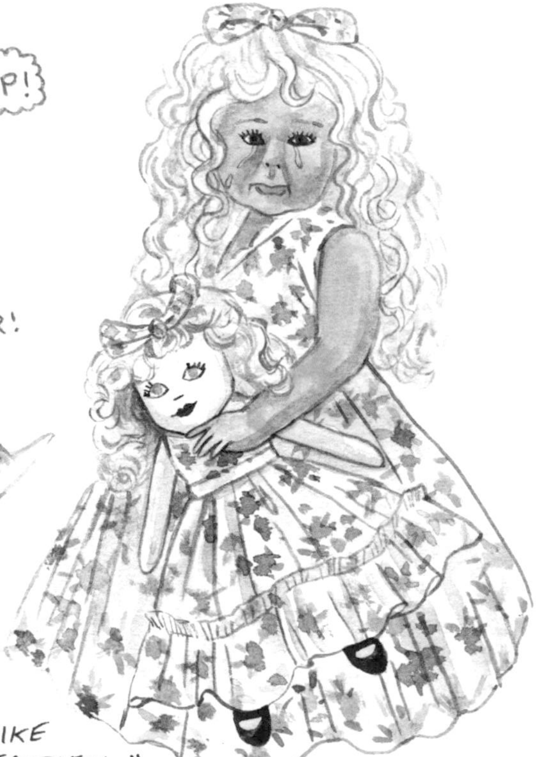

• HERE'S A TOY I CAN'T IMAGINE ANYONE WANTING: A BLONDE DOLL CRYING SEMEN-LIKE TEARS AND CLUTCHING A SMALLER DOLL OF HER OWN.

I APPROACH DOLLY FOR A CLOSER LOOK AND NOD AT THE OWNER, A SWEET, MIDWESTERN GRANDMOTHER TYPE. "SHE'S LOVELY," I SAY. THOSE TEARS REALLY LOOK LIKE JIZZ. "ISN'T SHE STUNNING?" "JUST BEAUTIFUL."

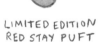

- IT'S IMPORTANT TO REMEMBER WE CAN MAKE A SWIFT EXIT IF THINGS GET AWKWARD. THE VENDORS ARE SOMEWHAT GLUED TO THEIR BOOTHS AND WON'T PURSUE US VERY FAR INTO THE AISLE.

- I LEAVE TIM'S SIDE TO GO INVESTIGATE A SALESMAN WEARING LITTLE RED SHORTS AND PLAYING HACKY SACK WITH A BADMINTON BIRDIE. DURING HIS DEMO HE LEANS IN TO CONFIDE, "I'M REALLY HUNGRY." I OFFER HIM A BANANA, HE SAYS HE'S NOT ALLOWED TO EAT IT, AND IT'S A MILLION TIMES MORE AWKWARD THAN IT NEEDS TO BE.

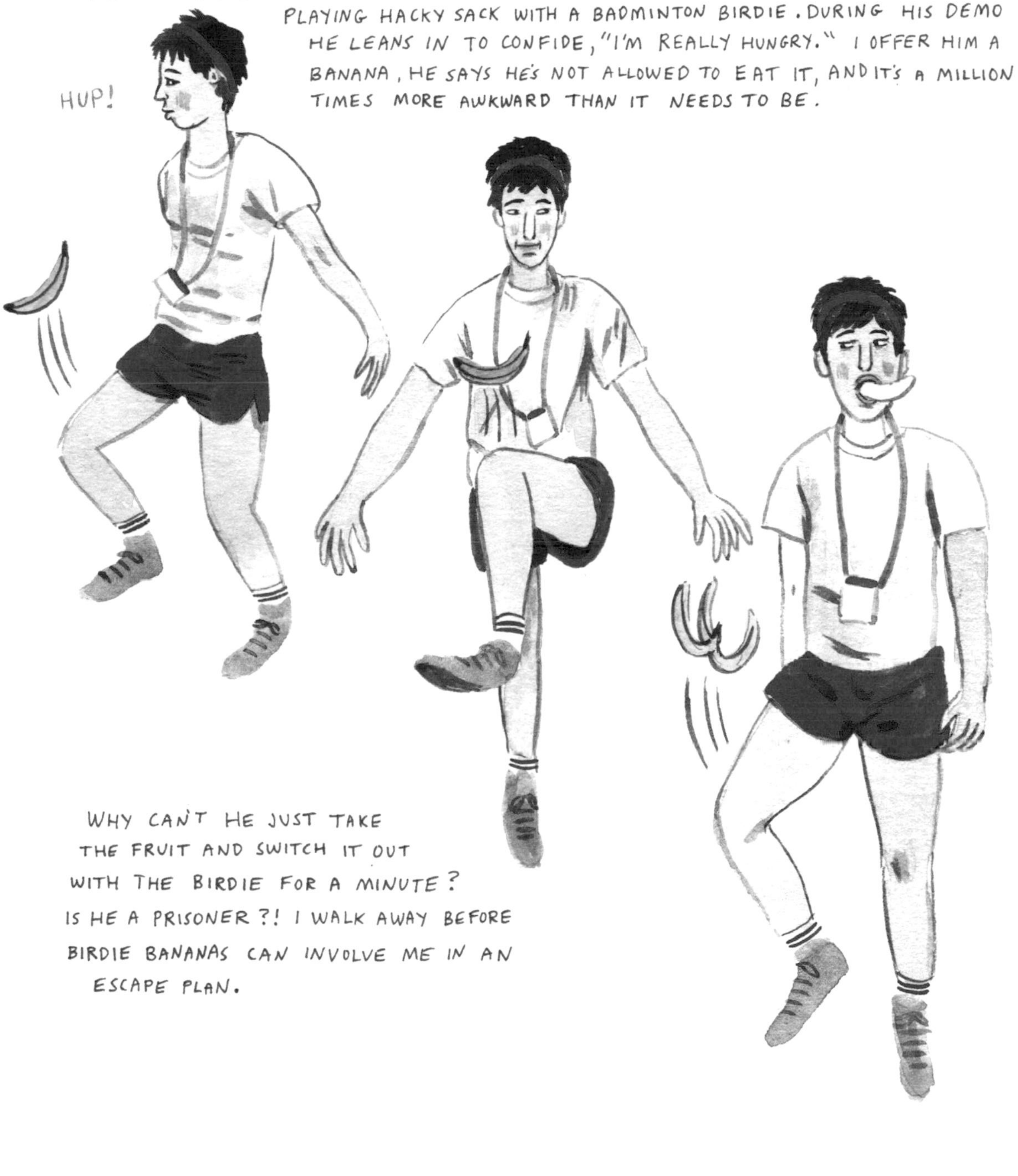
HUP!

WHY CAN'T HE JUST TAKE THE FRUIT AND SWITCH IT OUT WITH THE BIRDIE FOR A MINUTE? IS HE A PRISONER?! I WALK AWAY BEFORE BIRDIE BANANAS CAN INVOLVE ME IN AN ESCAPE PLAN.

• I FIND TIM IN THE STAR TREK COLOGNE BOOTH AND BLECCHH IT SMELLS CHEAP AND REPUGNANT. "SHIRTLESS KIRK" IS ESPECIALLY DISAPPOINTING, NOT EVEN WORTH IT AS A GAG GIFT.

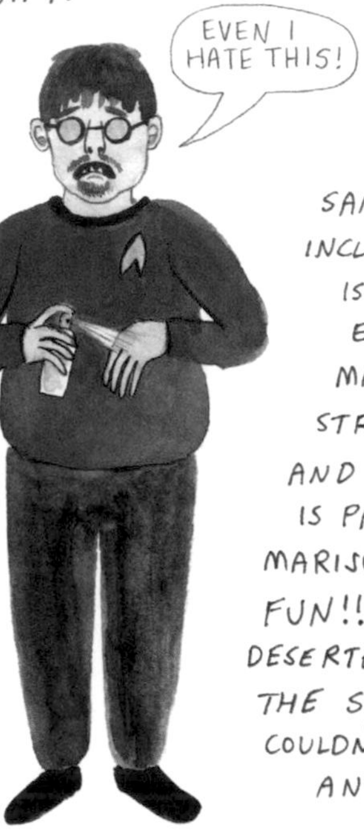
EVEN I HATE THIS!

• BUT HERE'S SOMETHING EVEN LESS DESIRABLE: "ABUNDANT HARVEST," A GAME FOR TEACHING CHILDREN AND ADULTS HOW TO MAKE WISE LIFE DECISIONS.

SAMPLE SCENARIOS INCLUDE "YOUR SPOUSE IS NOT PUTTING EFFORT INTO MAINTAINING A STRONG MARRIAGE" AND "YOUR FRIEND IS PASSING AROUND A MARIJUANA CIGARETTE." FUN!! THE BOOTH IS DESERTED, LIKE EVEN THE SALESPEOPLE COULDN'T TAKE IT ANYMORE.

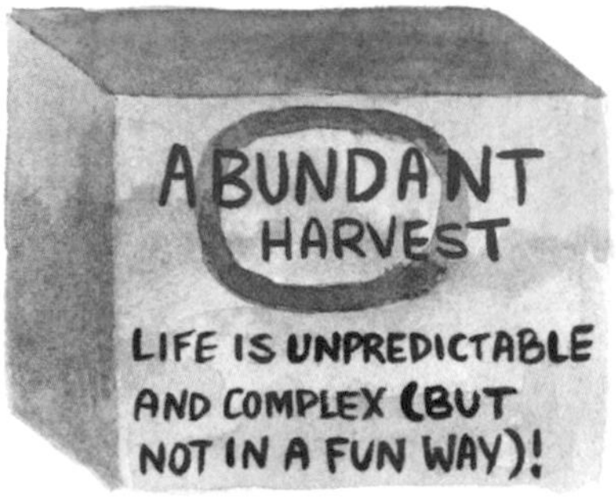
ABUNDANT HARVEST
LIFE IS UNPREDICTABLE AND COMPLEX (BUT NOT IN A FUN WAY)!

ORIGINAL BOARD GAME

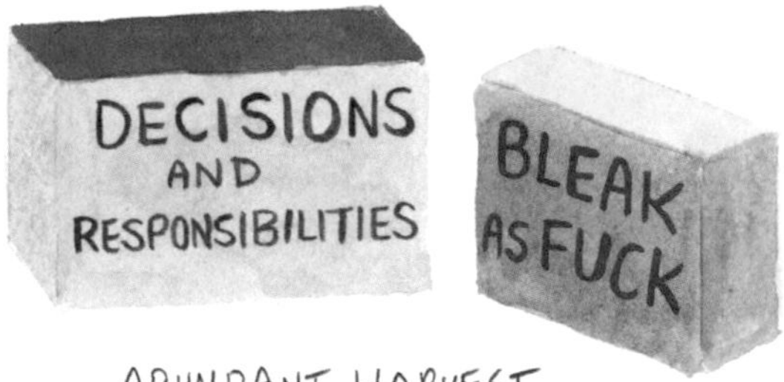
DECISIONS AND RESPONSIBILITIES
BLEAK AS FUCK

ABUNDANT HARVEST EXPANSION PACKS

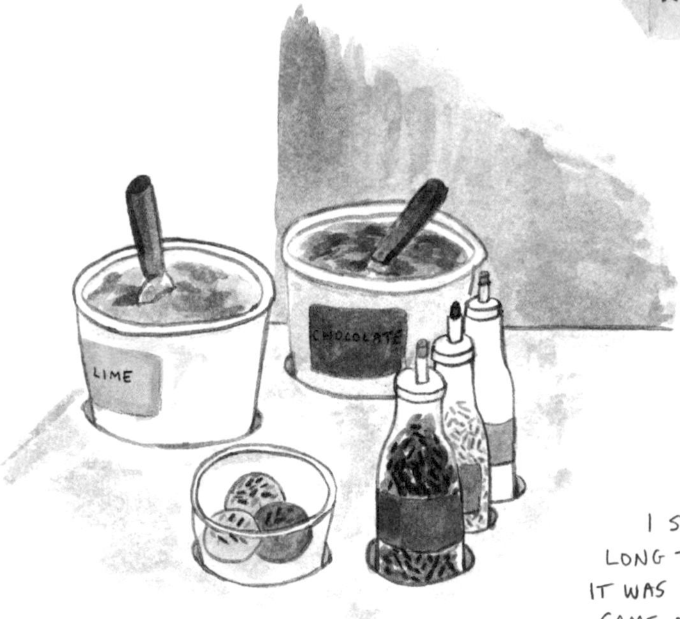
LIME
CHOCOLATE

• THERE'S A LOT OF CANDY AT THIS CONVENTION. I'M DOING A LOT OF PRETENDING TO BE INTERESTED IN TOYS SO THAT I CAN EAT PIECES OF CANDY.

←

I STARED AT THIS STUFF FOR A LONG TIME, TRYING TO FIGURE OUT IF IT WAS EDIBLE, BEFORE A SALESWOMAN CAME OVER AND TOLD ME IT WAS SOAP.

• I SQUINT AT AN "AMERICOOB" BANNER JUST TO MAKE SURE... NO, IT DOESN'T SAY "AMERIBOOB." THE BOOTH GUY EXPLAINS HOW THE TOY IS BASED ON THE VIKING GAME, KUBBSPEL, AND HE INVITES ME TO WEAR A PLASTIC VIKING HELMET WHILE TRYING OUT A GAME OF AMERICOOB IN THE AISLE.

I KNOCK A BLOCK (COOB?) OVER WITH A DIFFERENTLY SHAPED BLOCK (OR IS THIS ONE THE COOB?), I YELL "COOB!!" AND IT FEELS GOOD.

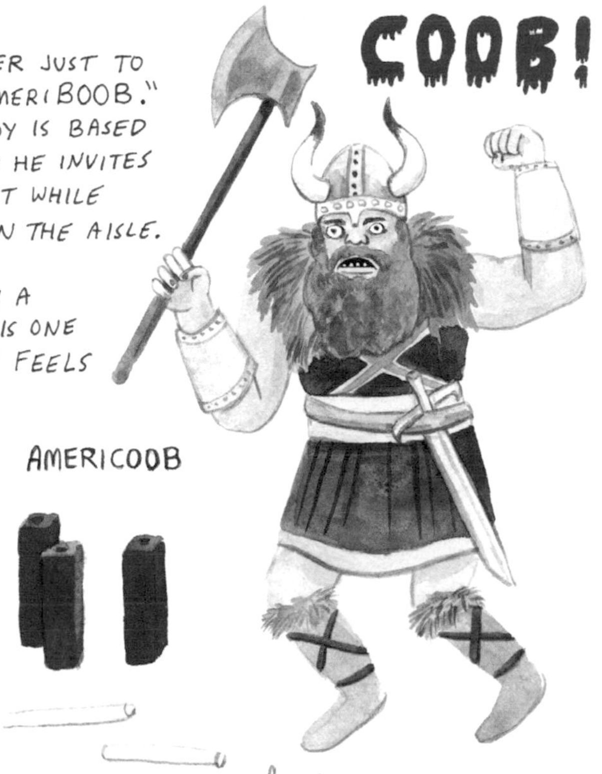
COOB!
AMERICOOB

IT HAS A BARE BONES THROW-A-THING-AT-A-THING CHARM. STILL, I WONDER IF THE WHOLE "ANCIENT NORSE WARRIORS" VIBE COULDN'T BE INCORPORATED MORE INTO GAMEPLAY ?

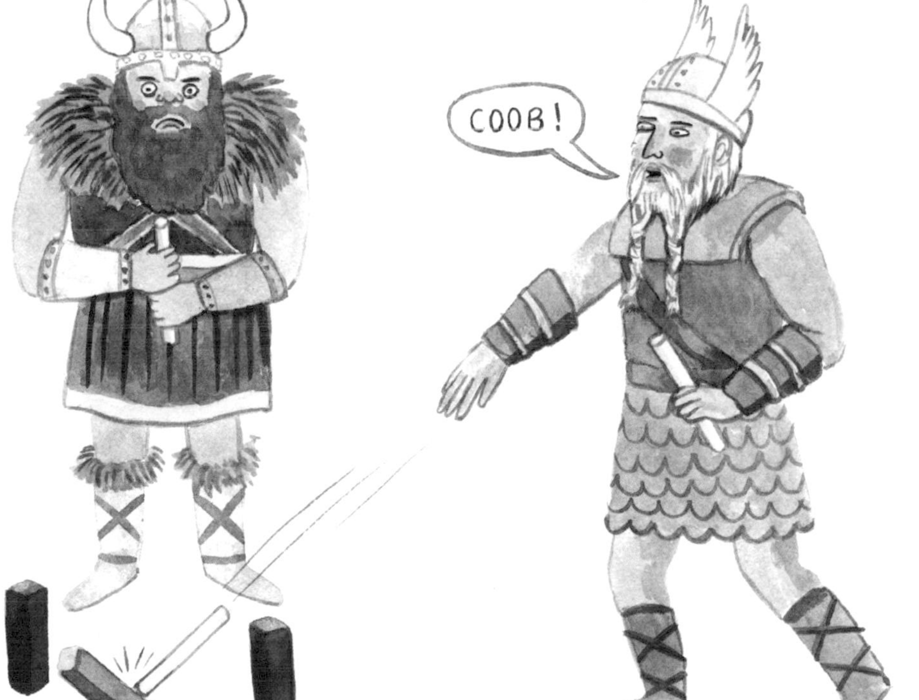
COOB!

- WE HEAD UPSTAIRS, WHERE ALL THE HEAVY HITTERS AND BIG BRANDS WENT NUTS DESIGNING ELABORATE BOOTHS. THE ALREADY CONFUSING TRADE SHOW SOCIAL DYNAMIC CHANGES UP HERE; INSTEAD OF BEING COURTED BY DESPERATE SMALL BUSINESS OWNERS, WE'RE MET BY ICY SUITS AT PODIUMS REQUESTING VENDOR ACCOUNT NUMBERS AND APPOINTMENTS. I REALIZE I'M THE VILLAIN HERE AND THESE PEOPLE ARE JUST TRYING TO MOVE WHOLESALE GOODS, BUT WHAT'S THE HARM IN LETTING ME CHECK OUT THE NEWEST PIRATE SHIP PLAY SET OR WHATEVER? SURE, I JUST SELL CHIA SEEDS, BUT I'M LOOKING TO BRANCH OUT.

- REACTIONS TO MY CHIA AFFILIATION HAVE BEEN MOSTLY NEUTRAL OR "OH COOL, LIKE THE CHIA PETS," BUT THE WOMEN GUARDING THE PLAYMOBIL ® COMPOUND ARE TOTAL DICKS ABOUT IT.

ONE OF THEM SAYS "CHIA?!" AND TURNS TO HER COWORKER WITH A SNEER. THEN BOTH OF THEM LAUGH IN OUR FACES. I'M STILL FUMING TEN MINUTES LATER. WHO DOES PLAYMOBIL THINK THEY ARE? THEY'RE NO LEGO, THAT'S FOR SURE!

LEGO

PLAYMOBIL IS FOR DUMB BABIES

APPOINTMENTS ONLY

- LEGO WON'T EVEN LET US INTO THEIR BOOTH. YOU NEED AN APPOINTMENT AND THE RECEPTIONIST WON'T GIVE US A PEEK EVEN THOUGH NOBODY'S AROUND. AT COMIC-CON, THEY PILE LEGOS ON THE FLOOR AND LET YOU SWIM IN THEM! JUST SAYIN'.

• THANK YOU, UNCLE MILTON INDUSTRIES, FOR LETTING US ENJOY YOUR "TARANTULA PLANET" CRITTERS. I'M A SUCKER FOR UGLY ANIMALS IN COSTUMES, AND HEY, WEIRD, THE SOCCER-THEMED TARANTULA IS WEARING THE SAME OUTFIT AS THAT BIRDIE BANANAS GUY FROM EARLIER!

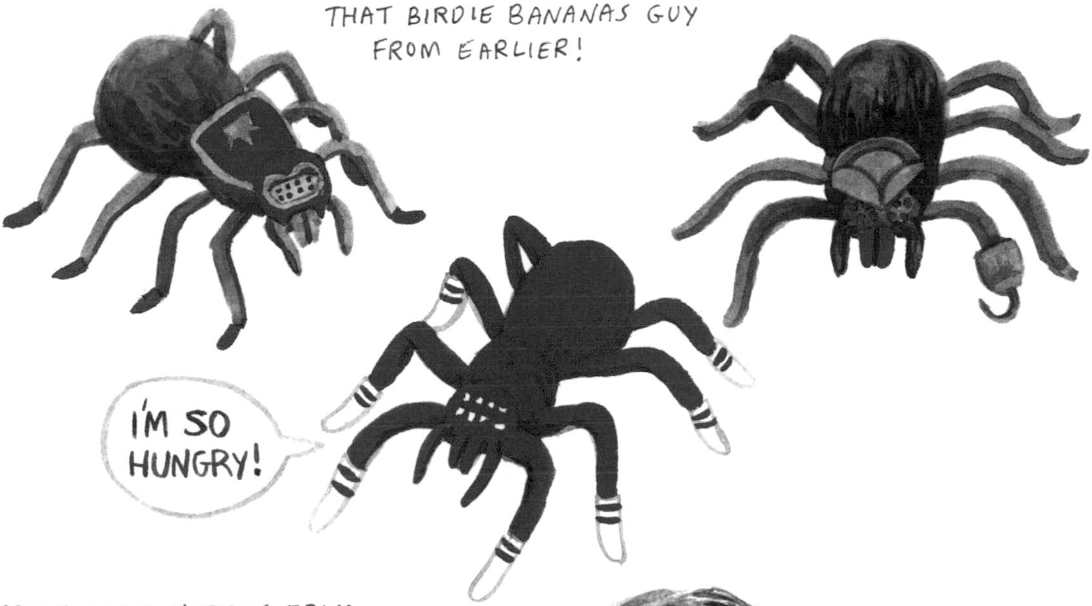
I'M SO HUNGRY!

• I SPY PLASTIC HORSES FROM ACROSS THE ROOM AND GET ALL SCREECHY. BREYERS! I CORNER A SALESLADY, "OH MY GOD, I'M SUCH A BREYER FAN! I SOLD MOST OF MY COLLECTION WHEN I MOVED TO NEW YORK, BUT I STILL KEEP A BUNCH IN THE CLOSET AT MY PARENTS' HOUSE!!" I NERD OUT OVER THEIR DISPLAYS FOR A WHILE.

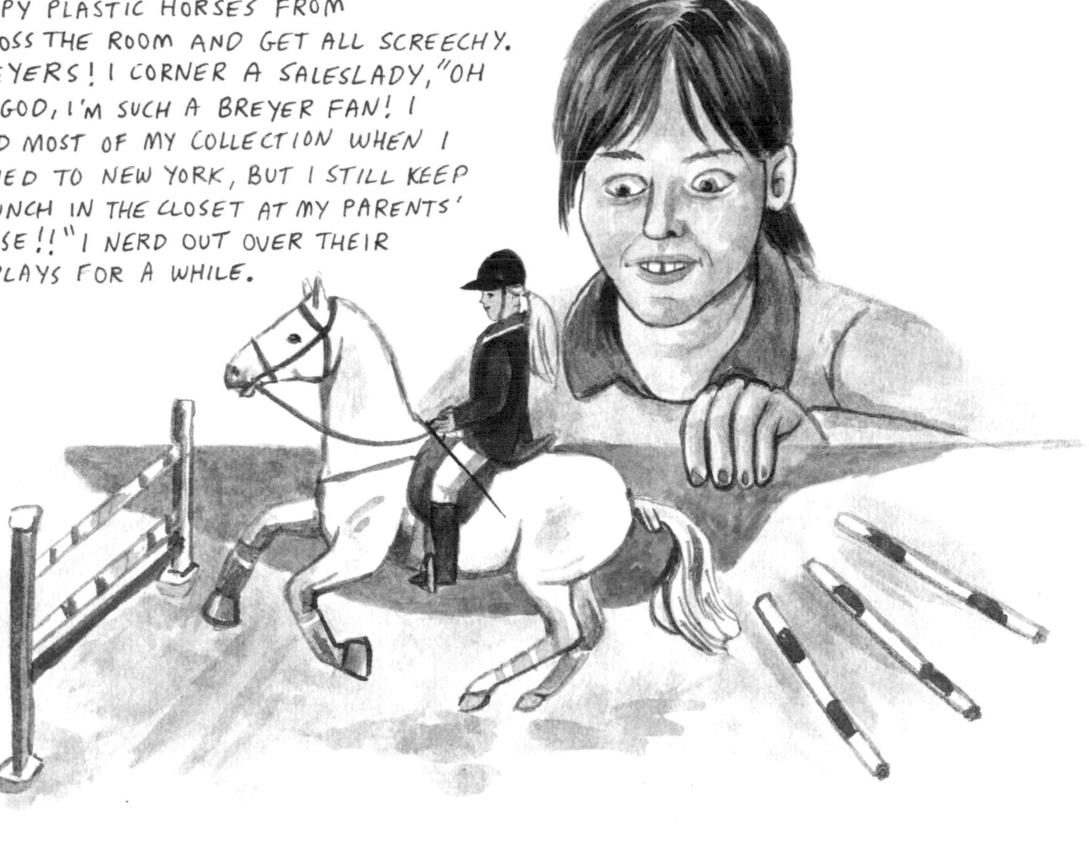

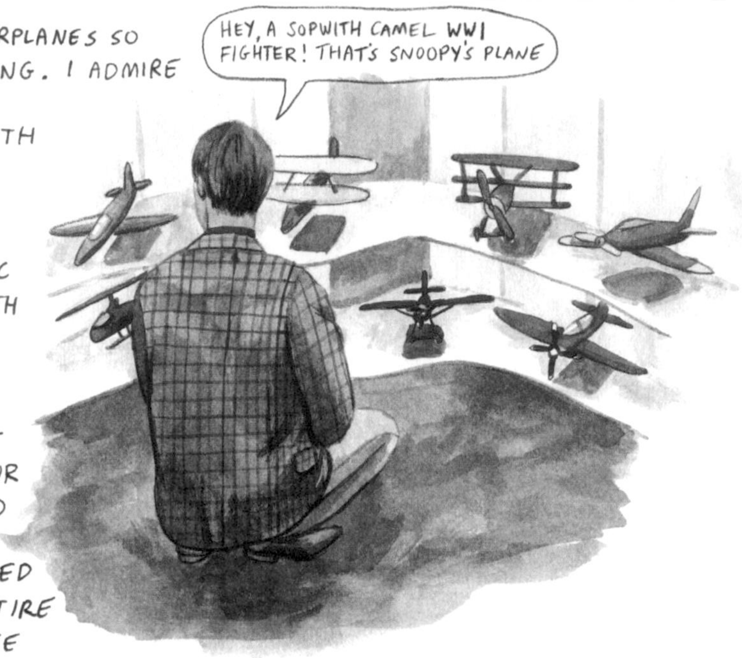
HEY, A SOPWITH CAMEL WWI FIGHTER! THAT'S SNOOPY'S PLANE

• NEXT WE CHECK OUT MODEL AIRPLANES SO TIM CAN TAKE A TURN GEEKING. I ADMIRE THE PLANES, PARTICULARLY A WOODGRAIN SPACE SHUTTLE WITH MOVING COMPARTMENTS, BUT THEY'RE NO MATCH FOR ACETATE EQUINES.

• I'M GOING TO GET NOSTALGIC FOR A MOMENT, SO BEAR WITH ME, BUT DO YOU REMEMBER YOUR FAVORITE TOYS AS A CHILD? AND MAYBE YOU WONDERED WHY ADULTS DIDN'T SEEM AS ENCHANTED WITH YOUR TOYS AS YOU WERE? I USED TO SWEAR I'D NEVER LOSE INTEREST IN MY TOYS; I FEARED IT WOULD MEAN LOSING MY ENTIRE SENSE OF SELF. BUT OF COURSE I GREW OLDER AND LEFT THOSE BELOVED THINGS BEHIND. I CAN PICK UP A BREYER, ADMIRE THE SMOOTH PLASTIC DETAILS, BUT... THAT'S IT. I'M NOT GOING TO SIT ON THE FLOOR WITH IT FOR HOURS, MAKING IT TALK TO OTHER TOYS, ACTING OUT MY LATEST CONFLICTS AND FANTASIES, FORMING PRETEND RELATIONSHIPS. I WISH I COULD ENJOY TOYS ON THAT LEVEL AGAIN.

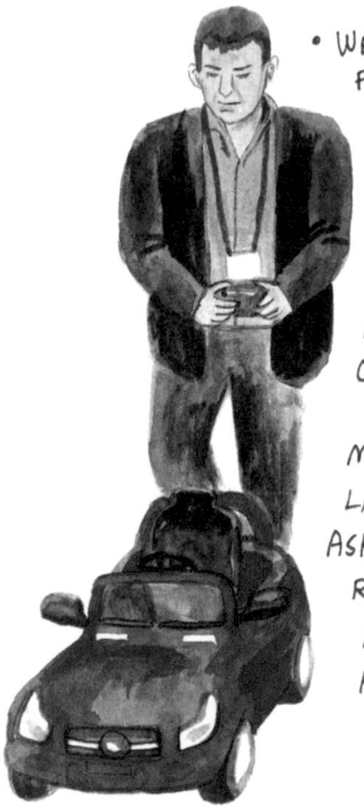

• WE WANDER AROUND FOR A FEW MORE MINUTES BEFORE ADMITTING WE'RE WORN OUT; WE CAN'T PLAY WITH TOYS ALL DAY LIKE WE USED TO. OUTSIDE THE JAVITS CENTER, WE SEE A MAN CONTROLLING A LARGE TOY CAR AND I ASK, "HEY CAN I GET A RIDE?" HE PRETENDS NOT TO HEAR ME. HE'S VERY SERIOUS.

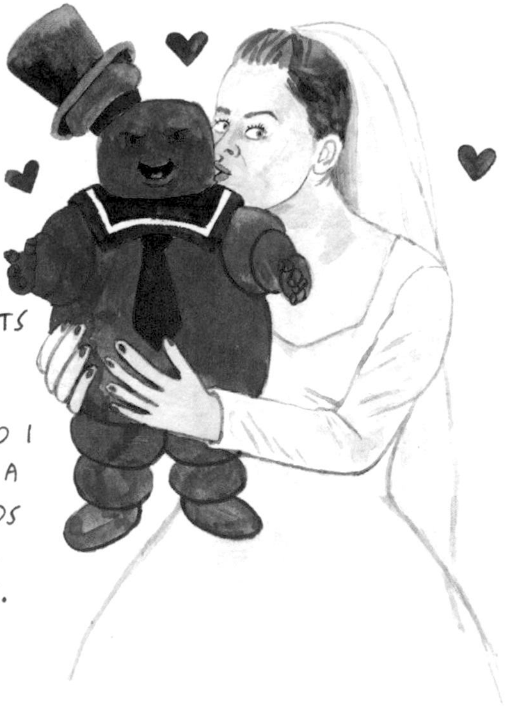

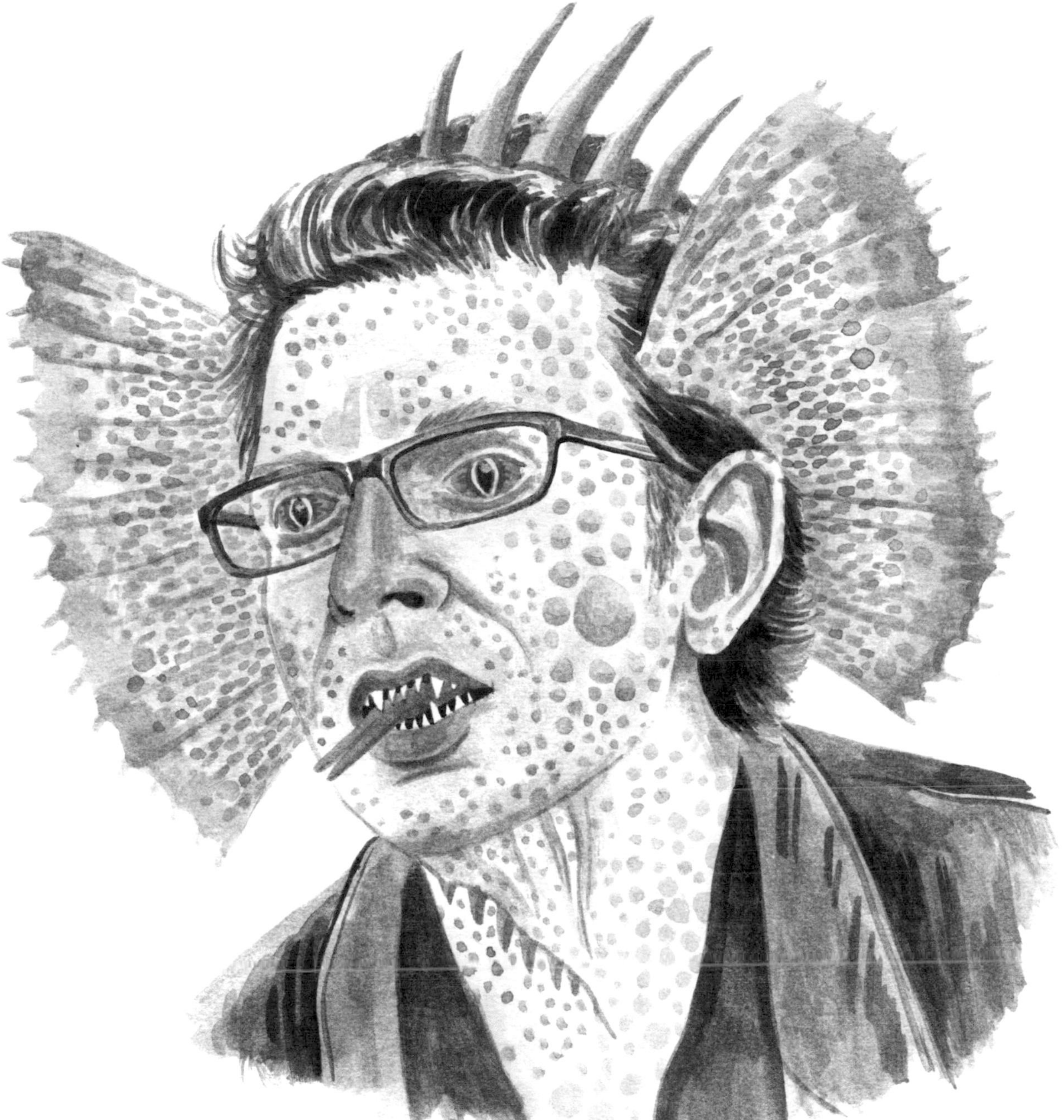

Jeff Goldblum in Jurassic Park

SMALL COMIC STRIPS

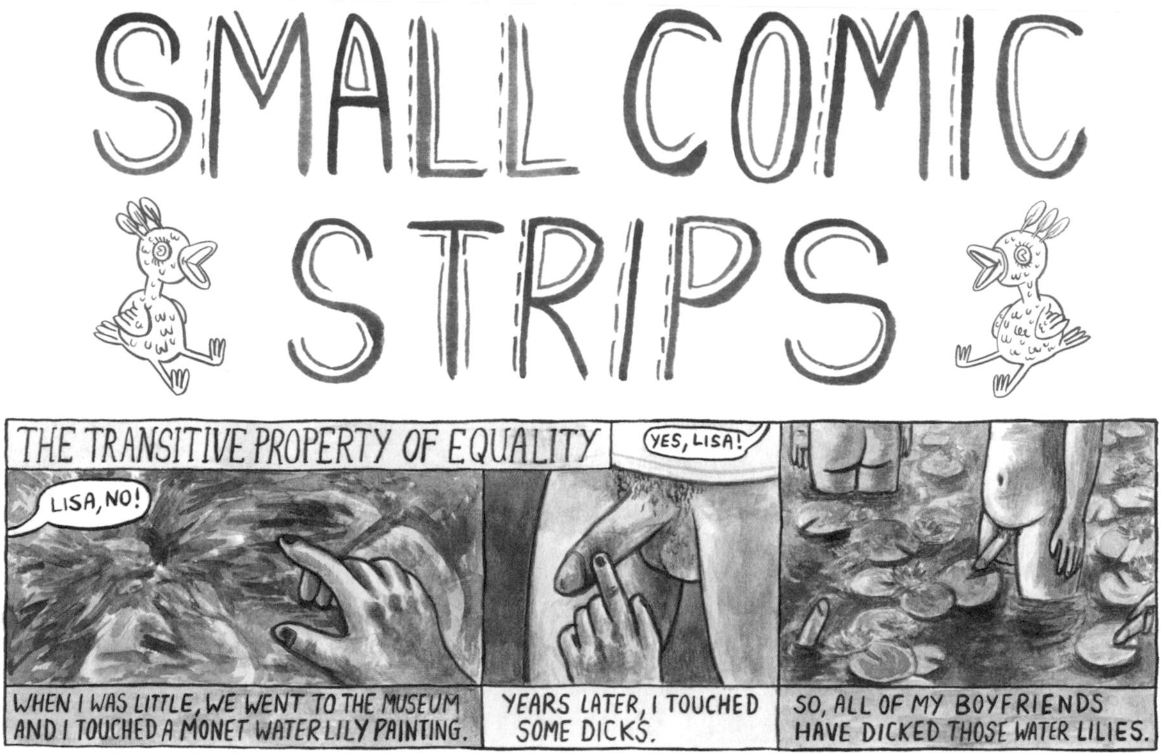
THE TRANSITIVE PROPERTY OF EQUALITY
LISA, NO!
WHEN I WAS LITTLE, WE WENT TO THE MUSEUM AND I TOUCHED A MONET WATER LILY PAINTING.
YES, LISA!
YEARS LATER, I TOUCHED SOME DICKS.
SO, ALL OF MY BOYFRIENDS HAVE DICKED THOSE WATER LILIES.

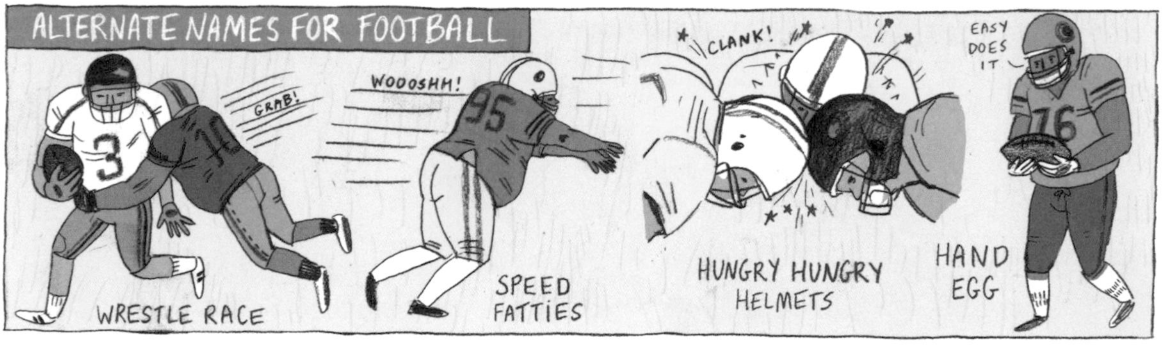
ALTERNATE NAMES FOR FOOTBALL
GRAB!
WRESTLE RACE
WOOOSHH!
SPEED FATTIES
CLANK!
HUNGRY HUNGRY HELMETS
EASY DOES IT
HAND EGG

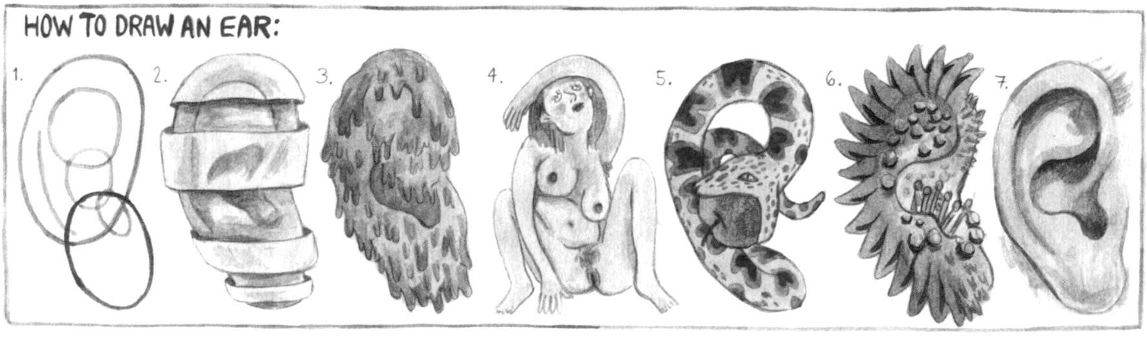
HOW TO DRAW AN EAR:
1.
2.
3.
4.
5.
6.
7.

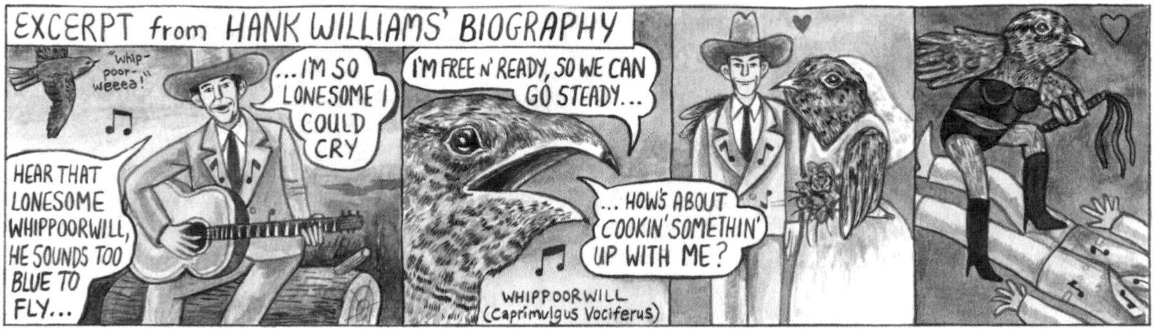
EXCERPT from HANK WILLIAMS' BIOGRAPHY
"whip-poor-weeea!"
HEAR THAT LONESOME WHIPPOORWILL, HE SOUNDS TOO BLUE TO FLY...
...I'M SO LONESOME I COULD CRY
I'M FREE N' READY, SO WE CAN GO STEADY...
... HOW'S ABOUT COOKIN' SOMETHIN' UP WITH ME?
WHIPPOORWILL (Caprimulgus Vociferus)

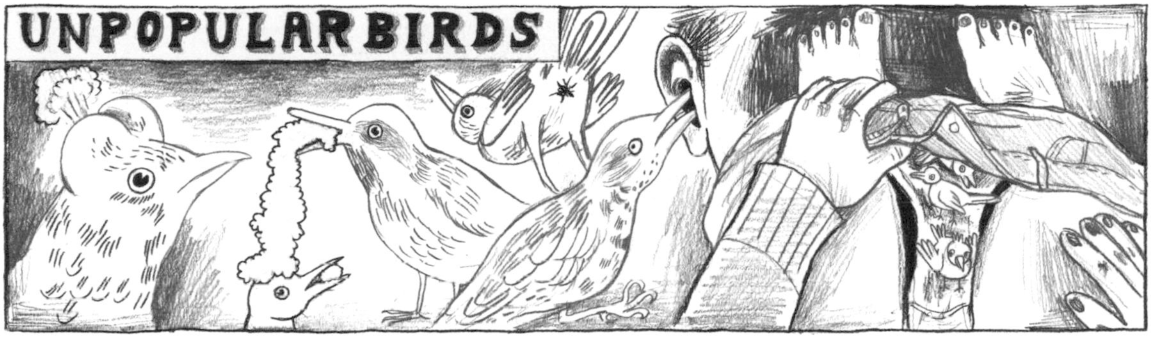
UNPOPULAR BIRDS

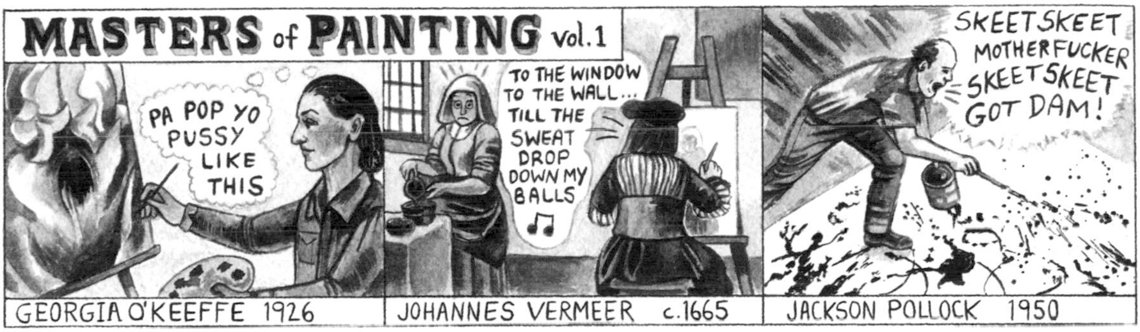
MASTERS of PAINTING vol. 1
PA POP YO PUSSY LIKE THIS
GEORGIA O'KEEFFE 1926
TO THE WINDOW TO THE WALL... TILL THE SWEAT DROP DOWN MY BALLS
JOHANNES VERMEER c.1665
SKEET SKEET MOTHERFUCKER SKEET SKEET GOT DAM!
JACKSON POLLOCK 1950

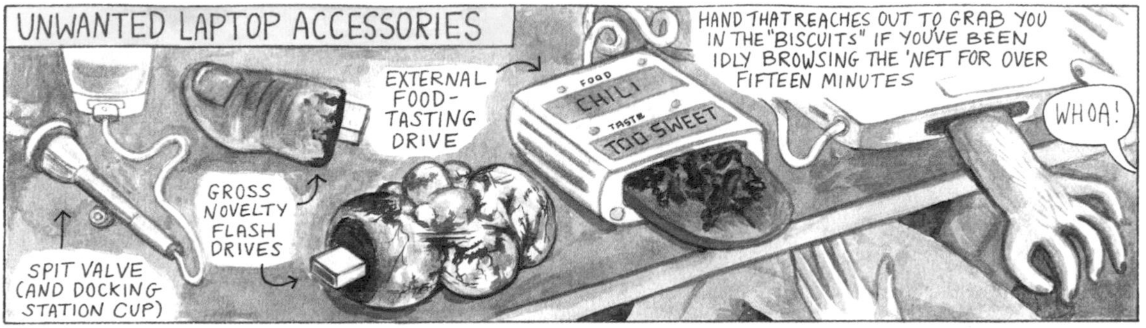
UNWANTED LAPTOP ACCESSORIES
SPIT VALVE (AND DOCKING STATION CUP)
GROSS NOVELTY FLASH DRIVES
EXTERNAL FOOD-TASTING DRIVE
FOOD
CHILI
TASTE
TOO SWEET
HAND THAT REACHES OUT TO GRAB YOU IN THE "BISCUITS" IF YOU'VE BEEN IDLY BROWSING THE 'NET FOR OVER FIFTEEN MINUTES
WHOA!

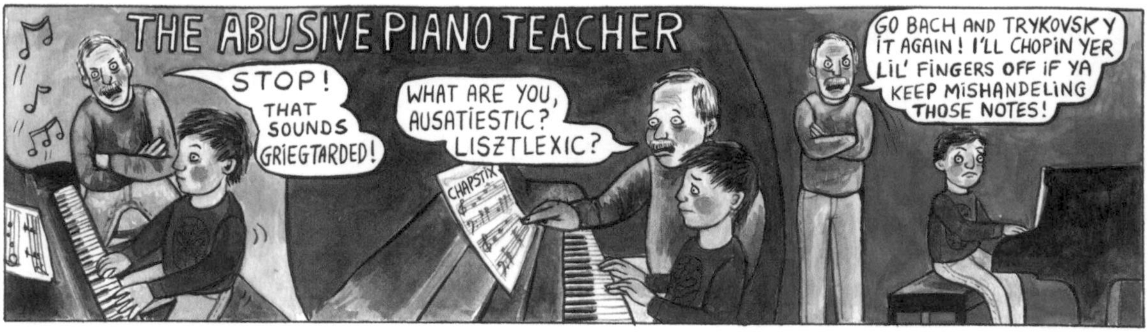
THE ABUSIVE PIANO TEACHER
STOP! THAT SOUNDS GRIEGTARDED!
WHAT ARE YOU, AUSATIESTIC? LISZTLEXIC?
CHAPSTIX
GO BACH AND TRYKOVSKY IT AGAIN! I'LL CHOPIN YER LIL' FINGERS OFF IF YA KEEP MISHANDELING THOSE NOTES!

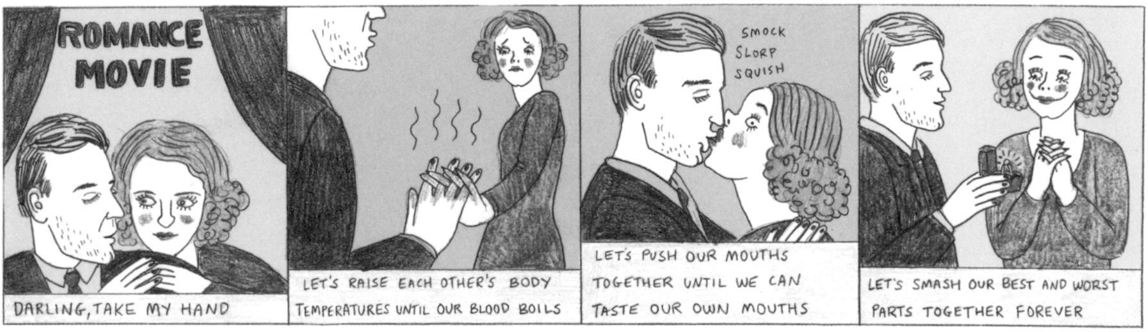
ROMANCE MOVIE
DARLING, TAKE MY HAND
LET'S RAISE EACH OTHER'S BODY TEMPERATURES UNTIL OUR BLOOD BOILS
SMOCK
SLORP
SQUISH
LET'S PUSH OUR MOUTHS TOGETHER UNTIL WE CAN TASTE OUR OWN MOUTHS
LET'S SMASH OUR BEST AND WORST PARTS TOGETHER FOREVER

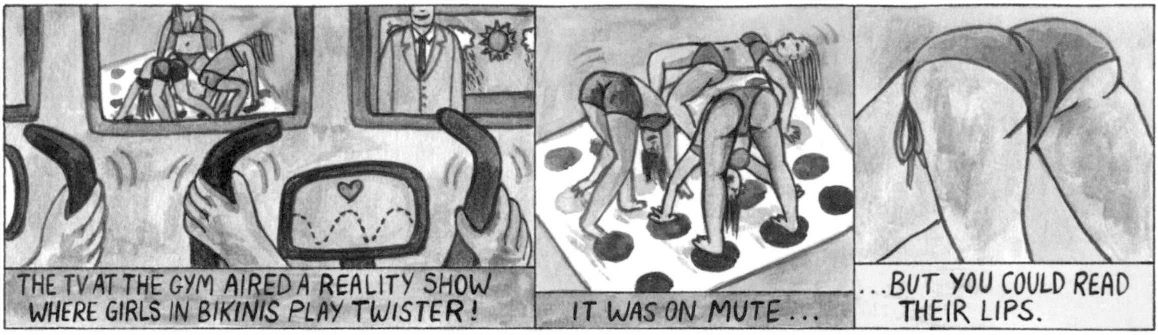
THE TV AT THE GYM AIRED A REALITY SHOW WHERE GIRLS IN BIKINIS PLAY TWISTER!
IT WAS ON MUTE...
...BUT YOU COULD READ THEIR LIPS.

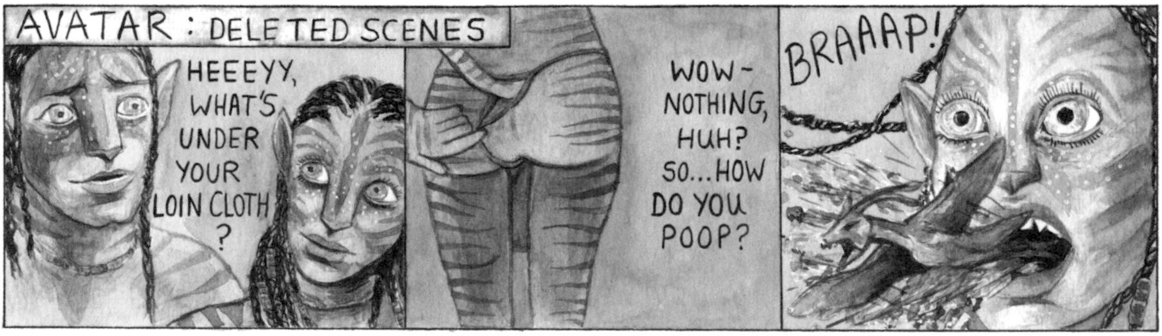
AVATAR : DELETED SCENES
HEEEYY, WHAT'S UNDER YOUR LOIN CLOTH?
WOW - NOTHING, HUH? SO... HOW DO YOU POOP?
BRAAAP!

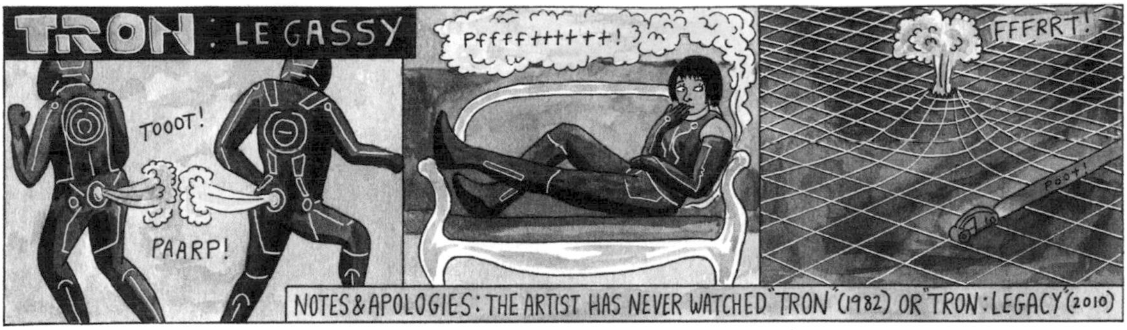
TRON : LE GASSY
TOOOT!
PAARP!
Pfffftttttt!
FFFRRT!
POOT!
NOTES & APOLOGIES: THE ARTIST HAS NEVER WATCHED "TRON" (1982) OR "TRON: LEGACY" (2010)

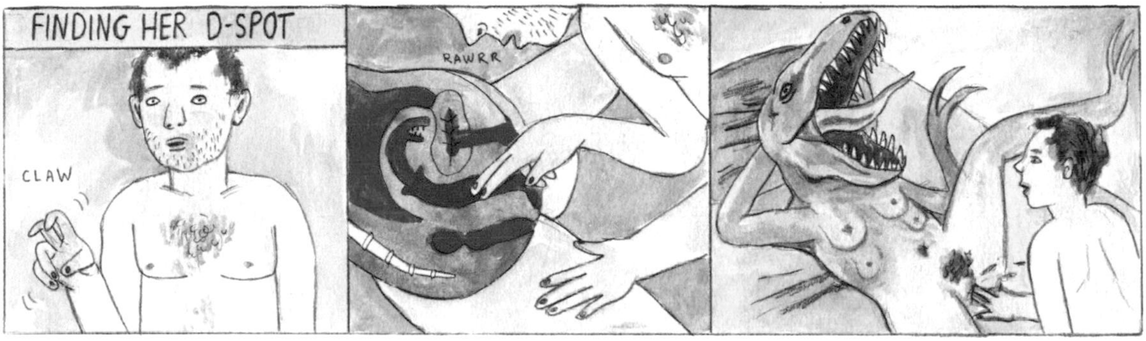
FINDING HER D-SPOT
CLAW
RAWRR

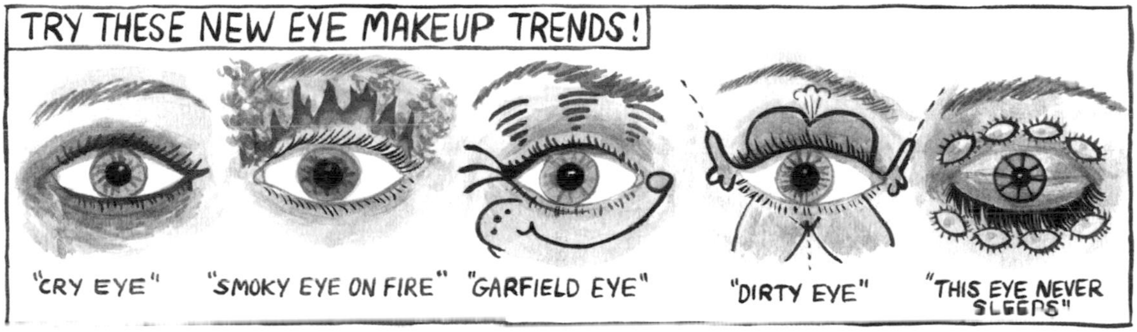
TRY THESE NEW EYE MAKEUP TRENDS!
"CRY EYE"
"SMOKY EYE ON FIRE"
"GARFIELD EYE"
"DIRTY EYE"
"THIS EYE NEVER SLEEPS"

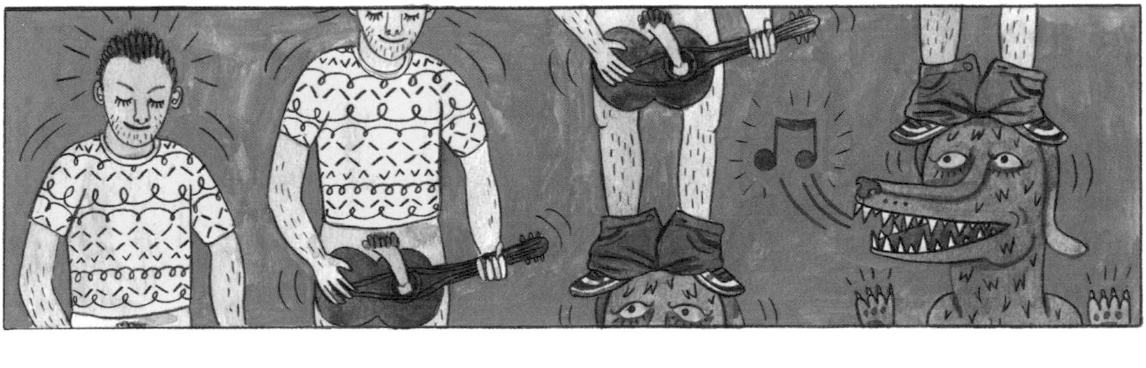

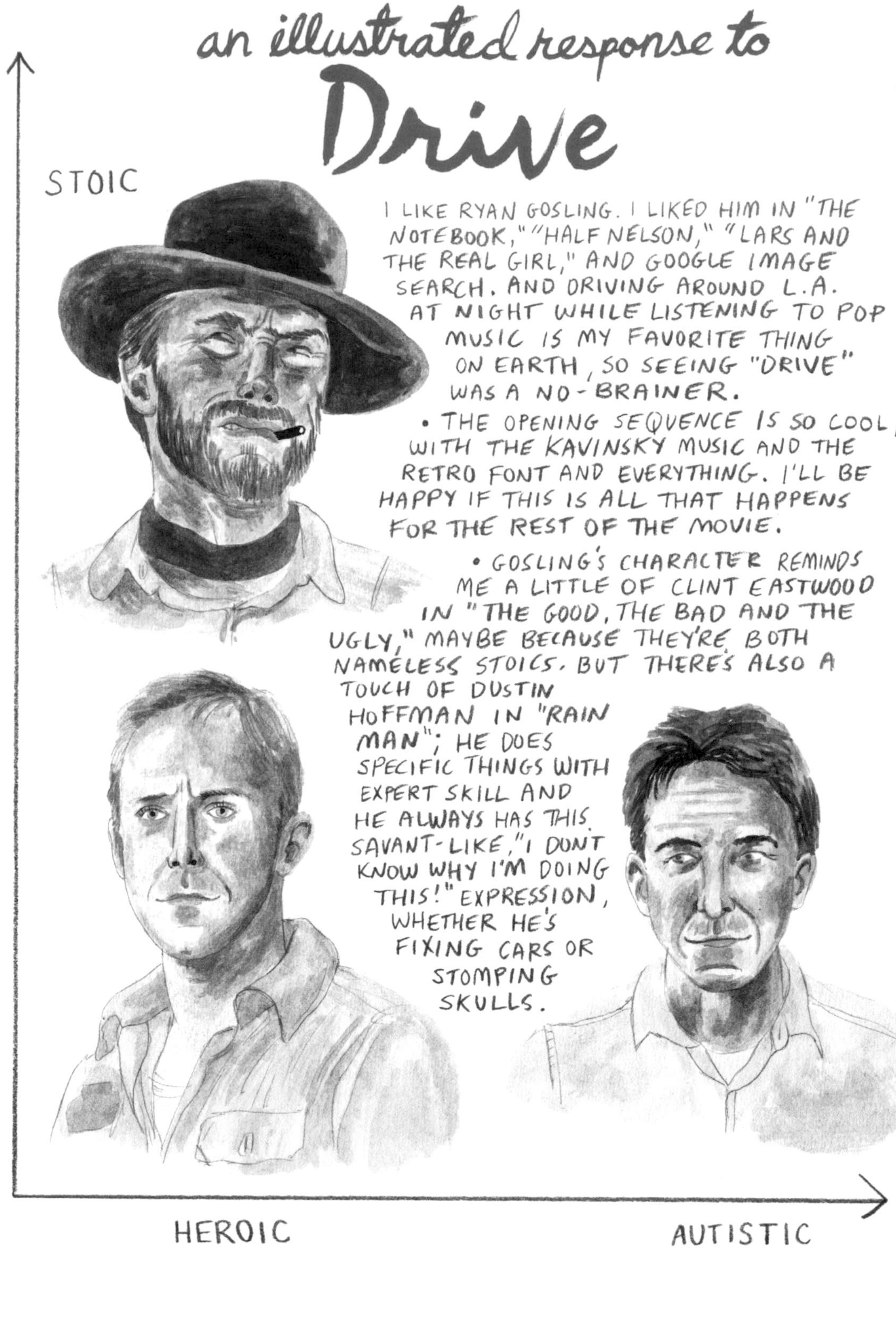
an illustrated response to
Drive
STOIC
I LIKE RYAN GOSLING. I LIKED HIM IN "THE NOTEBOOK," "HALF NELSON," "LARS AND THE REAL GIRL," AND GOOGLE IMAGE SEARCH. AND DRIVING AROUND L.A. AT NIGHT WHILE LISTENING TO POP MUSIC IS MY FAVORITE THING ON EARTH, SO SEEING "DRIVE" WAS A NO-BRAINER.
• THE OPENING SEQUENCE IS SO COOL, WITH THE KAVINSKY MUSIC AND THE RETRO FONT AND EVERYTHING. I'LL BE HAPPY IF THIS IS ALL THAT HAPPENS FOR THE REST OF THE MOVIE.
• GOSLING'S CHARACTER REMINDS ME A LITTLE OF CLINT EASTWOOD IN "THE GOOD, THE BAD AND THE UGLY," MAYBE BECAUSE THEY'RE BOTH NAMELESS STOICS. BUT THERE'S ALSO A TOUCH OF DUSTIN HOFFMAN IN "RAIN MAN"; HE DOES SPECIFIC THINGS WITH EXPERT SKILL AND HE ALWAYS HAS THIS SAVANT-LIKE, "I DON'T KNOW WHY I'M DOING THIS!" EXPRESSION, WHETHER HE'S FIXING CARS OR STOMPING SKULLS.
HEROIC
AUTISTIC

• BUT MAYBE I'M JUST THINKING ABOUT "RAIN MAN" BECAUSE THEY BOTH LIKE TOOTHPICKS.

• WE KEEP HAVING TO SECOND GUESS WHAT DRIVER ACTUALLY DOES. HE'S A GETAWAY DRIVER. NOW HE'S A COP! WAIT, NOW HE'S A STUNTMAN... AND A MECHANIC! NOW HE'S A U.S. MARSHALL AND A BOUNTY HUNTER! NOW HE'S A BEAUUU-UUTIFUL LADY!

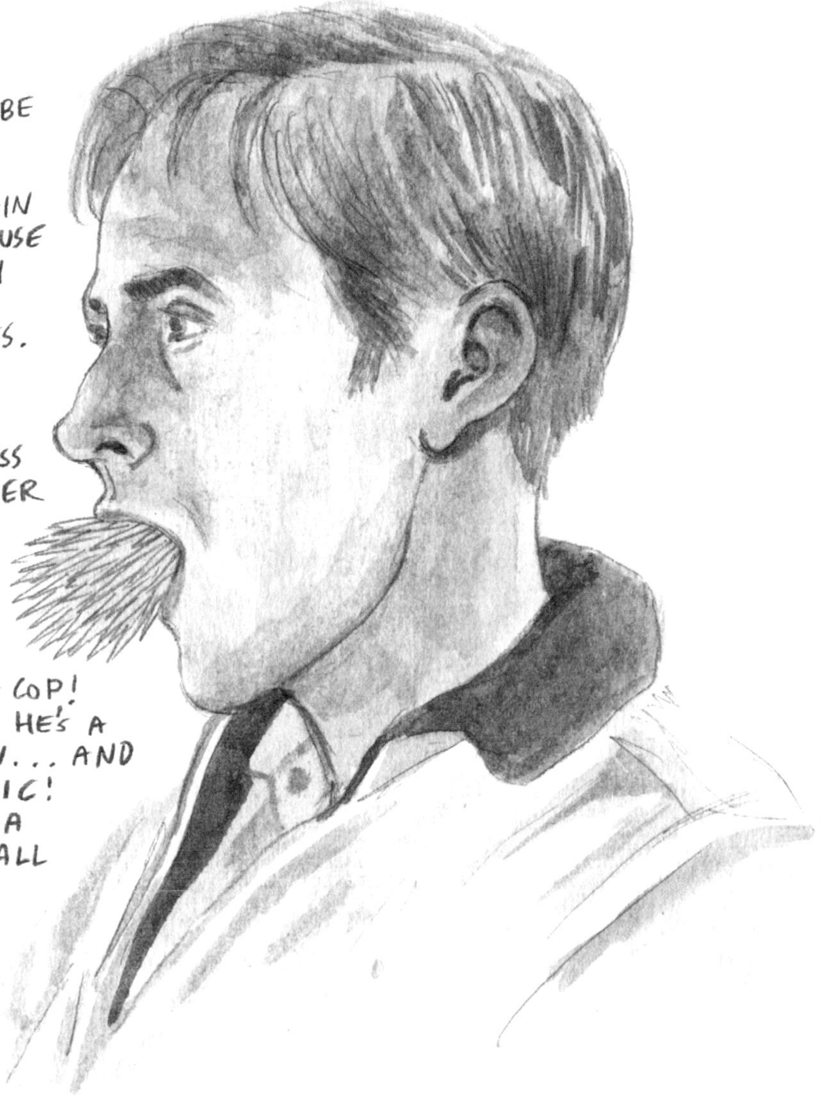

246 TOOTHPICKS

• I CAN TELL THIS THEME SONG, "A REAL HERO," IS GOING TO BE STUCK IN MY HEAD FOREVER. I KNOW IT'S INSPIRED BY CAPTAIN SULLY SULLENBERGER, BUT IT'S FUN TO PRETEND THE LYRICS ARE SUNG BY A GIRL WITH WEIRD STANDARDS FOR WHAT MAKES DUDES WORTH SINGING ABOUT. "YOU HAVE PROVED TO BE A REAL HUMAN BEING!! AND A REAL HERO... AND A REAL HUMAN BEING!!!" MAYBE SHE'S DATED A LOT OF ROBOTS?

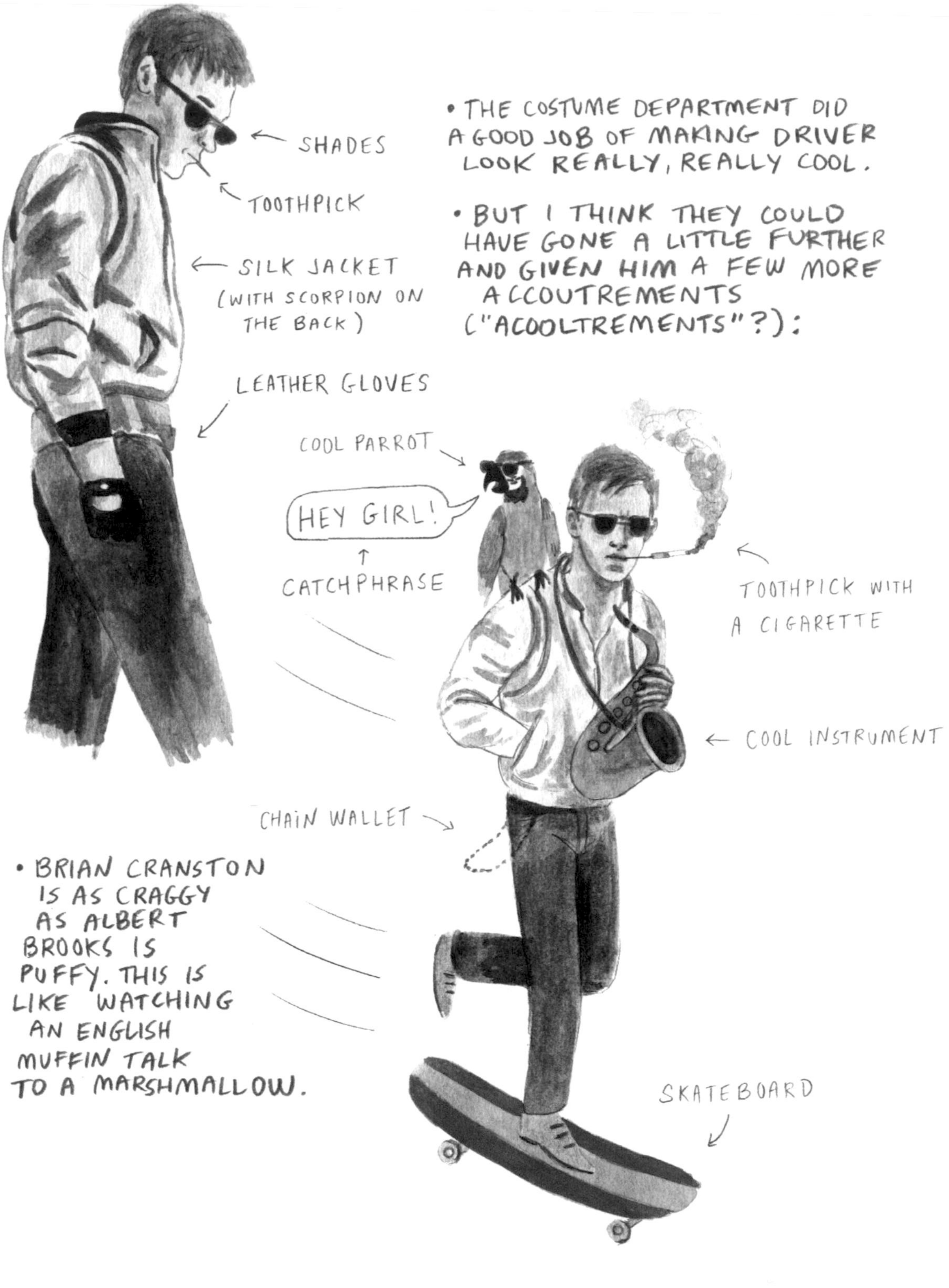
SHADES
TOOTHPICK
SILK JACKET (WITH SCORPION ON THE BACK)
LEATHER GLOVES
• THE COSTUME DEPARTMENT DID A GOOD JOB OF MAKING DRIVER LOOK REALLY, REALLY COOL.
• BUT I THINK THEY COULD HAVE GONE A LITTLE FURTHER AND GIVEN HIM A FEW MORE ACCOUTREMENTS ("ACOOLTREMENTS"?):
COOL PARROT
HEY GIRL!
CATCHPHRASE
TOOTHPICK WITH A CIGARETTE
COOL INSTRUMENT
CHAIN WALLET
• BRIAN CRANSTON IS AS CRAGGY AS ALBERT BROOKS IS PUFFY. THIS IS LIKE WATCHING AN ENGLISH MUFFIN TALK TO A MARSHMALLOW.
SKATEBOARD

- "CRANSTON & BROOKS" SOUNDS LIKE A BRAND OF MARMALADE I WOULD SPREAD ON AN ENGLISH MUFFIN. THEY SHOULD DO A MARKETING CAMPAIGN FOR THOMAS ENGLISH MUFFINS AND TALK ABOUT THEIR "BROOKS AND CRANNIES."

- THERE ARE SURPRISINGLY FEW CAR CHASES IN THIS MOVIE.

- CAREY MULLIGAN IS ADORABLE AND A FINE ACTOR, BUT HER CHARACTER IS BASICALLY "PRETTY BUG WAITING AROUND TO GET SQUISHED."

- CHRISTINA HENDRICKS IS ONLY IN THE MOVIE FOR LIKE TWO SECONDS! "HOW YOU GONNA FIT ALL THEM TITTIES INTO TWO SECONDS?" IS WHAT THE DIRTY DUMB PART OF MY BRAIN JUST THOUGHT.

SERENE PIXIE DREAM GIRL

• BROOKS JUST SLICED CRANSTON'S ARM OPEN, BUT AT LEAST HE WAS REALLY NICE ABOUT IT?

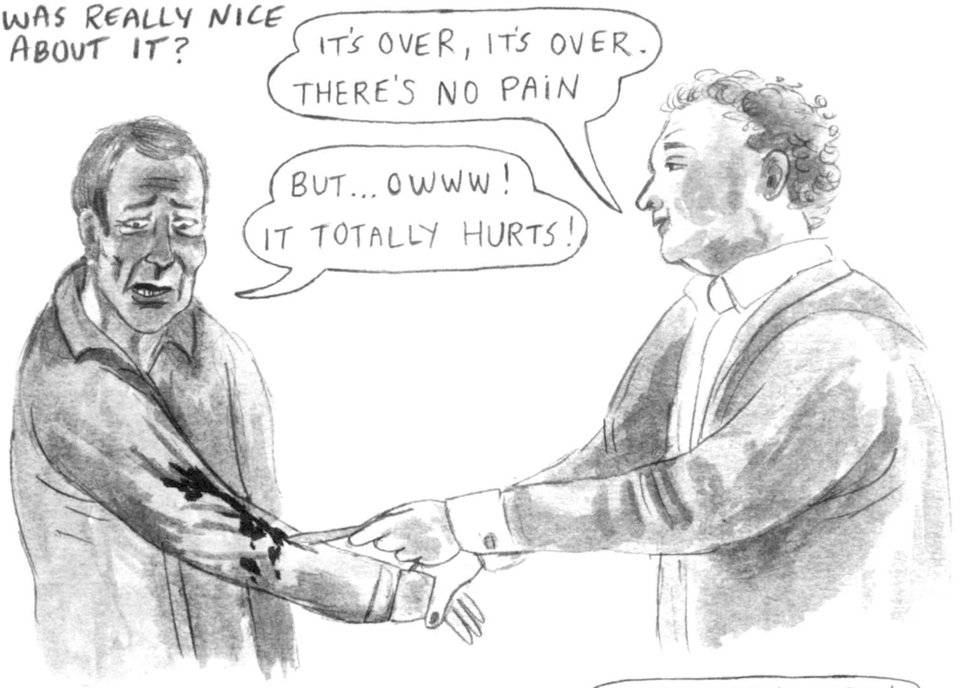
IT'S OVER, IT'S OVER. THERE'S NO PAIN
BUT... OWWW! IT TOTALLY HURTS!

• I HAD TO GET SOME BLOOD TESTS DONE A FEW HOURS BEFORE THE MOVIE, AND UNLIKE CRANSTON'S CHARACTER, I WAS A TOTAL SPINELESS WIENER ABOUT IT.

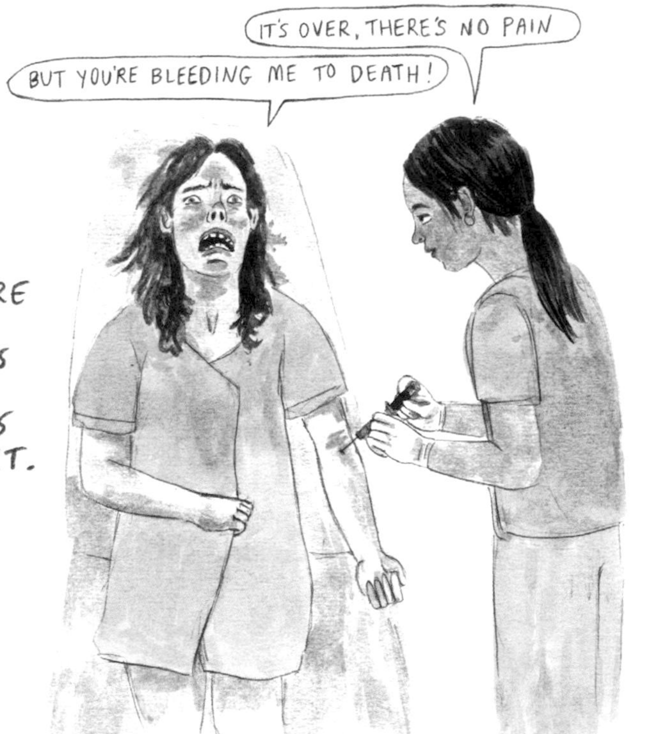
IT'S OVER, THERE'S NO PAIN
BUT YOU'RE BLEEDING ME TO DEATH!

Bleedy
Scrapey
Sharpy
Pokey
Jabby
my favorite knives

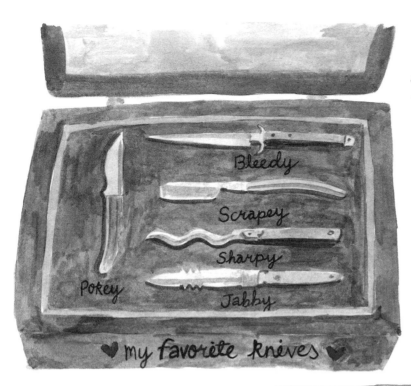

• BROOKS JUST WHIPPED OUT A COLLECTION OF THE PRETTIEST KNIVES I'VE EVER SEEN. WE'VE ALREADY WATCHED HIM STAB A BUNCH OF PEOPLE, BUT NOW WE KNOW FOR SURE THAT KNIFING IS HIS THING.

• NOW THE AUDIENCE IS ROARING WITH LAUGHTER BECAUSE DRIVER KEEPS WEARING HIS SCORPION JACKET EVEN THOUGH IT'S SOAKED WITH BLOOD.

• BEING NAMELESS IS THE COOLEST. FROM NOW ON, ALL OF YOU CAN JUST CALL ME "THE DRAWER."

• IT'S HARD TO MAKE FUN OF THIS MOVIE BECAUSE EVERY ACTION SEEMS SO DELIBERATE AND SMART. GOSLING AND THE DIRECTOR, NICHOLAS WINDING REFN, SEEM TOTALLY IN CONTROL OF HOW EACH CHOICE WILL BE PERCEIVED.

SO YOU'RE LIKE, "I DON'T CARRY A GUN, I DRIVE." BUT THEN IN THE NEXT PART YOU WILL TOTALLY SHOOT A GUN!
THAT WILL MAKE THE AUDIENCE FEEL SURPRISED!

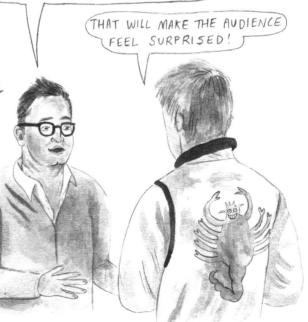

- FUN FACT: NICHOLAS WINDING REFN CAN'T DRIVE, IN FACT HE FAILED HIS DRIVING TEST EIGHT TIMES AND NEVER GOT A LICENSE. SO HE MADE A MOVIE ABOUT THE THING HE'S THE ABSOLUTE WORST AT.
- MY BOYFRIEND JUST SAID, "MY ULTIMATE MOVIE WOULD BE A REMAKE OF 'DRIVE,' STARRING ANDY SERKIS AS A STOIC, UNNAMED GETAWAY CHIMP." I USUALLY SAY NO WHEN HE ASKS ME TO DRAW STUFF, BUT FOR OBVIOUS REASONS:

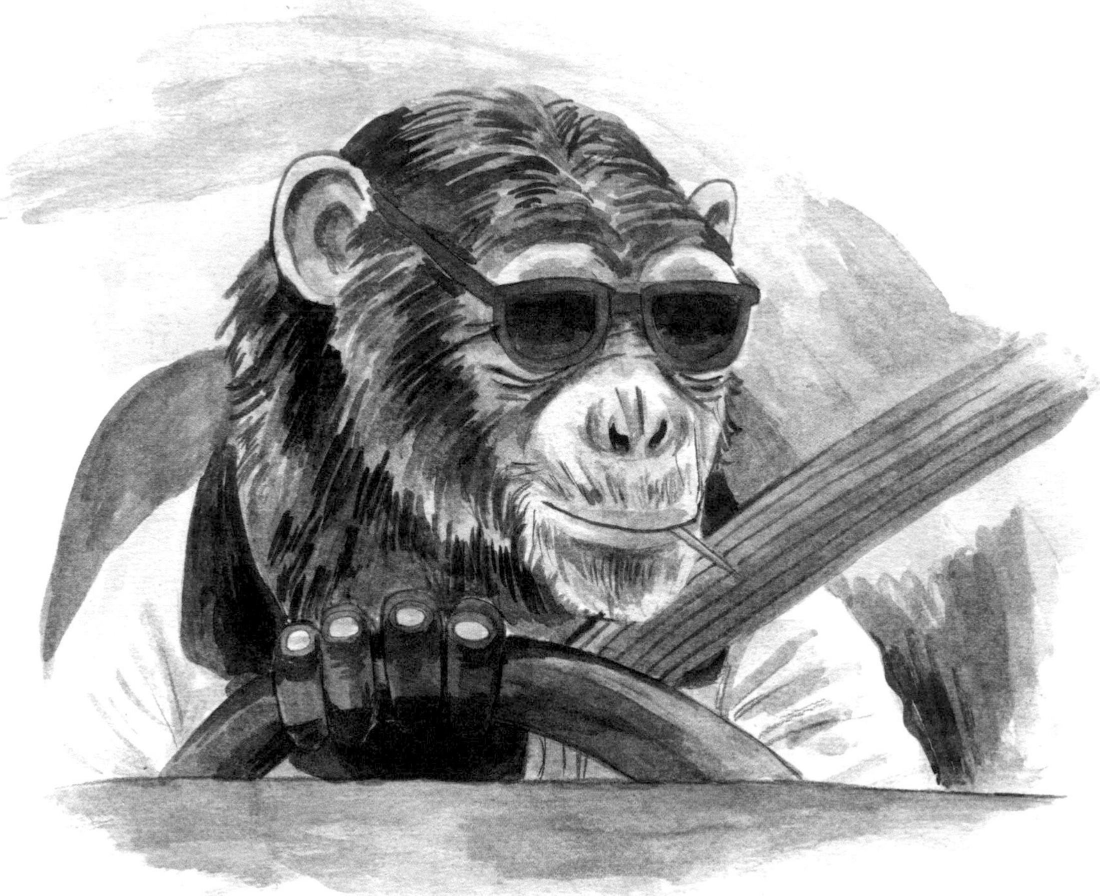

- IN CONCLUSION: "DRIVE" REFERENCES A DOZEN OTHER MOVIES AND IT'S SUPER STYLIZED, LIKE A LESS CAMPY TARANTINO FLICK. IT'S ALSO A TON OF FUN. I GIVE IT FIVE-OUT-OF-FIVE GOSLINGS!

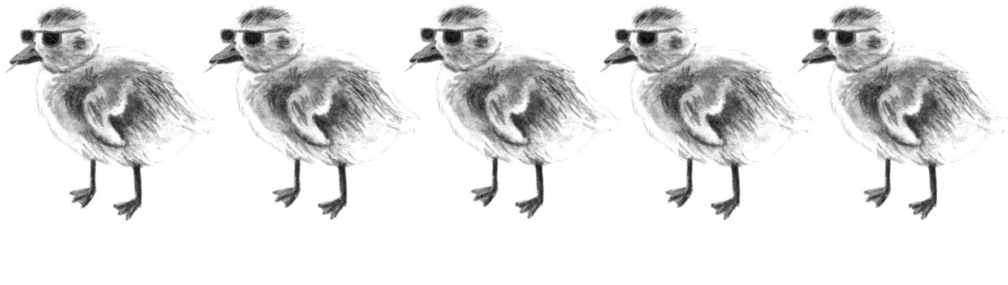

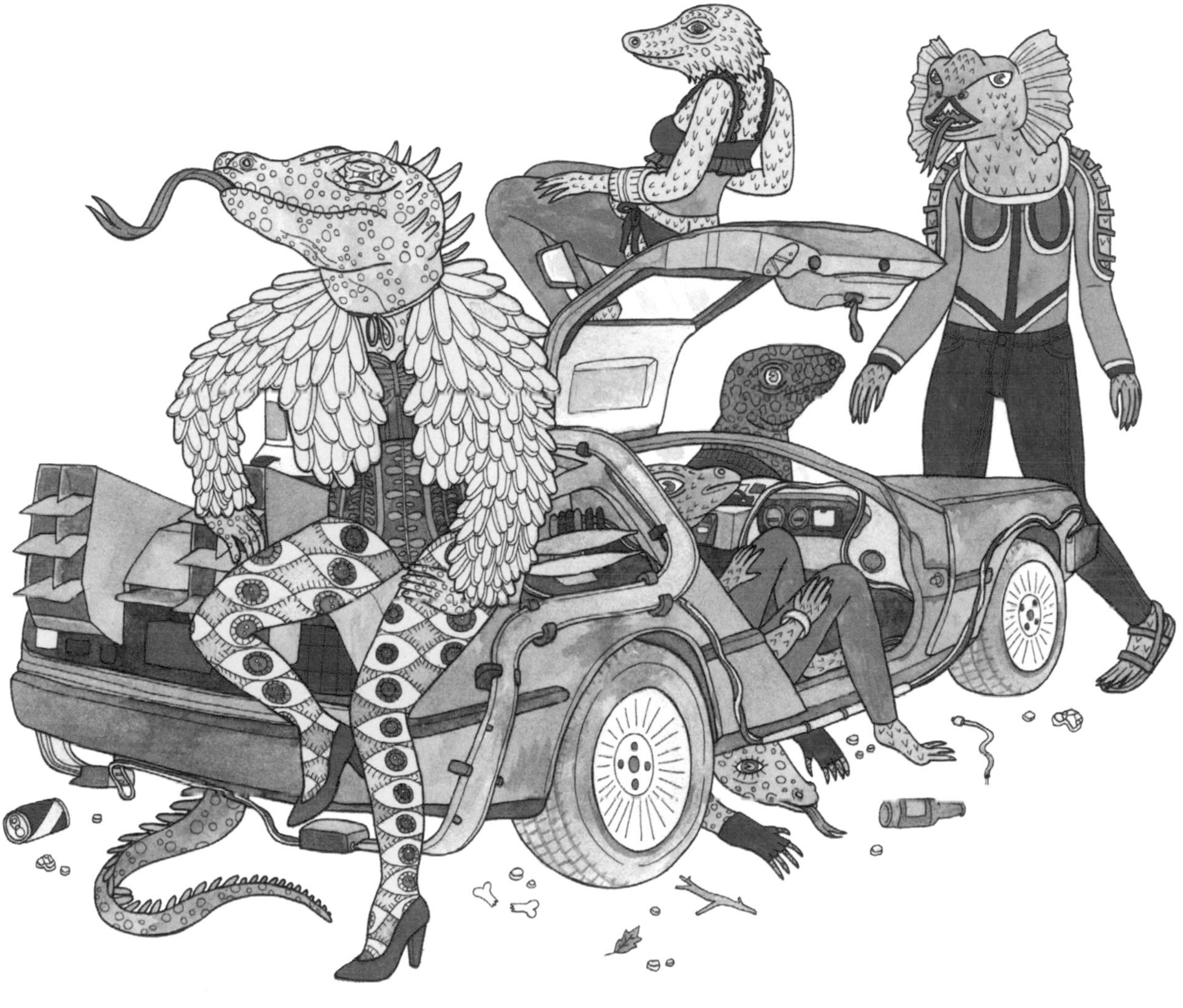

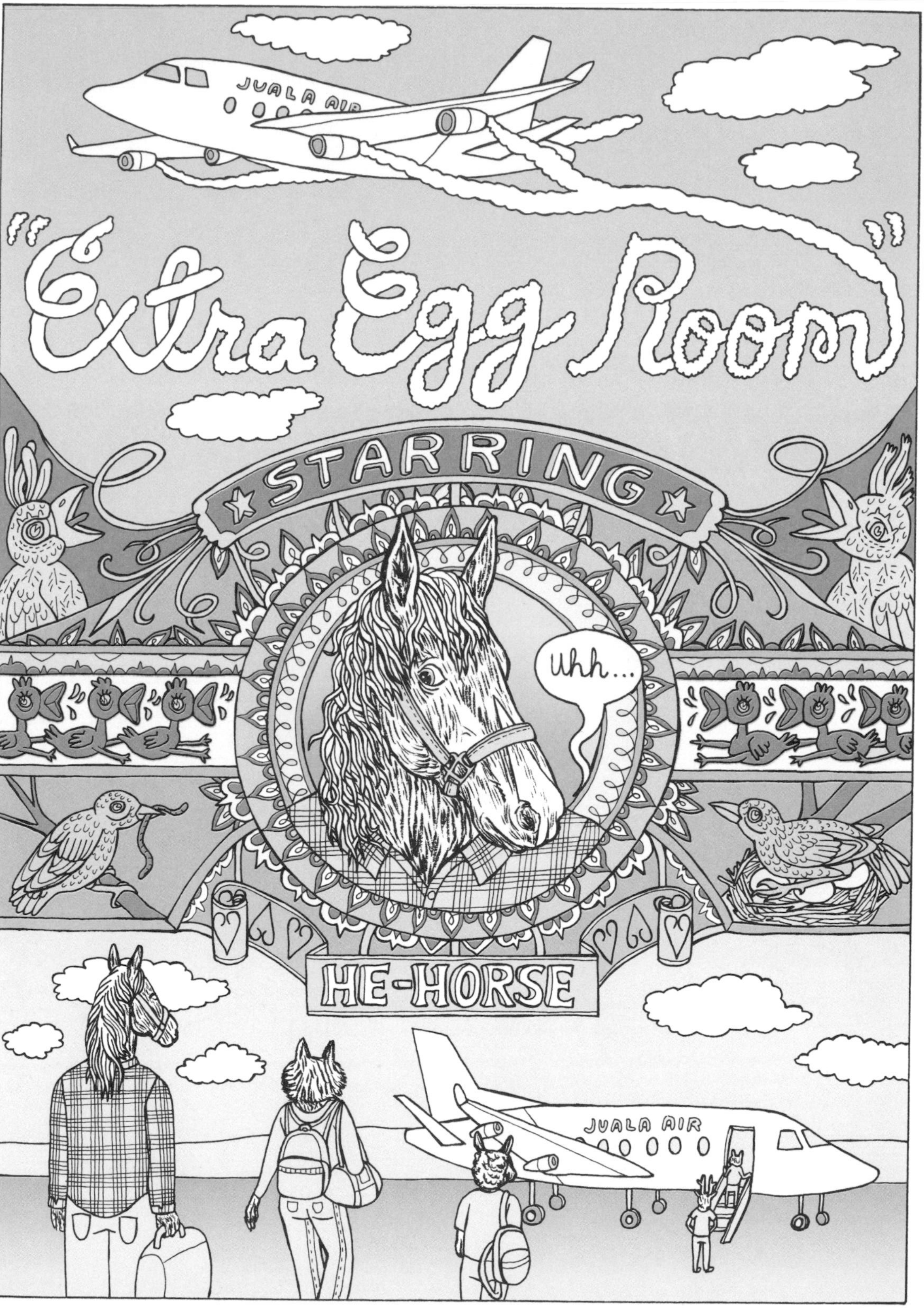
JUALA AIR
"Extra Egg Room"
STARRING
Uhh...
HE-HORSE
JUALA AIR

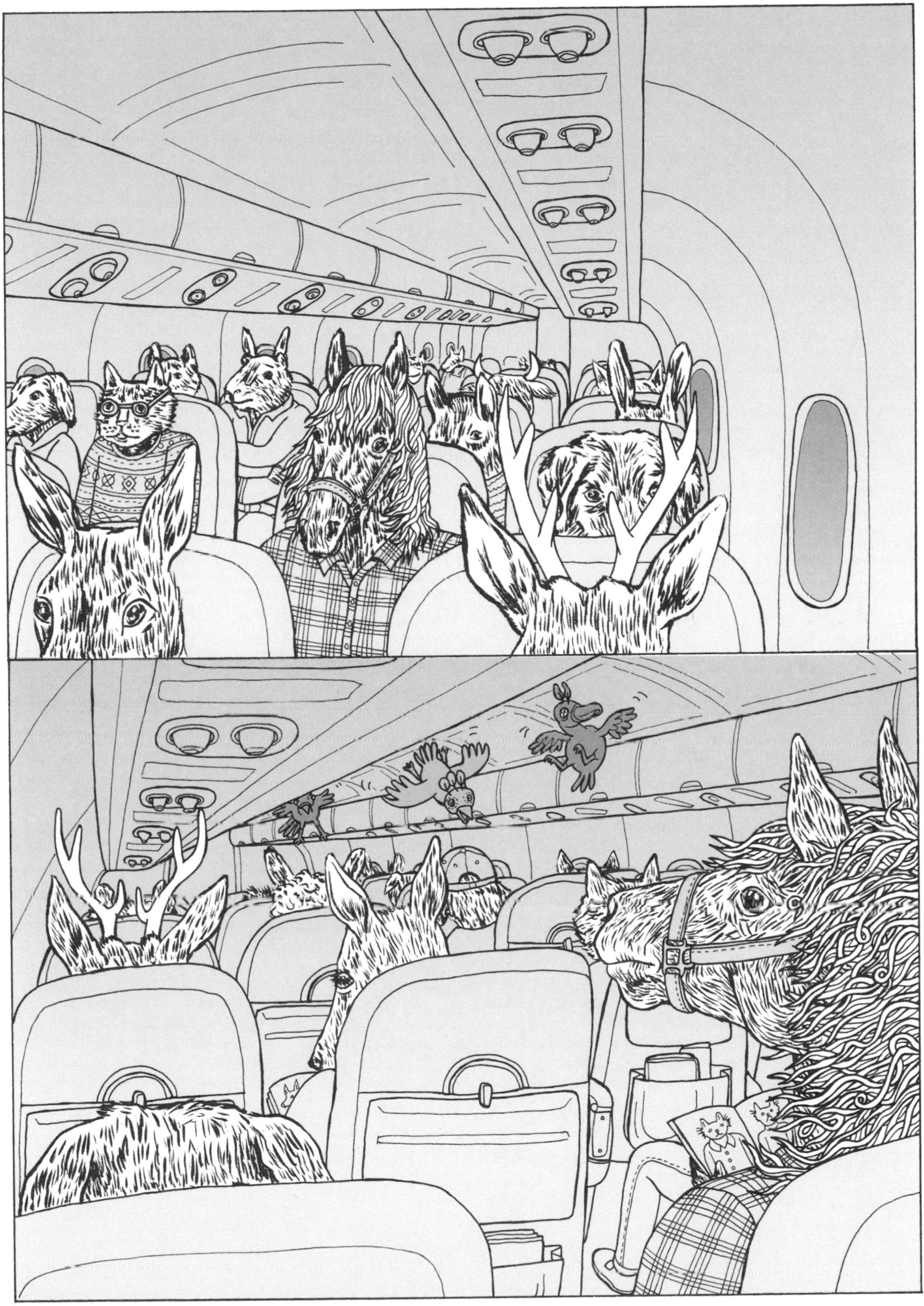

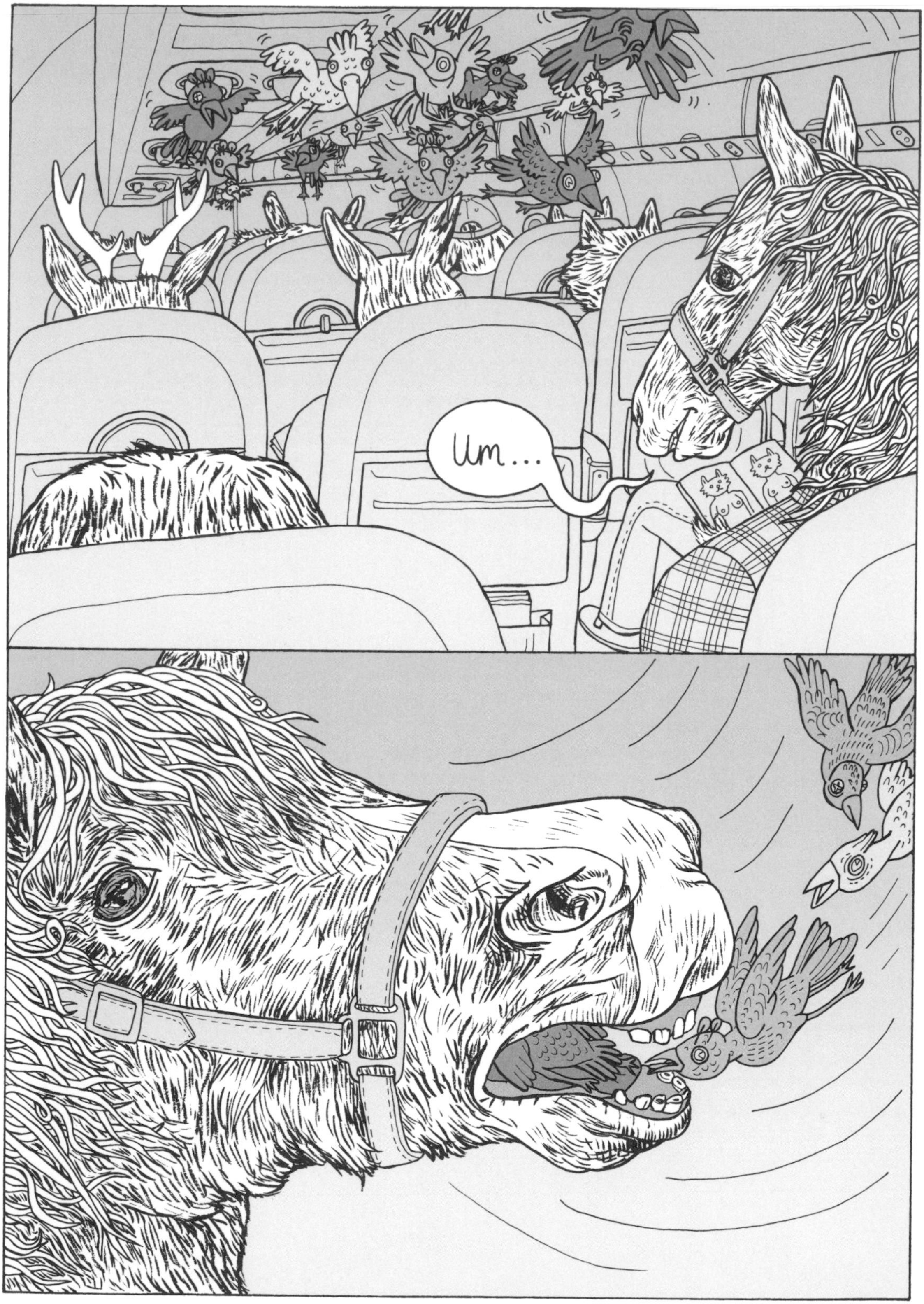
Um...

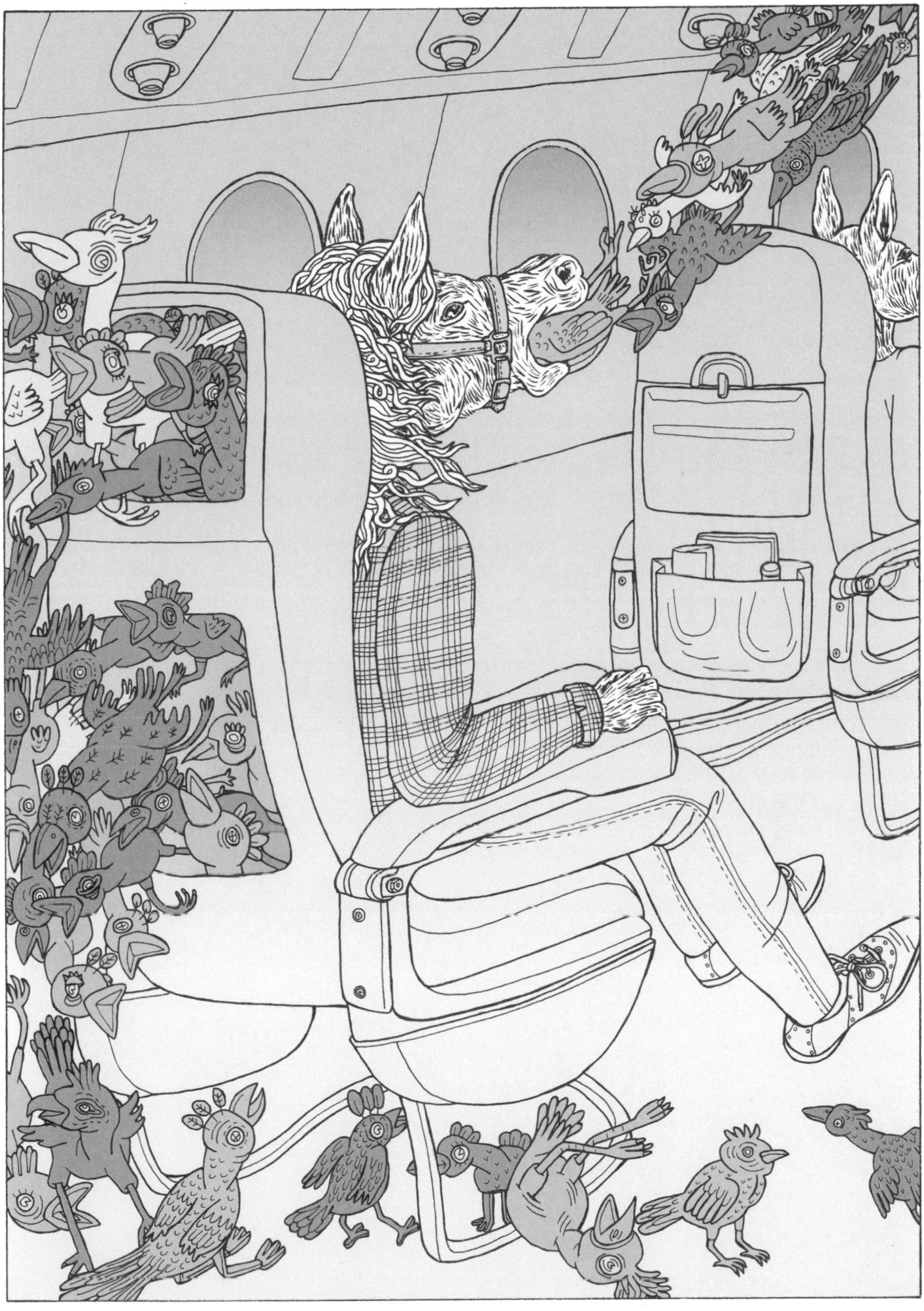

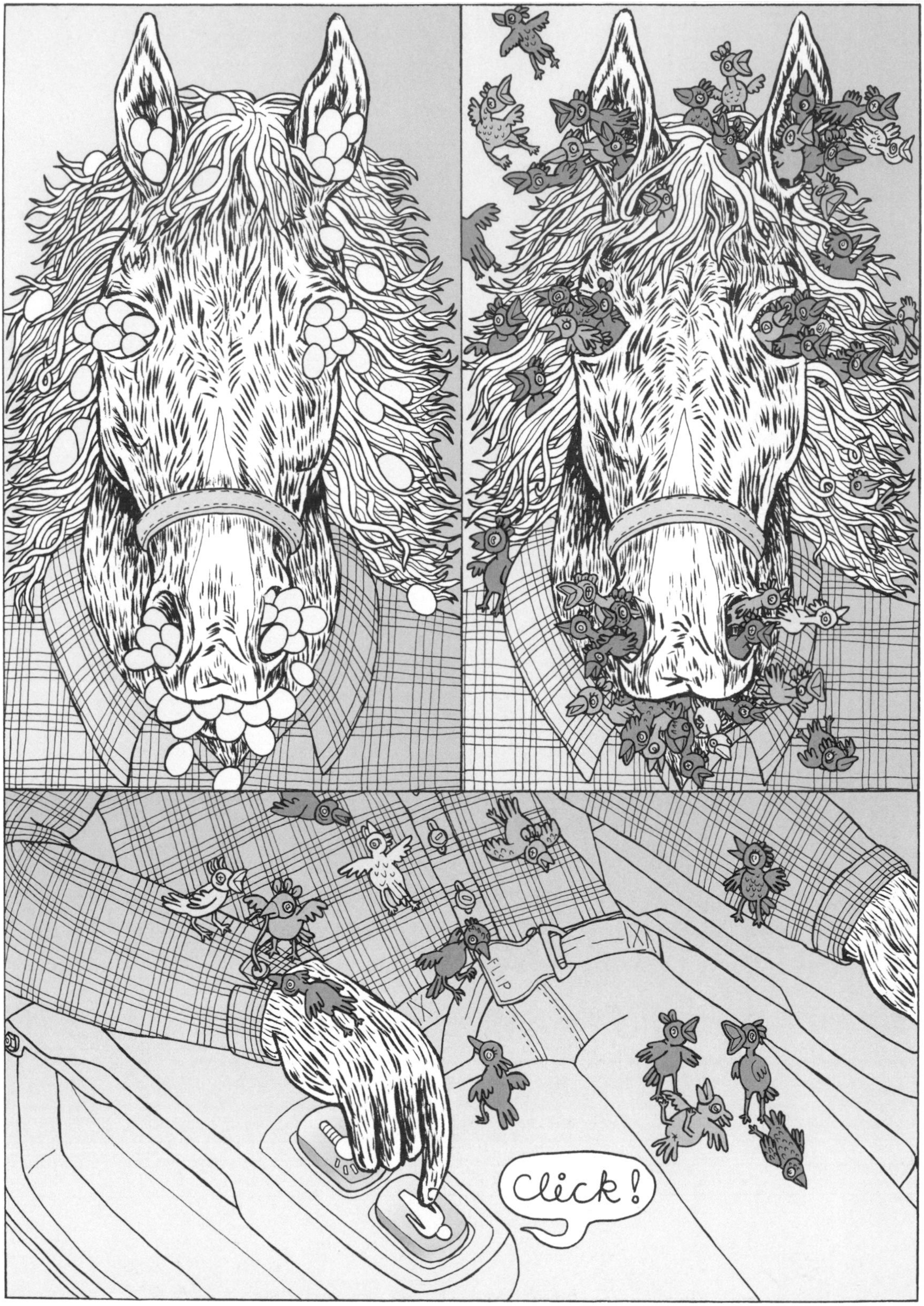
FLIP
Click!

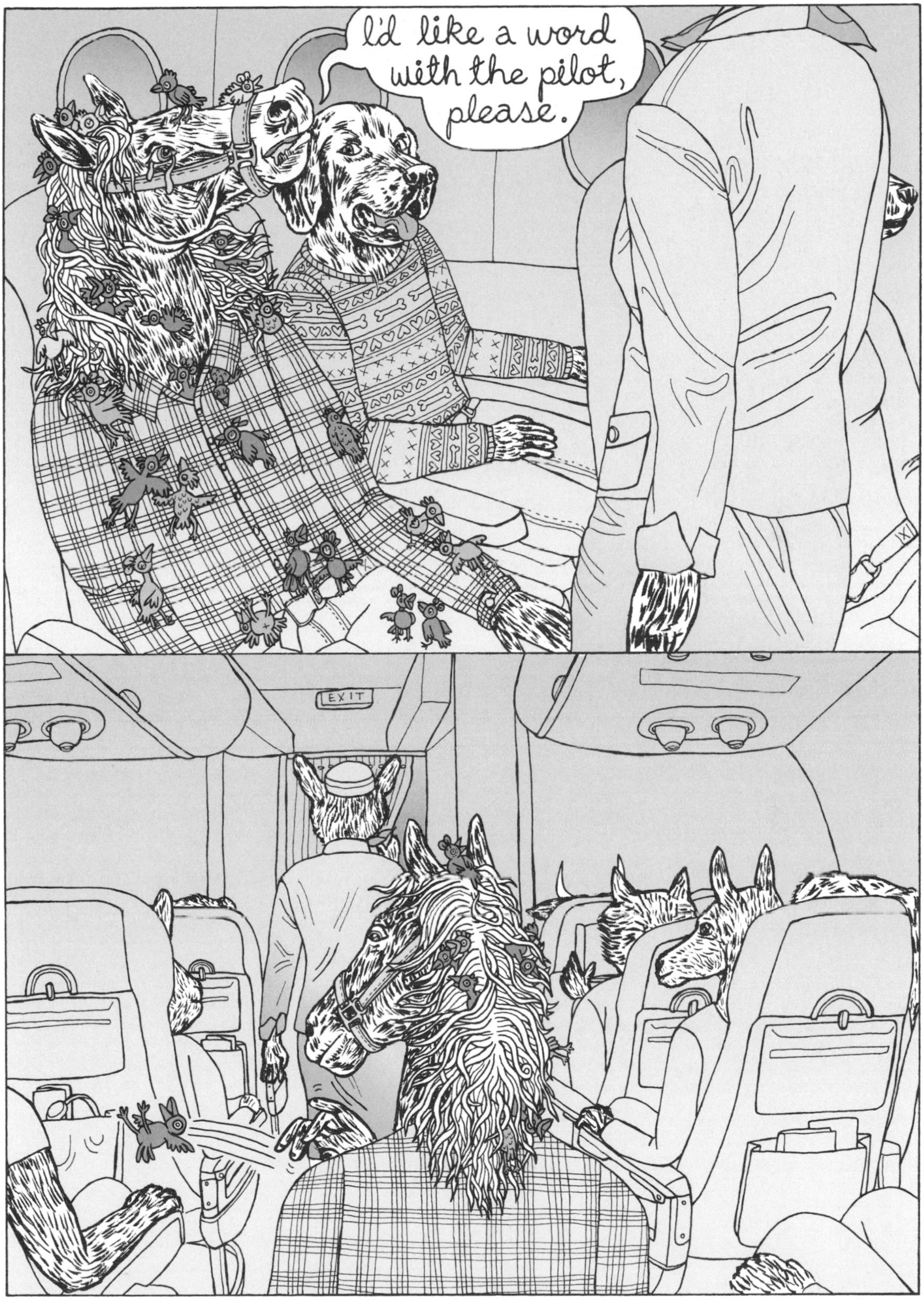
I'd like a word with the pilot, please.
EXIT

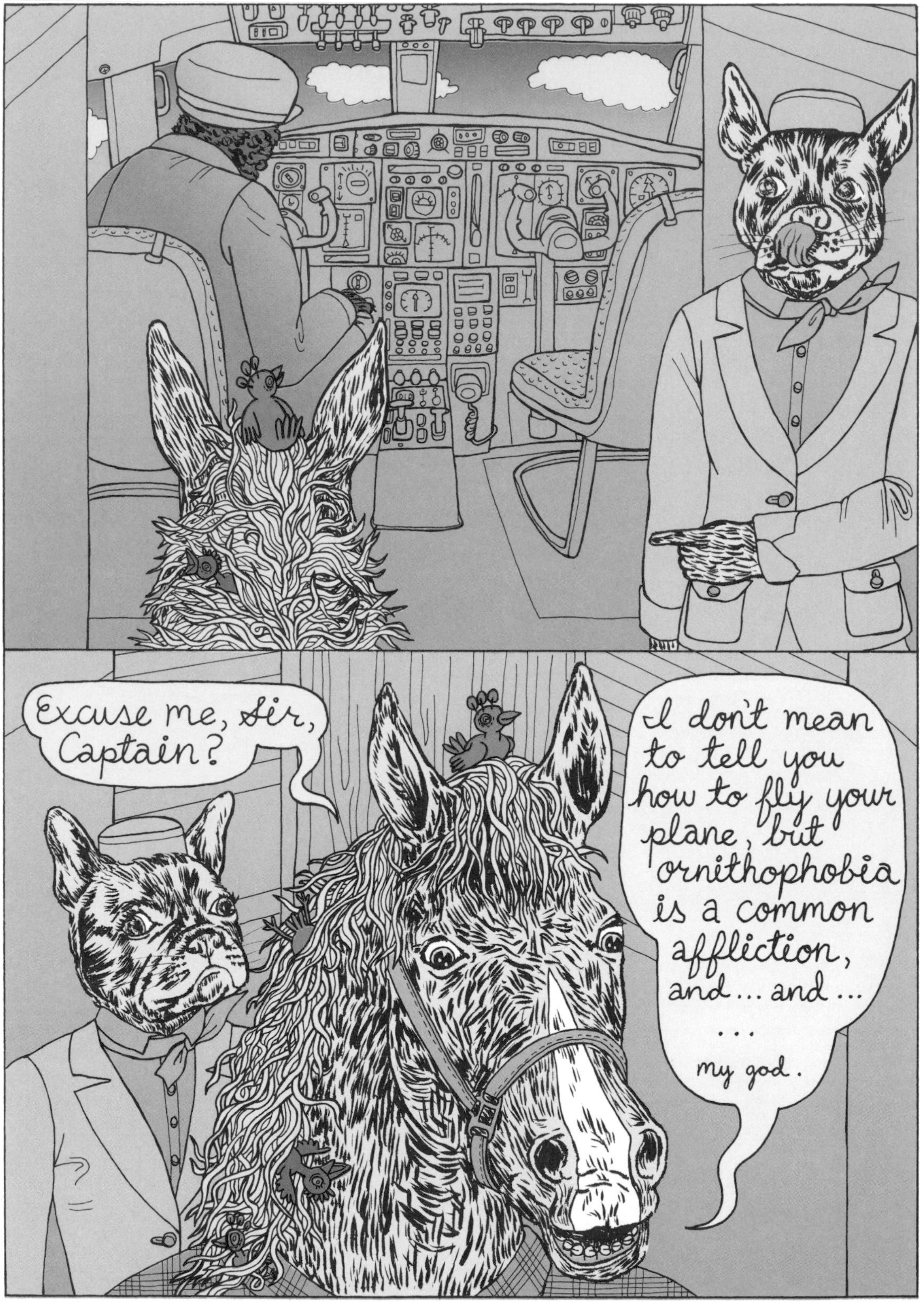
Excuse me, Sir, Captain?
I don't mean to tell you how to fly your plane, but ornithophobia is a common affliction, and... and... ... my god.

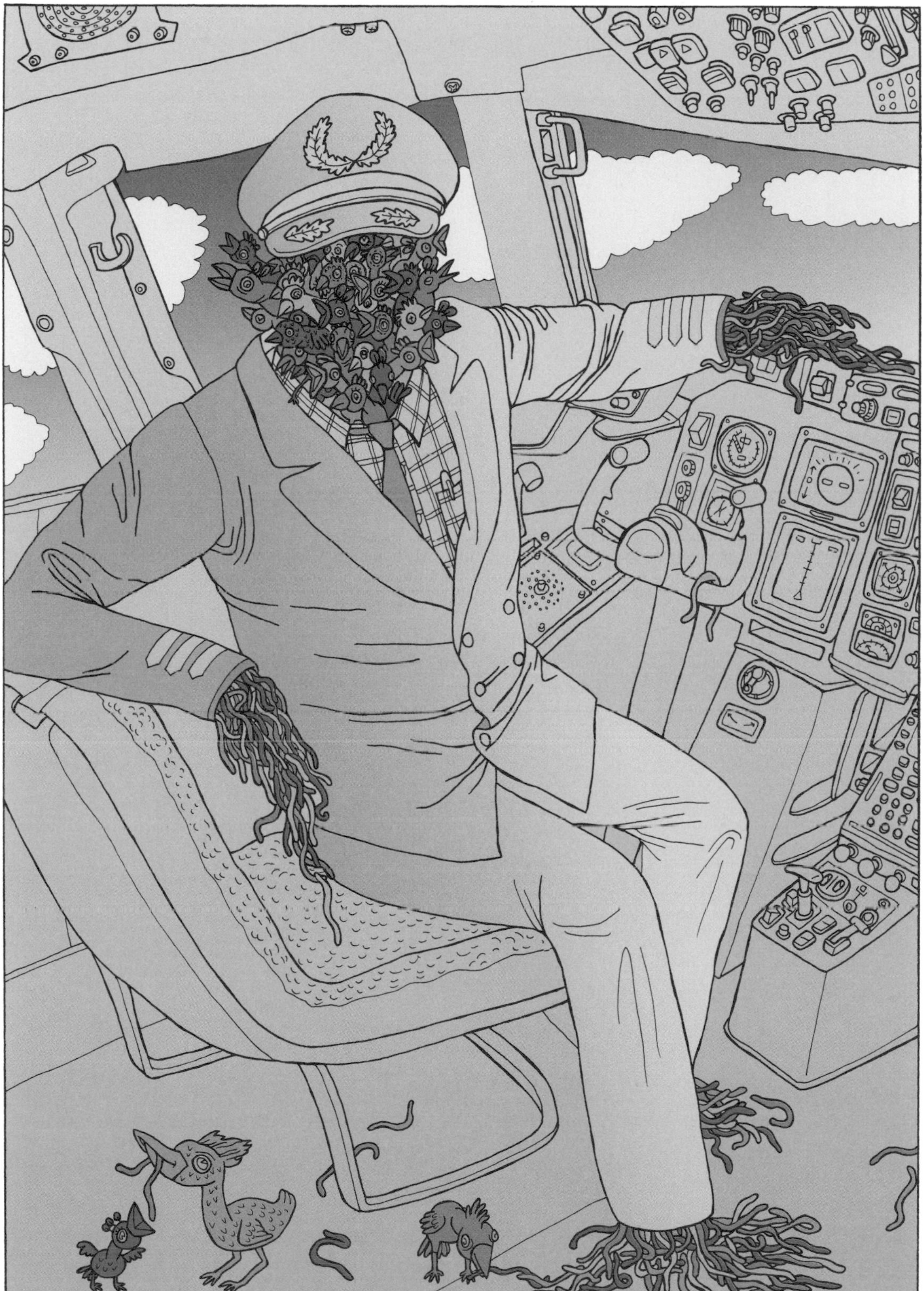

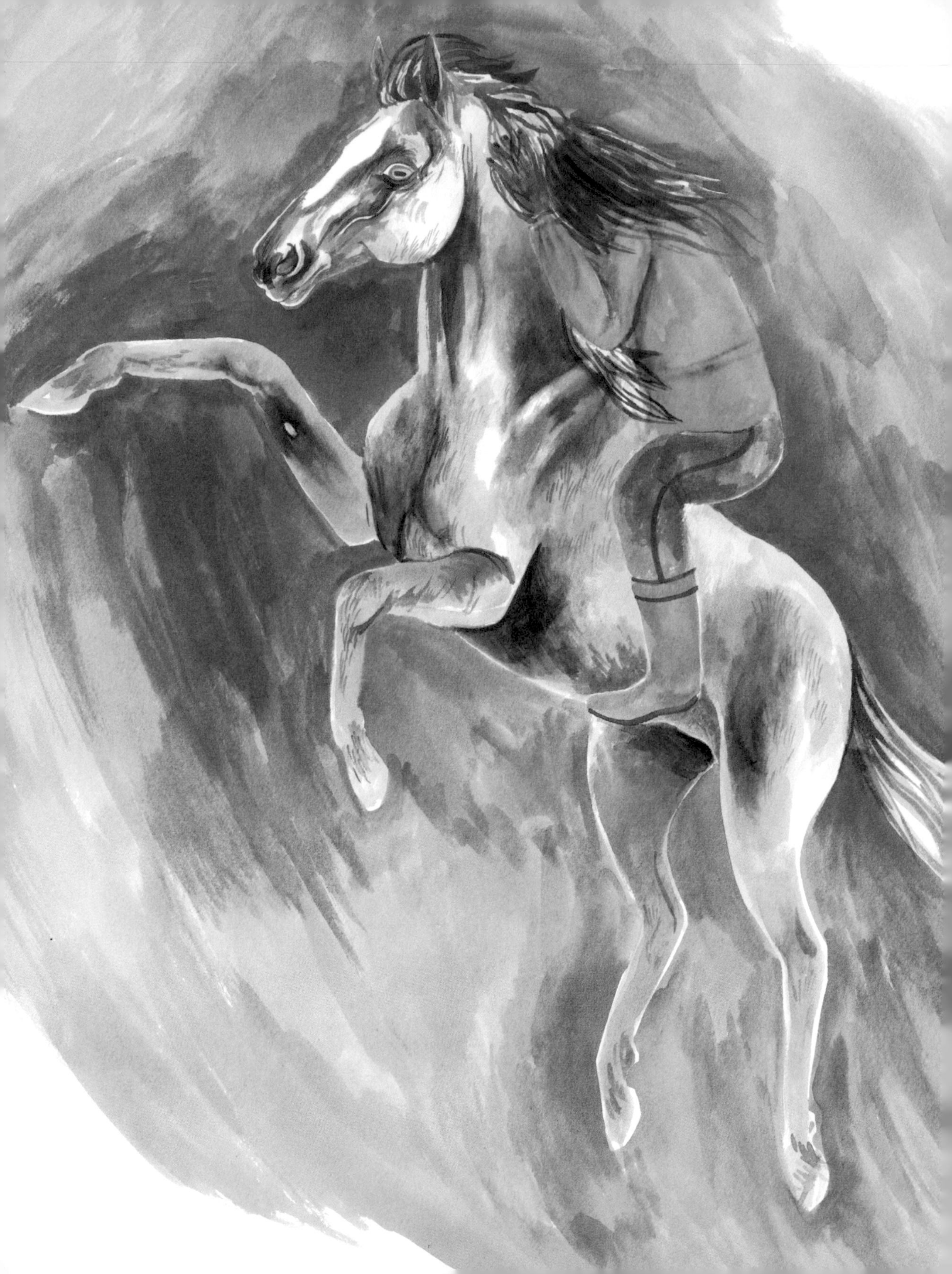

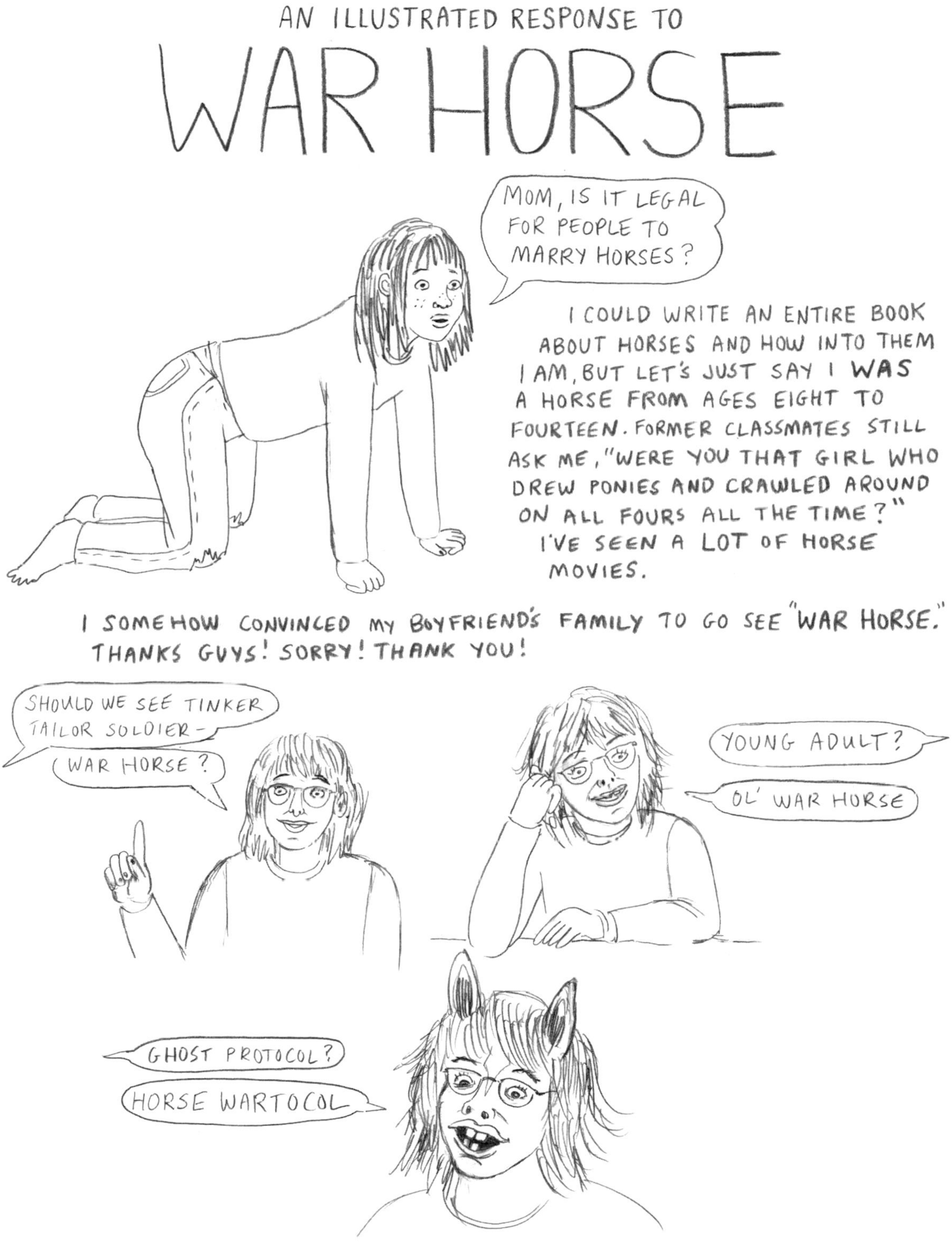
AN ILLUSTRATED RESPONSE TO
WAR HORSE
MOM, IS IT LEGAL FOR PEOPLE TO MARRY HORSES?
I COULD WRITE AN ENTIRE BOOK ABOUT HORSES AND HOW INTO THEM I AM, BUT LET'S JUST SAY I WAS A HORSE FROM AGES EIGHT TO FOURTEEN. FORMER CLASSMATES STILL ASK ME, "WERE YOU THAT GIRL WHO DREW PONIES AND CRAWLED AROUND ON ALL FOURS ALL THE TIME?" I'VE SEEN A LOT OF HORSE MOVIES.
I SOMEHOW CONVINCED MY BOYFRIEND'S FAMILY TO GO SEE "WAR HORSE." THANKS GUYS! SORRY! THANK YOU!
SHOULD WE SEE TINKER TAILOR SOLDIER-
WAR HORSE?
YOUNG ADULT?
OL' WAR HORSE
GHOST PROTOCOL?
HORSE WARTOCOL

REGARDLESS OF WHETHER THE MOVIE WAS GOOD OR BAD, I KNEW I'D ENJOY "BATTLE EQUINE" AS LONG AS THERE WERE ABUNDANT SHOTS OF SHINY HORSES GALLOPING THROUGH FIELDS. HERE'S MY REVIEW:

- SPIELBERG DOES US RIGHT AND STARTS OFF WITH NEWBORN COLT-FROLICKING.

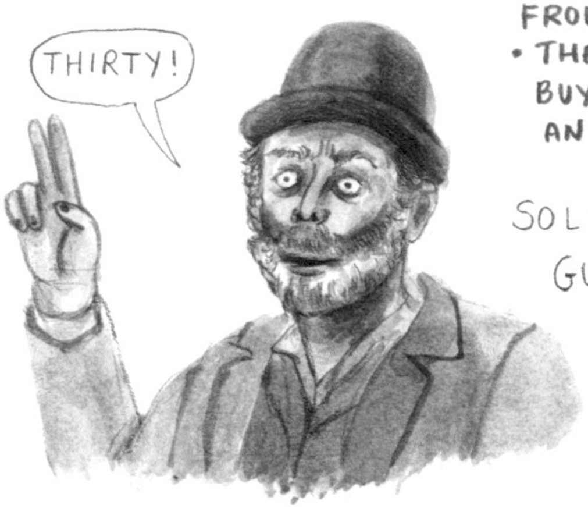
THIRTY!

- THE STORY GETS GOING WHEN AN OLD DRUNK BUYS WAR HORSE AT AN AUCTION. WHAT AND HOW MUCH IS A GUINEA?

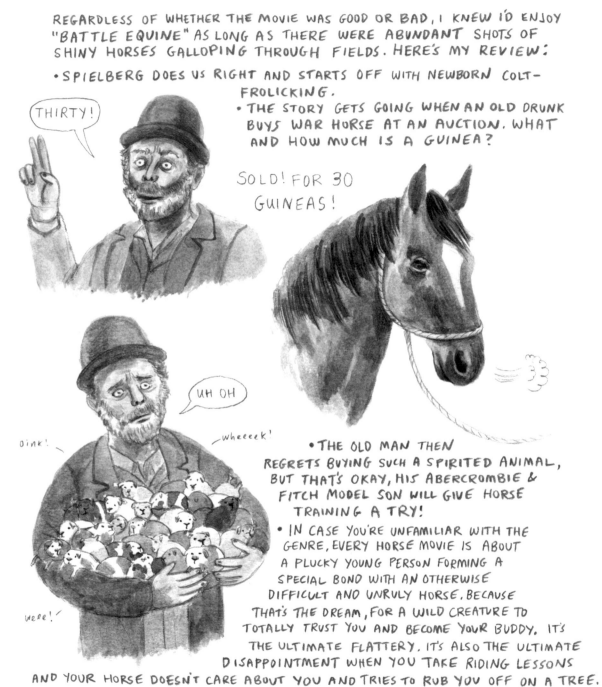

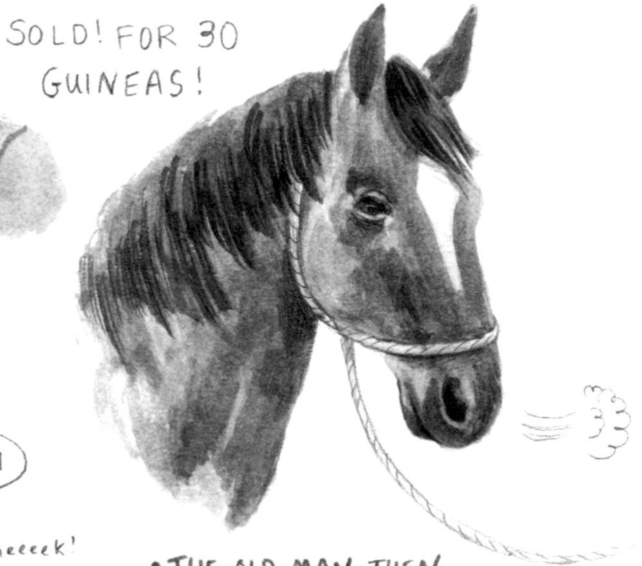
SOLD! FOR 30 GUINEAS!

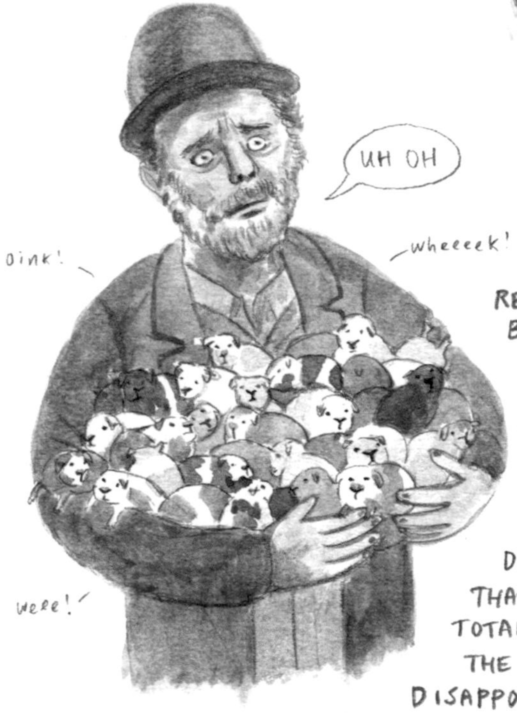
UH OH
oink!
wheeeek!
weee!

- THE OLD MAN THEN REGRETS BUYING SUCH A SPIRITED ANIMAL, BUT THAT'S OKAY, HIS ABERCROMBIE & FITCH MODEL SON WILL GIVE HORSE TRAINING A TRY!
- IN CASE YOU'RE UNFAMILIAR WITH THE GENRE, EVERY HORSE MOVIE IS ABOUT A PLUCKY YOUNG PERSON FORMING A SPECIAL BOND WITH AN OTHERWISE DIFFICULT AND UNRULY HORSE. BECAUSE THAT'S THE DREAM, FOR A WILD CREATURE TO TOTALLY TRUST YOU AND BECOME YOUR BUDDY. IT'S THE ULTIMATE FLATTERY. IT'S ALSO THE ULTIMATE DISAPPOINTMENT WHEN YOU TAKE RIDING LESSONS AND YOUR HORSE DOESN'T CARE ABOUT YOU AND TRIES TO RUB YOU OFF ON A TREE.
- IT'S LAME THEY NAMED HIM "JOEY" INSTEAD OF "WAR HORSE." COULDN'T THEY HAVE AT LEAST CHOSEN SOMETHING MORE HORSEY, LIKE "JOEY ME THE MO'HAY"?

• I'M ALSO BUMMED THAT WAR HORSE ISN'T MORE BAD-ASS AND THIS ISN'T A HORSE VERSION OF "RISE OF THE PLANET OF THE APES."

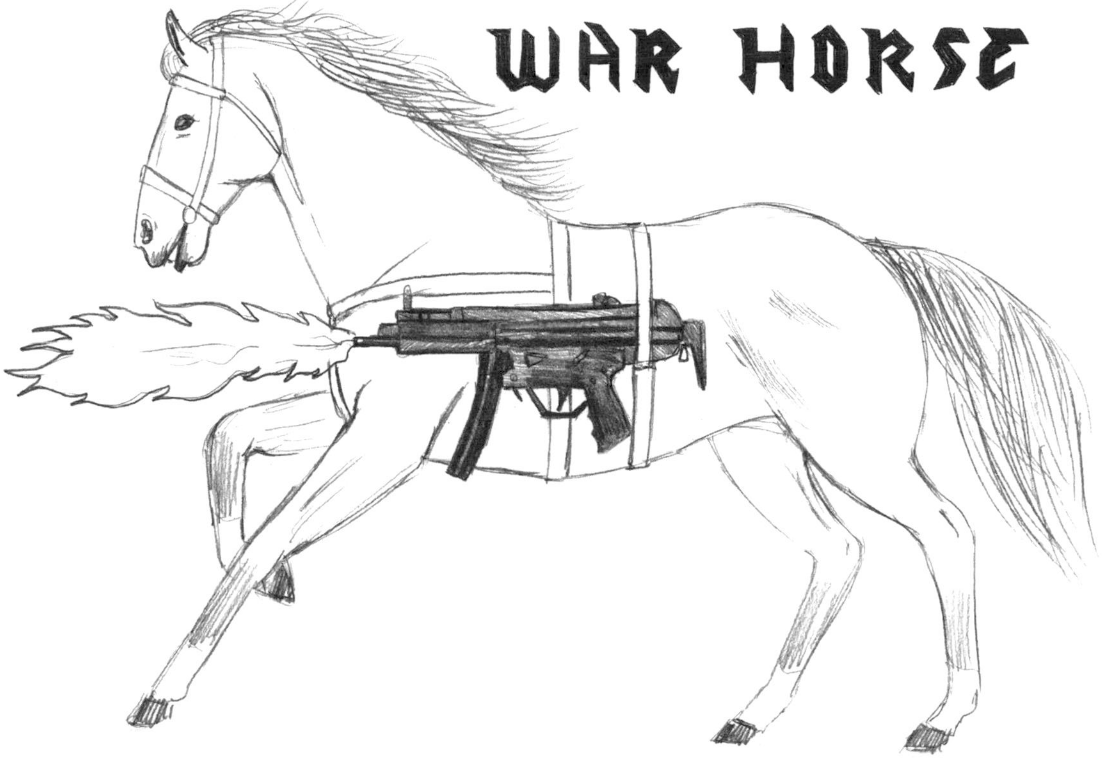
WAR HORSE

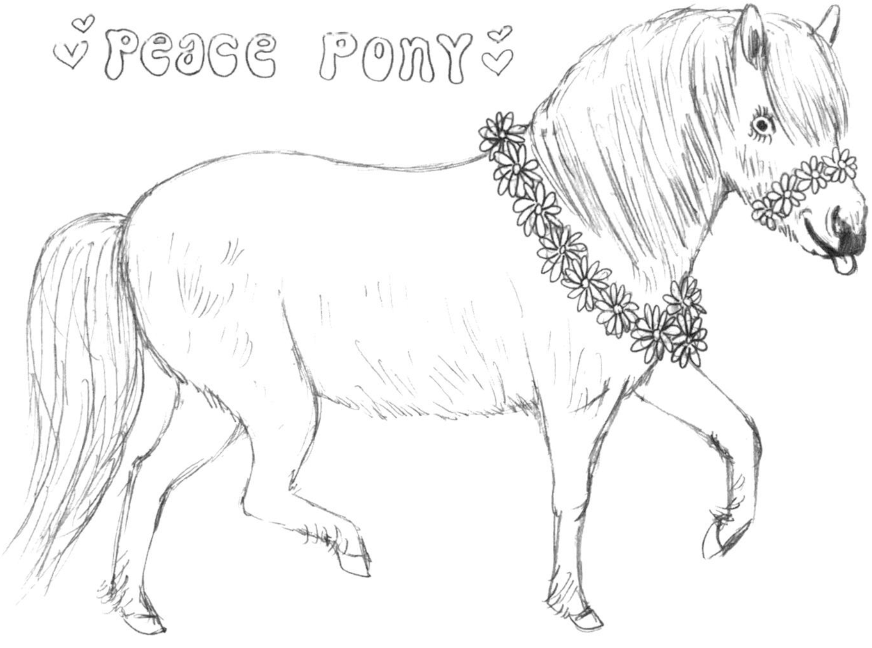
peace pony

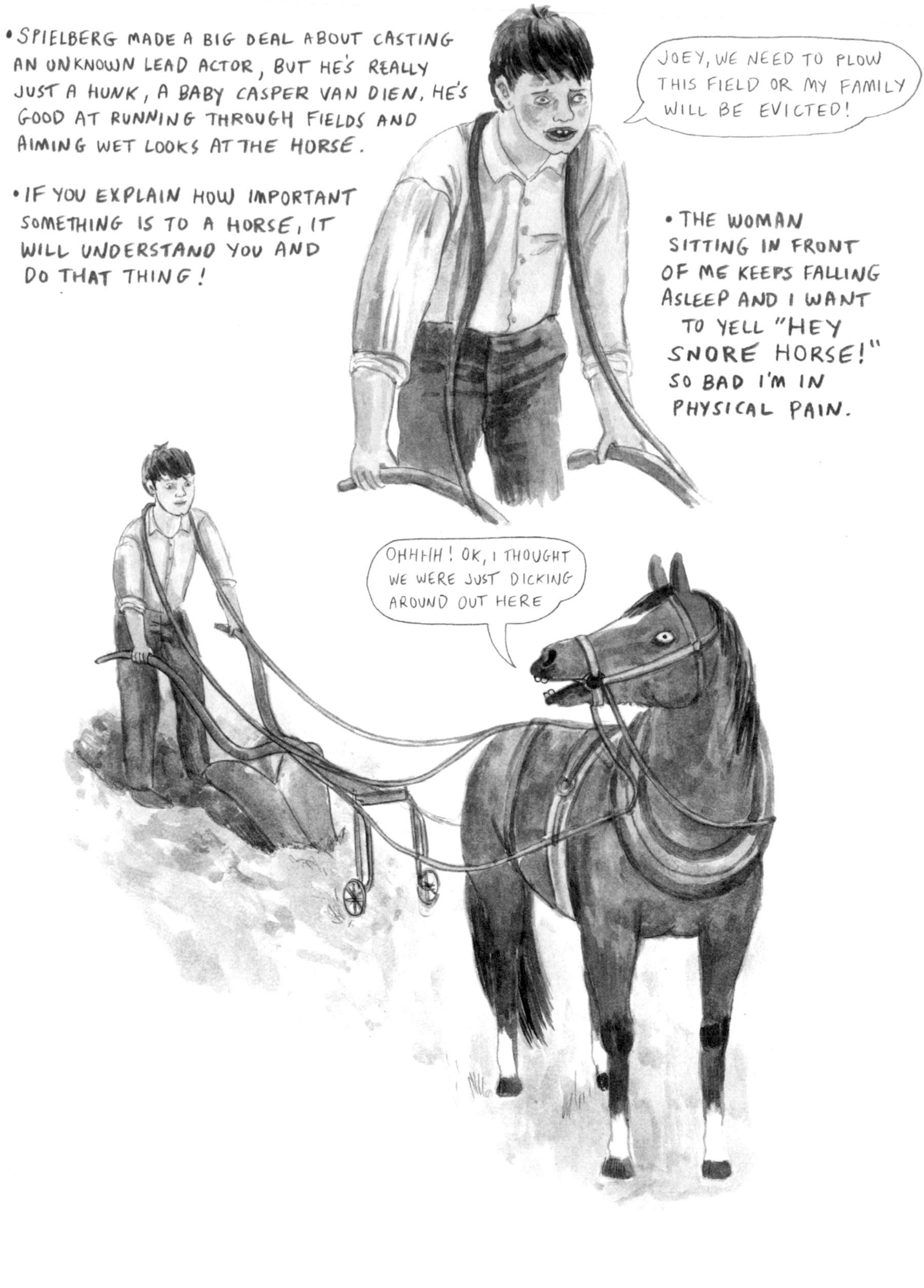
• SPIELBERG MADE A BIG DEAL ABOUT CASTING AN UNKNOWN LEAD ACTOR, BUT HE'S REALLY JUST A HUNK, A BABY CASPER VAN DIEN. HE'S GOOD AT RUNNING THROUGH FIELDS AND AIMING WET LOOKS AT THE HORSE.
JOEY, WE NEED TO PLOW THIS FIELD OR MY FAMILY WILL BE EVICTED!
• IF YOU EXPLAIN HOW IMPORTANT SOMETHING IS TO A HORSE, IT WILL UNDERSTAND YOU AND DO THAT THING!
• THE WOMAN SITTING IN FRONT OF ME KEEPS FALLING ASLEEP AND I WANT TO YELL "HEY SNORE HORSE!" SO BAD I'M IN PHYSICAL PAIN.
OHHHH! OK, I THOUGHT WE WERE JUST DICKING AROUND OUT HERE

• GOOSE! THERE'S A GOOSE THAT KEEPS CHASING AND CHOMPING PEOPLE AND SHOWING UP IN SCENES RANDOMLY. IT HAS MORE CHARISMA THAN ANYTHING ELSE IN THE MOVIE. GOOSE FOR BEST ACTOR!

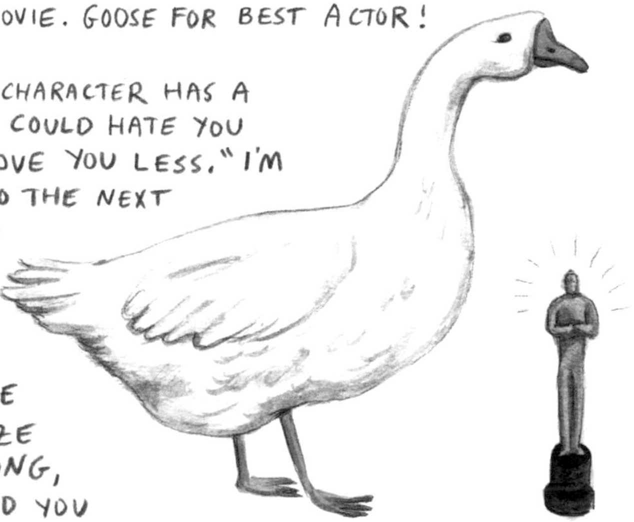

• OOH EMILY WATSON'S CHARACTER HAS A REALLY GOOD LINE: "I COULD HATE YOU MORE, BUT I COULDN'T LOVE YOU LESS." I'M TOTALLY SAYING THAT TO THE NEXT FRIEND TO FART IN MY PRESENCE.

• HORSES' FACES ARE EXPRESSIONLESS FOR THE MOST PART; THEY GAZE AT YOU OVER THOSE LONG, BEAUTIFUL NOSES AND YOU DON'T KNOW WHAT THEY'RE THINKING. I ASSUME THEY'RE PONDERING CARROTS AND WAYS TO DESTROY MANKIND, BUT WHO KNOWS?

• FOR MY COLLEGE SCULPTURE CLASS I MADE A PAIR OF CERAMIC HORSE HEADS, AND MY PROFESSOR GOT SUPER WORKED UP OVER HOW STRANGE AND ENIGMATIC HORSES ARE. AT ONE POINT SHE KEPT LOUDLY REPEATING: "WHAT IS IT ABOUT THEIR FACES? WHAT IS IT ABOUT THE FACE?!" WHILE ALL THE STUDENTS STARED BACK AT HER, STUNNED. WHAT IS IT ABOUT THE FACE?

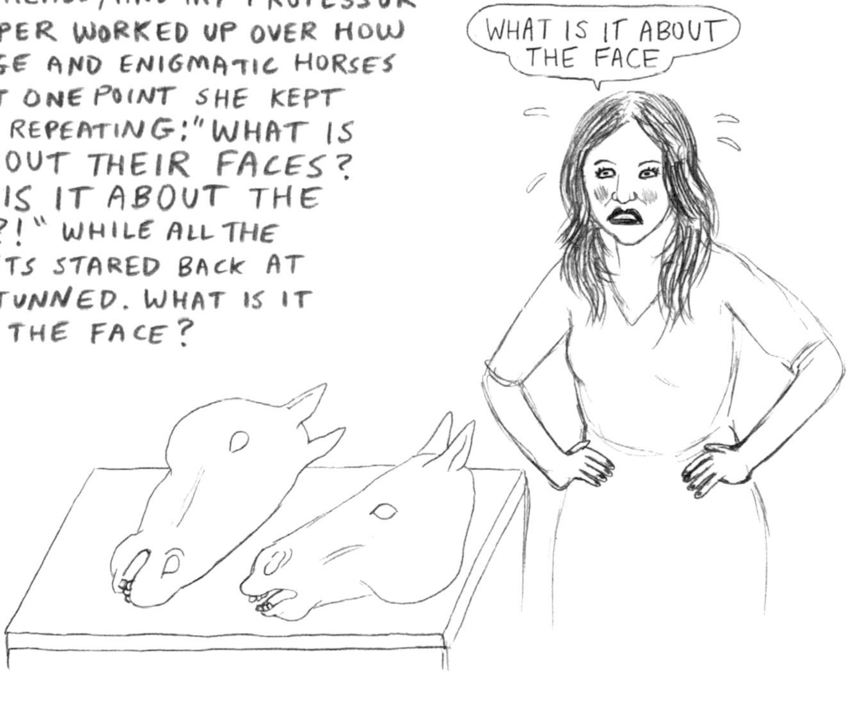
WHAT IS IT ABOUT THE FACE

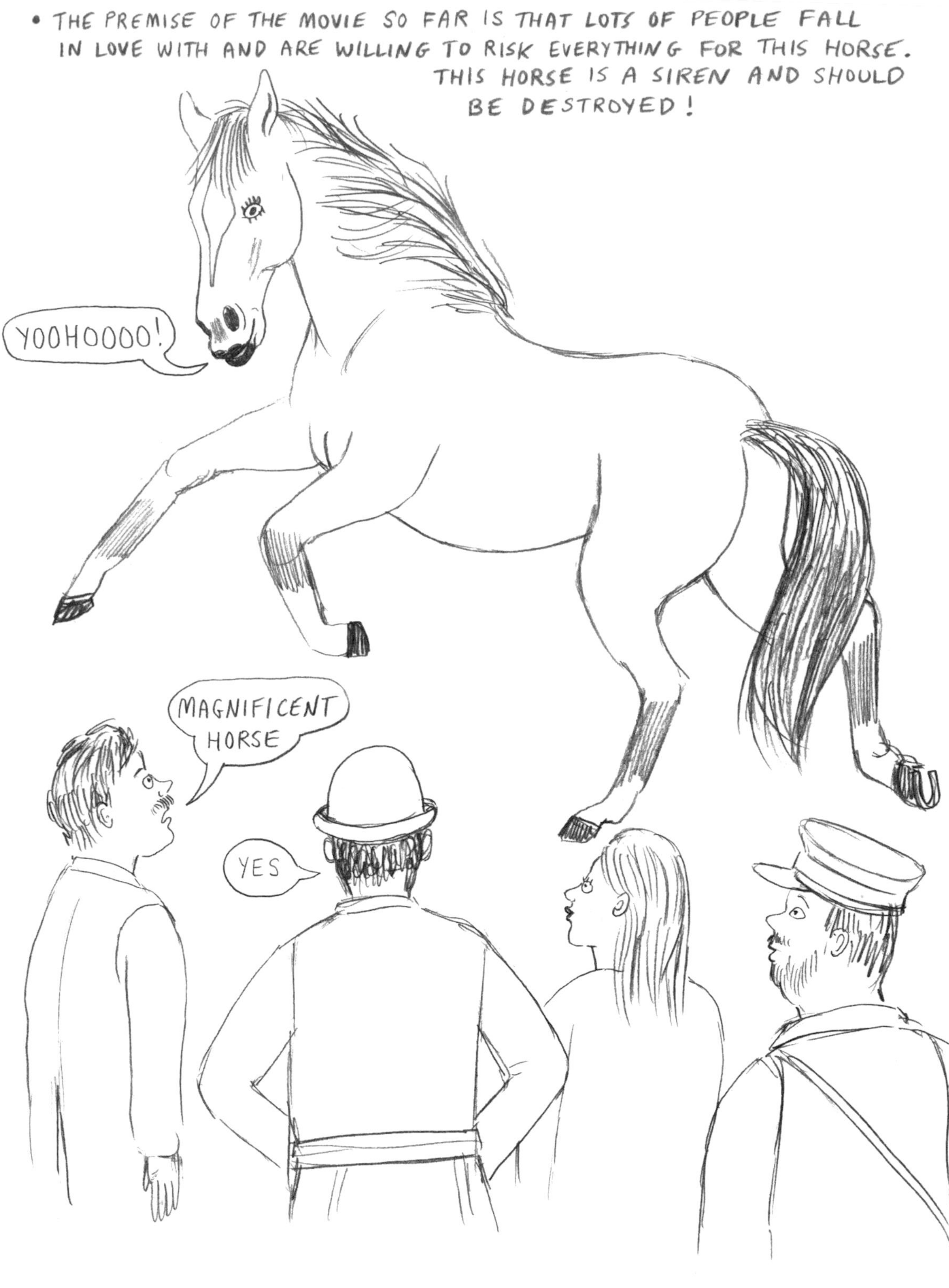
• THE PREMISE OF THE MOVIE SO FAR IS THAT LOTS OF PEOPLE FALL IN LOVE WITH AND ARE WILLING TO RISK EVERYTHING FOR THIS HORSE.
THIS HORSE IS A SIREN AND SHOULD BE DESTROYED!
YOOHOOOO!
MAGNIFICENT HORSE
YES

• BENEDICT CUMBERBATCH ONLY APPEARS ONSCREEN FOR A SECOND, BUT IT'S WORTH MENTIONING BECAUSE HE'S BENEDICT CUMBERBATCH.

• SOMETIMES WHEN I'M RIDING IN A CAR, I LOOK OUT THE WINDOW AND IMAGINE I'M RIDING A HORSE RUNNING ALONGSIDE THE ROAD AND WE'RE JUMPING OVER FENCES, MAIL BOXES, CUMBERBATCHES, AND STUFF.

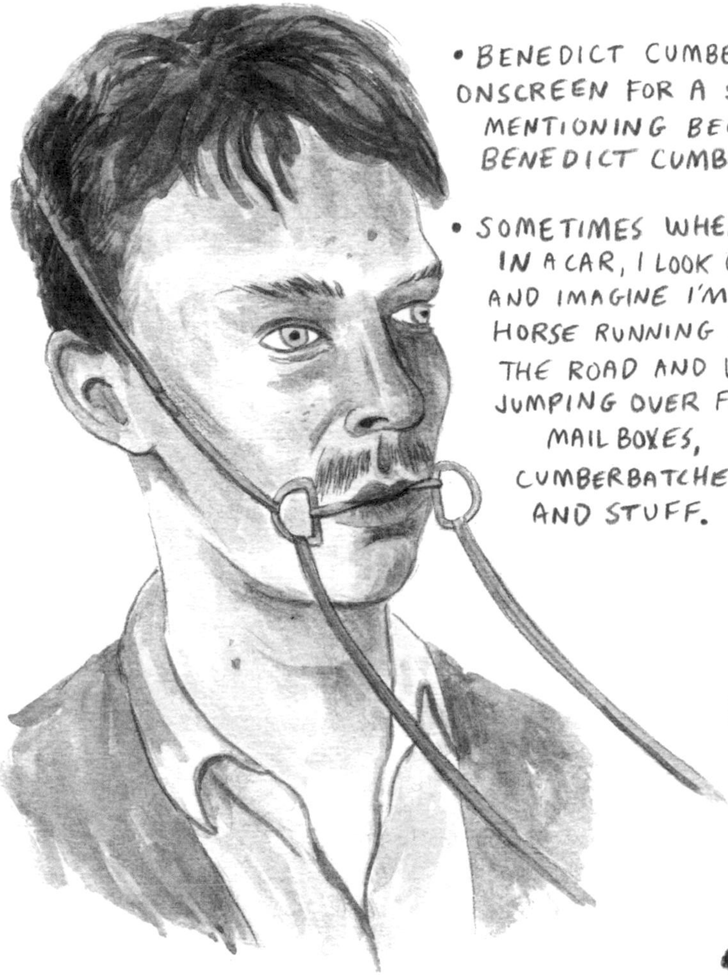

B. CUMBERBATCH

• AND ALSO SOMETIMES WHEN I'M JOGGING, I PRETEND I'M A HORSE, AND THEN IF I'M REALLY IN THE GROOVE, I MAKE QUIET RHYTHMIC CLUCKING NOISES TO MYSELF SO I'M ALSO THE RIDER? I'M RIDING MYSELF?

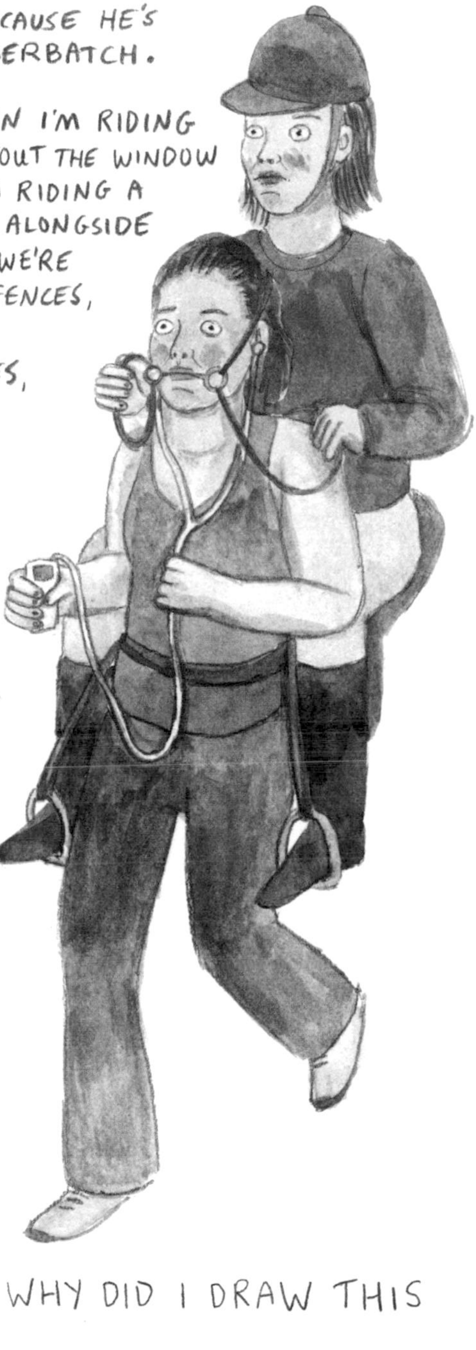

WHY DID I DRAW THIS

- I'M GLAD WAR HORSE DOESN'T TALK OUT LOUD OR HAVE THOUGHTS.
- SPIELBERG HAS SOME CLEVER WAYS OF HIDING THE CARNAGE OF WAR; WE SEE RIDERLESS HORSES JUMPING OVER CANNONS, THE SAILS OF A WINDMILL CONCEAL AN EXECUTION, ETC. IT'S A NON-GORE-HORSE APPROACH TO VIOLENCE.
- THE SOLDIERS' HORSES ARE MARCHING AGAINST THE BACKDROP OF A FIREY SUNSET AND ONE OF THEM IS POOPING! I SEE THE SILHOUETTES OF POOPS!

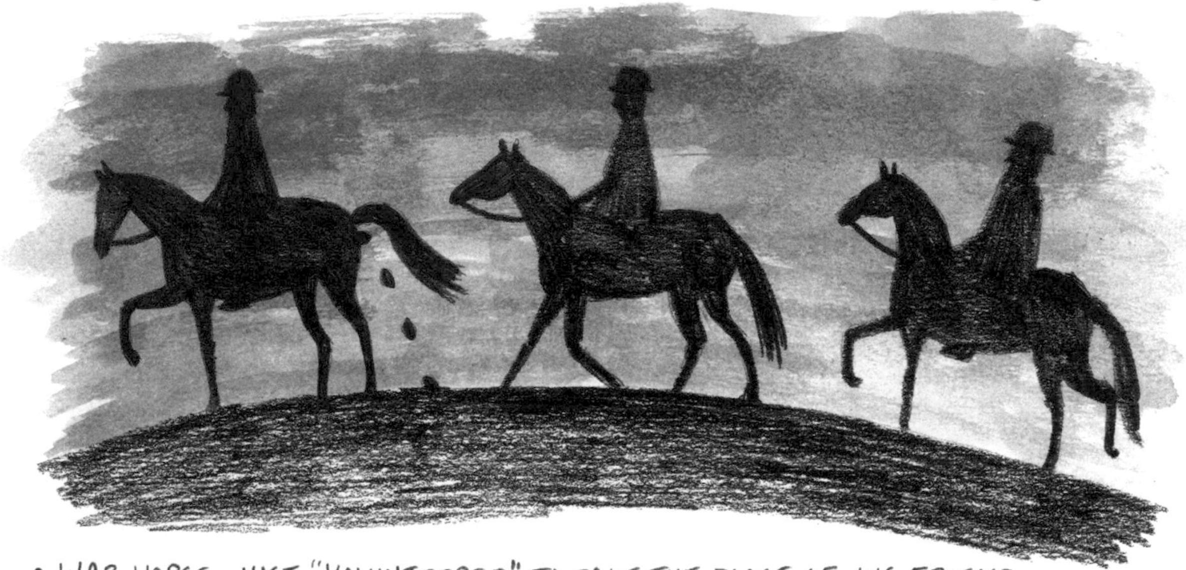

- WAR HORSE JUST "VOLUNTEERED" TO TAKE THE PLACE OF HIS FRIEND, WHO IN WAR HORSE'S OPINION WAS TOO SICK TO PULL A WAGON. DO HORSES HAVE THE ABILITY TO VOLUNTEER?
- I'M ALMOST CERTAIN THAT HORSES ONLY VOLUNTEER TO DO THEIR FAVORITE THINGS.

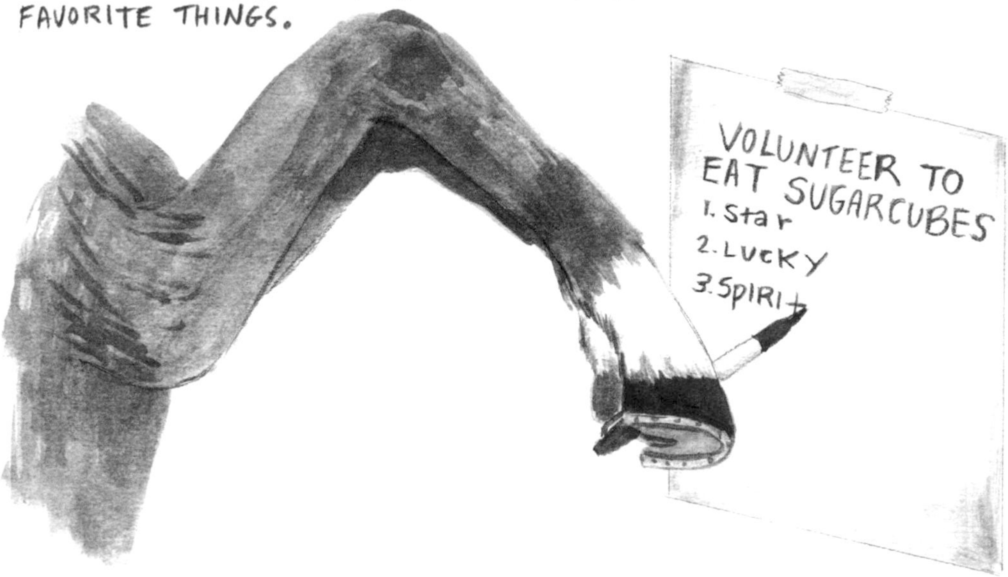
VOLUNTEER TO EAT SUGARCUBES
1. Star
2. Lucky
3. Spirit

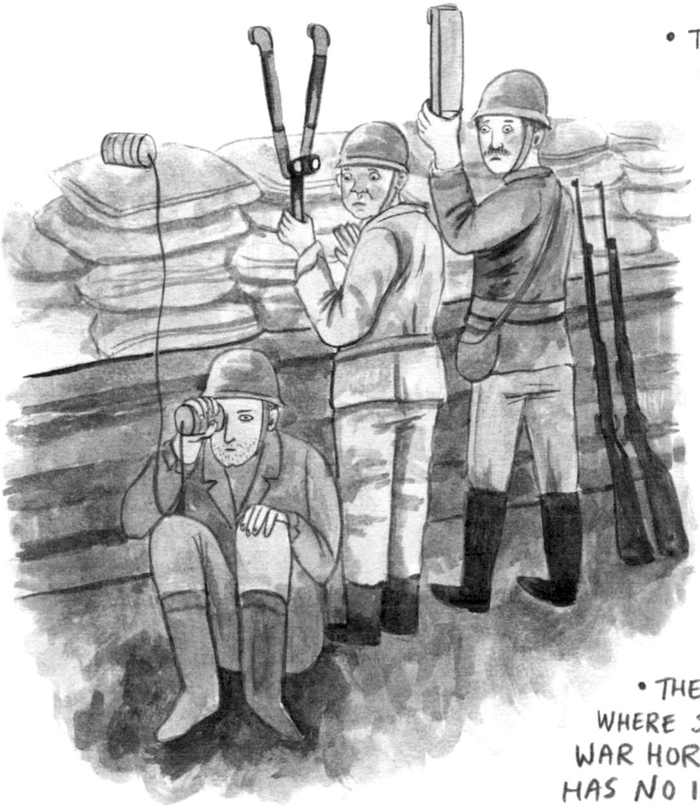

• THE OTHER HORSE JUST DIED!! OH NO, I'M CRYING, SHIT, SHIT, I'VE GOT FEELINGS DIARRHEA!

• OKAY, BUT THE SADDEST PART IS FOLLOWED BY THE BEST SCENE: WAR HORSE FACES OFF WITH A TANK, THEN GALLOPS THROUGH NO MAN'S LAND, LEAPING IN AND OUT AND OVER TRENCHES BEFORE GETTING TANGLED IN BARBED WIRE. I TRY TO START AN AUDIENCE CHANT, WAR HORSE WAR HORSE!, BUT IT DOESN'T CATCH ON.

• THE SOLDIERS ARE USING SO MANY DIFFERENT STYLES OF PERISCOPE! GOOD JOB, PROP MASTER.

• THERE ARE AT LEAST THREE SCENES WHERE SOMEBODY IS ABOUT TO SHOOT WAR HORSE FOR NO REASON, AND HE HAS NO IDEA! BECAUSE HE'S A HORSE.

• IN CONCLUSION: THIS IS A STANDARD HORSE FILM ABOUT PROJECTING HUMAN IDEALS, EMOTIONS, AND SYMBOLISM ONTO ANIMALS, WITH A DECENT WAR MOVIE SANDWICHED IN THE MIDDLE. THERE ARE ABOUT FOUR "PRETTY HORSEY RUNS REALLY FAST" SCENES, SO I GIVE IT 4-OUT-OF-5 HORSESHOES!

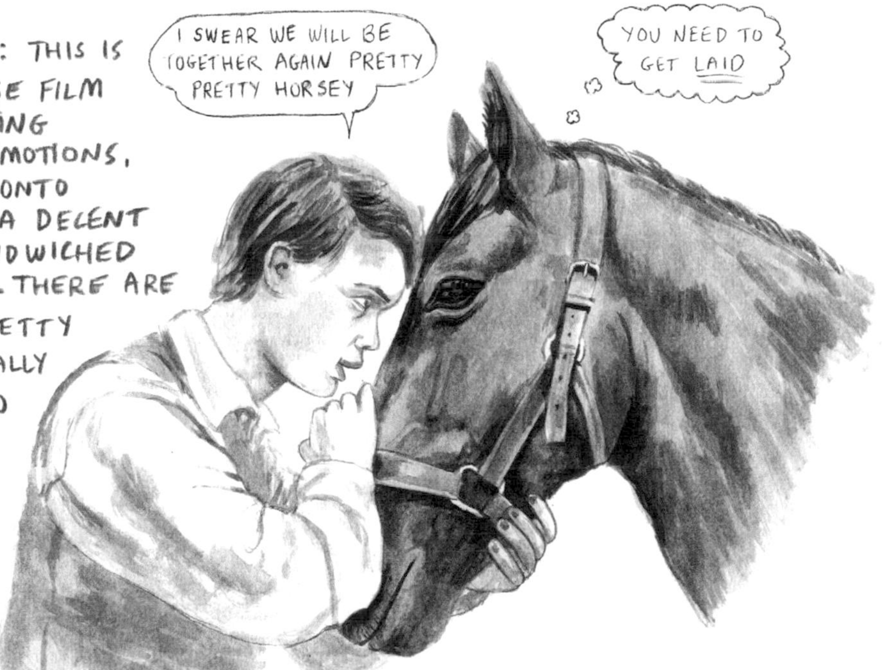
I SWEAR WE WILL BE TOGETHER AGAIN PRETTY PRETTY HORSEY
YOU NEED TO GET LAID

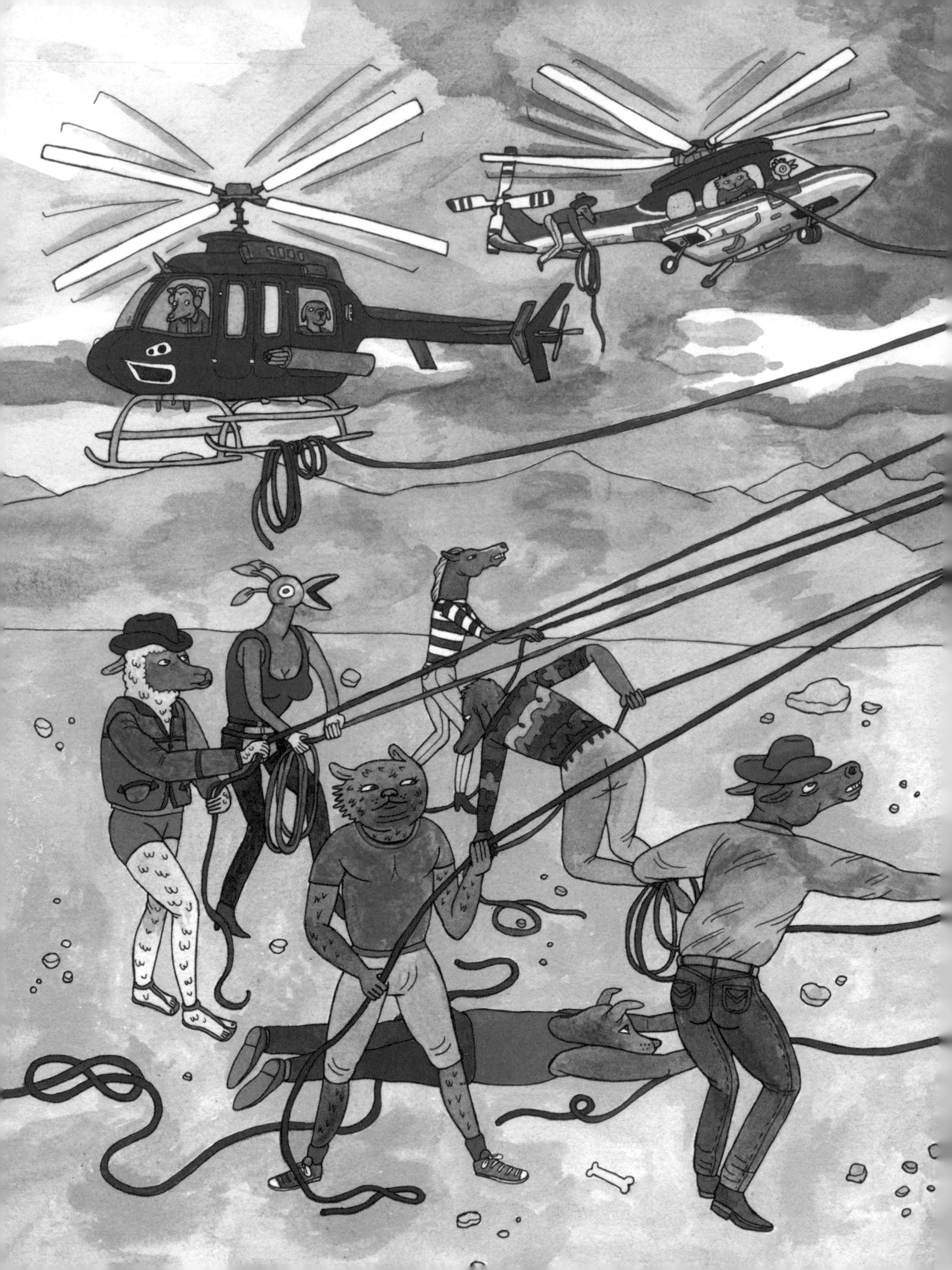

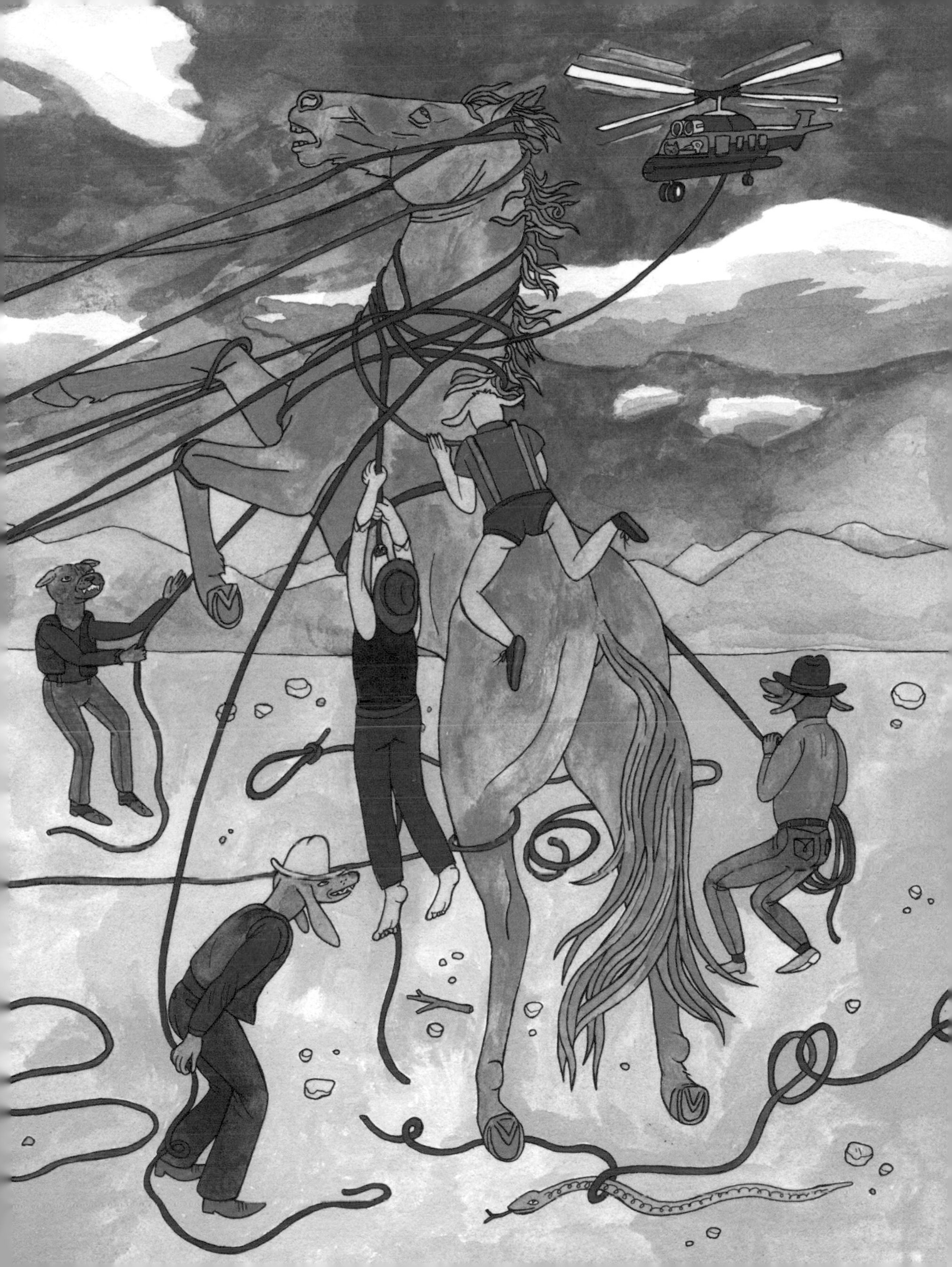

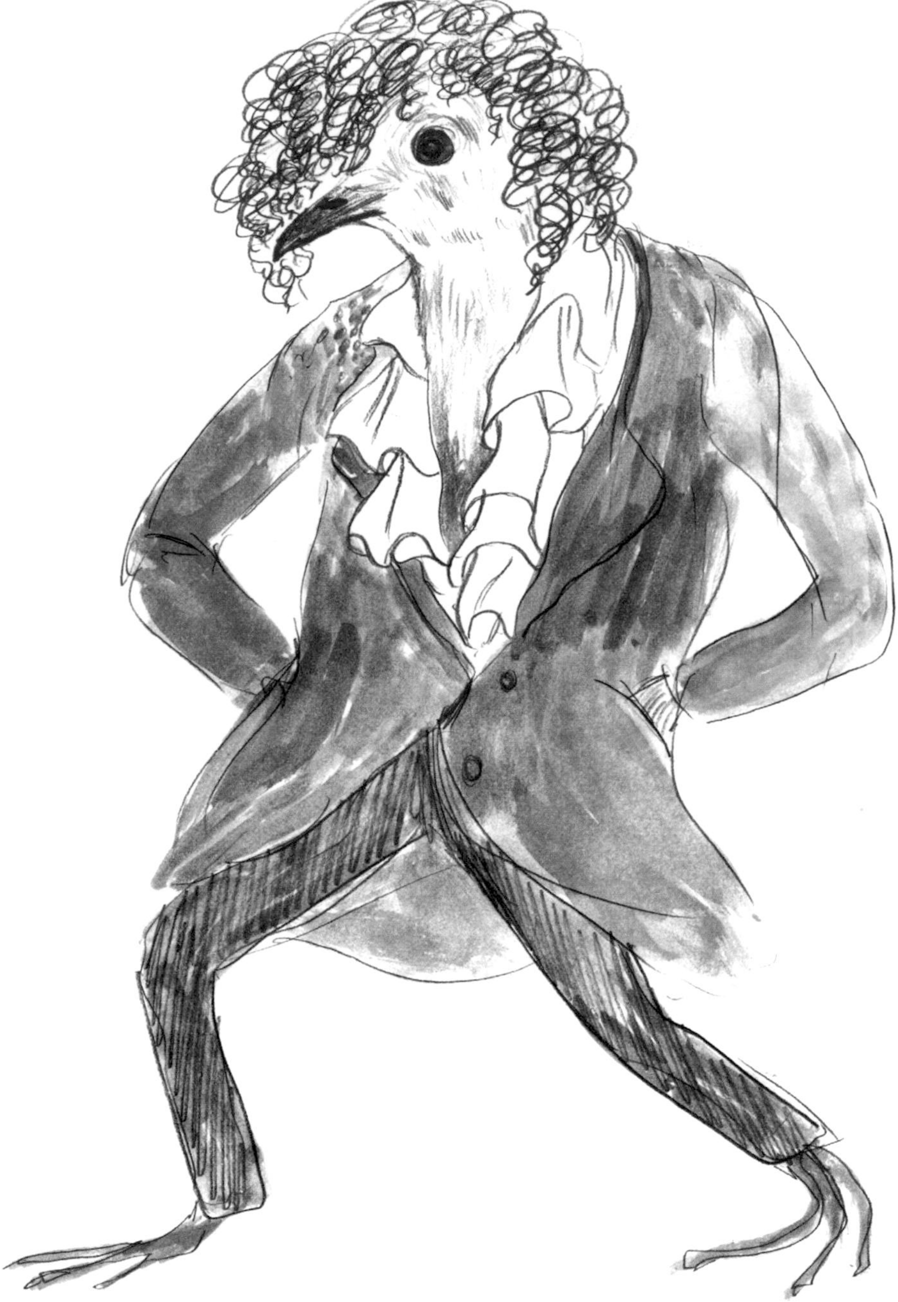

When Doves Cry

THE BACHELOR

A REALITY TV SKETCH BOOK

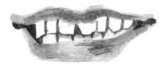

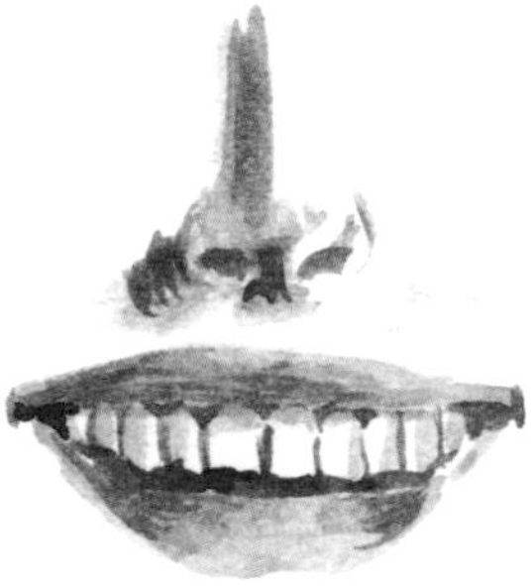

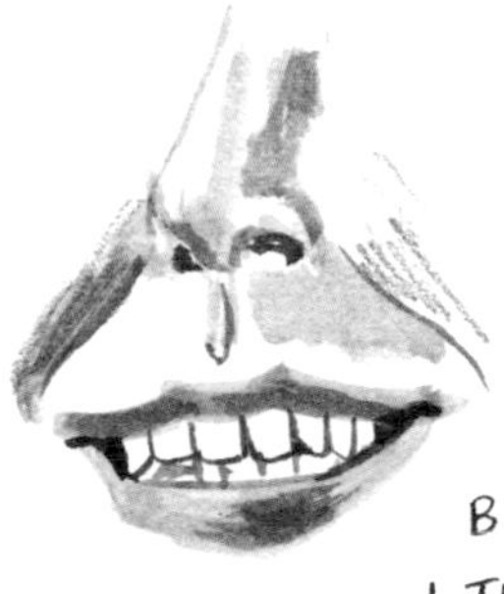

NICK

- ALL THE WOMEN ON THIS SHOW HAVE SO MANY SHARED FEATURES: BUTTON NOSES, HIGH CHEEKBONES, BLEACHED TEETH, BIG EYES. THEY'RE ALL WHITE, I THINK. IF YOU HAD PROSOPAGNOSIA, YOU'D JUST SEE AN OCEAN OF BLONDES AND BRUNETTES PLUS ONE REDHEAD.

- TELLING THE GIRLS APART COMES DOWN TO WEIRD SPECIFICS: NIKKI HAS FANG-LIKE TEETH, KACIE'S HAIR GETS PUFFY WITH THE HUMIDITY, RACHEL SUCKS HER LOWER LIP, SAMANTHA KEEPS SPILLING ICE CREAM IN THE JACUZZI, EMILY'S WANTED FOR MURDER, ETC.

EMILY

RACHEL

SAMANTHA

COURTNEY

• THESE PEOPLE DON'T TALK LIKE REAL PEOPLE! TOPICS OF CONVERSATION ARE LIMITED TO BEN THE BACHELOR AND FEELINGS TOWARD BEN THE BACHELOR. IF THEY DISCUSS WORK, POLITICAL BELIEFS, OR EVEN A BOOK OR MOVIE THEY LOVE, IT'S BEEN EDITED OUT.

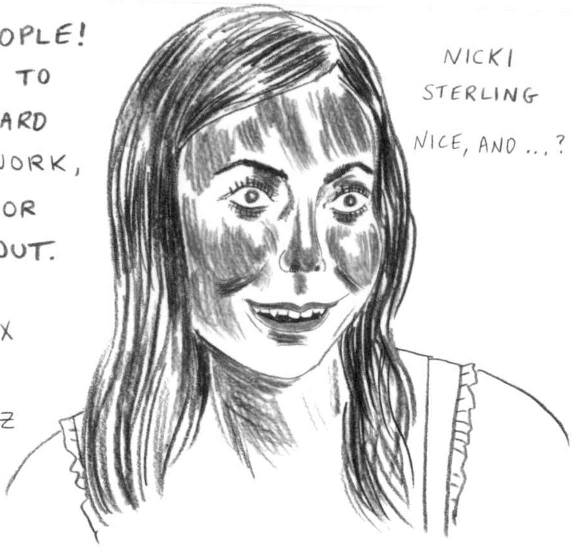

NICKI STERLING
NICE, AND ...?

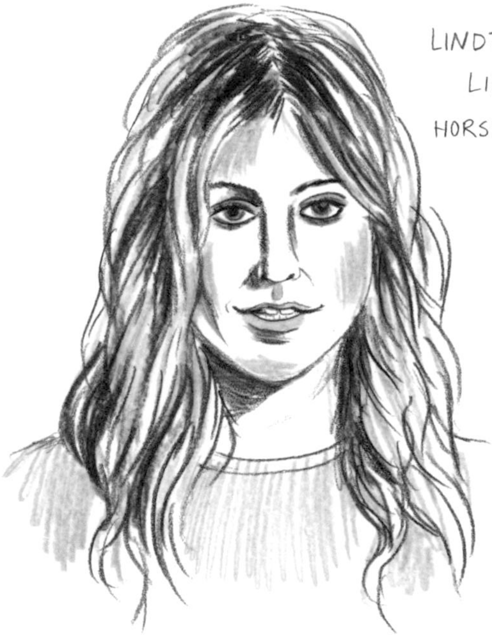

LINDZI COX
LIKES
HORSE Z Z Z

ARE THE WOMEN REALLY THIS BORING OR HAVE THE EDITORS PANCAKED THEIR PERSONALITIES AND ERASED THEIR OPINIONS?

• THIS FEELS LIKE WATCHING A CULT. BEN BEHAVES LIKE A CREEPY CAMP COUNSELOR; HE MAKES OUT WITH EVERYONE, TRIES TO KEEP THE PEACE IN THE MOST DETACHED WAY POSSIBLE, AND WOMEN WHO AREN'T 100% IN LOVE WITH HIM BY EPISODE FIVE ARE ELIMINATED. IT'S CONSIDERED OFFENSIVE FOR THE GIRLS TO ACKNOWLEDGE THAT BEN ISN'T THE ONLY MAN LEFT ON EARTH.

• BEN LOOKS LIKE SOMEONE BOILED ALL THE FLAVOR OUT OF JASON SCHWARTZMAN.

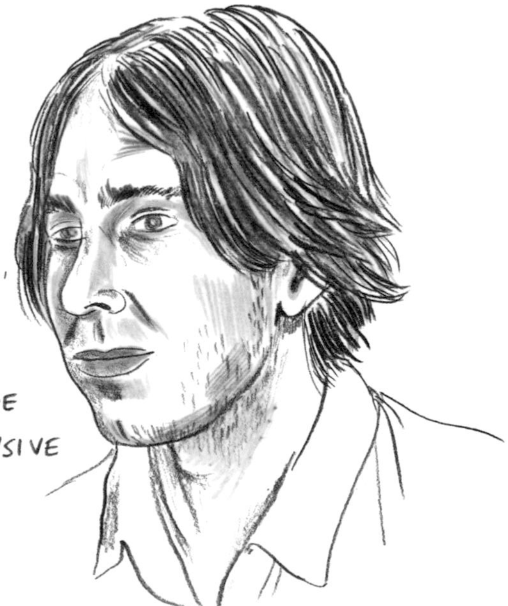

BEN FLAJELLY
TALL, DARK, AND FLOPPY

• SOME OF THE WOMEN EVEN MANAGE TO COMPLIMENT BEN'S AWFUL HAIR, THEY'RE SUCH DEVOTEES OF THE CULT OF BEN.

• MY FRIEND JULIA SUGGESTS, "WHEN BEN GOES BACK TO THE HOTEL AT NIGHT, HE JUST STANDS STILL IN A CORNER FACING THE WALL ALL NIGHT UNTIL THE PRODUCERS COME GET HIM THE NEXT MORNING." IT'S HARD TO IMAGINE HIM HAVING ANY KIND OF INTERNAL LIFE OR OFF-CAMERA EXISTENCE.

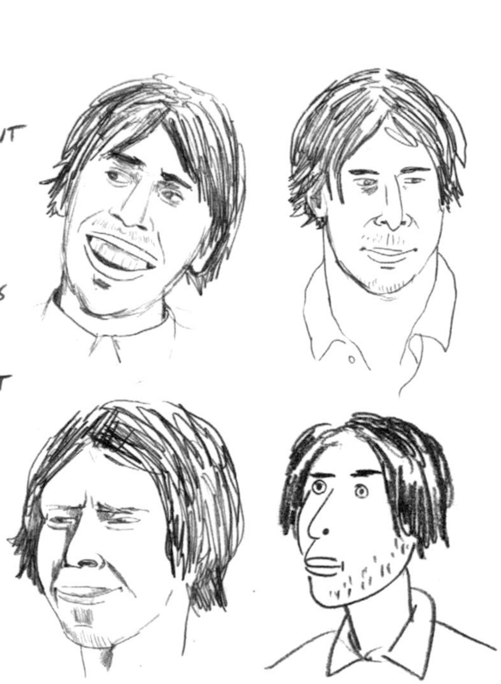

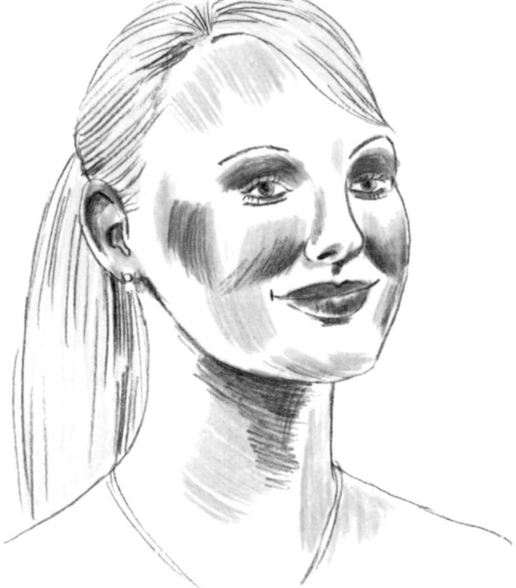

MONICA
DOESN'T GIVE A DAMN

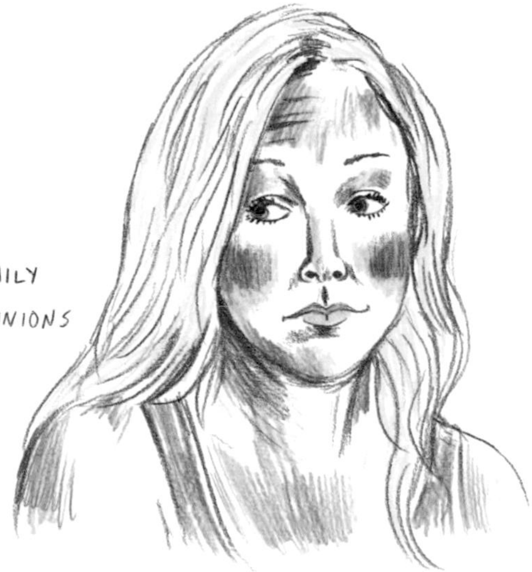

EMILY
HAS OPINIONS

• MY FAVORITE CONTESTANTS ARE THE ONES WHO DON'T NEED TO BE HERE. MONICA APPEARS TO FIND THE WHOLE THING FUNNY AND DOESN'T GIVE A HOOT ABOUT BEN.

• EMILY'S A PH.D. STUDENT WHO RAPS ABOUT EPIDEMIOLOGY. SHE SEEMS TOO SMART TO BE ON THIS SHOW. SHE TRIES TO WARN BEN ABOUT COURTNEY BEING DUPLICITOUS AND FROM THEN ON HE SEES EMILY AS A TROUBLEMAKER. HOW DARE SHE HAVE AN ORIGINAL THOUGHT!

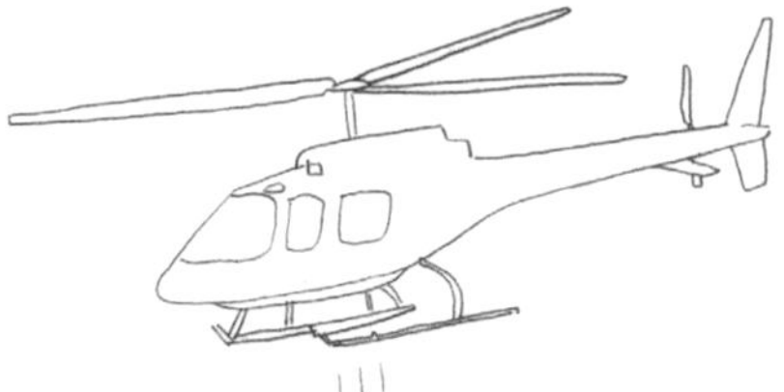

• THERE ARE HELICOPTERS IN EVERY EPISODE AND HALF THE DATES REVOLVE AROUND JUMPING OUT OF THEM, FALLING INTO POOLS OF WATER FROM GREAT HEIGHTS, STANDING CLOSE TO CLIFFS, AND CLIMBING TALL THINGS. THE "FALLING IN LOVE" METAPHOR IS PUSHED AND RE-STATED UNTIL IT'S AS STRINGY AND FLAVORLESS AS A TWO WEEK OLD PIECE OF GUM.

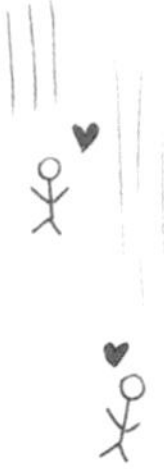

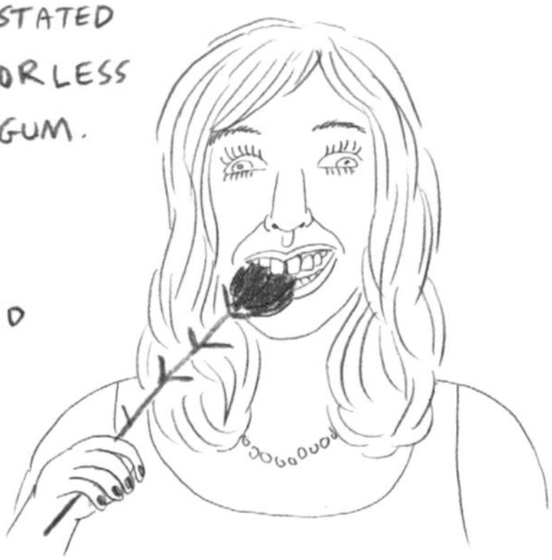

• THERE'S FOOD ON ALL THE DATES BUT I NEVER SEE ANYONE TAKE A BITE. THE WOMEN LOOK STARVED DURING THE ROSE CEREMONIES, BUT MAYBE THEY'RE JUST HUNGRY FOR ROSES.

• SOME OF THEIR FACES WARP IN FRIGHTENING WAYS WHEN THEY GET UPSET. CASEY IS JUST ANOTHER PRETTY GIRL UNTIL BEN BANISHES HER AND HER TEARS TRANSFORM HER INTO A GREMLIN.

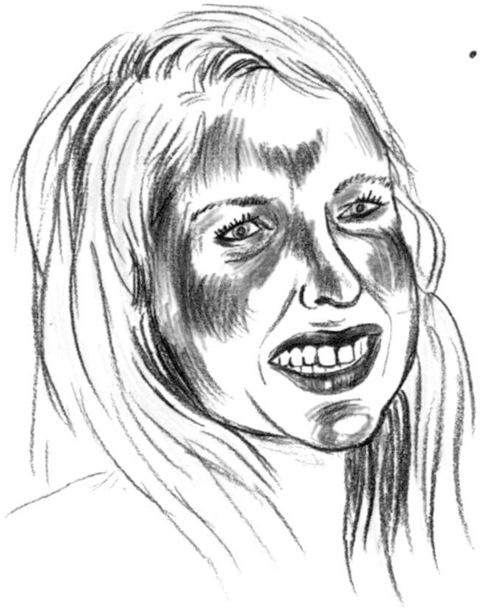

CASEY S

DO NOT GET WET OR FEED AFTER MIDNIGHT

• COURTNEY, THIS SEASON'S VILLAIN, STRUGGLES WITH NARCISSISTIC PERSONALITY DISORDER AND CONFIDENT MODEL SYNDROME. SHE'S LITHE AND WEIRD AND THE SHOW WOULD BE AN UNWATCHABLE SNOOZE WITHOUT HER.

• I PLACE A $5 BET ON COURTNEY TO WIN AFTER SHE SKINNY DIPS IN AN EARLY EPISODE.

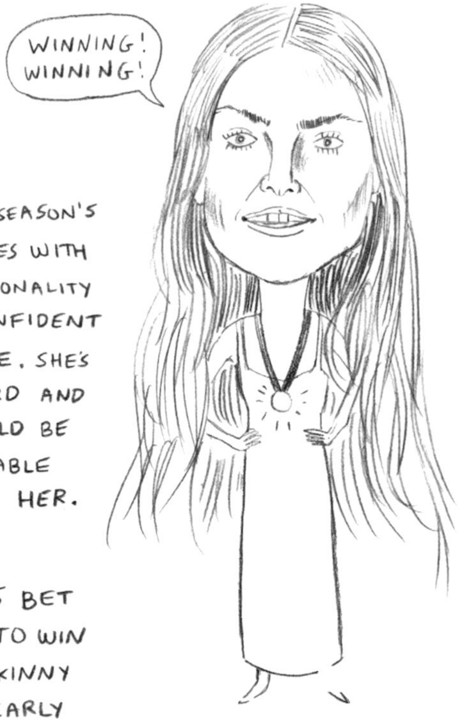
WINNING! WINNING!

THE MICHAEL PHELPS OF REALITY TV CONTESTANTS

COURTNEY

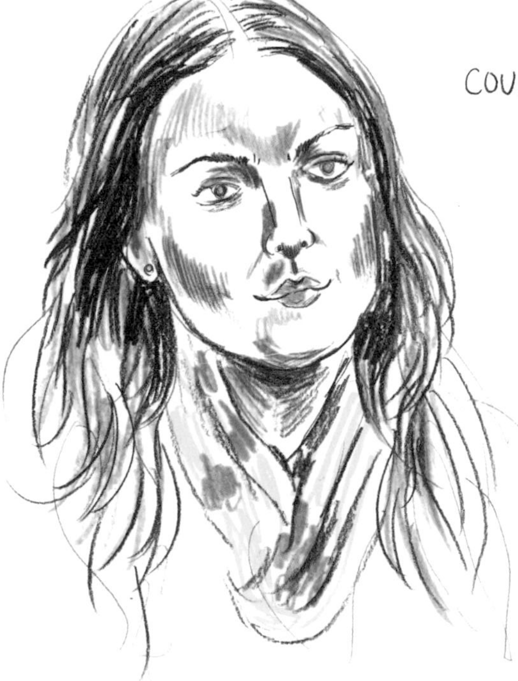

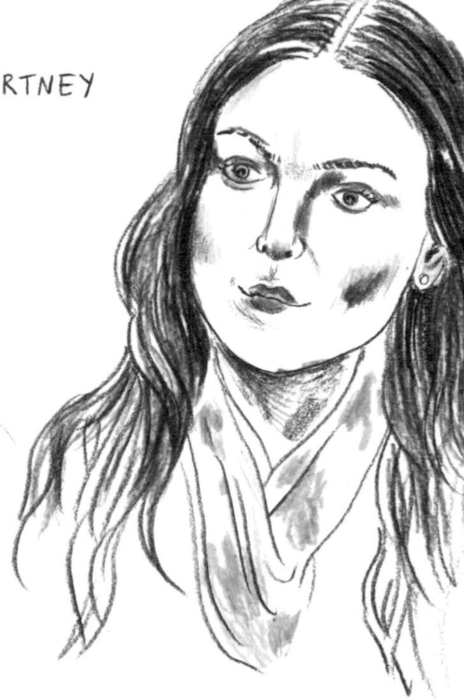

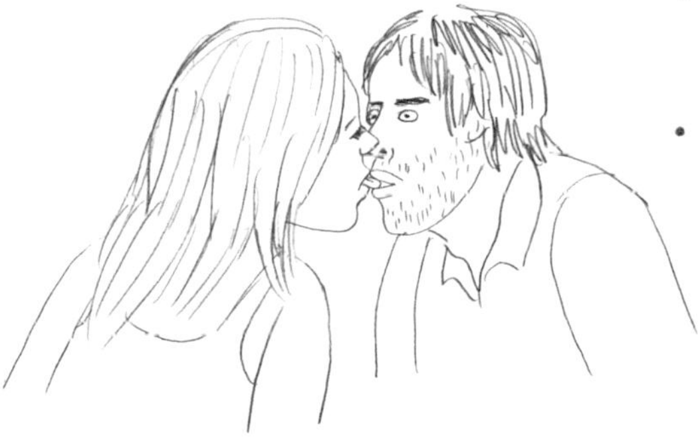

- THERE'S SO MUCH KISSING; I WONDER WHAT BEN'S BREATH SMELLS LIKE?
- I WANT TO KNOW WHAT HAPPENS DURING THOSE OVERNIGHT DATES. I'M GUESSING "DRY HAND JOBS" UNTIL I HAVE FURTHER INFORMATION.

- WHAT WOULD IT BE LIKE IF I COMPETED ON THIS SHOW? WHAT WOULD THE PRODUCERS DO TO MY PERSONALITY? I HOPE I NEVER FIND OUT.

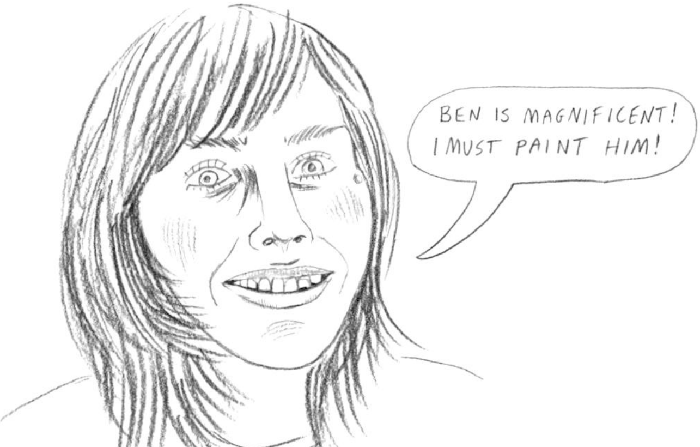
BEN IS MAGNIFICENT! I MUST PAINT HIM!

LISA H.

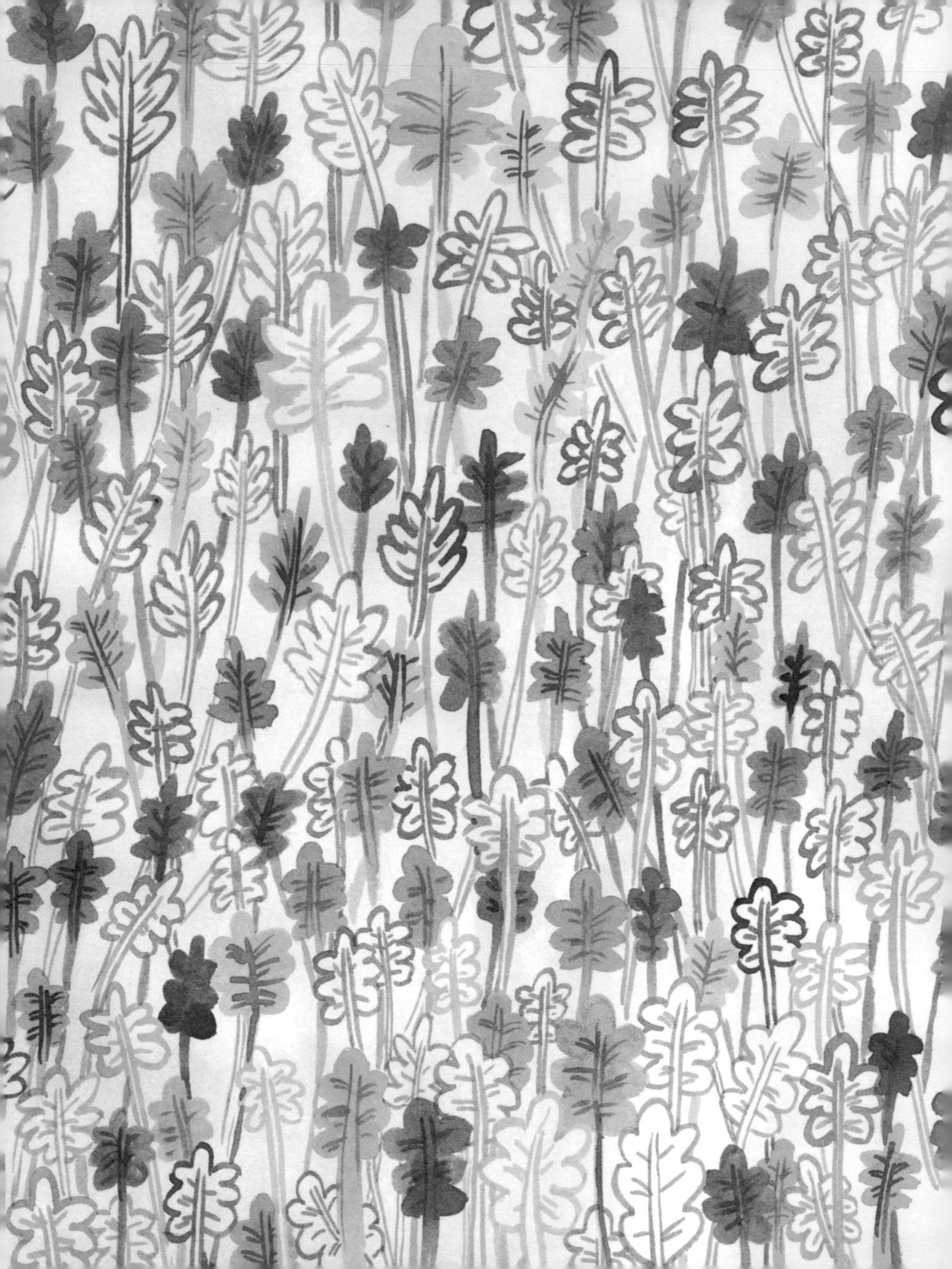

Control

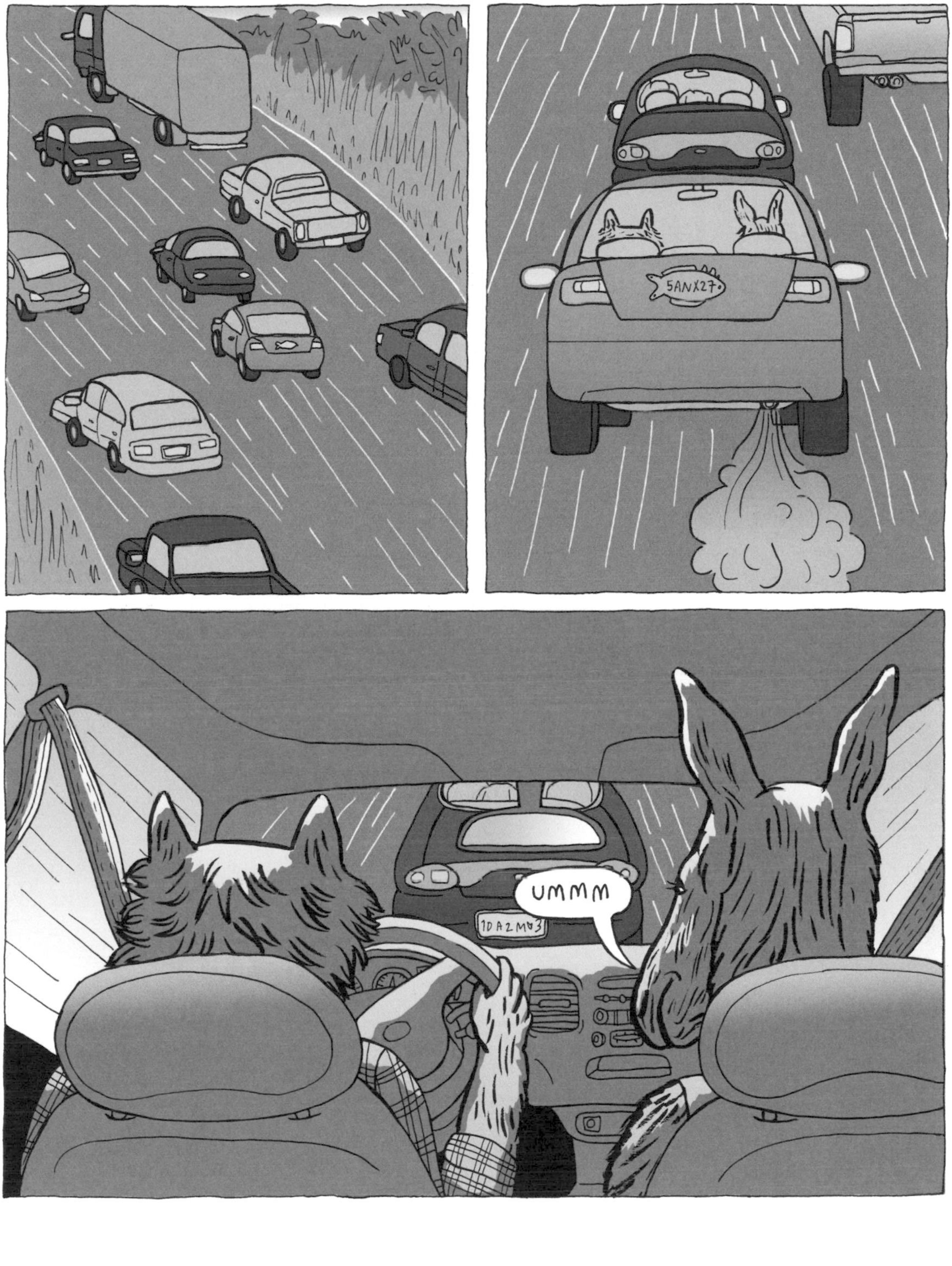
5ANX27
UMMM

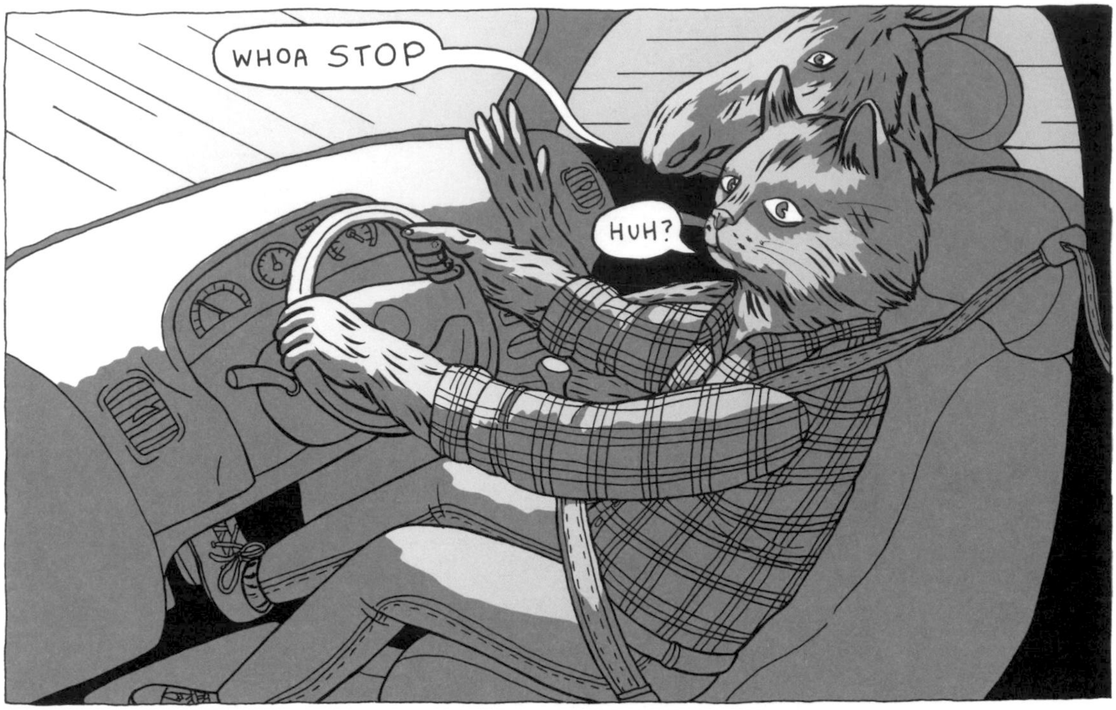
WHOA STOP
HUH?

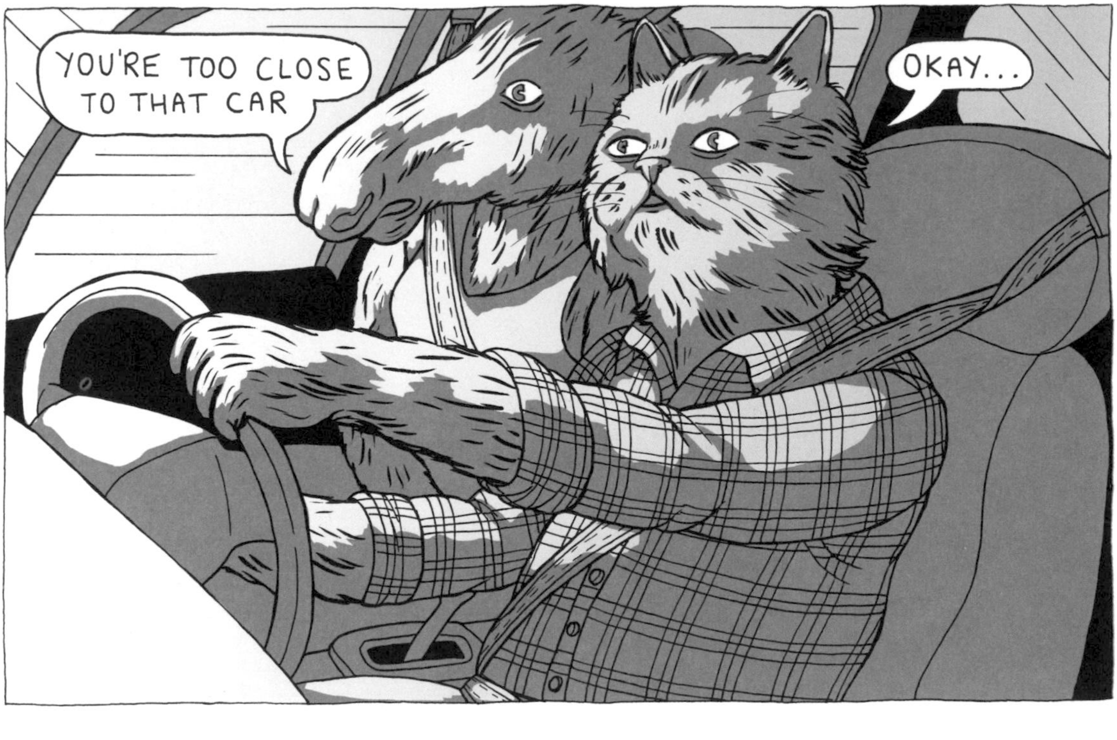
YOU'RE TOO CLOSE TO THAT CAR
OKAY...

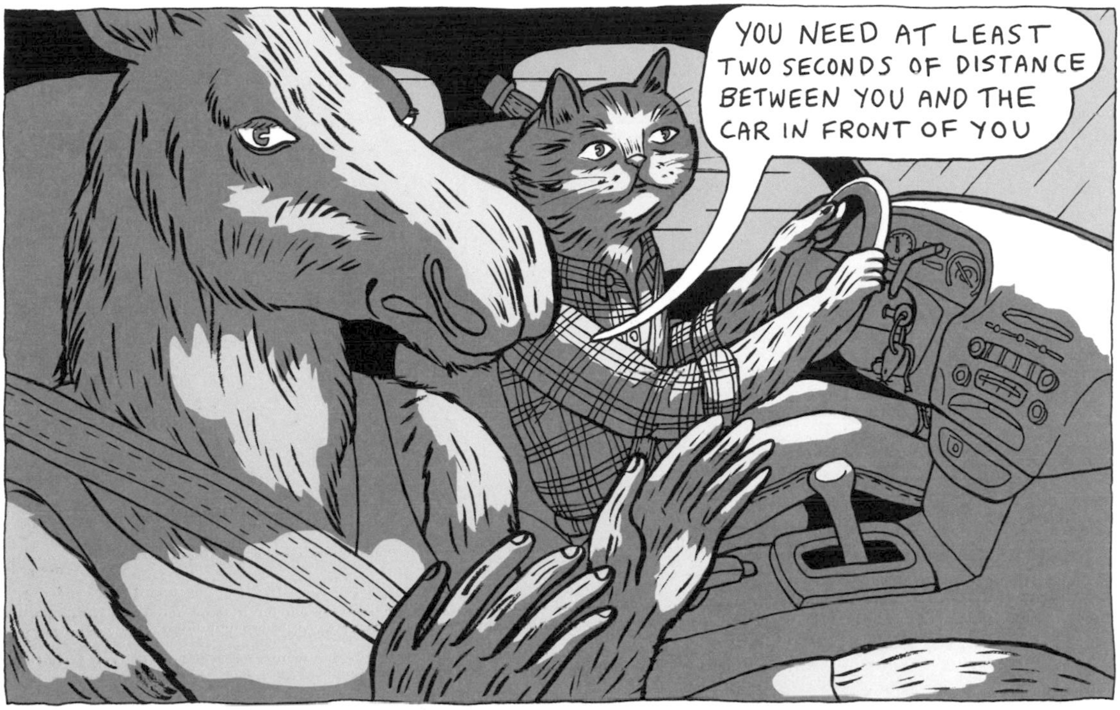
YOU NEED AT LEAST TWO SECONDS OF DISTANCE BETWEEN YOU AND THE CAR IN FRONT OF YOU

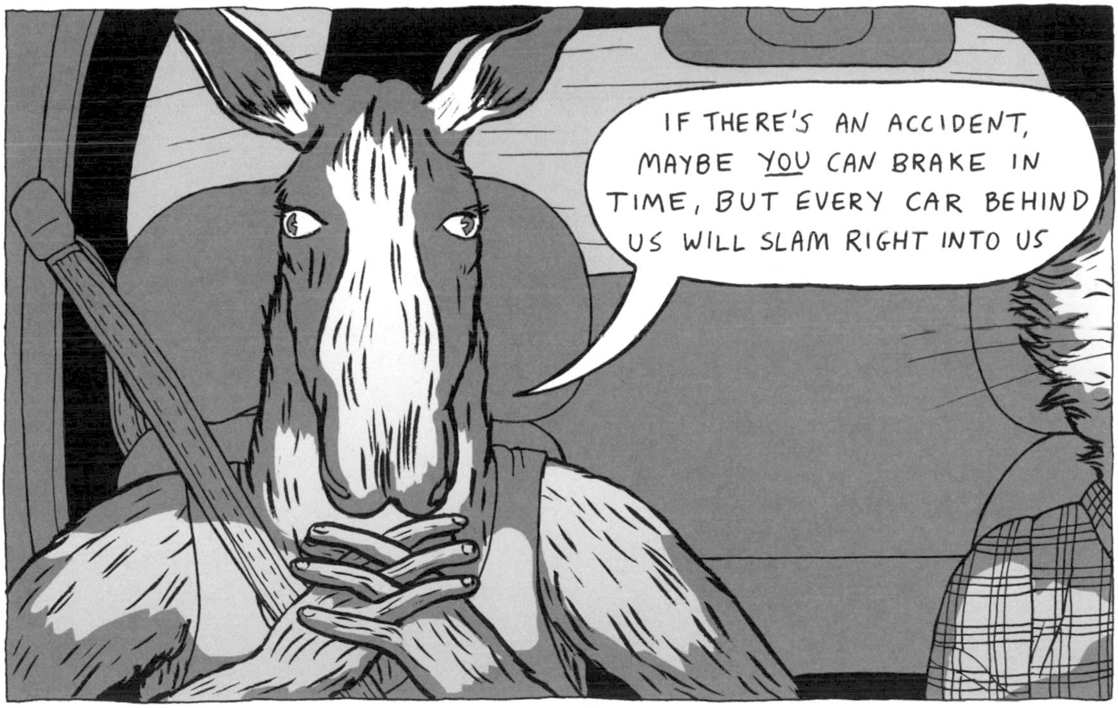
IF THERE'S AN ACCIDENT, MAYBE YOU CAN BRAKE IN TIME, BUT EVERY CAR BEHIND US WILL SLAM RIGHT INTO US

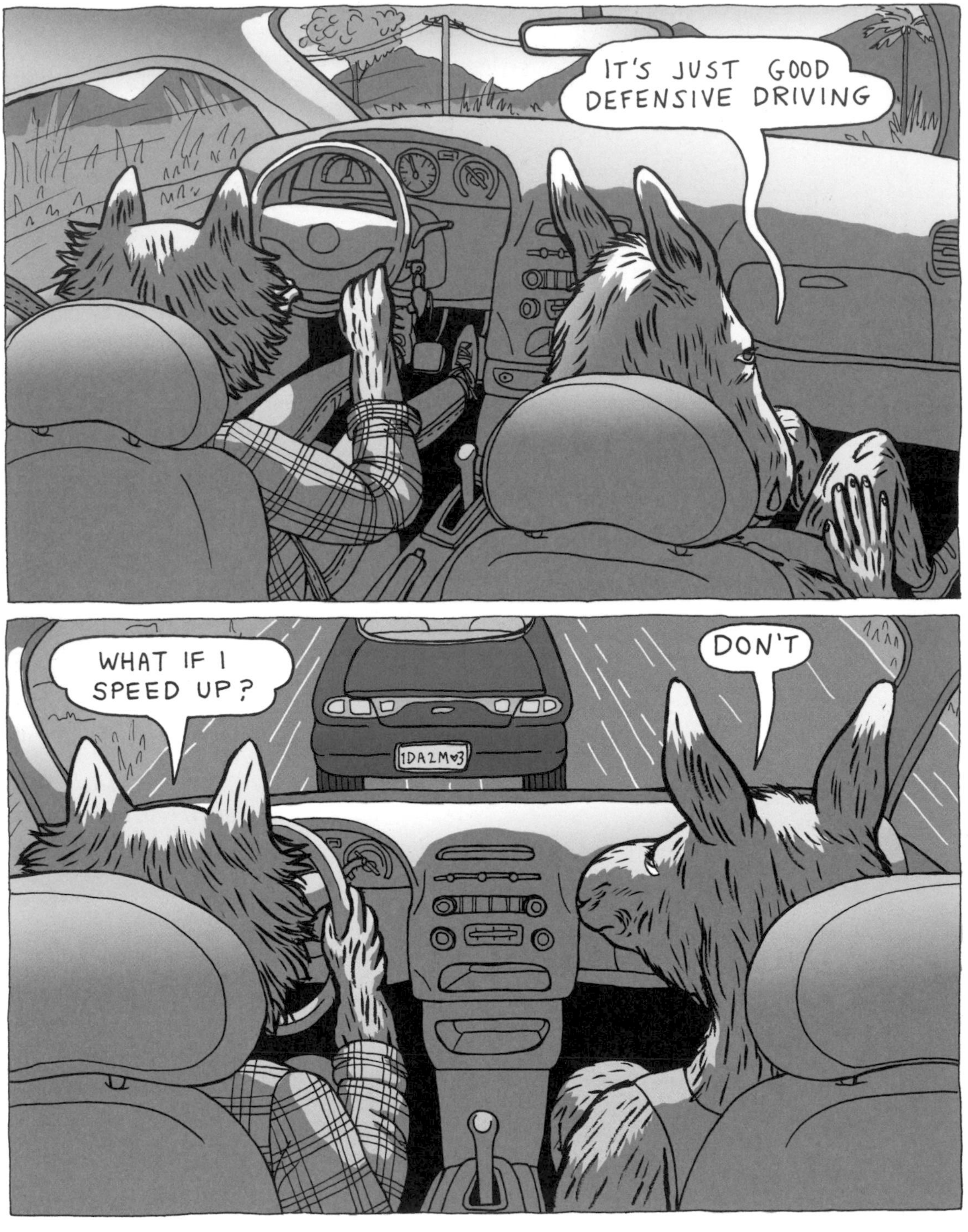
IT'S JUST GOOD DEFENSIVE DRIVING
WHAT IF I SPEED UP?
DON'T

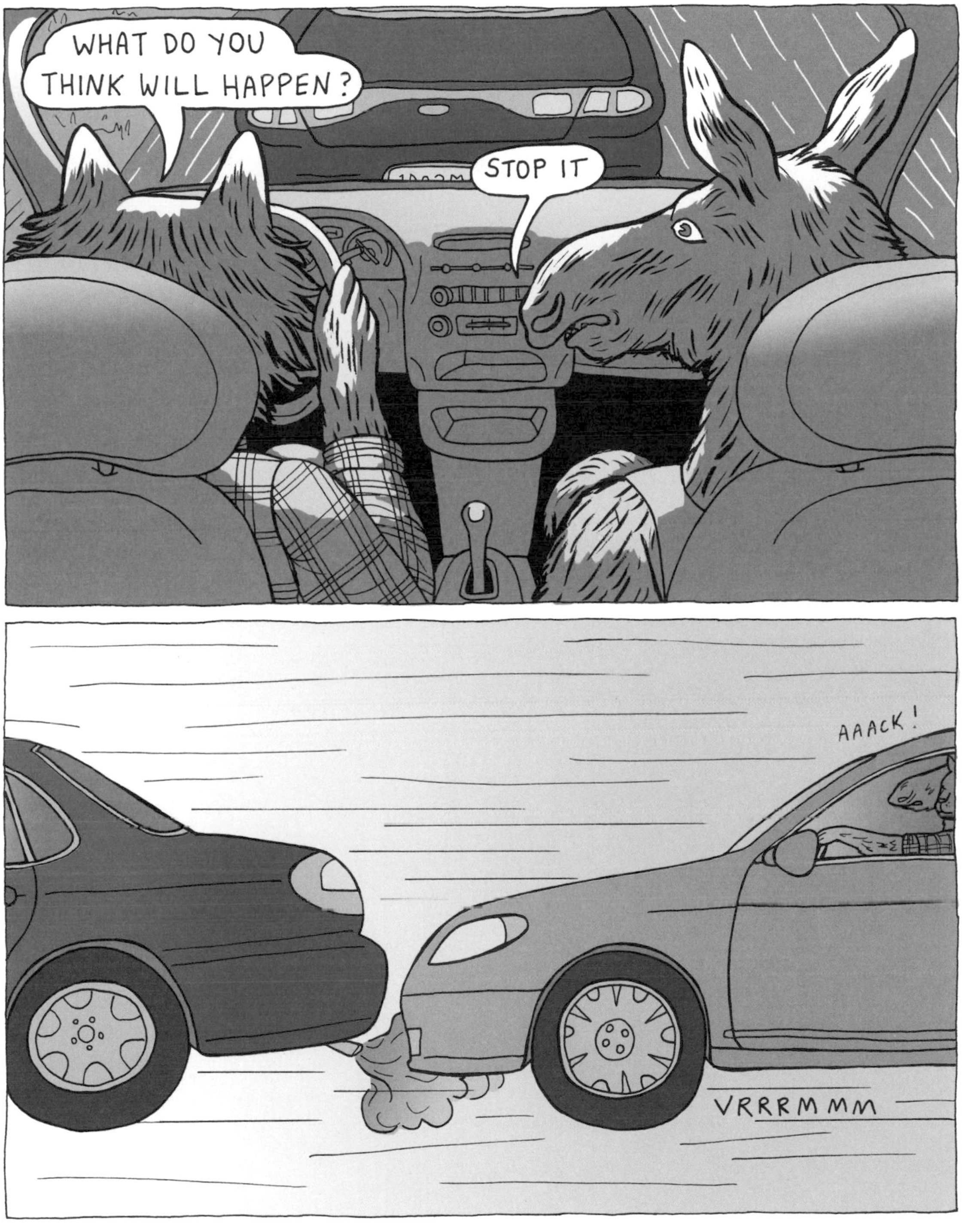
WHAT DO YOU THINK WILL HAPPEN?
STOP IT
AAACK!
VRRRMMM

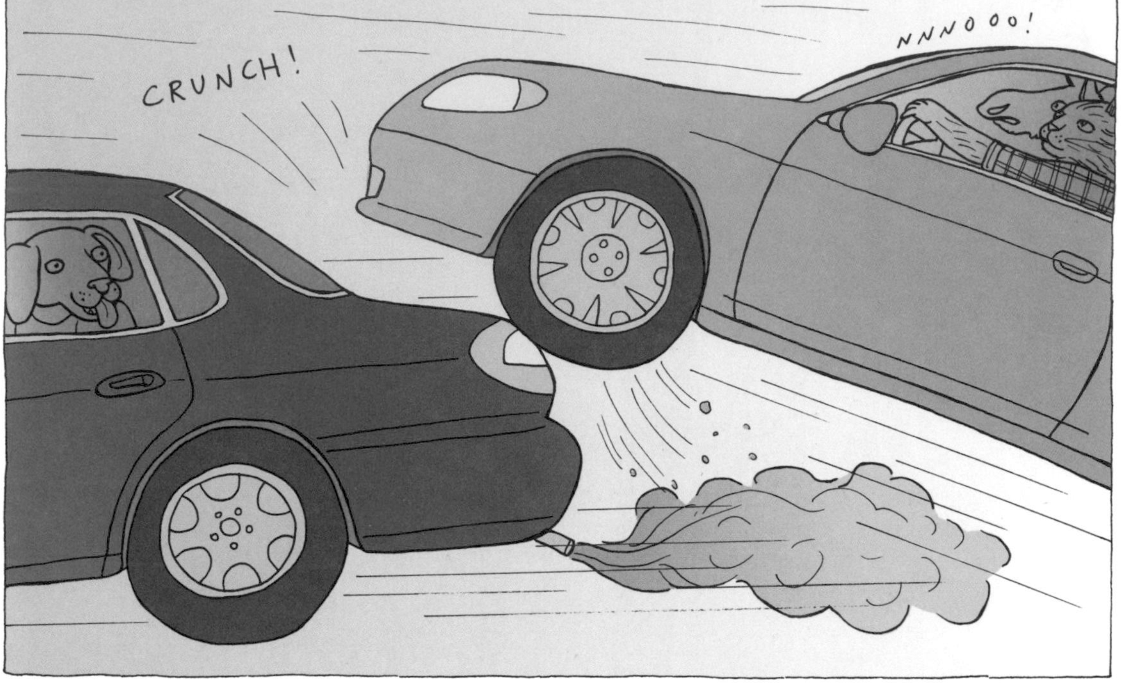
CRUNCH!
NNNOOO!

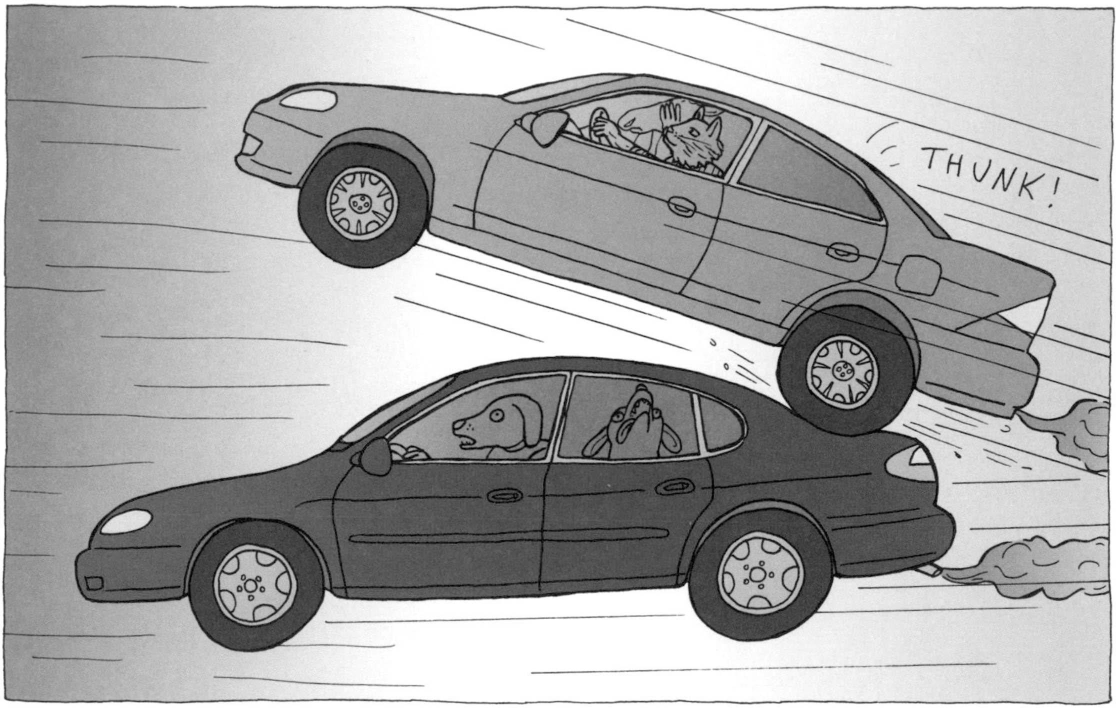
THUNK!

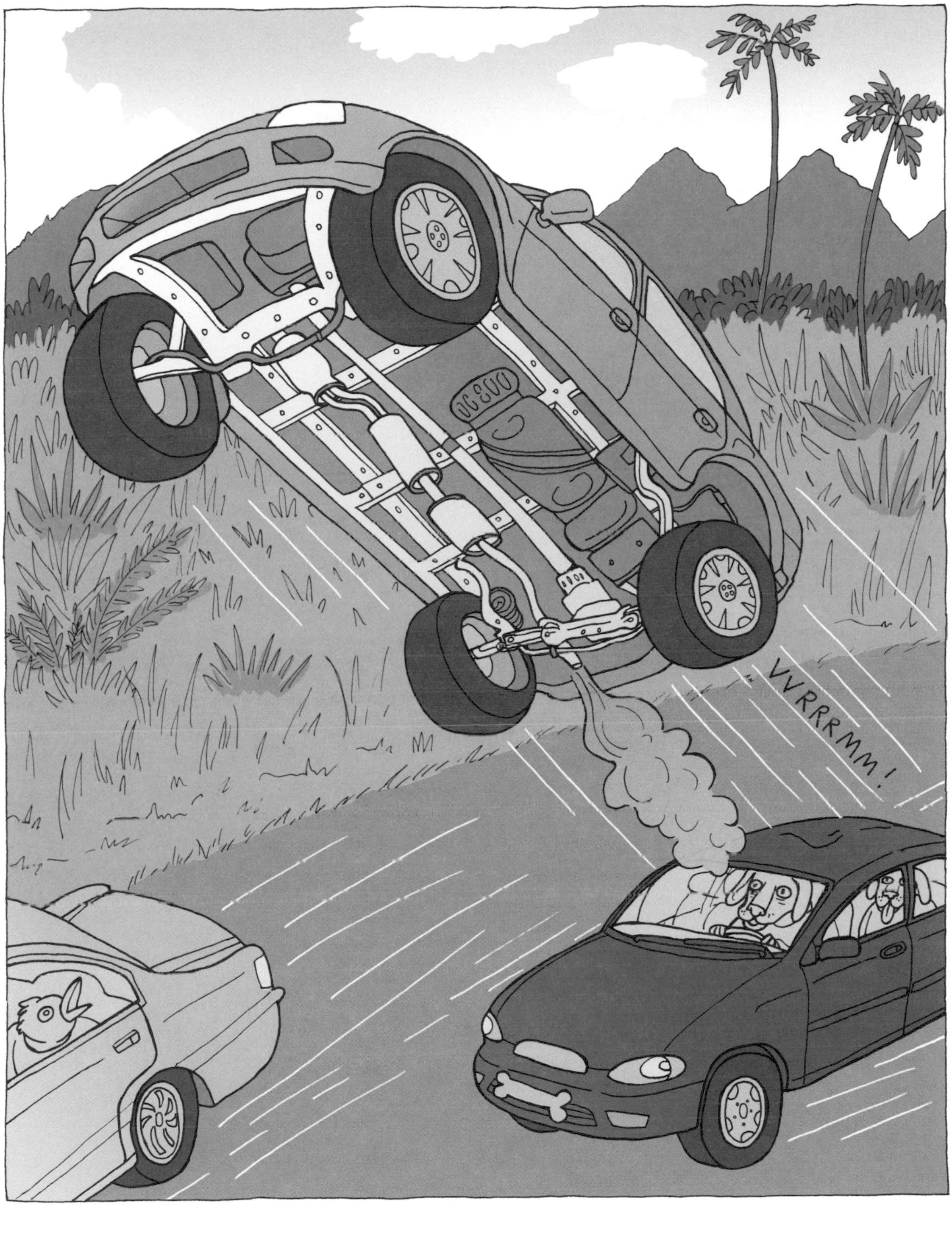
VVRRRMMM!

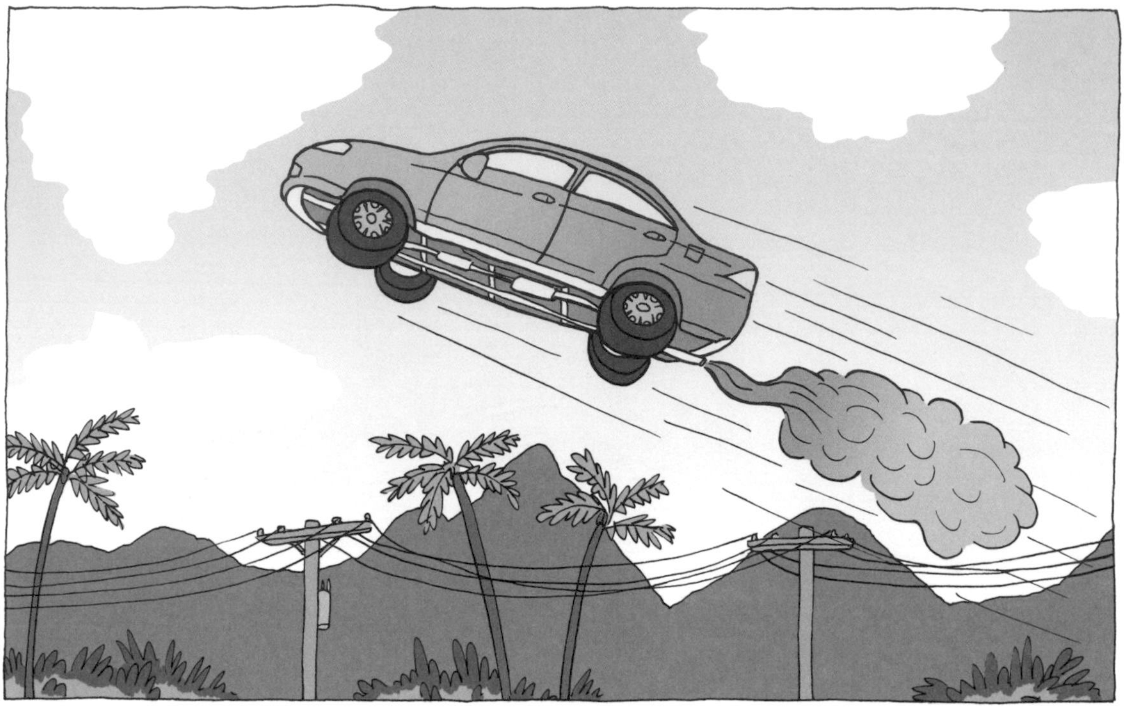

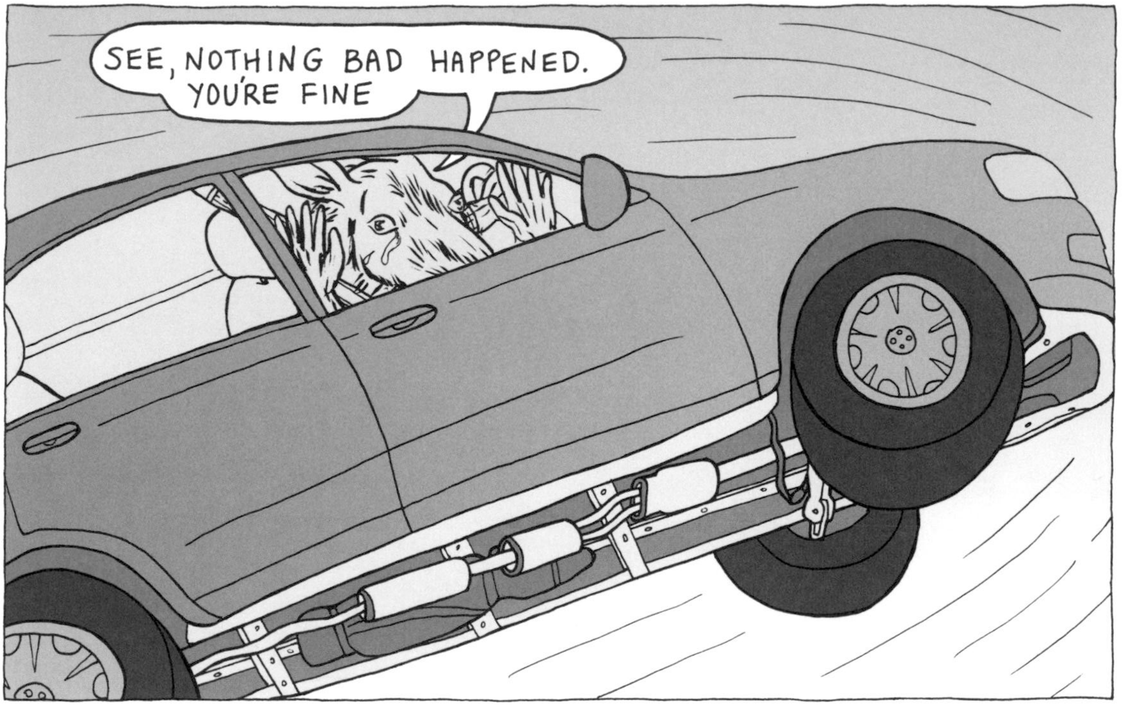
SEE, NOTHING BAD HAPPENED.
YOU'RE FINE

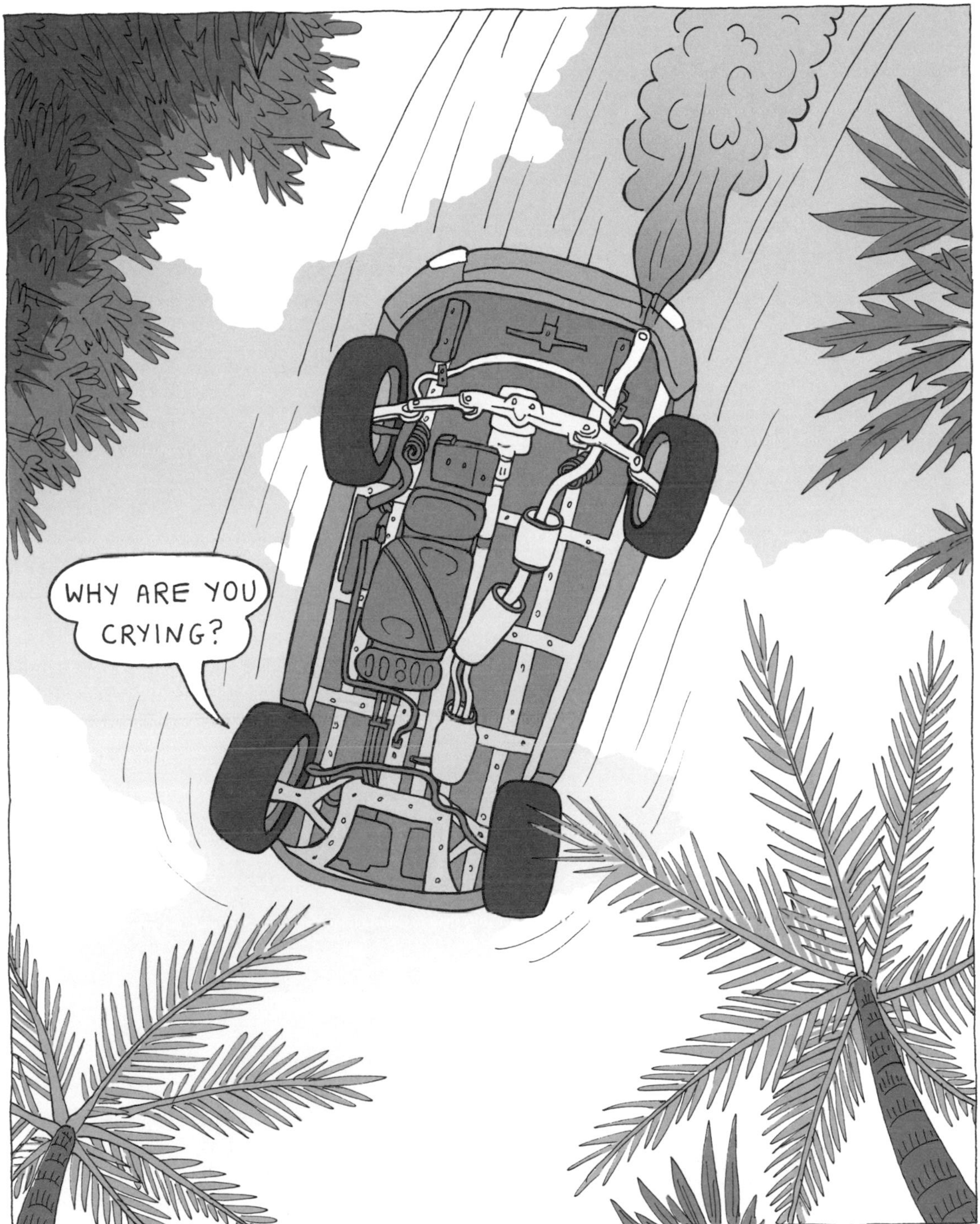
WHY ARE YOU CRYING?

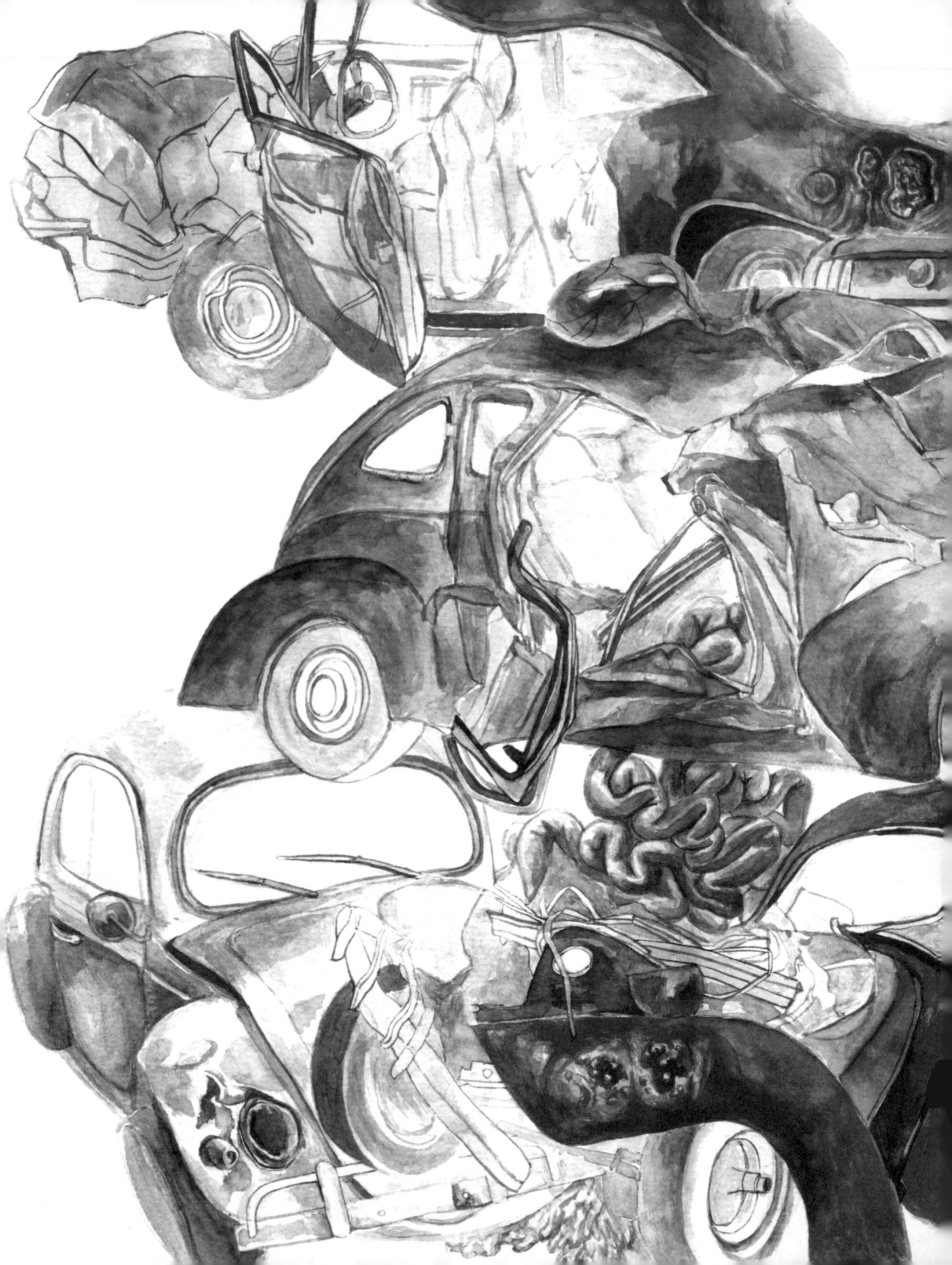

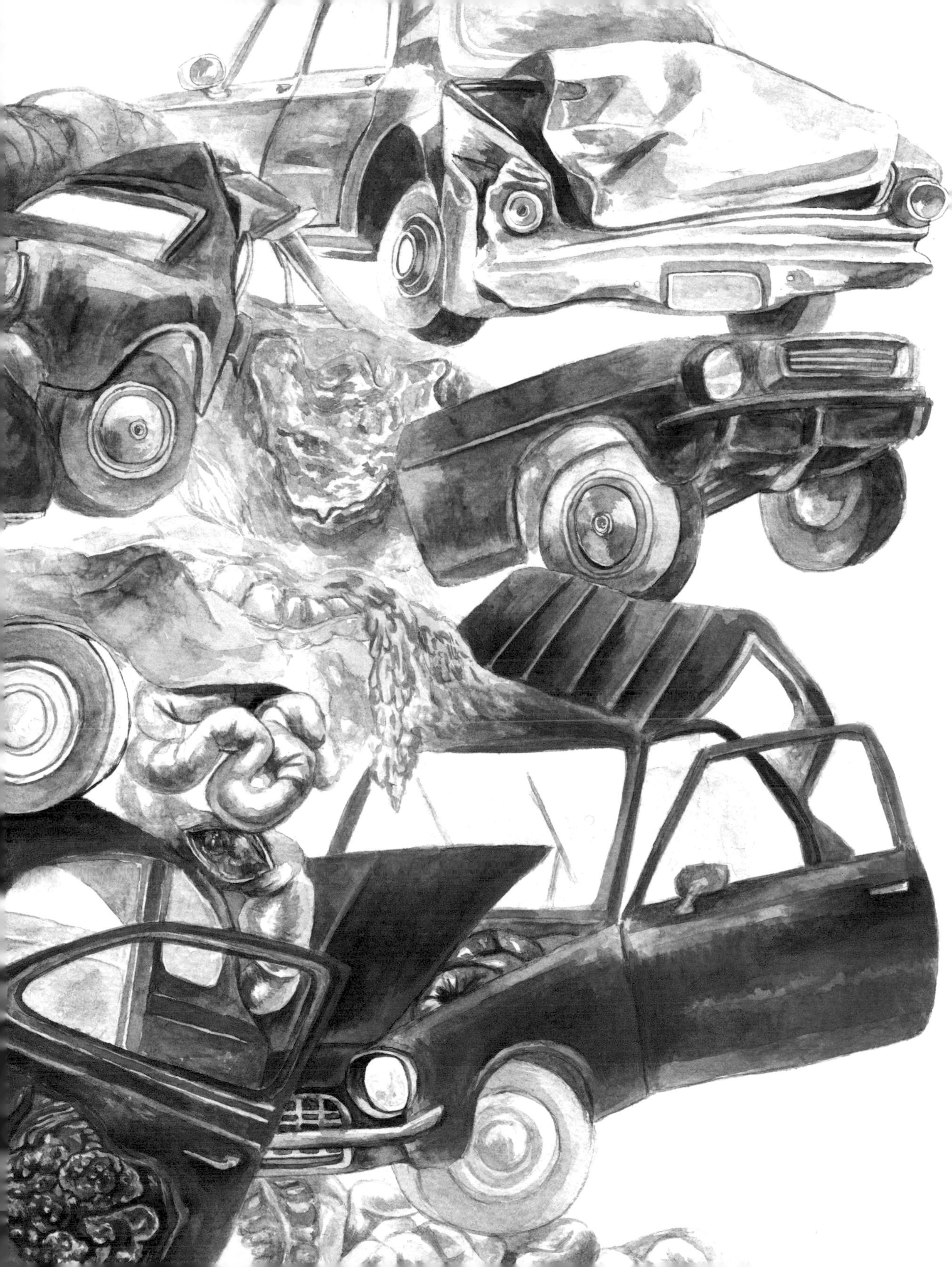

SPECIAL THANKS TO ALVIN BUENAVENTURA, DOMITILLE COLLARDEY, SARAH GLIDDEN, JULIA WERTZ, TIM KREIDER, MEREDITH KAFFEL, TRACY HURREN, TOM DEVLIN, PEGGY BURNS, AND EVERYONE AT D&Q.

FINGER PHOTOGRAPHY BY SAM WEBER.

REJECTED BOOK TITLES: SAVE A HORSE, RIDE A HANAWALT • A RUDE MIND • BLUNDER CABINET • A SUPPOSEDLY FUN THING THAT IS ACTUALLY PRETTY FUN • DICK LIZARDS AND BOOB DOGS: A MEMOIR • WHAT WE DRAW ABOUT WHEN WE DRAW ABOUT SEX BUGS

WWW.DRAWNANDQUARTERLY.COM   WWW.LISAHANAWALT.COM
FIRST EDITION: MAY 2013. PRINTED IN CHINA. 10 9 8 7 6 5 4 3 2 1

LIBRARY AND ARCHIVES CANADA CATALOGUING IN PUBLICATION: HANAWALT, LISA. MY DIRTY DUMB EYES/ LISA HANAWALT. ISBN 978-1-77046-116-1. 1. GRAPHIC NOVELS. I. TITLE. PN6727.H35M9 2013 741.5'973 C2012-907119-6 IT'S 44°F OUTSIDE RIGHT NOW. I HAVE TO PEE.

PUBLISHED IN THE USA BY DRAWN & QUARTERLY, A CLIENT PUBLISHER OF FARRAR, STRAUS AND GIROUX: 18 WEST 18TH STREET; NEW YORK, NY 10011; ORDERS: 888.330.8477. PUBLISHED IN CANADA BY DRAWN & QUARTERLY, A CLIENT PUBLISHER OF RAINCOAST BOOKS: 2440 VIKING WAY; RICHMOND, BC V6V 1N2; ORDERS: 800.663.5714 DOES ANYBODY READ ALL OF THIS? WHO ARE YOU? DISTRIBUTED IN THE UNITED KINGDOM BY PUBLISHERS GROUP UK: 63-66 HATTON GARDEN; LONDON; EC1N 8LE; INFO@PGUK.CO.UK

NOTE: THIS BOOK IS SCRATCH-'N'-SNIFF; HOWEVER, THE MICROFRAGRANCES ARE EXTREMELY SUBTLE. SEE IF YOU CAN DETECT THE AROMA OF "EGG WRAPPED IN NEWSPAPER" OR "WINTER GLUE."

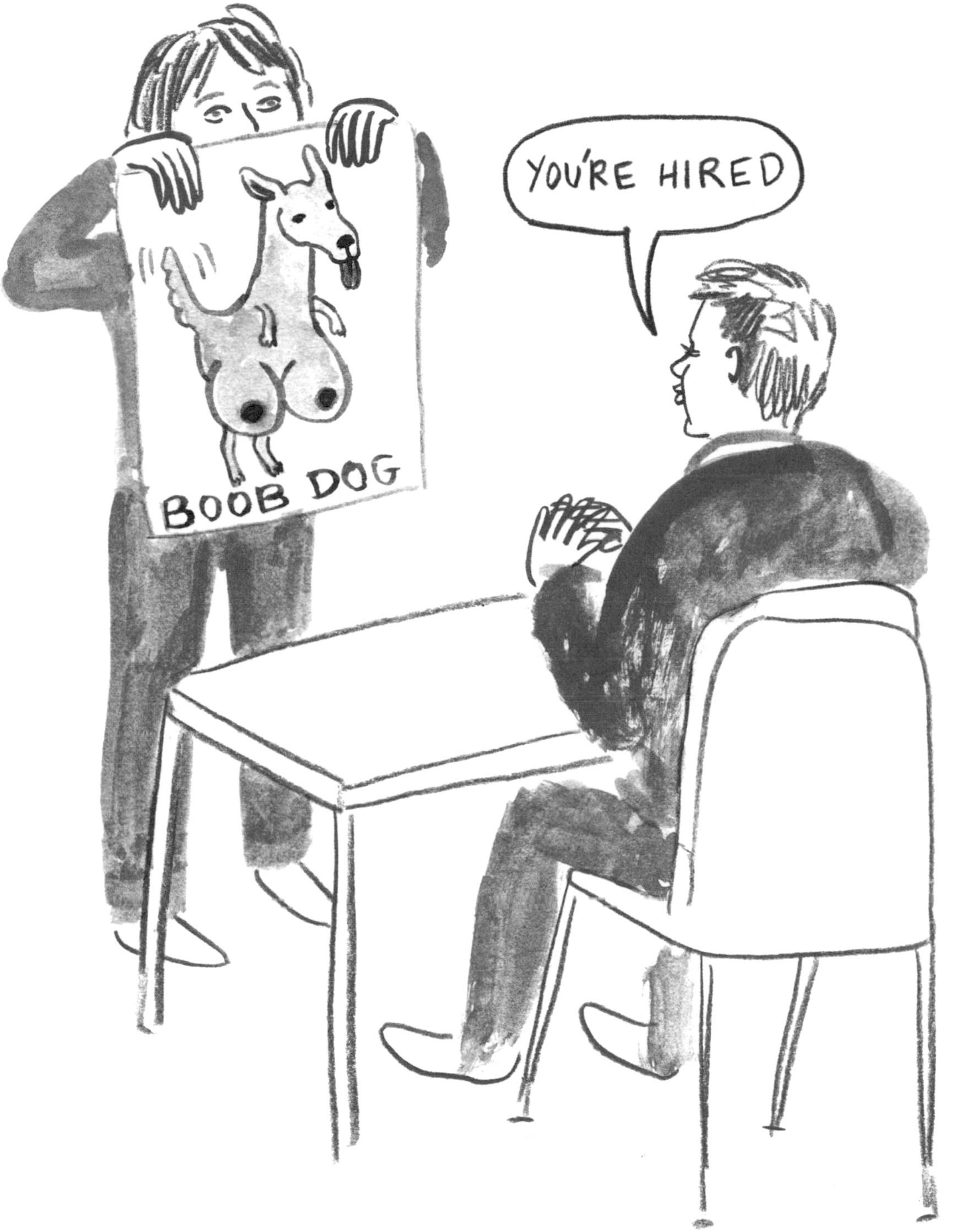
BOOB DOG
YOU'RE HIRED

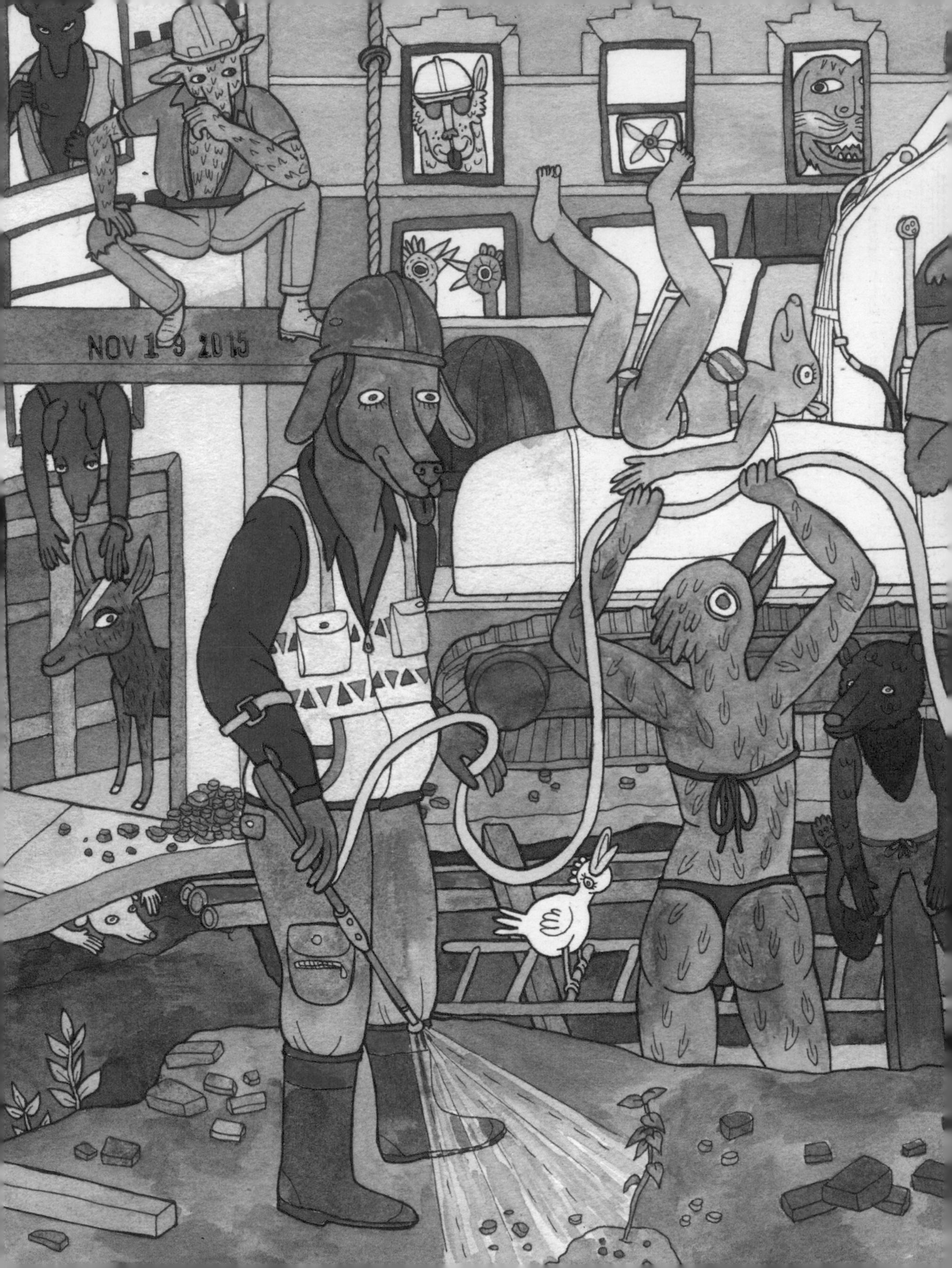